Pre-Modernity, Totalitarianism and the Non-Banality of Evil

Steven Saxonberg

Pre-Modernity, Totalitarianism and the Non-Banality of Evil

A Comparison of Germany, Spain, Sweden and France

palgrave
macmillan

Steven Saxonberg
Department of European Studies and International Relations
Comenius University
Bratislava, Slovakia

Center for Social and Economic Strategies
Charles University in Prague
Prague, Czech Republic

ISBN 978-3-030-28194-6   ISBN 978-3-030-28195-3   (eBook)
https://doi.org/10.1007/978-3-030-28195-3

Cover illustration: jcgwakefield / Getty Images

This Palgrave Macmillan imprint is published by the registered company Springer Nature Switzerland AG.
The registered company address is: Gewerbestrasse 11, 6330 Cham, Switzerland

This book is dedicated to Sylvia.

PREFACE

I would like to thank my colleagues at the Department of European Studies at the Faculty of Social Sciences at the Comenius University in Bratislava for their support, as well as Tomáš Sirovátka at the Institute of Public Policy and Social Work at the Masaryk University in Bratislava. Research for this book was also carried out at the Centre for Social and Economic Strategies at the Charles University in Prague. I would also like to thank the staff at the Department of Sociology at the University of Innsbruck, who were very supportive during my stay there as a guest professor in 2018. Further thanks goes to Birgit Pfau-Effinger, who arranged for me to be a guest professor at Hamburg University in 2012 and who arranged several more research stays for me there. During one of these stays, Tim Mueller generously arranged for me to use the facilities at the Hamburg Institute for Social Research. Bo Rothstein deserves my appreciation for inviting me for a research stay at Nuffield College at the University of Oxford in 2018. It goes without saying that both Nuffield College and the University of Oxford have an amazing library. I also benefited from visits to the Autonomous University in Barcelona. Both Marta Simó and Lluís Flaquer helped me arrange seminars and public lectures, where I could present my ideas on the Spanish Inquisition and get feedback. Manlio Cinalli joins this list as he very kindly invited me for a research stay at Science Po in Paris. Oscar Hidalgo was very helpful as a research assistant during the first year of the project. Stefan Olsson gave me great advice on the Swedish chapter. Last, but not least, I want to thank Peter Mayers, who did an amazing job as my proofreader despite the very tight deadline that we faced from Palgrave, which kept us both up late at night during the final weeks of this project.

Whenever I cite a text that was not originally in English, I tried to find an English version of that book to use its translation. When that was not possible, I translated the texts myself.

This book was supported by the Czech Science Foundation (GACR) under [grant number 15-16107S] and the Charles University Research Programme "Progres" Q18—Social Sciences: From Multidisciplinarity to Interdisciplinarity.

Bratislava, Slovakia   Steven Saxonberg

CONTENTS

CHAPTER 1

Introduction

"Nothing could be more totalitarian," I thought to myself as a student of economics while attending the Berliner film festival. No, the film was not about the horrors of Nazi Germany or the Stalinist Soviet Union; instead, it was about the Portuguese Inquisition, which in reality was an extension of the Spanish Inquisition. Of course, studying in what was then West Berlin, I was well-aware of the Nazi atrocities; and specializing in East European economies, I was well-aware of the great repression that people had suffered under Stalin. I never thought the Spanish Inquisition was more ruthless or "evil" than Hitlerism or Stalinism, but it still felt more *totalitarian*. In my view, the essence of totalitarianism is summed up in the statement that Janos Kádár, the Hungarian communist ruler, made to mark his break with totalitarianism: "[W]hereas the Rákosites [i.e., supporters of the previous totalitarian ruler] said that someone who is not on our side is against us, we say, those who are not against us, are with us" (Linz and Stepan 1996: 298). In other words, a totalitarian regime is not satisfied if the population merely accepts its rule passively; it demands that the population support it *actively*. Totalitarian regimes want your heart and "soul."

What struck me in the film is that it was not enough for the protagonists to be members of the Catholic Church and to attend mass; they had to convince the inquisitors that they truly *believed* in Church dogma. To prove their dedication to the one "true" doctrine, they had to tell the inquisitors when the last time was that they prayed (and the

© The Author(s) 2019
S. Saxonberg, *Pre-Modernity, Totalitarianism and the Non-Banality of Evil*, https://doi.org/10.1007/978-3-030-28195-3_1

answer had better be "today" or at least "yesterday"!); they had to tell them exactly which prayer they said; and they had to show them that they knew these prayers by heart. By contrast, no inquisitors forced people under the rule of Stalin to prove they had memorized sections of works from Marx, Lenin or Stalin, even if they had to join Party organizations (trade unions, student associations, women's associations, etc.), and even if they had to attend some demonstrations (such as the First of May) or in the case of students to pass exams in Marxism-Leninism. In fact, other than the university exams in Marxism-Leninism—which one only had to barely pass with a low grade—there was little control on what people actually thought, as long as they proved loyal to the Party in their actions. One reason why the communist system could fall so rapidly is that it was common for people to live double lives, in which they pretended to have one opinion publicly while harboring another one privately (e.g., Kuran 1991). Obviously, totalitarianism is an ideal-type, and no rulers can ever gain total control over everyone's thoughts. There will always be agnostics and nonbelievers.[1] Nevertheless, it seems to me that the Spanish Inquisition at least tried harder than other totalitarian regimes to ensure that the population truly believed in the dogma.

Having received my PhD in political science and my professorship in sociology, now I am able to return to the topic of totalitarianism. This is a topic that my original studies in economics allowed little time for contemplating. The more I have read about the Inquisition, the more I have been struck by how much modern totalitarian regimes seem to have borrowed from it. For example, the earliest mentions I have found about a "holocaust" were *not* criticisms aimed at Nazi Germany, but rather words of *praise* from Catholic priests, who savored the glorious "holocaust" that occurred when heretics in France were burned at the stake. Thus, the chronicler Albericus gleefully wrote that a "holocaust, very great and pleasing to God" took place on Friday, May 13, 1239, in which more than 180 Cathars were burned (Haskins 1902: 635–6). Yet, even though this inquisition in France had some totalitarian attributes, it did not create a totalitarian regime. However, it served as a model for the Spanish Inquisition, which *did* lead to the creation of a totalitarian regime. Moreover, since the inquisition in France was not *the* French Inquisition, but rather *an* inquisition that took place in that country, I do not capitalize the term. I do capitalize the Spanish Inquisition, however, because that is the name of the specific inquisition in question.

In addition, the manner in which agents of the Inquisition interrogated their victims shows remarkable similarities with how Stalin's secret police interrogated theirs. An example comes from Menachem Begin (1957), later Israeli Prime Minister, who describes his detention by the Stalinist secret police (after the Soviet invasion of Poland in 1939) as a process that was very similar to that used by the Spanish Inquisition. As with his counterparts under the Inquisition, he was not officially arrested; nor was he charged with any crime. As under the Inquisition, he was not told who his accusers were. And as under the Inquisition, he was told that if he confessed and told them everything he knew, he would be set free.

Similarly, one could argue that the Nazi dogma about Jews' constituting a dangerous race has its equivalent in the Spanish "purity-of-blood" statutes (*limpieza*). Moreover, even if the Nazi idea of forcing Jews into ghettos was not part of the Spanish Inquisition (since the Jews were instead all expelled in the Spanish case), there was nonetheless a Catholic tradition of forcing Jews to dress differently than Christians and of forcing them to live in separate ghettos. As will be discussed in later chapters, rulers in certain parts of Spain prior to the expulsion tried to implement these types of policies.

Finally, it is even possible to see parallels between how Stalin organized the Soviet Party-state system and how the Catholic Church tried to organize society. Perhaps it is not a coincidence that Stalin had originally studied to be a priest in the Orthodox Church. Of course, the Orthodox Church is not organized as hierarchically as the Catholic Church is. For example, it does not have an "infallible" pope. Nevertheless, anybody studying to be an Orthodox priest must have been well-aware of how the Catholic Church is organized. Thus, Stalin replaced the "infallible" pope with the "infallible" General Secretary and the Bible with the works of Marx and Lenin. Instead of priests, he had Party leaders, who had the right to "interpret" Truth for the "ignorant" masses. Moreover, as I have argued previously (Saxonberg 2001, 2013), under communist rule the state was not a mere tool of the Party. Instead, there were always tensions between the Party and state, even though many people went from positions in the one institution to positions in the other or held positions in both simultaneously. From this perspective, the tensions between the Catholic Church and the Spanish Catholic monarchs can be seen as paralleling the tensions between the Party and the state under communist dictatorships.

This chapter proceeds as follows: first it makes clear the main argument of the book; then it discusses the comparative approach; and finally, it defines totalitarianism.

MAIN ARGUMENT OF THE BOOK

Of course, showing some similarities between the regime in Spain during the Inquisition and modern totalitarian regimes like the Nazi and Stalinist ones is not the same as showing that modern totalitarian leaders *consciously* borrowed methods developed during the Inquisition. Nonetheless, these parallels strengthen my belief that Spain during the Inquisition was indeed totalitarian. Of course, even if all inquisitions had totalitarian elements, and even if there are parallels between Stalin's regime and the Catholic Church, this does not mean the Catholic Church always supports totalitarianism, or that all countries harboring inquisitions were in fact totalitarian. In fact, I argue in this book, the inquisition in France did not lead to a totalitarian regime, while the one in Spain did.

Since my main argument emphasizes the importance of state-building or at least country-building, I will also present a similar paired comparison of two modern cases—Sweden and Germany—in an attempt to explain why the one Germanic country became totalitarian but not the other. I will argue that the rulers of Germany and of Spain had much greater incentives to use totalitarian methods in order to unify their newly created states, whereas the rulers of France and of Sweden—countries that had existed for centuries—faced a very different situation.

My argument goes against mainstream thinking, which links totalitarianism to modernity (e.g., Agamben 1995; Bauman 1991; Giddens 1991; Heller 2010; Horkheimer and Adorno 1944). One could even argue I am guilty of "concept-stretching," inasmuch as the pre-modern, late-medieval societies in France and Spain differed greatly from modern societies in Germany and Sweden. However, any kind of theorizing about political-sociological phenomena requires some amount of abstraction, as well as a degree of reliance on ideal-types that emphasize similarities; and the similarities in question concern features which are found in both modern and pre-modern societies.

The usefulness of different kinds of ideal-types depends on what we want to explain. For example, in order to explain why dictatorships arose in the last century in such countries as Italy, Germany and Russia—in which the state tried to gain total control over the population in a manner qualitatively different from the control sought by other kinds of authoritarian regimes (such as monarchies)—scholars grouped these regimes together under the ideal-type of "totalitarian." Yet, it has always been widely recognized that important differences existed, such as between National Socialism in Germany and Stalinist rule in the Soviet Union (e.g., Kershaw 2000). National Socialism sees race as the main social division, while communist doctrine sees class as the main one (e.g., Aharony 2010; Fritzsche and Hellbeck 2009; Lefort 1998; Stanley 1987); National Socialism claims to be nationalist, while Marxism-Leninism claims to be internationalist; National Socialism seeks the dominance of one people over another, while at least in theory Marxism-Leninism seeks equality and progress for all humans (e.g., Ehret 2007); National Socialist doctrine is purely totalitarian, while Marxism has had democratic interpretations and has inspired democratic movements that played a major role in democratizing Europe and Latin America (e.g., Rueschemeyer et al. 1992). In addition, Kershaw (2008: 35ff.) argues that, while Stalinism was based on creating institutional structures and could "settle down" and become conservative after Stalin died, Hitlerism was based on charismatic leadership and the avoidance of any bureaucratic or institutional brakes on its radicalism. Despite these differences, however, both Nazi Germany and the Soviet Union under Stalin have served as model cases of totalitarianism; and if we want to find out how and why regimes in the twentieth century were able to carry out policies aimed at gaining total control over people, then it makes sense to group the two countries together.

While it is certainly fruitful to investigate the reasons why totalitarian regimes could develop in the 1920s and 1930s in such countries as Germany, Italy and the Soviet Union, it is even more fruitful to investigate whether it is possible to develop a social-scientific explanation for why totalitarian regimes can develop in pre-modern as well as in modern societies. By applying this "method of agreement" (Skocpol and Somers 1980), we can develop theories which are stronger and that apply across a broader range of cases. So, the question is whether pre-modern societies can really ever be totalitarian. Of course, this depends on how one defines the term "totalitarian": if one defines it in such a manner that aspects of modernity form part of its definition, then only modern societies can be totalitarian. However, if one uses a more general definition—as referring to a regime's attempt to gain total dominance over its population—then there is no reason why pre-modern societies cannot also be totalitarian.

Interestingly, definitions of "democracy" have *not* been linked to modernity in the way that definitions of totalitarianism have, even though the interwar period saw a great increase in the number of democratic regimes (initially) as well as the emergence of totalitarian ones (a little later). In fact, the term "democracy" comes from the ancient Greeks. Few would deny that Athens was democratic during a certain period, even if the type of democracy practiced there differed greatly from that seen in the modern era. A city-state could practice direct democracy in a manner unthinkable in a modern society. However, this does not mean that only Athens was democratic and that modern representative governments are not; rather, both systems are democratic. It does mean, though, that democracy takes different forms during different historical eras since this type of government comes into being during periods that have different levels of technological and economic development.

One could see it like this: on the one hand, we have a linear perspective on history, according to which history is going in a certain direction. Elias (1939/1976) describes the "civilization process" by which society becomes more rationalized—a process that Horkheimer and Adorno (1944/1988) see as part of the Enlightenment project. This line of thinking lies behind Bauman's (1991) *Modernity and the Holocaust*, in which he argues that the Holocaust was made possible by the logic of modern bureaucracy, in which desk murderers each carried out their small task without feeling any responsibility for the final outcome. This tradition of linking totalitarianism and the Holocaust to modernity also lies behind Arendt's (1963/2005) concept of the "banality of evil"; however, she also links totalitarianism to modernity in earlier texts, such as *The Origins of Totalitarianism* (Arendt 1948/1973).

On the other hand, even though society and technology are continuously developing, this does not mean that certain types of governance—democracy, totalitarianism and so on—can only arise in one historical era or during one stage of technological and economic development. Rather, it may simply mean that these types of governance take different *forms* in different eras. In a slave society (such as ancient Athens)—where tools were rather basic, industry was lacking, city-states predominated, and societies were much smaller—democracy was bound to take a different form from that seen in a highly industrialized society based on mass production and a high degree of specialization. Nevertheless, in ancient Athens the basic democratic principle of one person one vote was followed for those who were citizens. (Of course, women and slaves could not vote, but neither could they during the first decades of America's democracy; yet, the USA is still often considered the first modern democracy.) Similarly, pre-modern societies obviously did not have the technology for running mass campaigns via radio and film the way the Nazis and communists did. Most people in the sparsely populated rural societies of the pre-modern era were illiterate, and neither the printing press nor radio had yet been invented; so a totalitarian regime in such a society could not use mass media to spread its propaganda. In an era in which the nobility, crown and Church vied for power, while the bourgeoisie was small and underdeveloped and political parties had not yet emerged, a totalitarian party could not emerge to create a one-party state. Still, none of these features should form part of the *definition* of totalitarianism; rather, the technological tools mentioned are simply instruments which a regime trying to gain totalitarian power can use during a certain stage of socio-economic development.

This point can also be put in Marxian terms: as the forces of production evolve and the economic base changes, the political superstructure will have different means available to control society. Of course, orthodox Marxists have not put much emphasis on the autonomy of the state. As institutionally oriented neo-Marxists have argued, however, the state is "relatively autonomous" from the dominant class (cf. Block 1977; Dahlkvist 1978; Miliband 1969; Poulantzas 1978).

Similarly, I argue that greatly varying types of rule can emerge under any type of "means of production," but that the ways in which such rule is implemented are dependent on the level of technological development (i.e., the development of the forces of production). Under capitalism, for example, we have huge variations in types of democracy (presidential systems, parliamentary systems, majoritarian versus proportional and mixed systems, majoritarian systems with one round and with two rounds, etc.); and we have great variation in nondemocratic systems as well (fascist and communist regimes, monarchies, military juntas, etc.). Similarly, as will be discussed later, medieval times saw a great variation in types of rule. In addition, feudalism—at least in the form in which lords ruled over serfs—was not so prominent in three of the four countries in this study. It is true that, in the German territories, serfs did not fully gain freedom from their manorial lords until well into the 1800s (Jacob 1963: 17–20); however, serfdom in France had disappeared to a large extent by the time that country's inquisition started in the thirteenth century (cf. Ladurie 1978: 36, 44). Like their counterparts in

France, moreover, serfs in Sweden gained their freedom rather early, as serfdom was abolished already in 1335 (Bägerfeldt 2003: 18, 2004: 93). Furthermore, some scholars argue that the Spanish territories never had a fully feudal system (e.g., Lourie 1966: 55). This is not to deny that all four countries experienced certain aspects of feudalism, such as the existence of guilds or of a landowning nobility, but the details reveal great variation among the four countries even during the medieval period that traditional Marxism considers to be "feudal." The important point is that, given the much lower level in the late medieval period of the forces of production (i.e., of technological development), a totalitarian regime in that era was bound to be different than one in the twentieth century.

This also means that people who commit "evil acts" in a pre-industrial medieval society might be expected to behave somewhat differently than those who (according to Arendt) carried out evilness in a banal way in Nazi Germany. Nevertheless, as the title of this book implies, new historical studies make it clear that evilness under the Nazi regime was nowhere near as "banal" as Arendt claims.

Thus, in addition to showing that pre-modern societies such as Spain during the Inquisition could be totalitarian, and besides analyzing why some countries become totalitarian but not others, this book will analyze the reasons why some people have been willing to commit "evil" acts for totalitarian regimes. In so doing, the book will criticize both the idea that totalitarianism is something "modern" and the notion that evilness under totalitarian regimes is "banal."

This chapter proceeds as follows: first, it discusses the comparative methodology that I employ. Then it defines "totalitarianism." Next, it presents my theoretical framework for analyzing totalitarianism and develops criteria for determining whether a country is totalitarian. Chapter 2 then shows that Spain during the Inquisition meets these criteria, whereas France during its inquisition does not. In so doing, the chapter demonstrates that Spain shares many traits with Germany under Nazi rule. Afterward, Chap. 3 sets out my framework for explaining why people under totalitarian rule are willing to commit "evil" acts. It shows that, just as totalitarianism forms part of a state-building process, so does the application of "evil" policies. In developing this analytical framework, Chap. 3 also criticizes Arendt's banality-of-evil thesis. Subsequent chapters present my empirical case studies, after which I present my conclusion.

COMPARATIVE METHODOLOGY

This book follows the tradition of such authors as Theda Skocpol (1979) and Barrington Moore (1966) in applying a comparative historical political-sociological analysis. In contrast to historical studies that place the emphasis on uncovering new empirical information, a historical political-sociological analysis usually relies on available studies for the empirical evidence—as the goal is to *theorize* past events rather than to question certain empirical details about them. All four of the cases in this book have been thoroughly researched; consequently, I have no ambition to add to our empirical knowledge about them.

In this book, I have applied a research strategy known as the *method of difference* (Skocpol and Somers 1980). This involves comparing countries that are as similar as possible but which have different outcomes. Thus the two medieval countries which I compare, Spain and France, had several points in common. Both of the two neighbors were Latin and Catholic, and both had infamous inquisitions. Both were kingdoms based on at least semi-feudal systems in which the landholding nobility had special powers. However, the inquisition in France came first, and its procedures became a basis for the methods later used by the Spanish Inquisition. Nevertheless, Spain became totalitarian but France did not.

Some might argue that the two cases are not comparable since the inquisition in France was instigated by the pope (hence my use of the term "inquisition in France" rather than "French Inquisition"), while the Spanish Inquisition was run by the crown.[2] However, this book will show that this division is somewhat exaggerated. In France, the initiative for action against heretics came originally from a local ruler, Count Raymond V of Toulouse, who attacked the Cathars in 1178. He tried to get the French king to support him; and had such support been forthcoming, the result would have been a non-papal inquisition under the control of the crown. But, he failed to get the king's support, so he turned to the Holy See (Wakefield 1974: 83ff.). Yet, to be able to carry out the crusade against the Cathars, the pope needed the help of the French king in the form of soldiers. The king in turn only obliged reluctantly and only during certain periods. Thus, we have a situation in which local rulers and clergy interacted with both the crown and the papacy in a complicated relationship.

In Spain, the idea of instituting the Inquisition and expelling the Jews came from the local Church leaders. In the mid-fifteenth century, Dominican monks living in Spain pressured the crown to take action. The papal nuncio, Niccolo Franco, then residing at the court of Castile, supported the demands of the local clergy (Prescott 1841: 277). A Dominican monk, de Torquemada, played an especially important role in convincing the Spanish crown to instigate an inquisition, which he infamously went on to head as the first Grand Inquisitor (Prescott 1841: 279). The monarchy eventually agreed to set up the Inquisition, but it had to turn for approval to Pope Sixtus IV, who issued a bull for an inquisition in 1478 (Kamen 1985: 30). Even though King Ferdinand and Queen Isabella chose the Grand Inquisitor, the Inquisition was self-financing through its confiscations. It did have to hand over the confiscated property to the crown, which kept some of the treasures, but the crown returned the rest to the Inquisition. The Inquisition became relatively autonomous, and it sometimes prosecuted people working for the monarchs. Although the rulers tried in vain to protect these people, the Inquisition sometimes gained the pope's support for the prosecution of royal staff. For example, King Philip reluctantly yielded to the Church, handing over his personal confessor, de Carranza, to the Inquisition in 1559, after the pope had threatened the king with excommunication (Atkinson 1934: 104). Similarly, the Inquisition often came into conflict with popes over its prosecution of clergy (e.g., Kamen 1985: 157ff.). At certain times the popes intervened more in the affairs of the Inquisition (when they felt stronger); at other times they did so less (when they felt weaker). Thus Church-crown relations were complicated, as each institution influenced the other—just as Party-state relations were complicated in Nazi Germany and under the communist regimes.[3]

Of course, arguing that Spain represents a case of pre-modern totalitarianism does not imply it is the only such case. For example, Barrington Moore (1958: 59ff.) sees Calvinist Geneva as a case of pre-modern totalitarianism, while Stanley (1987: 177–207) sees the rule of King Shaka over the Zulus in southern Africa in the nineteenth century as a non-European, pre-modern case of totalitarianism. This book concentrates on Spain because it is the best-known and most studied case—which means the largest amount of literature is available for analyzing it. Hopefully, this monograph will encourage more studies on non-modern forms of totalitarianism.

For the modern cases, this book compares two Germanic countries that are sort of neighbors (although separated by the sea): Germany and Sweden. The Nazis in Germany based their power on a racial ideology, but racialist notions were by no means restricted to that country. In Sweden, for example, there was a political consensus in the 1920s on the need for research on race biology. Consequently, Uppsala University established the world's first research institute devoted to racial hygiene. Its founding had gained near unanimous support in parliament from both left and right. In Sweden, as in Germany, myths were strong about a glorious past when pre-Christian Germanic gods ruled the planet, and there was a strong belief in the need for racial purity. National socialists regarded both Swedes and Germans as "Aryans," and if anything saw Swedes as the more homogeneously Aryan of the two. Both countries also had strong Lutheran traditions. In Sweden, the official state church was Lutheran, while Germany was the birthplace and homeland of Luther (although unlike Sweden it had a sizable Catholic minority). Both countries were quite highly industrialized, with strong social democratic parties and well-organized workers; and both were parliamentary democracies based on proportional representation.

In *States and Social Revolutions*, Skocpol (1979) recommends combining the method of difference with the method of agreement. The latter method involves comparing countries that are as different as possible but which have similar outcomes. This book follows her advice, in that it shows how the same mechanisms which allowed Germany to become totalitarian also allowed Spain to do so—even though the two cases are separated by centuries, and even though one country was medieval and "feudal" while the other was modern, capitalist and industrialized. Spain was also Catholic, whereas Germany was predominantly Lutheran. However, despite these differences, people in both countries were willing to commit "evil" acts. Similarly, even though the Swedish and French cases are separated by many centuries and by a huge gap in levels of technological and economic development, and even though their religious composition differed (France being Catholic and Sweden being Lutheran), the outcome was the same in both cases: neither country became totalitarian.

My main focus in the French case is on the years between 1209 and 1323—that is, on the period between the Albigensian Crusades and the end of Bernardo Gui's term as head inquisitor. The French inquisition began after the pope called for a crusade in the Albi region to wipe out the Cathar Christian sect. This sect believed in celibacy and vegetarianism, and it claimed that there are two gods: one good and one evil. Gui became famous for writing the handbook for inquisitors—*Practica inqui sitionis heretice pravitatis*—instructing them on how to extract confessions. After

his time at the head of the French inquisition, the body lost its importance. My main focus in the Spanish case is on the period between 1492
and 1600—that is, between the country's unification and the end of the
next century. (The sixteenth century marked the height of the Spanish
Inquisition and its repression in society.) In the Germanic cases, finally, I
concentrate on the years between 1800 and 1945. In Sweden in 1809,
after a coup overthrew the king in response to the loss of Finland to Russia,
the state started carrying out important administrative reforms in order to
modernize the country. The nineteenth century was also important for
Germany, because of the failed revolution of 1848, the rise of romanticism
and anti-Semitism and the unification of the country. Obviously, the comparison of the two countries concludes in 1945, when World War II
(WWII) ended and the Nazi regime collapsed. Even though I concentrate
on certain historical periods, I find it necessary at times—since I am con-
ducting a historical analysis of the evolution of the four countries—to take
up events from earlier periods which clearly influenced later developments.

DEFINING TOTALITARIANISM

Those linking totalitarianism to modernity often define it in such a way
that it *must* be modern, in the sense of having traits that are only possible
in industrialized societies based on mass production and mass communica-
tion (e.g., Bauman 1991). Yet if modernity is part of the definition, then
there is no way to investigate whether regimes in other eras were totalitarian. The question is whether the modern aspects of classical totalitarian
regimes really were essential to totalitarianism, or whether instead they
arose simply because such regimes existed in the modern era. For example,
in one of the classic texts on the definition of totalitarianism, Friedrich
(1964: 52) claims that totalitarian regimes are based on a "single mass
party" comprising up to 10 percent of the population. If political parties
are essential for totalitarianism, then only modern societies can be totalitarian, as previous societies did not have such institutions. However, if
political parties are just a means to an end—that is, if they furnish a means
that aspiring leaders can use to create a totalitarian society—then they may
simply help to explain in some cases how a totalitarian movement was able
to acquire and maintain power (rather than forming part of the definition
of what makes a society totalitarian). Instead of requiring the existence of
a mass party, a more open definition—one which would not necessitate
that totalitarian regimes be modern—would require the existence of an

organization which pressures society into accepting the regime's ideology. Moreover, at least one pre-modern organization penetrated society more deeply than any modern mass party has done: Friedrich's definition requires only that at least 10 percent of the population belong to a mass party, while *100 percent* of the population had to belong to the Church under the Spanish Inquisition.

The real essence of totalitarianism, as indicated by the word itself, concerns rather the aspiration to have *total* control over people's thoughts and to force the population to support the regime *actively* (e.g., Arendt 1948/1973). Similarly, Linz (1975/2000) emphasizes the need for a totalizing ideology which instills the regime with a higher purpose. Raymond Aron (1969: 193) argues that, under totalitarian regimes, "[t]he monopolistic party is animated or armed with an ideology on which it confers absolute authority and which consequently becomes the official truth of the state." While most social scientists today go back to the classic texts of authors like Arendt and Friedrich for definitions of totalitarianism, there has been a distinct trend toward putting greater emphasis on the role of ideology and the attempts of totalitarian regimes to establish such hegemonic control over society that it becomes difficult even to think outside of the official ideological framework (e.g., Carstensen and Schmidt 2016; Thompson 2002; Tibi 2007).

Thus, it seems clear that a totalitarian regime must have a *totalizing ideology*, which it uses to try to gain hegemony over society; and that it must operate through *ideological organizations*, such as parties in the modern era and the Church in medieval Europe. In order to gain support for its ideology, it needs a "carrot"—either a political religion for people to believe in or (in the case of a theocracy) a religion that is politicized. Moreover, since it is never possible to get an entire population to believe unquestioningly in a doctrine, the regime must also have a "stick"—that is, some kind of oppressive apparatus with which it can make people live in fear.

Scholars of totalitarianism often refer to the totalizing practices of a totalitarian regime as a *political religion*. Linz (1996: 104) states that "[p]olitical religion is conceived by the rulers as a means of legitimation of a movement and a political system." The idea, as Voegelin (2007, 3rd edition) originally developed it, is that as the world becomes more secularized and traditional religions—such as Catholicism—provide less of a moral guideline, a moral vacuum emerges, which leaves an opening in society for dictators to emerge, who preach inner-worldly political religions that replace the traditional religions. Herz (1996: 162) comments that, in claiming that totalitarianism arises in modernity because society decays after the Church loses its spiritual influence, "Voegelin's ideas remain… merely a variant of the [anti-modernist Catholic philosophy of] Renouveau Catholique." Roberts (2009: 388) notes that "[t]he phenomenological, associated especially with Voegelin, suggests that modern political religion offers an experience fully comparable to traditional religious experience."

In contrast to those who contend that totalitarianism emerges because of the decline of religion, I argue that religions themselves can form the basis for totalitarian regimes. That was not just the case in medieval Spain; it is also true in the case of modern religious movements like Islamic State in Iraq and Syria (ISIS). Whereas political religions have to replace God with race (as in Nazi Germany), class (as in the Soviet Union under Stalin) or something else, overtly religious totalitarian regimes can base themselves on their claim to be guardians of the will of God. With the rise of Islamist movements such as Islamic Brotherhood, Al Qaeda and ISIS, there has been a growing literature portraying these movements are totalitarian in nature (e.g., Bale 2009; Boroumand and Boroumand 2002; Hansen and Kainz 2007; Heck 2017; Tibi 2007, 2010; Zekulin and Anderson 2016). These movements demand total obedience to theocratic rulers, and they allow for no dissenting opinions. Rather than referring to the doctrine of a theological totalitarian regime as a political religion, it makes more sense to follow Tibi (2010) in calling it a "politicized religion," or as Payne (2005: 171) calls it "an extreme politicisation of traditional religion." Maier (1996) reflects that totalitarian regimes have "pure doctrines," "'holy' (or at least canonically valid) books and testaments; there are heretics and 'inquisitions,' care for 'faith' and 'morals' guarded by punishment; there are heresies, dissidents and renegades, apostates and proselytes, etc." All of these traits hold as much for "politicized religions" like that in Spain under the Inquisition as they do for the Nazi and Stalinist political religions.

The idea that Catholicism in certain eras can have totalitarian tendencies[4] is borne out by the Vatican's criticism of the claim of Nazi and Fascist movements in the 1930s to be totalitarian. The Holy See countered that the Church is the organization that *really* deserves to have total control. In discussing the Church's response to fascism, Gentile (2006: 160–1) comments: "Most Catholic scholars, however, felt certain that a clash between totalitarianism and Catholicism was in any case inevitable, because each of the two systems claimed for itself total control over every aspect of individual and collective life." In addition,

> the pope contrasted the totalitarian supremacy of the church with political totalitarianism, stating that "if there is a totalitarian regime—*de facto* and *de jure*—it is the regime of the church, because man belongs entirely to the church, and must belong to it, given that man is a creature of the Good Lord."

Nevertheless, the fact that the Catholic Zentrum party was one of the main parties supporting the Weimar Republic shows that Catholicism cannot be associated unequivocally with totalitarianism. Rather it shows that, like all religions, Catholicism can be interpreted in a variety of ways.

Of course, while theocracies can become totalitarian, not all religions lead to totalitarianism. First, some religions by their nature are more tolerant than others. As Bale (2009: 75) observes, religions such as Jainism or Taoism are extremely unlikely to "produce violent extremists." Polytheistic religions like those in ancient Greece and Rome were relatively tolerant, as they were "often willing and able to incorporate the deities of other peoples they encountered into their own pantheons, thereby avoiding the unnecessary generation of religion-based hostility and conflict." Bale adds that "the three Near Eastern monotheistic religions are almost bound to engender animosity or conflict, since their followers generally believe that only their God is the true god, that all other gods are false gods, and that anyone who does not convert to their religion or accept their God is consigned to Hellfire for eternity." Yet, even among these three, there is a difference: between Judaism, which is not a missionary religion, and both Christianity and Islam, which are. In the case of the missionary religions, "it is the duty of their followers to spread their faith throughout the world...." Consequently, missionary religions are more likely to lead to totalitarianism, as they proclaim the need for everyone in the world to believe in their one "true" faith.

Second, religions and ideologies are open to different interpretations. Consequently, Boroumand and Boroumand (2002: 12) argue,

> the religious references which Khomeini used to justify his rule were literally the same as those invoked a century earlier by an eminent ayatollah who was arguing for the legitimacy of parliamentarism and popular sovereignty on Islamic grounds. Koranic verses lend themselves to many different and even contradictory interpretations.

The same is obviously true of Catholicism and Christianity, as most Christian societies throughout history have not been totalitarian. Since not everyone will believe in the religion, and since even some believers may think they are following the "true" religion while actually deviating from the accepted interpretations of Truth, totalitarian regimes need a stick with which to beat the population into submission. Describing the totalitarian tendencies of communist regimes, Versluis (2006: 9) observes:

> For the Communist Party in power, nothing is "as great a menace as is heresy." The enemy, in a potential form, will always be there; the only friend will be the man who accepts the doctrine 100 per cent. If he accepts only 99 per cent, he will necessarily have to be considered a foe, for from that remaining 1 per cent a new church can arise. Communism enforces on people a numbing intellectual deadness generated by fear of the state Inquisition. In place of Christian faith, it substitutes doctrines of "historical inevitability" and "progress" on earth, but it functions similarly to the Spanish Inquisition.

This quote makes the link between the Spanish Inquisition and modern totalitarianism clear.

Grieder (2007: 563–4) reflects that the most important theorists of totalitarianism, such as Arendt and Aron, emphasize the role of *fear* in keeping the population in line. Brzezinski (1956) claims that Stalin spread terror in society by instigating a "permanent purge." Maier (1996: 194) notes that the Nazis spread anxiety among the population by making everyone live in fear that the authorities would uncover an unknown Jewish grandfather; while the Bolshevik movement spread fear with its periodic purges. In both cases, moreover, those who survived could experience the positive feeling of belonging to society's "ingroup." In other words, terror has the function both of making the costs of dissidence too high to contemplate and of creating a feeling of belonging among those not included in the punished group. The Spanish case shows that widespread fear could even be used in pre-modern times when there was no bureaucratic apparatus from which to purge people.

In summary, I define a state as totalitarian if it meets the following criteria:

- It has a totalizing ideology with which it seeks to legitimize its rule.
- It has organizations capable of helping it enforce its rule.
- It bases itself on a political religion or a politicized religion.
- It creates an atmosphere of fear in order to deter would-be dissenters.

Chapter 2 explains why Spain under the Inquisition and Germany in the Nazi era meet these criteria, but France under its inquisition and Sweden in the "modern" era do not.

EXPLAINING TOTALITARIANISM: THE ROLE OF STATE-BUILDING

As noted in the introduction, the most common explanation for the rise of totalitarianism links it to the mechanisms of modernity. According to this view, a type of modern instrumental rationality has allowed rulers to establish an efficient and far-reaching bureaucracy, and enabled desk murderers to carry out their tasks without feeling responsible for the consequences of their actions. Thus, "evil" becomes banal. However, such an approach cannot explain how pre-modern countries such as Spain could become totalitarian. In addition, as I argue in this book, the banality-of-evil thesis is not persuasive.

Another common argument is cultural: that is, Germany had an especially authoritarian and anti-Semitic culture (e.g., Shirer 1960; Weiss 1996). For example, Erich Fromm argues (1941/1969) in his famous book *Escape from Freedom* that the authoritarian Lutheran heritage was to blame for the willingness of Germans to embrace National Socialism. As a psychologist, he especially emphasized the Lutheran style of child-raising, with its demand for total obedience. Fromm's book has great insights, but his approach cannot explain why Sweden did not become totalitarian since that country was *more* purely Lutheran than Germany. In Sweden the State Church was Lutheran, and all citizens were automatically made members at birth, although as adults they could request to leave the Church. Until the 1990s, in fact, the Church carried out such official state tasks as registering the residence of all inhabitants. Foreigners coming to Sweden did not register with the police or the tax authorities, but rather with the State Church. Until the 1800s, it was not even legal in Sweden to belong to a different church, and until the 1900s, one could not hold any public office unless one was a member. Germany, by contrast, has a large Catholic population in parts of the country, such as Bavaria. Moreover, Austria also embraced National Socialism, and it is a Catholic country. Furthermore, it is hard to argue that Germany was more "Germanic" than Sweden, as the latter country had proportionally fewer immigrants, fewer members of minority groups and far fewer Jews. In any case, this approach cannot explain why Catholic Spain became totalitarian but Catholic France did not.

Similarly, one common view explains the rise of the Nazis as resulting from the *Sonderweg* (special path) of development that Germany supposedly underwent; but this approach too runs afoul of the fact that Spain became totalitarian as well. This argument emphasizes the strength of the aristocratic Junker class and the weakness of the German bourgeoisie and of German liberalism, which resulted in the country's following a more authoritarian path (for critical discussions of this view, see Evans 2005; Kocka 2018; Ping 2012). A further problem with the "special path" argument is that, by its nature, it can only be applied to one country; so it cannot explain the rise of totalitarian regimes elsewhere. In addition, as several authors have pointed out, German elections were actually more democratic in the late 1800s than British ones were (although the British parliament had more power than the German one since the cabinet needed its confidence). Consequently, it is not clear that Germany historically was more authoritarian than "normal" European countries were (Berman 2001; Möller 1982).

Some neo-Marxist theorists, applying their notion of the relative autonomy of the state, argue that fascist parties could come to power in countries where the capitalist class was too weak to keep power and the working class too weak to take it. A situation of this kind enables "Bonapartist" dictators to emerge and to gain considerable autonomy from both classes (cf. Block 1977; Dahlkvist 1978; Miliband 1969; Poulantzas 1978). This can also help explain why fascist parties did not come to power in Sweden, as the working class was stronger and less divided in that country than in Germany. However, while such an argument is fruitful for explaining the Nazis' rise to power, it still has difficulty explaining why Spain became totalitarian but not France. It also has trouble explaining why the German variant of totalitarianism became racist and genocidal, but not the Italian one did not. Finally, it fails to take into account institutional factors that could either facilitate or inhibit totalitarian rule.

Numerous studies have also analyzed the importance of actors' decisions in Hitler's rise to power—such as the decision to make him chancellor, the decision of some parties to let the previous governments fall and so on. Similarly, other studies have analyzed the issue of who voted for the Nazis (Childers 1983; Falter 1991) or who became party members (e.g., Brustein 1996). Such approaches are valuable for helping us understand how an authoritarian movement could come to power, but that in itself is not enough to explain why the country became totalitarian. For example, even if Trump does not espouse a fascist ideology—in fact, it is questionable whether he has any ideology at all other than self-love—he still clearly has authoritarian tendencies. Yet, despite these tendencies, his prospects for establishing a totalitarian dictatorship are far less favorable than Hitler's were. Already within his first year of power, Hitler was basically able to overturn almost all of the democratic institutions in Germany (Kershaw 2008). Trump, on the other hand, has not even been able to repeal Obama's healthcare reform or to build the wall on the Mexican border. When Trump proposed a ban on Muslims' visiting the country, his first two proposals were overturned by the courts. Even if Trump were to espouse an openly totalitarian ideology, it is extremely unlikely he would be able to institute a totalitarian regime, because the structural-institutional hindrances to doing so are too great.

My main argument is that totalitarianism has come about as part of a state-building strategy. Thus, in Spain, the Crown used Catholicism as a way to homogenize society around a Catholic ideology, in order to legitimize its power over the newly united country. Meanwhile, France at the period of its inquisition had already long been an established country, in the sense that there was a French king and French territory.

Although France was not yet a modern state with a modern bureaucracy when the inquisition was instituted, the country was already what Hastings (1997: 29) calls a "traditional state" based on a kingdom. After becoming countries, both Spain and France had regions where people spoke different languages and different dialects. The type of bureaucracies and the degree of centralization have also changed over time, as have the borders. As Elias (1939/1976) notes, the Middle Ages were not static, and countries such as France went through a long period of gradual development and centralization. In France during the period of this study, much of the country's southern territory was indeed under the crown, but relatively autonomous and run by vassals. Spain provides a stark contrast to France. Until the period of the Spanish Inquisition following the union of the crowns of Castile and Aragon, a Spanish country did not exist. Meanwhile, France was a country during the time of its inquisition, and a relatively well-established one by the criteria of its time; so its inquisition did not form part of any state-building strategy. The population in both countries spoke a variety of dialects and languages, but this posed a particular problem for the rulers of Spain since that country had been united only recently. It, therefore, made more sense for them to use

Catholicism than to use language as a way to homogenize the country. After all, it was not a problem to force the populations of the Portuguese and Italian territories to become homogeneously Catholic when they came under Spanish rule since these populations were already mostly Catholic. Portugal had a Jewish population, but the Spanish rulers expelled those Jews who did not convert, and they extended the Spanish Inquisition to the area in order to maintain control over those who did. It would have been much more difficult to unite these populations around the Spanish language, especially since at that time the Spanish language itself was not completely unified. Consequently, the crown used the Inquisition as a way to legitimize the rule of the "Catholic monarchs" and to create a united country with a homogenized Catholic-Spanish culture. Moreover, they did this in an area that had previously consisted of separate kingdoms with three important religions, and in which some regions had previously had Muslim majorities.

Where the modern cases are concerned, Sweden had already been a country for hundreds of years. At the helm of a well-established state, its rulers did not have to take any special actions to recruit a loyal bureaucracy, as they already enjoyed great legitimacy and could count on the bureaucracy's already being loyal to this old state. In addition, despite racist tendencies, the Swedish state had no pressing need to determine who was Swedish and who was not, or to find an outgroup to use as a scapegoat. Furthermore, with its "policy legacy" of consensus, the country democratized through an evolutionary process, which had the support of all of the political parties as well as the monarchy; as a result, there were no strong forces opposed to the regime in the 1920s and 1930s. Moreover, the country's comparatively inclusionary path of state development had traditionally afforded representation to the peasantry in parliament, as one of the four estates. This meant that the peasants, who often held racist and authoritarian views, could still be coopted into supporting democracy, due to the great influence which a peasant-based party was able to wield within the democratic system. From 1932 until WWII began, this party joined the social democrats in a coalition government that took the first steps in developing the Swedish model of social welfare.

The German state, by contrast, was created quickly in the 1870s when Bismarck succeeded in uniting the German kingdoms after Prussian victories on the battlefield. Bismarck had to battle against strong regional identities centered on the various kingdoms. (In fact, even some of the original Nazi leaders in the early 1920s favored Bavarian independence.)

Creating a new country required Bismarck to take actions to gain the loyalty of the state bureaucracy, which prompted him to introduce special welfare programs to favor civil servants (*Beamten*). In addition, as loyalty was such a pressing issue, coming from a conservative background and showing strong loyalty and obedience to the Kaiser became a more important criterion than merit for recruitment to the bureaucracy.

Consequently, when the imperial regime collapsed after losing World War I (WWI), the new democracy inherited a bureaucracy that was basically hostile to the republic and its values. Not only did the conservative bureaucracy make it more difficult for democratic governments to rule during the Weimar Republic; it also made it easier for the Nazis to gain power and to govern, as the Nazi regime had greater legitimacy in the eyes of many bureaucrats than the Weimar Republic had had.

As rulers of a new state, Germany's leaders also had to decide who belonged and who did not. Should the state be based on religion, ethnicity/race or language? Bismarck had good reason to think the Poles and French living in German territory might not be loyal to the new state in case of war. For racist reasons, moreover, he questioned the loyalty of Jews. To begin with, Bismarck also fought against Catholics in his "culture war" (*Kulturkampf*), but then he relented and decided against using religion as the line of demarcation. (He was still against Jews, but by then they were considered to be a race as much as a religious group.)

In contrast to Sweden, this new, less stable state also felt it necessary to ban the socialist parties—including the largest party, the social democrats—because Bismarck and the Kaiser feared they would try to overthrow the state. (In contrast, when Sweden democratized, all of the right-wing parties and even the king trusted the social democrats.) To a large extent German society united behind the Kaiser during WWI, as even the social democrats voted in favor of the bill to finance the war, although the vote split the party. However, once the Kaiser lost the war, the regime quickly lost legitimacy, and he abdicated in the face of a revolutionary uprising of workers and soldiers. Strikingly enough, even though the social democrats came to power because of the revolution, their leaders actually were against revolutionary change; and they wanted the monarchy to continue. Thus, the new republic was born through a revolution that none of the major parties really wanted. Many of the right-wing parties looked for a scapegoat to deal with the humiliation of defeat and the resulting Versailles Treaty, with the suffering caused by hyperinflation, and so on. This made it easier for anti-democratic, anti-Semitic parties to chal lenge the republic and to blame the Jews for the calamities once the Great Depression broke out. Promising to make Germany a strong and united country once again, they were able to gain legitimacy among a large part of the population and of the bureaucracy.

Interestingly, while Swedish kings relied historically on support from peasants, which strengthened the latter and encouraged them to build their own party eventually—whereby they were integrated into the democratic process—German monarchs relied on the support of the nobility, which kept both the peasants and the burghers rather weak. As a consequence, there were no farmers' parties for peasants to turn to, except in the case of Bavaria; so many of them turned to the Nazis (whereas in Bavaria most supported the peasant party). Of course, peasants were not the only important class to support fascist movements, but they played an important role. Moreover, as will be discussed in Chap. 6, they presented the greatest threat of fascism in the Swedish case. Thus, the difference between the ways the two states were formed, as well as between being a well-established state and a new one, were extremely important for the divergent dynamics seen in Germany and Sweden.

While emphasizing the role of state-building, this book does not deny the importance of actors in creating policies. It does not take a deterministic view; instead, it merely shows that the issue of state-building has been an extremely influential underlying factor with which political actors must deal. A theoretical discussion now follows, after which I turn to Sweden and then to Germany. In addition to questioning the claim that totalitarianism is something modern, this book contests the claim that evil is banal. Thus, I define evilness in the next section, although I also discuss theories explaining the causes of state-supported evilness in Chap. 3. For now, it suffices to explain what I mean by the term "evil," and to give a very brief account of how I will explain in Chap. 3 why totalitarian regimes have an incentive to induce parts of the population to commit "evil" acts.

EVILNESS

My political-sociological approach emphasizes the role of state-building and the need for newly created states to legitimize themselves. I argue throughout this book that totalitarian states tend to pressure parts of the population to commit "evil" acts as part of their legitimation process. That is, the new state, lacking legitimacy, tries to unite the population around an ideology, as well as against an outgroup that it claims poses an existential threat to the country. Many theorists of totalitarianism empha-size the role of modernity in making possible the emergence of totalitarian regimes that engage in "evil" acts. For example, Bauman (1991) argues that the uniqueness of the Holocaust lay in its factory-style mass killing. Gerlach (2016) and Mann (2005), by contrast, point out that a large pro-portion of the slaughter was not carried out in this manner: soldiers, police and SS troops shot hundreds of thousands of people, and many victims died of hunger. Moreover, they note that even the murders in the concen-tration camps were not only desktop murders, as many of the perpetrators dealt with the victims personally. In any case, the killing factories were indeed unique and they obviously could not exist in pre-modern times—when factories did not exist, and the industrial division of labor (which the Nazis used in the killing factories) did not exist either. Nevertheless, geno-cide is definitely not just a modern phenomenon, and neither is totalitari-anism. However, genocide and totalitarianism took a different form in the past.

In *The Iliad*, for example, Homer depicts Agamemnon, king of Mycenae and leader of the Greek army, urging his brother to renounce any thought of mercy:

> So soft, dear brother, why?
> Why such concern for enemies? I suppose you got
> such tender loving care at home from the Trojans.
> Ah would to god not one of them could escape
> his sudden plunging death beneath our hands!
> No baby boy still in his mother's belly,
> not even he escape-all Ilium blotted out,
> no tears for their lives, no markers for their graves! (6.55–60,
> translation used from Homer 1990)

Konstan (2007: 174) comments:

> It is a commonplace that, in ancient Greece, those who were vanquished in war were wholly at the mercy of the victors and that there were no con-straints, apart from spontaneous pity or calculated self-interest, that pre-vented conquerors from inflicting on those they defeated the annihilation or enslavement of their entire population and the destruction of their city.

Of course, in Spain during the period of the Inquisition, the state did not engage in genocide—at least not in the sense of committing mass murder. Nevertheless, it did wipe out entire cultures and ethnic groups in its territory, by forcing all Jews and Muslims to leave the country or convert, and then repressing those who converted in a manner that eliminated their cultural and ethnic traditions. Even if this does not technically amount to genocide (in the sense of mass murder taking place), it still fits the definition of "evil" used in this book.

I personally do not like the term "evil," as it is normative and has religious implications; but since there is an important discourse about what causes evil behavior, I feel forced to use the term, especially since I want to criticize the banality-of-evil thesis. I subscribe to Vetlesen's (2005: 2) definition: "[T]o do evil,…is to *intentionally inflict pain and suffering on another human being, against her will, and causing serious and foreseeable harm to her.*" Similarly, Waller (2007) defines "*human evil as the deliberate harming of humans by other humans.*" (Italics in the original for both quotes.) As I am interested in evil acts committed in the name of a totalitarian regime, I would add Waller's (2007: 14) point that evil refers "to the deliberate harm inflicted against a defenseless and helpless group targeted by a political, social, or religious authority…." Thus, I will argue in Chap. 5 that Spain during the first century of the Inquisition meets these criteria.

In Chap. 3, I discuss theories of evilness and criticize the banality-of-evil thesis. Here, it suffices to give a very brief summary of my approach. My explanation is based on the notion that totalitarian regimes have an incentive to encourage the population to commit "evil" acts because doing so helps them in their state-building process and grants greater legitimacy to their attempt at building the new state. I agree with the socio-psychological theories that emphasize the following steps as being necessary for inducing people to participate in "evil" acts:

1. leaders label groups of people as being the "other"
2. then the leaders take steps to dehumanize these people
3. the leaders present these dehumanized groups of people as presenting an existential threat to society

However, these socio-psychological approaches by themselves cannot explain why states would *want* to mobilize people to perform such acts. I claim that mobilizing society against the "other" and presenting groups as an existential threat are strategies that rulers of recently created states find useful as a way of gaining legitimacy for their regimes because they enable them to pose as saviors against a dangerous enemy. I further maintain that the mere fact of creating a new state raises the issue of who belongs and who does not belong to the ingroup (and to the outgroup). Long-established states, by contrast, already enjoy great legitimacy, and they do not face the ingroup/outgroup issue to the same extent as newly founded states.

My approach incorporates cultural approaches but does not use them as a simple causal explanation in which people commit "evil" acts because they have a culture of "eliminationist anti-Semitism" or other type of cultural prejudice. Rather, as I see it, culture provides a background which rulers can utilize in certain circumstances in order to convince the population that an outgroup poses an existential threat. When a new state is created, and people feel anxiety over the future of this unstable new state, its rulers have an incentive to try to gain legitimacy by playing upon existing prejudices and pointing out a certain group as an existentially threatening "other." Then, by taking progressive steps to dehumanize the outgroup while consolidating their power, the rulers gain legitimacy for their actions and convince an increasing number of people that they should engage in evil acts against the outgroup in order to ensure their own survival. In contrast, stable states that have existed for centuries find it much more difficult to convince the population that an outgroup constitutes an existential threat; therefore, even if cultural prejudices against an outgroup exists in such a society, its rulers have difficulty convincing the population to engage in measures against that group.

SUMMARY AND CONTENT OF THE BOOK

Chapter 2 shows why medieval Spain during the period of the Inquisition meets the criteria for totalitarianism, while France during its inquisition does not. That chapter argues that Spain's totalitarian side had a lot in common with Nazi Germany's, even if totalitarianism under pre-modern conditions necessarily differed from totalitarianism under modern conditions. Sweden, for its part, developed into a parliamentary democracy, so there is little reason to present evidence that it was not totalitarian; accordingly, Chap. 2 focuses on the other three countries. Chapter 3 develops a theoretical framework for explaining why people living under totalitarian regimes are willing to commit "evil" acts, and it explains why totalitarian regimes have incentives to pressure people into committing such acts. Thus, Chaps. 1, 2 and 3 establish the framework for the book, after which the empirical case studies follow. The first empirical case, set out in Chap. 4, is that of France, since it was one of the first countries to have an inquisition. (The Spanish Inquisition later used tools devised during the French inquisition.) In that chapter, I show that, since France was one of the most well-established countries by the standards of the time, the French crown did not have the same incentive as the Spanish one to resort to totalitarian terror in order to legitimize its rule. In fact, rather than unifying the country, the inquisition in France sharply divided it, as large portions of the population opposed the inquisition.

Chapter 5 then explains how the Spanish Inquisition helped the country become totalitarian, while the inquisition in France did not have this effect. I argue that the Catholic monarchs, Ferdinand and Isabella, decided to use Catholicism as a homogenizing strategy in order to give legitimacy to their newly created state. This new state embarked on a mission to make the world more Catholic. In general, there had been some fear in the air, as the previous decades had witnessed widespread disorder, which the newly created regime was able to reign in. Jews were also seen as an existential threat, as they could induce newly converted Christians to revert to Judaism; moreover, there had already been riots against Jews in the previous two centuries because local clergy had blamed them for such calamities as the plague. The *conversos*, moreover, represented a threat to the new order, as some of the wealthiest among them had begun marrying into aristocratic families, thereby threatening the claim of the latter to having "better" and "purer" blood than the peasantry (and thus being entitled to rule). The peasants could now claim that their blood, unlike that of the nobles, was untainted by "Jewish blood." Meanwhile, once the Islamic territories were conquered, Muslims came to represent an existential threat, because even if they could be pressured to convert to Catholicism, they might still side with invading Muslim armies from the Ottoman Empire or Morocco.

Chapter 6 focuses on Sweden. As a long-established state, Sweden had a population and bureaucracy that were loyal; thus, its rulers had no need to find an outgroup against which to aim popular sentiment in order to unify the country; nor did they need to create a totalitarian ideology in order to ensure their rule. Furthermore, the bureaucracy was much more autonomous in Sweden than in Germany; so, even if German bureaucrats were not in fact robots who simply followed orders blindly, it is true that they faced much more pressure than their Swedish counterparts to be obedient to the regime. Thus, Swedish bureaucrats could take greater policy initiatives, such as making entry easier for Jewish refugees when the Holocaust become known.

Anti-Semitism and racism were widespread in Sweden at the turn of the century, and Sweden became the first country in the world to establish an institute for race biology. Myths of Aryan superiority were also strong. Up until the late 1930s, it was also a common theme that Jews were racially too different ever to become "true" Swedes. Some social democrats in Sweden, in contrast to their German counterparts, even expressed anti-Semitic views openly until the late 1920s. Yet, no eliminationist ideology ever emerged in Sweden, except among a small group of Nazi supporters in the 1930s. In the Swedish case, then, culture did matter somewhat; but it is also important that, due to the long-established nature of the Swedish state, the country's rulers saw no need to identify any racial outgroup against which to campaign.

Not only did Sweden benefit from the fact that its state was well-established, it also benefitted from the *way* in which the latter developed. The degree of autocracy in Sweden varied over time, but Swedish kings were generally more tolerant and democratic than their counterparts in Prussia or later in united Germany. In addition, Germany before its unification had developed in a feudalistic and highly decentralized manner, and many of the rulers of its various states had sought support from the nobility sooner than from the peasantry (cf. Moore 1966). Sweden, by contrast, had been more centralized, and its kings had often allied themselves with the peasants in order to limit the power of the nobles. The pre-democratic Swedish parliament thus had four estates, of which the peasantry was one. Thus, peasants always wielded more influence in Sweden than they did in the German states; and they felt more included. Then, when Sweden democratized, the peasants formed their own parties (which then united into one), so that they were represented in the new democratic order. The Farmers' Party did have racist and authoritarian elements, but in 1932 the social democrats were able to coopt it into joining a coalition government that started building the modern welfare state. Consequently, in contrast to their counterparts in Germany, peasants in Sweden who held racist views did not turn to fascist-nationalist parties; instead, they stayed loyal to the Farmers' Party.

In addition, the way in which Sweden modernized helped ensure its democratic stability. It was a stable country that had existed for many centuries, so its regime enjoyed great legitimacy, and a policy legacy of consensus had emerged. This contrasted greatly with the many divisions that arose in Germany after its unification (at various times Bismarck saw Jews, liberals, Catholics and social democrats as enemies of the Reich). Whereas none of the major political parties in Germany wanted the German revolution or the Weimar Republic, *all* of the Swedish political parties supported the democratic reforms. While the German emperor had to abdicate, causing ill will in the conservative parties and among several social groups (the Junkers, the military, portions of the wealthy bourgeoisie, etc.), the Swedish king retained his office and supported the democratization process, helping to ensure the legitimacy of the democratic regime.

Chapter 7 analyzes Nazi Germany. It shows how, in an attempt to ensure that civil servants would be loyal to the new country, Bismarck limited recruitment to applicants with conservative views and provided relatively generous social provisions for those who held such positions. The chapter also discusses the dilemmas Bismarck faced in deciding who belonged to the state and who the outgroup should be. Furthermore, it discusses the rise of anti-Semitism and its influence on the imperial regime. Then it briefly discusses the problems the Weimar Republic faced, including its lack of legitimacy, the Versailles Treaty that its leaders felt forced to sign, the opposition it met from bureaucrats, and its lack of support from peasants. As I show in the chapter, these issues helped the Nazis gain legitimacy for their rule. They were then able to use this legitimacy to persuade that public that the Jews were to blame for the ills of the Weimar Republic. They were also able to exploit existing prejudices, thereby creating an atmosphere that encouraged actions against Jews. By portraying Jews as the existential enemy, the regime succeeded at inducing bureaucrats to commit evil acts and to take great initiative in doing so. Thus, the evilness of such bureaucrats was not banal. It was not the case either, however, that Germans were simply acting out eliminationist cultural values they had inherited from the past.

Finally, Chap. 8 provides a short summary and a discussion of future research.

Notes

1. Aharony's (2010) study of concentration camps shows that, even under these most inhumane conditions, the Nazis were not able to gain total control over the inmates, who created underground self-help organizations and the like. Yet, there is no doubt the Nazis at least tried to gain total control over their victims.

2. Authors such as Anderson (2002: Chap. 5), Kamen (1985: 3, 33), Pérez (2005) and Yerushalmi (1970: 320) claim that the French inquisition was "papal," whereas the Spanish Inquisition was run by the crown.
3. For a discussion of party-state relations under the communist dictators, see Saxonberg (2001).
4. For a discussion of the totalitarian tendencies of Christianity and especially Catholicism, see Freeman (2003).

REFERENCES

Agamben, G. (1995). *Homo Sacer: Sovereign Power and Bare Life* (D. Heller-Roazen, Trans.). Stanford: Stanford University Press.
Aharony, M. (2010). Hannah Arendt and the Idea of Total Domination. *Holocaust and Genocide Studies, 24*(2), 193–224.
Anderson, J. M. (2002). *Daily Life During the Spanish Inquisition*. Westport: Greenwood Press.
Arendt, H. (1948/1973). *The Origins of Totalitarianism*. San Diego: Harvest.
Arendt, H. (1963/2005). *Eichmann and the Holocaust*. London: Penguin.
Aron, R. (1969). *Democracy and Totalitarianism* (V. Ionescu, Trans.). London: Weidenfeld and Nicolson.
Atkinson, W. C. (1934). *Spain: A Brief History*. London: Methuen.
Bägerfeldt, L. (2003). *När Sverige blev till: an annorlunda teori om Svea rikes vagga*. Fälköping: Lars Bägerfeldts förlag.
Bägerfeldt, L. (2004). *När Sverige blev en stat: Övergången från rike to stat i början av medeltiden*. Falköping: Lars Bägerfeldts förlag.
Bale, J. F. (2009). Islamism and Totalitarianism. *Totalitarian Movements and Political Religions, 10*(2), 73–96.
Bauman, Z. (1991). *Modernity and the Holocaust*. Oxford: John Wiley & Sons.
Begin, M. (1957). *White Nights: The Story of a Prisoner in Russia*. London: MacDonald.
Berman, S. (2001). Modernization in Historical Perspective: The Case of Imperial Germany. *World Politics, 53*(3), 431–462.
Block, F. (1977). The Ruling Class Does Not Rule: Notes on the Marxist Theory of the State. *Socialist Revolution, 33*, 6–28.
Boroumand, B., & Boroumand, R. (2002). Terror, Islam, and Democracy. *Journal of Democracy, 13*(2), 5–20.
Brustein, W. (1996). *The Logic of Evil: The Social Origins of the Nazi Party, 1925–1933*. New Haven: Yale University Press.
Brzezinski, Z. (1956). *The Permanent Purge*. Cambridge, MA: Harvard University Press.
Carstensen, M. B., & Schmidt, V. A. (2016). Power Through, Over and in Ideas: Conceptualizing Ideational Power in Discursive Institutionalism. *Journal of European Public Policy, 23*(3), 318–337.

Childers, T. (1983). *The Nazi Voter. The Social Foundations of Fascism in Germany, 1919–1933*. Chapel Hill: University of North Carolina Press.

Dahlkvist, M. (1978). *Staten, socialdemokratin och socialismen*. Lund: Prisma.

Ehret, U. (2007). Understanding the Popular Appeal of Fascism, National Socialism and Soviet Communism: The Revival of Totalitarianism Theory and Political Religion. *History Compass, 5*(4), 1236–1267.

Elias, N. (1939/1976). *Über den Prozess der Zivilisation. Soziogenetische und psychogenetische Untersuchungen* (Vol. 2). Frankfurt: Suhrkamp Verlag.

Evans, R. J. (2005). Zwei deutsche Diktaturen im 20. Jahrhundert? *Aus Politik und Zeitgeschichte, 1–2*, 3–9.

Falter, J. W. (1991). *Hitlers Wähler*. Munich: C.H. Beck.

Freeman, C. (2003). *The Closing of the Western Mind: The Rise of Faith and the Fall of Reason*. London: Pimlico.

Friedrich, C. J. (1964). The Unique Character of Totalitarian Society. In C. J. Friedrich (Ed.), *Totalitarianism*. New York: Grosset & Dunlap.

Fritzsche, P., & Hellbeck, J. (2009). The New Man in Stalinist Russia and Nazi Germany. In M. Geyer & S. Fitzpatrik (Eds.), *Beyond Totalitarianism: Stalinism and Nazism Compared*. Cambridge: Cambridge University Press.

Fromm, E. (1941/1969). *Escape from Freedom*. New York: Avon Books.

Gentile, E. (2006). New Idols: Catholicism in the Face of Fascist Totalitarianism. *Journal of Modern Italian Studies, 11*(2), 143–170.

Gerlach, C. (2016). *The Extermination of the European Jews*. Cambridge: Cambridge University Press.

Giddens, A. (1991). *The Consequences of Modernity*. Stanford: Stanford University Press.

Grieder, P. (2007). In Defence of Totalitarianism Theory as a Tool of Historical Scholarship. *Totalitarian Movements and Political Religions, 8*(3–4), 563–589.

Hansen, H., & Kainz, P. (2007). Radical Islamism and Totalitarian Ideology: A Comparison of Sayyid Qutb's Islamism with Marxism and National Socialism. *Totalitarian Movements and Political Religions, 8*(1), 55–76.

Haskins, C. H. (1902). Robert Le Bougre and the Beginnings of the Inquisition in Northern France. *The American Historical Review, 7*(4), 631–652.

Hastings, A. (1997). *The Construction of Nationhood: Ethnicity, Religion and Nationalism*. Cambridge: Cambridge University Press.

Heck, A. (2017). Images, Visions and Narrative Identity Formation of ISIS. *Global Discourse, 7*(2–3), 244–259.

Heller, A. (2010). Radical Evil in Modernity: On Genocide, Totalitarian Terror and the Holocaust. *Thesis Eleven, 101*(May), 106–117.

Herz, D. (1996). The Concept of "Political Religions" in the Thought of Eric Voegelin. In H. Maier (Ed.), and J. Bruhn (Trans.), *Totalitarianism and Political Religions. Volume I: Concepts for the Comparison of Dictatorships*. London: Routledge.

Homer. (1990). *The Iliad* (R. Fagles, Trans.). New York: Penguin.

Horkheimer, M., & Adorno, T. (1944/1988). *Dialektik der Aufklärung*. Frankfurt am Main: Fischer.

Jacob, H. (1963). *German Administration since Bismarck: Central Authority versus Local Autonomy*. New Haven: Yale University Press.

Kamen, H. (1985). *Inquisition and Society in Spain in the Sixteenth and Seventeenth Centuries*. Bloomington: Indiana University Press.

Kershaw, I. (2000). *The Nazi Dictatorship: Problems and Perspectives of Interpretation*. London: Bloomsbury.

Kershaw, I. (2008). *Hitler, the Germans and the Final Solution*. New Haven: Yale University Press.

Kocka, J. (2018). Looking Back on the *Sonderweg*. *Central European History, 51*(1), 137–142.

Konstan, D. (2007). Anger, Hatred, and Genocide in Ancient Greece. *Common Knowledge, 13*(1), 170–187.

Kuran, T. (1991). Now Out of Never: The Element of Surprise in the East European Revolution of 1989. *World Politics, 44*(1), 7–48.

Ladurie, E. L. (1978). *Montaillou: Cathars and Catholics in a French Village 1294–1324* (B. Bray, Trans.). Middlesex: Penguin.

Lefort, C. (1998). The Concept of Totalitarianism. In *Papers in Social Theory*. Coventry: Warwick.

Linz, J. (1975/2000). *Totalitarian and Authoritarian Regimes*. Boulder: Lynne Rienner.

Linz, J. (1996). The Religious Use of Politics and/or the Political Use of Religion Ersatz Ideology Versus Ersatz Religion. In H. Maier (Ed.), and J. Bruhn (Trans.), *Totalitarianism and Political Religions. Volume I: Concepts for the Comparison of Dictatorships*. London: Routledge.

Linz, J. J., & Stepan, A. (1996). *Problems of Democratic Transition and Consolidation: Southern Europe, South America, and Post-Communist Europe*. Baltimore: John Hopkins University Press.

Lourie, E. (1966). A Society Organized for War: Medieval Spain. *Past & Present, 35*(Dec.), 54–76.

Maier, H. (1996). Concepts for the Comparison of Dictatorships: 'Totalitarianism' and 'political religions'. In H. Maier (Ed.), and J. Bruhn (Trans.), *Totalitarianism and Political Religions Volume I: Concepts for the Comparison of Dictatorships*. London: Routledge.

Mann, M. (2005). *The Dark Side of Democracy: Explaining Ethnic Cleansing*. Cambridge: Cambridge University Press.

Miliband, R. (1969). *The State in Capitalist Society*. New York: Basic Books.

Möller, H. (1982). Referate. In *Deutscher Sonderweg – Mythos oder Realität?* Munich: R. Oldenbourg Verlag.

Moore, B. (1958). *Political Power and Social Theory*. Cambridge, MA: Harvard University Press.

Moore, B. (1966). *Social Origins of Dictatorship and Democracy*. Boston: Beacon Press.

Payne, S. G. (2005). On the Heuristic Value of the Concept of Political Religion and Its Application. *Totalitarian Movements and Political Religions*, *6*(2), 163–174.

Pérez, J. (2005). *The Spanish Inquisition: A History*. New Haven: Yale University Press.

Ping, L. L. (2012). Gustav Freytag, the *Reichsgründung*, and the National Liberal Origins of the *Sonderweg*. *Central European History*, *45*, 605–630.

Poulantzas, N. (1978). *Political Power and Social Classes* (T. O'Hagan, Trans.). London: Verso.

Prescott, W. H. (1841). *The History of the Reign of Ferdinand and Isabella* (Vol. 1). London: Routledge.

Roberts, D. D. (2009). 'Political Religion' and the Totalitarian Departures of Inter-War Europe: On the Uses and Disadvantages of an Analytical Category. *Contemporary European History*, *18*(4), 381–414.

Rueschemeyer, D., Stephens, E. H., & Stephens, J. D. (1992). *Capitalist Development and Democracy*. Chicago: University of Chicago Press.

Saxonberg, S. (2001). *The Fall*. London: Routledge.

Saxonberg, S. (2013). *Transitions and Non-Transitions from Communism: Regime Survival in China, Cuba, North Korea, and Vietnam*. Cambridge University Press.

Shirer, W. L. (1960). *The Rise and Fall of the Third Reich*. New York: Simon & Schuster.

Skocpol, T. (1979). *States and Social Revolutions: A Comparative Analysis of France, Russia, and China*. London: Cambridge University Press.

Skocpol, T., & Somers, M. (1980). The Uses of Comparative History in Macrosocial Theory. *Comparative Studies in Society and History*, *22*(2), 174–197.

Stanley, J. L. (1987). Is Totalitarianism a New Phenomenon? Reflections on Hannah Arendt's Origins of Totalitarianism. *The Review of Politics*, *49*(2), 177–207.

Thompson, M. R. (2002). Totalitarian and Post-Totalitarian Regimes in Transitions and Non-Transitions from Communism. *Totalitarian Movements and Political Religions*, *3*(1), 79–106.

Tibi, B. (2007). The Totalitarianism of Jihadist Islamism and its Challenge to Europe and to Islam. *Totalitarian Movements and Political Religions*, *8*(1), 35–54.

Tibi, B. (2010). The Politicization of Islam into Islamism in the Context of Global Religious Fundamentalism. *Journal of the Middle East and Africa*, *1*(2), 153–170.

Versluis, A. (2006). *The New Inquisitions: Heretic-Hunting and the Intellectual Origins of Modern Totalitarianism*. Oxford: Oxford University Press.

Vetlesen, A. J. (2005). *Evil and Human Agency.* Cambridge University Press.

Voegelin, E. (2007). *Die Politischen Religionen* (3rd ed.). Munich: Wilhelm Fink.

Wakefield, W. L. (1974). *Heresy, Crusade and Inquisition in Southern France 1100–1250.* Berkeley: University of California Press.

Waller, J. E. (2007). *Becoming Evil* (2nd ed.). Oxford: Oxford University Press.

Weiss, J. (1996). *Ideology of Death: Why the Holocaust Happened in Germany.* Chicago: Ivan R. Dee.

Yerushalmi, Y. H. (1970). The Inquisition and the Jews of France in the Time of Bernard Gui. *The Harvard Theological Review, 63*(3), 317–376.

Zekulin, M., & Anderson, T. D. (2016). Contemporary Terrorism and the True Believer. *Behavioral Sciences of Terrorism and Political Aggression, 8*(3), 1–20.

Cases of Totalitarianism

In the previous section I argued that, for a regime to be totalitarian, it must meet the following criteria:

- It has a totalizing ideology with which it seeks to legitimize its rule.
- It has organizations capable of helping it enforce its rule.
- It bases itself on a political religion or a politicized religion.
- It creates an atmosphere of fear in order to deter would-be dissenters.

Below follows a discussion on the extent to which the four cases meet these criteria.

TOTALIZING IDEOLOGY

Since Sweden was a pluralist democracy in the 1920s and 1930s, it is obvious that the regime in that country did not have a totalizing ideology; instead, Sweden was a pluralist society, in which political parties with different ideologies could compete with each other. Thus, Sweden will not be considered in this section as a possible case of totalitarianism. It is also quite obvious that National Socialism was a totalizing ideology. Adhering to the doctrine of social Darwinism, the Nazis depicted history as a racial struggle of survival of the fittest; and they portrayed Aryans—among them Germans—as the superior master race, whose duty it was to take over the world. Furthermore, Nazi doctrine emphasized the need for unquestioning

© The Author(s) 2019
S. Saxonberg, *Pre-Modernity, Totalitarianism and the Non-Banality of Evil*, https://doi.org/10.1007/978-3-030-28195-3_2

loyalty and obedience to the Führer, who would lead the country to glory. It is more questionable, on the other hand, whether the French or Spanish regimes had totalizing ideologies.

Some authors have claimed that Church doctrine, in general, was totalitarian in the medieval era, in that the pope expected the population to adhere to Catholic doctrine without question. For example, Trachtenberg (1943/2001: 11) claims the Church became increasingly intolerant of Jews during the Crusades, given "…the dogmatic enmity of the Church underscored by the religious and cultural nonconformity of the Jewish people within what was essentially a *totalitarian civilization*…." (emphasis added). In addition, "[t]he Church was, in principle, a totalitarian power, seeking to exercise unlimited dominion in the temporal and spiritual realms, not always unchallenged, but with its confidence in its divine election to this role unshaken. Like all totalitarian powers, it refused to tolerate difference, independence of thought or action, for these imperiled its own position" (p. 171).

As the French kings claimed to be upholding Catholicism in France, this gives some basis for thinking the country may have had totalitarian tendencies. However, the very fact that Jews were allowed to live there for most of the period of the inquisition shows that France could not have been completely totalitarian since it allowed a people to live within its bounds who held different beliefs than those held by its rulers. It is true the Jews were eventually expelled (in 1306), but they were allowed back into the country in 1315; then they were expelled again (in 1322), and then allowed back in again (in 1359) (Yerushalmi 1970). Yet, in contrast to the Spanish expulsions, the French expulsions were undertaken for political and economic rather than ideological reasons: economic in that they enabled the king to confiscate Jewish property; and political in that they enabled him to get the townsmen to agree—in return for the expulsion of the Jews—to pay taxes to the royal treasury.[1] As the country was expanding, namely, the Jewish population could not provide enough money to finance the treasury; and in order to be able to tax the towns, the king needed their support (Barkey and Katznelson 2011).

Meanwhile, when it came to the religious beliefs of the rest of the population, the inquisition in France was never as thorough as the Inquisition in Spain was. It also mostly sought out Cathar strongholds: that is, it repressed groups that openly opposed Catholic doctrine, but it did not try to find out what everyone was thinking. Furthermore, in contrast to the Spanish Inquisition, it did not demand conformity of lifestyle. Basically, in

France, the monarchy used the inquisition when possible as a way to increase its power—as when it repressed the Templar Knights in order to avoid paying back loans to them. Nonetheless, the inquisition was not central to the regime; it was not even something the regime asked for. The regime wanted greater political power, but it did not try to steer the thoughts of the population to the extent that totalitarian regimes do.

In Spain, by contrast, the Catholic monarchs introduced the Inquisition as a way to unify the country around an ideology; thus, it played a central role for building the newly created state. The Inquisition actively sought out those who dared even privately to harbor thoughts that were not completely consistent with Church orthodoxy. Weitz (2003: 111) observes that

> National Socialism's political principle of totality corresponds to the ideological principle of the organically indivisible national community. It does not tolerate within its sphere the development of any political ideas at variance with the will of the majority.

Few would dispute Weitz's account of Nazi Germany; yet, he could just as well be describing Spain under the Inquisition. In Spain during the sixteenth and seventeenth centuries, even differences in lifestyle could lead to repression, as the Inquisition exercised control over all aspects of one's life. Thus, Jews who converted came under suspicion of not being "true" believers if they kept *any* of their old traditions, even if those traditions did not in any way contradict belief in Catholic doctrine. For example, washing one's hands before eating or after going to the toilet was enough to get a person accused of being a secret Jew; so was refusing to eat pork (Friedman 1987). The Inquisition was so concerned about persecuting people who might once in their life have committed what Orwell termed "thought crimes" that it sometimes punished alleged heretics for things they had said decades earlier (Roth 1995/2002: 217). Its desire for thought control was thus even greater than Hitler's, as the Nazi dictator complained of the harm done by people who denounced others for acts they had committed many years before (Gellately 1980: 679–80). Thus, it was not enough in Spain to be a passive supporter of the regime; everyone had to adhere to the ideology *actively*; and one had to make sure one had avoided any expression of doubt toward the ideology at any time in one's life. As Rawlings (2006: 16) writes of the Spanish Inquisition: "In the eyes of the Catholic hierarchy, the end justified the means: to extend the mission of the Church and enforce an absolute adherence to its structures of belief."

Organization

Even if a regime has totalitarian aspirations, it cannot attain such aspirations without an organization to carry them out. The Nazis, of course, had the National Socialist German Workers' Party and its related organizations (the Hitler Youth, women's organizations, etc.) to help spread its ideology, and it also had paramilitary organizations such as the SA and SS. Both France and Spain had the Catholic Church and the inquisitions as organizations to promote "correct" thinking, but Spain was much better organized in this regard.

In Spain, inquisitors would arrive in a town or village and arrange for the reading after a Sunday mass of an "edict of faith," which all local residents had to attend. Everyone in the area had to swear an oath of allegiance to the Holy Inquisition.

> The local inquisitor then read aloud the edict, comprising a long list of heresies against the Catholic faith (Jewish, Islamic, Illuminist, Lutheran etc.). This was followed by an invitation to all those present to acknowledge their own sins as well as to denounce their friends and neighbours for engaging in such offences. (During its early years the Inquisition permitted those who confessed during an initial 30-to 40-day period of grace to be reconciled to the Church without penalty.) The congregation was under moral obligation to comply with the inquisitor's wishes. Denunciations to the Inquisition were commonly based on long-standing disputes between members of the local community rather than on verifiable evidence of heresy. The fear of being exposed to public scrutiny by their neighbours (rather than fear of the Inquisition *per se*) prompted many false confessions of guilt. The collaboration of ordinary people was thus fundamental to the Inquisition's work on the ground and particularly so in areas where social discord was rife. (Rawlings 2006: 30–1)

After the inquisitors finished their work and coerced all the accused to confess their "sins" of having harbored unacceptable thoughts, they would organize a large public event—the *auto de fè*—with the entire population of the area being present. At these spectacles, the "guilty" were paraded around in special clothing, so that the population could mock them. Those who refused to confess despite being tortured, as well as those who were accused of being "relapsed heretics," were then handed over to secular authorities to be burned at the stake. The fact that an accused person normally could not be found innocent, and the fact that the inquisitors demanded a confession even if the person was innocent, shows how totalitarian the system was. In this sense, it was similar to the show trials in the communist-led countries in the early 1950s, where communist activists were coerced into making false confessions. The Inquisition, just like the Communist Party, could not be wrong, and it was not enough to confess having been guilty of committing a "thought crime"; one also had to *admit* that one was wrong, and to reconcile oneself to the Church or face a horrifying death at the stake. Moreover, the entire population of the area was involved in the process. First, they had to attend mass and to swear an oath of allegiance to the Inquisition; then they had to denounce friends and neighbors and to confess any heretical thoughts they might once have had at some point. Finally, they had to attend the public festival where the verdicts were read and the "guilty" paraded around (for descriptions of the *auto de fé*, see, e.g., Kamen 1985; Pérez 2005; Rawlings 2006; Roth 1995/2002). In fact, Nalle (1987) calculates in her study of the Tribunal of Cuenca that just two percent of denunciations came from Inquisition officials, with the rest coming from the public. She concludes that "while in the field, the Inquisitors almost always learned of a religious crime because a local resident brought the information directly to the court" (p. 567).

The inquisition in France, by contrast, did not organize such mass mobilizations. It was also less interested in public spectacles, although in later years it did organize a few *autos de fé*. Yet, even these events were not on the same scale as those in Spain (Lea 1888: 123ff.). In fact, these *autos de fé* seem to have been so rare that Lea is the only source I could find that even mentions them. In addition, the inquisition in France was less centralized and unified, and it did not enjoy the same kind of organizational support. In fact, at times different Catholic orders fought against each other over control of the inquisition. Friedlander (2000) describes how, in the fourteenth century, the Franciscans tried to counteract Dominican control over the inquisition, as they thought the Dominicans were being overly repressive and had abused their powers. On several occasions, the Franciscans convinced the kings to intervene against Dominican excesses. This kind of infighting did not take place in more totalitarian Spain.

When the inquisition came to an area, then, it was much more thorough in Spain than in France; but the question is: how comprehensive was its coverage? An inquisition concentrated in just a few areas would not have been powerful enough to make a country totalitarian. In France, the inquisition was nowhere near as comprehensive as in Spain. Even though it eventually operated in northern France, it concentrated, to begin with on the Cathar strongholds in the southern parts of the kingdom (which were a semi-independent duchy), and its activities never covered the entire country.

Of course, the Inquisition was not able to visit every single village in Spain; however, one must keep in mind that it was not the only tool of thought control in the country. Every village had a church, and every Spaniard had to be a member of the church; so the churches exercised some control and they could contact inquisition officials. Statistics show that, in 1611, Galicia had 388 *familiares* (lay servants of the Holy Office working for the tribunal, who could bear arms to protect the inquisitors) and 100 *comisarios* (local parish priests who gave information to the Inquisition and worked on its behalf), or one inquisition official per 241 households. These inquisitional officials were present, though, in fewer than 6.4 percent of the towns and villages. In Valencia in 1567, on the other hand, there were 1638 *familiares*, or one for every 42 households. In Barcelona in 1600 there were 815 *familiares*, or one for every 110 households (Kamen 1985: 145). Meanwhile, Rawlings (2006: 28) notes, there were 10,000–12,000 *familiares* in Castile in the mid-1500s. In Valencia in 1567, the proportion of *familiares* was much higher: at 1638 there was one per 42 households. "Over half were to be found in the sparsely populated countryside in small settlements of less than 1000 people where other forms of social control were at their weakest." Cruz (2000: 53) calculates that, at the end of the fifteenth century, Aragon had a maximum of 1215 *familiares*, or one for every 154 inhabitants. In another publication, dealing with the district of Seville, Cruz (1997) writes that people working for the Inquisition were present in 111 cities or villages, and absent in 94.

While these totals might not seem high, they actually compare quite well with Nazi Germany's. For example, Burleigh (2000b: 303) writes, there was only around one Gestapo officer in Nazi Germany for every ten thousand people. Moreover, "in 1937, the Düsseldorf district Gestapo headquarters had a staff of 291 persons, policing a population of four million. Forty-nine of these people were administrators." Zukier (1994: 435) notes that "in September 1941, there were 150 *Gestapo* officials in Würtzburg in charge of a population of nearly three million people distributed over 14,115 square kilometers." Of course, other organizations in addition to the Gestapo were involved in repression in Nazi Germany, such as the SS, the Nazi Party, national organizations and so on. Similarly, local Church authorities and government agents in Spain were also involved in reporting those who committed heresy or did not follow correct norms of behavior.

These examples show that we cannot measure totalitarian rule simply by the number of agents working for the repressive apparatus. After all, there are never enough agents for it to be possible to carry out totalitarian policies without the active cooperation of the population. This does not mean that everyone in the population believes in the ideology. What it *does* show is that Spain was similar to Germany. It shows that, when the rulers create an atmosphere of fear and combine it with an ideology that legitimizes turning people in, parts of the population will be willing to support the repression for ideological reasons, for personal reasons (getting rid of competitors, taking revenge on people they do not like, etc.) or for a combination thereof.

Thus, when it comes to the engagement of the population, Burleigh (2000b: 304) points out in reference to Würzburg that

> 57 percent of cases of "race pollution" were initiated by ordinary citizens, with only one case resulting from Gestapo investigations. Yet, no laws required people to denounce others and in May 1933 the regime made punishment for malicious denunciation more stringent.

Similarly, Zukier (1994: 435) explains that

> *Gestapo* files reveal that most cases were initiated not by agents or paid informers but by denunciations from ordinary citizens not connected to the *Gestapo* apparatus. Uncoerced collaboration was the "key relationship" and so widespread that it not only made the police system possible but rendered the professionals' work "almost superfluous."[2]

Similar to Nazi Germany's organs of repression, the Spanish Inquisition was based on denunciations from ordinary residents. As noted, moreover, the number of officials serving the Inquisition seems to have been much higher than the proportion of Gestapo in Nazi Germany. In Spain, the Church was active in supporting the Inquisition—and there was a church in every village. It is true that, in the first days of the Inquisition, the Church hierarchy considered it to be a problem that many clerics in the smaller villages were not very knowledgeable about Church doctrine. As Kamen notes, over four-fifths of the population lived outside the reach of

the large towns, and some villagers were combining traditional superstition with Catholicism out of ignorance. Consequently, beginning in the
1540s, the Church started to focus its attention on wiping out superstition in the rural areas (Kamen 1985: 199f.).[3] The Church considered it so
important to get everyone even in the smallest of villages to think cor-
rectly that,

> [r]ather than lightening its sentences because of the low degree of religious
> understanding in rural areas, the Inquisition in fact increased its punish-
> ments in order to achieve a greater disciplinary effect. Thus every type of
> expression—whether mumbled by a drunkard in a tavern or preached by an
> ignorant priest from the pulpit—that could be taken to be offensive, blas-
> phemous, irreverent or heretical, was carefully examined by the Holy Office
> and acted upon....Prisoners were asked to recite in Castilian the Our Father,
> Hall Mary, Credo, Salve Regina and the ten commandments, as well as
> other statements of belief. (Kamen 1985: 203)

This shows the regime considered it criminal not to be knowledgeable
about its ideology. As a result, records show, only about 40 percent of
those interrogated in 1550 were able to repeat the basic prayers; by the
1590s, however, the figure had risen to almost 70 percent. In order to
spread its doctrine, the Church established schools and made it mandatory
to attend services and recite the prayers at mass (Kamen 1985: 204). By
contrast, as already noted, the inquisition in France was never nearly as
widespread, and most areas were untouched by it. Thus, France under its
inquisition fails to meet the organizational criterion for totalitarianism.

Political Religion

Political religions give legitimacy to totalitarian regimes, as secular rulers
use religious motives to make their subjects true believers and to offer
them salvation (e.g., Burleigh 2000a; Ley and Schoeps 1997; Roberts
2009; Vondung 2005). As Burleigh (2000a: 5) points out, when a totalitarian government creates a political religion, hopes of salvation get dis-
placed from hopes of eternal life to hopes for the present life. For the
Nazis, evil was externalized and embodied in the Jews. Germans could
receive redemption as the racially elected people (p. 11). Vondung (2005:
88) notes that the Nazis presented themselves "[i]n forms that bore
resemblance to organisational and ritual forms of the Christian churches."

Party organizations such as the SS resembled religious orders, while *Ordensburgen* had ceremonial halls that resembled monasteries. They developed special holidays, festivals and ceremonies which resembled Christian ones. Hitler also viewed the world in apocalyptic terms, with history as a struggle between two universal forces of "light" and "darkness" (p. 92). Jews were the enemy and survival depended on their destruction (p. 93; Vondung 1997 makes similar statements). Bärsch (2002) argues that the Nazis saw the battle between Germans and Jews in apocalyptic terms—as similar to that between Christ and the anti-Christ— and adds that giving the "Heil Hitler" salute was a way of showing piety.

Of course, the Catholic monarchs in Spain did not introduce a political religion; instead, they relied on a politicized religion, using the Church and the Inquisition as a means to gain control over how people thought. Political religions are supposed to follow religions in promising salvation while also instilling fear with apocalyptic visions. These elements were also present in the Spanish Inquisition. Maureen Flynn (1991: 290) argues that the Spanish Inquisition produced anxiety and reminded citizens "of eternal suffering..., which influenced the Inquisition in its dramatic production of the Last Day [sic]." When watching the spectacle of the *autos de fe*, people lived through "their own apprehensions of the Final Judgment" (p. 295). She further describes how the apocalyptic emphasis of the Inquisition led to salvation:

> [I]t was fear of hell and its torments brought on by centuries of meditation on the Apocalypse that produced the Inquisition's frightful theater of cruelty. Standing on platforms erected in the center of urban life, victims of the *autos de fe* embodied the sin that weighed on the minds of the public. With their acts of contrition, they purged communities of religious guilt and with their blood, they appeased the wrath of a vindictive God. Around the pyre, true believers satisfied desires for vengeance on traitors to their faith at the same time that they empathized with the corporal suffering. Chroniclers observed the populace waiting and weeping, praying and rejoicing. Said one inquisitor, "and the people left more appeased and repentant as a result of the exhibition". (p. 296)

As already noted, the inquisition in France did not rely on such large spectacles and mobilizations. It did not even organize any *autos de fe* until the end of the inquisitional period, and these were not on the same scale as those in Spain. In addition, although at times Jews were expelled, they were eventually let back in again a few decades after each expulsion. This made Catholicism less totalitarian in France than in Spain, where the entire population had to adhere to Church doctrine.

Fear

It is not very controversial to claim that the Nazis used fear and terror as one of their mechanisms for maintaining power. The SA, the SS and the Gestapo could arrest anyone at will, and everyone knew about the existence of concentration camps. Of course, until WWII began, the camps were not used for exterminating people, but everyone knew they were highly unpleasant places (cf. Aharony 2010). Therefore, Burleigh (2000b: 303) posits when analyzing Nazi rule, "[w]hat should not be entirely overlooked is that the combination of a police force liberated from all legal restraints and licensed denunciation meant a climate of fear." He adds that everyone feared that everyone else was an informer.

Even if the Nazis used terror and fear as a weapon, the regime targeted people who either opposed the regime or belonged to the "wrong" races, religions or political groups. This contrasted with Stalin's purges, which often targeted Bolsheviks who had long been loyal Party members. Hitler's only purge against insiders was his elimination of the leadership of the SA in the early stages of Nazi rule; the Nazi leader thought the SA was trying to gain too much power for itself, thereby threatening his rule. Thus, Tsao (2002: 602) notes:

> The lack of a close parallel for this in the Nazi dictatorship is a reflection of a basic difference in the two totalitarian regimes, namely, that acquiescent Germans outside the proscribed categories of targets—and certainly the Nazis themselves—were largely immune from the violence of Hitler's terror, while Stalin's struck most ferociously at the most loyal of Bolsheviks— including (and for a time, especially) the agents of his secret police.

It is more controversial to make these claims about Spain under the Inquisition. In order to instill a general feeling of fear and also to mobilize support, the Spanish regime engaged in mass mobilizations similar to those staged by modern totalitarian movements. However, rather than the kinds of mass demonstrations that the Nazis and Communists organized, the main public spectacle was the *auto de fe*:

The function of the ceremonial *auto de fe* was essentially pedagogical: to publicly proclaim the supremacy of the Catholic faith by cleansing the Church of its most abhorrent enemies. It was both a theatre for the condemnation of those accused of heresy as well as an occasion for a public sermon...addressed to an audience of thousands of spectators. In this way the *auto* resembled a communal "act of faith" in which sinners and believers took part. By witnessing the sentencing of those who contravened the code of orthodoxy, the public reaffirmed their rejection of those who did not conform to the Old Christian model and their acceptance of the dominant order....[T]he purpose of the *auto de fe*,...was to instill *salutary fear* [my emphasis]. Non-participation in the celebration of Catholic hegemony implied non-conformity and withdrawal from the community of believers— a potentially offensive form of behavior that might lead to inquisitorial investigation, social exclusion and ultimate damnation. (Roth 1995/2002: 39–40)

Of course, almost all religions engage in some types of mobilization, such as holding masses; but the *auto de fe* represents a more totalitarian type of mobilization. It was based largely on fear since all who attended knew they could be the next victims. Weitz (2003: 139) sees direct parallels between the *autos de fe* under the Spanish Inquisition and the book burnings in Nazi Germany: both were mass mobilizations aimed at cleansing society of perceived evils. However, the fear factor was much greater for the *autos de fe* than for the Nazi book burnings. In Spain during the sixteenth and seventeenth centuries, all that it took to destroy a person's life was the desire of a couple of angry people to take revenge on him or her for something. Moreover, attendance was basically mandatory, and the goal was to promote support for the ruling ideology.

People throughout society feared being accused of heresy and brought before the inquisitors. Kamen (1985: 45) notes that, in the sixteenth century, the Jesuit Juan de Mariana wrote that the Inquisition seemed very oppressive to Spaniards at first, because children were being punished for their parents' crimes. People could not talk freely because there were informants in all of the cities, towns and villages.

As in the Soviet Union under Stalin, even the ideological guardians in Spain lived in fear. In the words of one *converso* in Toledo, writing in 1538: "[P]reachers do not dare to preach, and those who preach do not dare to touch on contentious matters, for their lives and honour are in the mouths of two ignoramuses, and nobody in this life is without his policeman" (cited in Kamen 1985: 164).

Gitlitz (2000: 60) concludes:

> Fear was pervasive, for any action could be misconstrued, and the watchers were everywhere. The purity-of-blood statutes [banning those of Jewish ancestry from holding public offices or other positions in society] required people to mask their past; the Inquisition required them to be circumspect about their present.... [Furthermore, t]hey had to be a private person and simultaneously wear a public persona....For intellectuals, and for conversos of any rank or station or religious predilection, survival required habits of thought which prepared one to give [an] autobiographical account on demand.

In such a climate of fear, people had to fear their friends and neighbors. The Inquisition was totalitarian both in scope (it included the entire population) and in aim (it forced adherence to its ideology). When inquisitors arrived in a district, the entire local population was required to attend the meeting which they called. After listening to a sermon, "everyone was obliged to swear a solemn oath of allegiance to the Holy Inquisition." Then the inquisitor read a list of heresies against the Catholic faith, after which all were encouraged to confess their own sins and to denounce their friends and neighbors.

> Denunciations to the Inquisition were commonly based on long-standing disputes between members of the local community rather than on verifiable evidence of heresy.
> The fear of being exposed to public scrutiny by their neighbours... prompted many false confessions of guilt. The collaboration of ordinary people was thus fundamental to the Inquisition's work on the ground and particularly so in areas where social discord was rife. (Rawlings 2006: 30–1)

This shows a similarity with modern totalitarian regimes, where personal gain as well as ideology mattered. For example, one study of denunciations in the city of Düsseldorf showed that 37 percent of the denunciations were motivated by private animosities, while only 24 percent were based on political beliefs (it was not possible in the remaining 39 percent of cases to establish motives) (Mann 1979: 974). As theorists of political religion have argued, not everyone under a totalitarian regime has to believe in the ideology; however, everyone acts in an environment that promotes and legitimizes certain types of behavior. Thus, Vondung (2005: 93) states, "even if the perpetrators were not themselves confident believers, a political religion offers at least a formal justification for their doings."

While fear was widespread in Spain, it was less so in France. For one thing, the inquisition in France was not as all-encompassing. In the beginning, it was concentrated mostly in the south; and even there, as will be discussed in Chap. 4, it met with widespread opposition even within parts of the Church. Consequently, Lea (1888: 117) observes:

> Heretics throughout the North were comparatively few and scattered; the chroniclers of the period [i.e., the thirteenth century] take no note of their discovery and punishment, nor even of the establishment of the Inquisition itself. That a few friars should be deputed to the duty of hunting heretics was too unimpressive a fact to be worthy of record.

Chapter 5 will show that in contrast to the inquisition in France— which met with widespread opposition—the Inquisition in Spain became genuinely popular. Indeed, it was established in the first place due to popular pressure in part. As a papal inquisition, moreover, the French inquisition did not enjoy the same kind of support from the Crown as the Spanish one. In fact, French kings often tried to prevent the inquisition from becoming too oppressive. Thus, Friedlander (2000: 69) notes, in 1247 King Louis IX appointed the first *enquêteurs-réformateurs*—agents charged with investigating and correcting abuses. In 1247 they went on their first mission to investigate abuses.

Nonetheless, even if the inquisition in France never became as far-reaching and totalitarian as the Inquisition in Spain, some totalitarian ideas were already developing in the former country. Concerning the inquisition in northern France, Haskins (1902: 644) writes: "Information was freely offered against others, parents even denouncing their children and children their parents, husbands their wives and wives their husbands." As Joseph P. Strayer remarks:

> Continuing pressure, the use of torture, the imposition of social and economic disabilities, and a nicely graded set of penalties that encouraged the weak to betray the strong in return for immunity or token punishments were the techniques that led to the disintegration of the heretical sects. All these techniques were used by European states of the later Middle Ages. Modern totalitarian governments have made few innovations; they have simple been more efficient. (excerpt published in Chalk and Jonassohn 1990: 117)

In sum, although France did not become totalitarian, the inquisition there served as a model for the Inquisition in Spain, which carried the former's methods to a more totalitarian extreme.

SUMMARY

Even though many authors have linked totalitarianism to modernity, this chapter shows that pre-modern societies, such as Spain under the Inquisition, could also be totalitarian. In addition, even though inquisitions *can* lead to totalitarian rule, they need not do so. In Spain, where the Inquisition was part of a state-building process, it led to totalitarianism, while in France, where the papal inquisition was not part of such a process, it did not lead to totalitarianism. Spain had a lot of totalitarian tendencies similar to those later seen in Nazi Germany. However, existing as it did in a pre-modern society with a very different level of forces of production, Spanish totalitarianism also had some important differences from totalitarianism in Nazi Germany. Nevertheless, these differences did not make Spain less totalitarian. This chapter has given little space to Sweden, because during the period in which Germany came under Nazi rule, Sweden evolved into a stable parliamentary democracy. Obviously, therefore, it was not totalitarian. Since this book discusses the reasons why some regimes become totalitarian and induce their populations to commit "evil" acts, the next chapter discusses my theoretical framework for explaining evilness. Later chapters present case studies of the four countries and a brief final chapter sets out my conclusions.

NOTES

1. This will be discussed in Chap. 4, which focuses on France.
2. For a discussion, see also Berger (1993).
3. The Inquisition also began to focus on the Muslim *Moriscos*.

REFERENCES

Aharony, M. (2010). Hannah Arendt and the Idea of Total Domination. *Holocaust and Genocide Studies, 24*(2), 193–224.

Barkey, K., & Katznelson, I. (2011). States, Regimes, and Decisions: Why Jews were Expelled from Medieval England and France. *Theory and Society, 40*(5), 475–503.

Bärsch, C. E. (2002). *Die politische Religion des Nationalsozialismus.* Munich: Wilhelm Fink Verlag.

Berger, R. J. (1993). The "Banality of Evil" Reframed: The Social Construction of the "Final Solution" to the "Jewish Problem". *The Sociological Quarterly, 34*(4), 604.

Burleigh, M. (2000a). National Socialism as a Political Religion. *Totalitarian Movements and Political Religions, 1*(2), 1–26.

Burleigh, M. (2000b). *The Third Reich: A New History.* London: Macmillan.

Chalk, F., & Jonassohn, K. (1990). *The History and Sociology of Genocide: Analyses ad Case Studies.* New Haven: Yale University Press.

Cruz, G. C. (1997). Los Comisarios de la Inquisición de Sevilla en el Siglo XVIII. In E. G. Fernández (Ed.), *El Centinela de la Fe.* Sevilla: Universidad de Sevilla.

Cruz, G. C. (2000). *Los Familiares de la Inquisición.* Valladolid: Junta de Castilla y León.

Flynn, M. (1991). Mimesis of the Last Judgment: The Spanish Auto de fe. *The Sixteenth Century Journal, 22*(2), 281–297.

Friedlander, A. (2000). *The Hammer of the Inquisitors: Brother Bernard Délicieux & the Struggle Against the Inquisition in Fourteenth-Century France.* Leiden: Brill.

Friedman, J. (1987). Jewish Conversion, the Spanish Pure Blood Laws and Reformation: A Revisionist View of Racial and Religious Antisemitism. *The Sixteenth Century Journal, 18*(1), 3–30.

Gellately, R. (1980). The Gestapo and German Society: Political Denunciation in the Gestapo Case Files. *Journal of Modern History, 60*(4), 654–694.

Gitlitz, D. (2000). Inquisition Confessions and Lazarillo de Tormes. *Hispanic Review, 68*(1), 53–74.

Haskins, C. H. (1902). Robert Le Bougre and the Beginnings of the Inquisition in Northern France. *The American Historical Review, 7*(4), 631–652.

Kamen, H. (1985). *Inquisition and Society in Spain in the Sixteenth and Seventeenth Centuries.* Bloomington: Indiana University Press.

Lea, H. C. (1888). *A History of the Inquisition of the Middle Ages: Volume 2.* London: Sampson Low, Marston, Searle, & Rivington.

Ley, M., & Schoeps, H. (Eds.). (1997). *Der Nationalsozialismus als politische Religion.* Frankfurt: Philo Verlagsgesellshaft.

Mann, R. (1979). Politische Penetration und gesellschaftliche Reaktion: Anzeigen zur Gestapo im nationalsozialistischen Deutschland. In R. Mackensen & S. Felizitas (Eds.), *Deutsche Gesellschaft für Soziologie und der ad-hoc-Gruppen beim 19. Deutschen Soziologentag.* 17–20 April, Berlin.

Nalle, S. T. (1987). Inquisitors, Priests, and the People During the Catholic Reformation in Spain. *The Sixteenth Century Journal, 18*(4), 557–587.

Pérez, J. (2005). *The Spanish Inquisition: A History*. New Haven: Yale University Press.

Rawlings, H. (2006). *The Spanish Inquisition*. Oxford: Blackwell.

Roberts, D. D. (2009). 'Political Religion' and the Totalitarian Departures of Inter-War Europe: On the Uses and Disadvantages of an Analytical Category. *Contemporary European History, 18*(4), 381–414.

Roth, N. (1995/2002). *Conversos, Inquisition, and the Expulsion of the Jews from Spain*. Madison: University of Wisconsin.

Trachtenberg, J. (1943/2001). *The Devil and the Jews: The Medieval Conception of the Jew and Its Relation to Modern Antisemitism*. New Haven: Yale University Press/Varda Books.

Tsao, R. T. (2002). The Three Phases of Arendt's Theory of Totalitarianism. *Social Research, 69*(2), 579–619.

Vondung, K. (1997). Die Apokalypse des Nationalsozialismus. In M. Ley & J. H. Schoeps (Eds.), *Der Nationalsozialismus als politische Religion*. Frankfurt: Philo Verlagsgesellshaft.

Vondung, K. (2005). National Socialism as a Political Religion: Potentials and Limits of an Analytical Concept. *Totalitarian Movements and Political Religions, 6*(1), 87–95.

Weitz, E. D. (2003). *A Century of Genocide: Utopias of Race and Nation*. Princeton: Princeton University Press.

Yerushalmi, Y. H. (1970). The Inquisition and the Jews of France in the Time of Bernard Gui. *The Harvard Theological Review, 63*(3), 317–376.

Zukier, H. (1994). The Twisted Road to Genocide: On The Psychological Development of Evil During the Holocaust. *Social Research, 61*(2), 435.

CHAPTER 3

Explaining Evilness

In addition to the issue of when countries become totalitarian, this book deals with the corollary issue: when do states induce people to commit "evil" acts? Since the best-known thesis about the relationship between totalitarianism and evilness comes from Arendt's (1963/2005) argument about the "banality of evil," this chapter begins by critically analyzing her idea. Her argument has had great influence on such important works as Bauman's (1991) *Modernity and the Holocaust*. Linking totalitarianism to modernity, Bauman claimed the division of labor made the Holocaust possible, because of how it allowed desktop bureaucrats to participate in mass murder without feeling any responsibility for their actions. Given the factory-like nature of the slaughter, the various cogs in the machine often did not even realize what the results of their actions were, as each person was only involved in one small part of the Holocaust. After discussing the banality-of-evil thesis, this chapter goes on to criticize Milgram's famous experiments, the results of which he claimed support Arendt's theory. The last part of the chapter takes up alternative social-psychological and cultural explanations for evilness.

CRITIQUE OF ARENDT

Arendt developed her concept of the banality of evil while attending the hearings of Adolf Eichmann. Eichmann had been *SS-Obergruppenführer* ("Senior Group Leader") at the RSHA (*Reichssicherheitshauptamt*; i.e.,

© The Author(s) 2019
S. Saxonberg, *Pre-Modernity, Totalitarianism and the Non-Banality of Evil*, https://doi.org/10.1007/978-3-030-28195-3_3

Reich Main Security Office) in its Jewish section. After spending much of the 1930s doing research on German and international Jewish organizations and the alleged international Jewish conspiracy, he developed the Nazis' strategy for how to deport Jews, and eventually, he became responsible for facilitating mass deportations and managing the logistics involved. In 1961, the Israeli secret police, the *Mossad*, captured Eichmann, who was hiding in Argentina and brought him to Jerusalem to be tried for crimes against humanity as well as other crimes. Eichmann's ordinariness and his lack of outwardly obvious demonic features shocked Arendt into developing the notion that evilness can be banal. Much recent research has criticized Arendt. The main criticism is that she accepted Eichmann's self-defense too readily, as it was in his interest—to minimize his guilt and escape execution—to portray himself as a nonideological person who was merely following orders.

As Bernstein (2008) points out, Arendt did not actually claim to have a theory capable of explaining *all* of the evil that took place under Nazi rule. Rather, her thesis on the non-banality of evil was specifically directed at Eichmann. Nevertheless, since her concept has inspired such great debate, it is worth taking it seriously as a theory that at the very least can explain the behavior of a large proportion of the perpetrators at the lower and middle levels—that is, those who were not the top decision-makers. In this section on the banality of evil, I limit myself to discussing Eichmann and his colleagues, as Eichmann was the focus of Arendt's argument. Moreover, since I discuss Eichmann and those around him in detail here, the chapter on Germany will not mention them. Instead, I will only consider the banality-of-evil thesis in that chapter insofar as it pertains to those who did the actual killing in the field.

Even though some critics of Arendt have emphasized the issue of following orders, Arendt was a bit more nuanced. I see three basic components to her banality-of-evil argument. First, rather than being charismatic and demonic, Eichmann was rather *ordinary* and *"banal."* Second, he was *motivated by a sense of duty* rather than by ideology (which does not necessarily mean he only followed orders). Arendt reluctantly admits at times that in fact, he took initiative, and she concedes that people who are loyal and who perform their duty can also do more than the minimum demanded of them. Nevertheless, it is easy to understand why many critics maintain she accepted Eichmann's argument that he was merely following orders because she greatly downplays each case where Eichmann took any initiative. Third, because Eichmann was a banal person who blindly accepted his duty, he was *unable to think*. Reflecting on the banality-of-evil thesis in an article published 8 years after her famous book, *Eichmann in Jerusalem*, Arendt (1971: 417) sums up her argument in three points:

> However monstrous the deeds were, the doer was neither monstrous nor demonic, and the only specific characteristic one could detect in his past as well as in his behavior during the trial and the preceding police examination was something entirely negative: it was not stupidity but a curious, quite authentic inability to think. He functioned in the role of prominent war criminal as well as he had under the Nazi regime; he had not the slightest difficulty in accepting an entirely different set of rules. He knew that what he had once considered his duty was now called a crime, and he accepted this new code of judgment as it were nothing but another language rule.

Ordinary and Banal

Concerning the first point—about Eichmann's being ordinary and "banal"—it is easy to understand the amazement of many people when they actually saw Eichmann at the trial. Indeed, he looked amazingly normal. As Baehr (2010: 139) summarizes: "Hannah Arendt's famous argument in *Eichmann in Jerusalem* was that Eichmann was not a demon on a mission from Hell, but a crass, ludicrous, pathetic individual" (cf. Culbert 2010: 148). Yet, Eichmann was actually a very good actor and role player—which is something that a truly banal person would have trouble pulling off. So at the trial, he tried to look banal and harmless, but in other situations, he portrayed himself very differently. In the 1930s, he was internationally known and feared by Jewish organizations. He was so proud of his efforts to expel German Jews to Palestine that, when the Third Reich incorporated Austria after the *Anschluß* in 1939, he asked the Jewish entrepreneur and author Adolf Böhm to add a chapter about him in a third volume of Böhm's series on the history of the Zionist movement (Stangneth 2014: 31–2, 2016: 8–9).

Thus, far from wanting to be a simple, loyal, unknown bureaucrat, Eichmann clearly desired fame and recognition. During his time in charge of deportations in Vienna, witnesses reported that he acted "like a young god" (ibid.). Eichmann soon became very well-known throughout Europe for his role in the "Jewish question," and he took such pleasure in his power that he was known as "the Czar of the Jews" (Stangneth 2016: 11ff.). In fact, as Stangneth (2014: 52–3, 2016: 26) observes, it was important for Eichmann to be in the spotlight so that Jews would be afraid of him; otherwise, his negotiating cards would have been weaker. Moreover, not only was his fame helpful for negotiating purposes, it also gave him great personal pleasure. Far from being content to be an anonymous bureaucrat, Eichmann sought and loved attention. Indeed, he craved admiration so much that, while in the Israeli prison, he admitted that what made him suffer most after the war was his need to be anonymous in order to avoid capture (2014: 143, 2016: 101). Stangneth also notes that "[i]n Argentina, Eichmann had explained with pride and pedantry exactly why his name had become a symbol even before the war. He knew his collection of press cuttings like the back of his hand, but he now [at the trial] claimed that 'until 1946, I had next to no public profile'" (2014: 464, 2016: 364). In other words, Eichmann was well-known during the Nazi era; being well-known helped make him a better and more feared negotiator, and he was proud of his power and fame. So even if he was not highly charismatic, and even if he did not look like a demon, neither was he a faceless bureaucrat who was simply doing his duty.

Later, in the late 1950s, when he met exiled Nazis in Argentina as part of the "Dürer Group," Eichmann showed great pride in his role in annihilating Jews. Willem Sassen, leader of the group and a Dutch former SS man, interviewed Eichmann for a project that aimed to show the Holocaust was a "Jewish lie" (Stangneth 2014: 268ff., 2016: 205ff.). Stangneth (2014 in German, 2016 English translation) published a careful study in which she gained access to almost all of the taped interviews and their transcripts. She notes that Sassen and his group wanted to interview Eichmann precisely because he was the only surviving Nazi who had been high enough to have detailed knowledge about the Holocaust, and who could therefore, offer "proof" that it never took place. In his first interviews with Sassen, Eichmann claimed that the number of Jews killed was greatly exaggerated. However, in the final interviews, to the horror of Sassen and those around him, Eichmann not only admitted that the number killed was around 6 million, but he also showed great pride in his role in the slaughter. He shouted: "I have no regrets!" Then he added that, if the Nazis had succeeded in murdering all 10.3 million Jews in Europe, then "[w]e would have fulfilled our duty to our blood and our people and to the freedom of the peoples, if we had exterminated the most cunning intellect of all human intellects alive today" (2014: 391–2, 2016: 303).

Cesarani (2005: 197) gives another example of Eichmann's obvious pride in his role in exterminating Jews. He notes that Eichmann's associate,

Dieter Wisliceny, claimed that back at the headquarters of the RSHA in Berlin in March 1945, Eichmann had said: "I will laugh when I leap into the grave because I have the feeling that I have killed 5,000,000 Jews. That gives me great satisfaction and gratification."

Not only did Eichmann take great pride in his work, he also greatly enjoyed exercising his power. The most infamous case was when Himmler wanted to call off the Holocaust. Himmler understood Germany would lose the war, and he was hoping to negotiate a settlement with the Western allies that would allow him to replace Hitler and to become the leader of a Germany allied with the Western powers against the Soviet Union. Eichmann decided, however, to go against his orders and to order the Jews of Budapest to go on a long death march (now that there were no trains to transport them). A Hungarian Jew, Rudolf Israel Kasztner, who had been negotiating with Eichmann about the possibility of letting some trains with Jews escape to Switzerland, described Eichmann's reaction after ordering the march:

> Eichmann reveled in the cruel disappointment of the stricken Jews, who had hoped Hungary would be able to wriggle out of the war like Bulgaria or Romania with their core Jewish communities intact. When he announced the astounding news that Budapest's Jews would trek to the Reich, Kasztner thought: "In that moment he seemed to be the happiest man on earth. He was in his element again." (Cesarani 2005: 190)

Burleigh (2011: 417) gives another example of how Eichmann enjoyed using his power. In Vienna, whenever he encountered Jews working at the headquarters of the *Sicherheitsdienst*, "Eichmann was wont to scream, 'Pig, stand against the wall when you address me.'" Not exactly the behavior of a banal man!

Duty Rather Than Ideology?

Now comes Arendt's second point. In *Eichmann in Jerusalem* (1963/2005), she abandons her previous emphasis on the importance of ideology (cf. Kohn 2002; Miller 1998: 57; Mommsen 2001: 229). In her previous book, *The Origins of Totalitarianism* (1948/1973), she had argued that ideology plays a major role for totalitarian regimes; in *Eichmann in Jerusalem*, however, she claims that a sense of duty rather than a belief in ideology was decisive. She goes so far as to maintain that

Eichmann was not even anti-Semitic. For example, she writes (1963: 26) that this

> was obviously also no case of insane hatred of Jews, of fanatical anti-Semitism or indoctrination of any kind. He [Eichmann] "personally" never had anything whatever against Jews; on the contrary, he had plenty of "private reasons" for not being a Jew hater.

Furthermore, "he did not enter the Party out of conviction, nor was he ever convinced by it—whenever he was asked to give his reasons, he repeated the same embarrassed clichés about the Treaty of Versailles and unemployment..." (p. 33).

However, Arendt does admit that persons who do their duty are often willing to go far beyond what they are required to do. The important thing is that they take these steps out of loyalty and a sense of duty, rather than out of belief in the ideology. In her words, (1963: 137)

> [m]uch of the horribly painstaking thoroughness in the execution of the Final Solution—a thoroughness that usually strikes the observer as typically German, or else as characteristic of the perfect bureaucrat—can be traced to the odd notion, indeed very common in Germany, that to be law-abiding means not merely to obey the laws but to act as though one were the legislator of the laws that one obeys. Hence the conviction that nothing less than going beyond the call of duty will do.

It is possible Arendt is correct that Eichmann did not join the Nazi Party on account of its anti-Semitism. Nonetheless, this does not mean he lacked radical anti-Semitic feelings. In fact, it seems few people joined the Party solely because of its anti-Semitism; however, it is unlikely they would have joined if they had objected to it. As Cesarani (2005: 33–4) remarks:

> For Eichmann, like millions of Austrians and Germans, dislike of Jews was quite unremarkable. It was so unremarkable that many other things were more impressive. Nor was this animosity necessarily attached to or directed at individual Jews....Anti-Jewish programmes of social exclusion, economic discrimination, denaturalization and state-sponsored emigration were commonplace. You didn't need to be a fanatical, racial anti-semite to join the Nazis; although Nazi policy on the Jews wouldn't put you off, either. There were other equally or more pressing reasons for becoming a Nazi: to reverse the humiliation of Versailles, to check the threat of Communism and curb

the socialists, to make your country politically stable and economically vibrant, to enjoy comradeship with like-minded men, to march, to wear a handsome uniform. Eichmann was probably being quite honest when he said that at the moment he joined the Nazi Party, he didn't hate Jews.

Eichmann was so good at propagating the lie at his trial that he was not a fanatical anti-Semite that even some of Arendt's critics accept the assertion. For example, Miller (1998: 57–8) writes that

> Eichmann was not a Nazi fanatic but a Hitler fanatic—a distinction without a difference, since Hitler was a fanatical anti-Semite. To be sure, if Hitler had changed his mind and said that all Jews should be given apartments on the Riviera, Eichmann would have zealously carried out those orders as well.

Historical research makes it clear, though, that Eichmann was in fact, a fanatical anti-Semite. Thus, Lozowick (2001: 217) notes, Arendt was mistaken to suggest anti-Semitism did not matter for Eichmann when he joined the Nazi Party. Before Kaltenbrunner convinced him to join, according to Arendt, Eichmann had been just as willing to join a nonpolitical club. However,

> Eichmann and many of his closest colleagues were affiliated with nationalistic, anti-Semitic organizations before they joined the party of the SS, and earlier than 1932, so that opportunism was not their main motive [for joining the Nazis]. Perhaps the best illustration of Arendt's carelessness on this point is that of the Schlaraffia club in Linz: Arendt would have us believe that this was a harmless *bürgerlich* club, committed to having fun, and that Eichmann was about to join when Kaltenbrunner carried him off to join the SS. Eichmann himself, *after the war*, told a different tale: What had impressed him about the Schlaraffia members was that they accepted no Jews.

Moreover, Eichmann did not simply join the Nazis. Soon he got a position at the Jewish section of the RSHA. Anybody joining the Jewish section had to know it was a fanatically anti-Semitic organization. Eichmann himself went to great lengths to propagate anti-Semitic myths. He gave numerous lectures where he displayed charts he had drawn showing the alleged ties of Jewish organizations in connection with their "international conspiracy." To give just a few of many examples, Lozowick (2000: 31) mentions a lecture that Eichmann gave on November 1, 1937, at a meeting for training employees at the *Sicherheitsdienst*. Its title was: "World

Jewry: Its Political Activity, and the Implications of the Activity on [sic] the Jews Residing in Germany." Lozowick (pp. 31–2) comments that the speech showed "[i]t was absolutely clear to him that there was a worldwide Jewish conspiracy, and the more facts he learned about the Jews, the more he was convinced of this." Since Jews were penetrating all areas of German society and all areas of people's lives, it was necessary to take "defensive measures."

Because of his rabid anti-Semitism, Eichmann took great pride in his attempts to liquidate all of the Jews in Europe. There were many examples of people trying to get exemptions from deportation, which Eichmann angrily turned down. To take one such example, Cesarani (2005: 133) reports the case of the "Aryan" Jochen Klepper, who was married to a Jewish woman. Klepper tried to use his connections to save her and their daughter, so he talked to his friend, Wilhelm Frick, who was Minister of the Interior. Frick recommended that he ask Eichmann; but when he visited Eichmann at his office, Eichmann refused to make an exception in their case. Klepper, his wife and their daughter then committed suicide. In fact, "Eichmann consistently intervened to limit the types of Jews and the number of Jews who could be exempted from deportation" (p. 147). He even went so far as to complain to the foreign office that the Jewish "enemies of the Reich" had been trying to arrange to "escape the fate they deserve" (p. 156). Cesarani also notes that the Auschwitz commander, Rudolf Höss, wrote in his memoir that, when he met with Eichmann around 1942–1943, Eichmann was "completely obsessed with the idea of destroying every single Jew that he could lay his hands on....Any compromise, even the slightest, would have to be paid for bitterly at a later date" (ibid.).

Cesarani (2005: 192) further notes that

Eichmann turned savagely against his opponents, Jewish, and non-Jewish. He ordered Dannecker to lead raids by SD [*Sicherheitsdienst* or RSHA] and [Hungarian fascist] Arrow Cross militia on safe houses, looking for Jews with false papers. He told Kasztner that he wanted to punish Wallenberg for obstructing the foot marches. His tirades against the Swedish envoy [who protected Jews by giving them Swedish passports] became notorious. After Eichmann was heard to say that "it was his intention to put to death by shooting," the person whom he called "the Jewish dog, Wallenberg," the Swedish minister in Budapest lodged a complaint with [SS-*Brigadeführer*] Veesenmayer. (ibid.: 192)

Finally, Cesarani (2005: 272) underlines that, at Eichmann's trial, the prosecutors presented his notes to the transcripts of his interview with Sassen, the Dutch former SS officer mentioned above. Eichmann wrote in these notes that, if his colleagues had tried to prevent the deportations in Hungary in 1944, this would have prevented him from reaching the "goal that he aspired to 'in my uncompromising fanaticism'…which was to free Hungary of all its Jews." Here, then, he even admitted to being *fanatical* about his anti-Semitism.

Cesarani (2005: 361) adds that Arendt ignored evidence that Eichmann was a fanatical anti-Semite with a strong pro-Nazi ideological affinity, who had been socialized in a German-nationalist environment under a father who was part of a right-wing, German-nationalist network. Eichmann joined the Nazi party when it was forbidden in Austria, and he did so while working for a Jewish-owned company. Later in the 1930s, he gave lectures about the alleged international Jewish conspiracy. Thus, "[d]espite all the evidence of Eichmann's right wing and anti-Semitic background, [Arendt] reduces his decision to careerism—though she does not explain how becoming a Nazi would help his career in a firm run by Jews or in an embattled party still far from Power" (2005: 347).

Other studies of Eichmann and his colleagues reach the same conclusions, as well as offering many examples of how they were ideologically charged zealots who would stop at nothing to pursue their goal of exterminating the Jews. Miller (1998: 58) asserts that "Arendt believed that Eichmann was so much the bureaucratic man that he *never realized what he was doing*"[emphasis in original]. Yet, as Lozowick (2000: 128) concludes, "[i]n contrast to what Arendt contended, even low-ranking people in the department understood that Jews sent to the East were being murdered." Lozowick points out that the Reich Main Security Office, department IV B 4, did not even use the euphemism *Sonderbehandlung* (special treatment) for the genocidal activities, reserving that term for executions of individuals at the camps. Instead, preferring to use "a euphemism for the euphemism," they spoke of *SB-Fälle* (SB cases). "The need to do so in this particular case would seem to indicate the strength of the instinct to conceal and repress what was happening. This is not consistent with the conjecture that they did not understand what they were doing was wrong." Lozowick cites an employee at the department (2000: 133):

Wöhrn took pride in his Jew-hatred and declared it openly. He justified everything that was happening to the Jews, and was sorry only that the action being taken against them was not energetic enough. Once one of the secretaries asked why so many Jews were being sent to camps, and his answer was that "there's a lot of room there." In this he was like Günter, who told another secretary that "We don't hate the Jews, we despise them."

So much for the banality of evil.

Since Arendt wants to portray Eichmann as a person without strong ideological beliefs, she tries to downplay the cases in which he took initiative. A typical instance was when Eichmann visited Palestine and co-authored a highly anti-Semitic report. Without providing any evidence, Arendt asserts that he did this because he was "ordered" to do so (1963: 62). Yet, given that he was a fanatical anti-Semite himself, and given that he worked for one of the centers of anti-Semitic policy in the Reich, he would have hardly needed any orders to write such a report!

Arendt mentions other cases where Eichmann took great initiative, but she always tries to qualify them. Take the deportations from Vienna that Eichmann organized, for which the Nazi regime subsequently rewarded him with a higher position in Berlin. Eichmann showed great ability in implementing a new plan for deportations in this case, and the regime duly showed its appreciation. Arendt tries to downplay his role here by claiming that the real instigator of the idea was somebody else (1963: 43). It is hard to know, however, how much of any idea here came from any particular person, as the planners cooperated in a group. Yet, even if Eichmann "only" took somebody else's idea, the creativity he showed in putting it into practice obviously impressed his superiors. In addition, in order to convince the Jews of Vienna to leave peacefully, he had to be a masterful liar and role player. A really banal person would not have been capable of that.

Moreover, recent historical studies cast doubt on Arendt's attempt to minimize the initiative Eichmann took in developing the Vienna model for deporting Jews. Lozowick (2000: 38), for instance, agrees that Eichmann's task in Vienna was originally rather limited. However, Eichmann took the initiative to broaden his role and to develop methods for deporting the Jewish population of the city:

> While the SD was looking for channels of operational activity, Eichmann found one, or perhaps, took advantage of the situation and created one. In the framework of a given direction of policy set by his superiors, he acted not as a drab bureaucrat carrying out orders, but rather as a very diligent,

very violent bureaucrat who was very successfully taking advantage of a for-tuitous moment. His personal initiative was on such a scale that, even months later, his erstwhile colleagues in Berlin still did not understand how much had had changed. The importance of this point for our discussion cannot be exaggerated: what put Eichmann at center state, and won him rapid promotion, was precisely his ability to perform on a plane higher than that of a drab bureaucrat.

Similarly, Safrian (1993/2010: 30–1) points to the letter that Eichmann's supervisor wrote to justify Eichmann's promotion from his position in Vienna to a higher one in Berlin. According to this letter, written in 1938, Eichmann was an "energetic and impulsive person [possessing] great abilities for independent administration of his area of expertise; capable especially of discharging organizational and negotiating tasks independently and extremely well; and recognized as a specialist in his area of expertise…."

Interestingly, Arendt (1963: 94) does admit that Eichmann was will-ing at one point to take an initiative that went contrary to his orders. This was when he redirected a group of Roma from Russian territory to the ghetto of Łódź. She emphasizes, though, that this was the "first and last time" he "took an initiative contrary to orders." Yet, she also admits that Eichmann "sabotaged" Himmler's orders to end the Holocaust by ordering the foot marches in the fall of 1944 (p. 145). Since she wants to downplay any initiative on Eichmann's part, she claims he was "cov-ered," since he "can probably show some telegram. Müller and Kaltenbrunner must have covered him." However, even if Eichmann perhaps *could have* found some document to cover him, the point is that he could also have decided to follow Himmler's orders. In fact, then, he had a choice, and as usual, he chose the most fanatical and murderous path possible.

Despite Arendt's claim that Eichmann was a banal person who rarely took initiative, and who was motivated by a sense of duty rather than ide-ology, she points out that when he was about to be hanged, he said that he was a *Gottgläubiger*. She admits this was a way "to express in common Nazi fashion that he was no Christian and did not believe in life after death" (1963: 252). Thus, as Gerlach (2001: 439) observes, Eichmann showed his ideological adherence to the SS even at his death. This makes him seem highly unlike the banal and nonideological person that Arendt makes him out to be.

The Inability to Think

The third component of the banality-of-evil thesis concerns the *inability to think* (cf. Clarke 1980: 417ff.; Kohn 2002). Arendt rightly points out that Eichmann often spoke in clichés. She observes (1963: 49):

> The longer one listened to him, the more obvious it became that his inability to speak was closely connected with an inability to think, namely, to think from the standpoint of somebody else. No communication was possible with him, not because he lied.

The mere fact that she writes Eichmann did not lie indicates that she was surprisingly willing to take everything he said at face value. Many observers have pointed out that Eichmann lied quite often in the hearings (e.g., von Lang 1986; Safrian 2010: 220; Stangneth 2014, 2016). Yet, leaving aside the issue of Eichmann's veracity, the fact that Eichmann often spoke in clichés does not mean he could not think. In fact, it even seems to contradict Arendt's argument that Eichmann did not believe in the ideology. People who believe strongly in an ideology are likely to use clichés concerning issues surrounding that ideology. However, *given their ideological framework*, they can still be quite capable of thinking and of coming up with solutions to problems, even if they are not willing to question the basic tenets of their ideology. If this is what Arendt meant by the inability to think, then the political-religion and politicized-religion framework is much more suitable than the banality-of-evil framework.

Within the Nazi ideological framework, Eichmann was able to think and to make decisions—all of them in support of the Holocaust. In fact, Eichmann's superiors had such respect for his creative abilities that they gave him permission to initiate experiments. He took advantage of this opportunity to establish the first forced-labor camps in Austria (in Doppl and Sandhof) (Stangneth 2014: 33–4, 2016: 10).

Eichmann was also willing to take initiatives to figure out how to murder Jews. The following case makes this clear. On July 16, 1941, after the invasion of the Soviet Union had led to a great increase in the number of Jews to deal with, *Sturmbannführer* (SS Major) Rolf-Heinz Höppner wrote a summary of a meeting that SS officers had held in Warthegau. Höppner noted their plans for sending all 300,000 Jews in the area to a camp in Łódź. Höppner reasoned that many of the Jews would starve to death, so it might be better to "liquidate" them; but the problem was that the head of the ghetto opposed such ideas, as he was making a large profit from the cheap labor. In response, Eichmann's department drew up a document that Reinhard Heydrich (head of the *Sicherheitsdienst*) used to get Göring to sign a new operational order allowing the murders. They wanted Göring to sign it rather than Himmler, as Göring represented the state (a state order had greater legitimacy, even though the SS belonged to the Nazi Party) (see, e.g., Lozowick 2000: 53–4; Safrian 1993/2010: 75).

A few months later Franz Rademacher, a foreign office legation councilor, called Eichmann because the German ambassador in Belgrade had sent a telegram to the foreign office insisting that at least all male Jews in Serbia be arrested and removed because they were carrying out acts of sabotage and rebellion. The ambassador wanted them to be deported to Romania, but the foreign office refused. The ambassador then complained that, if his request was refused again, the only alternative would be to deport the Jews to Russia or to the *General government* in Poland. Eichmann replied that the military was responsible for maintaining order, so it should simply shoot the Jews (Burleigh 2000: 634; Safrian 1993/2010: 79). So much for the notion that Eichmann did not take initiative or feel responsible for killing anyone!

Yet another example: Dr. Wetzel, the official in charge of racial policy in the national ministry for the occupied eastern territories, wrote a draft letter to his superior on October 25, 1941, about the gassing of Jews. The quantity of gas available, Wetzel explained, was insufficient for the purpose. He received a reply suggesting that a chemist be sent to Riga to take care of the problem locally. "Wetzel noted that Eichmann had approved of this" (Safrian 1993/2010: 101). In late 1941 and early 1942, gas vans were sent to Łódź, Riga and Minsk. They were to be used in the murder of Jews, Roma and Sinti who had been deported from Germany, Austria and the Protectorate, and who were considered unfit to work. The allegedly banal Eichmann

personally managed the negotiations with the responsible institutions at the target locations. All clues suggest his having proposed or supported this killing method in his discussions with Gestapo and ghetto administrative personnel in Łódź, with SS organizations in Minsk, with the officials of the Ostministerium [Ministry for the Eastern Occupied Territories], and having advanced its adoption in cooperation with central SS offices in Berlin. (p. 110)

At least within the framework of the ideology, then, Eichmann was obviously capable of thinking. However, Arendt adds another stipulation about thinking: the inability to put oneself in other people's shoes. She bases this on Eichmann's strange attempt to gain sympathy from the judges for his failure to get a promotion within the SS—a promotion he felt was his rightful due (1963: 49). While it is true that at times he had trouble understanding the judges' thinking, his entire defense was based on the lie that he had no responsibility for the murders of the Jews, that he had just been following orders and that he was not even an anti-Semite. His ability to lie so well that he even convinced Arendt indicates that, at least to some extent, he was able to put himself in other people's shoes. For example, he was able to portray himself completely differently when detained in a cell in Jerusalem than how he had done when meeting exiled Nazis in Argentina. In fact, a large part of his career in the Nazi era was based exactly on his ability to put himself in other people's shoes. He could hardly have convinced the *Judenräte* (Jewish Councils) to cooperate with him during the deportations if he were unable to understand how the Jewish leaders were thinking.

Precisely because Eichmann was a good liar and was able to put himself in other people's shoes, he became an excellent negotiator. Stangneth (2014: 343, 2016: 265) comments that "Eichmann was clearly proud of the tricks and lies he used to achieve his aims" when negotiating with Jewish organizations. "I loved playing an open hand against all the Jewish political functionaries," he told Sassen. Stangneth (2014: 468, 2016: 367) concludes:

> In power, Eichmann played treacherous games with his victims' hopes of finding a way out of their situation, in order to gain the respect and assistance of his old comrades, he confirmed their expectations that National Socialism could be separated from the imperative to exterminate. In Israel, he tried to serve what he saw as a 'Jewish instinct,' the desire to understand and gather knowledge. Like a mirror, he reflected people's fears and expectations, whether they were fearing for their own lives.

These examples contradict Arendt's assertion that Eichmann suffered from "thoughtlessness and a lack of imagination" (Ezrahi 2010: 154; cf. Marrus 2001: 211). Such a person would not have been able to play "an open hand"; nor would he have been able to create rumors and myths about himself (such as that he had been born in Palestine—see Stangneth 2014, 2016) in order to gain prestige.

LeBor and Boyes (2005: 12) sum up Eichmann's position:

> [T]here was always scope of initiative. A bureaucracy cannot function if people simply follow orders. It needs guidelines and strategies, then individual bureaucrats must decide on what to do with their power. Especially the SS functioned like this. The orders that Eichmann had "were vague and left space for interpretation. Eichmann, however, used his bureaucrat's freedom to perform overzealously rather than to exercise mercy."

Lozowick (2001: 218) concludes that "Eichmann and his staff were arrogant, brutally violent, malicious—and innovative."

Berkowitz (2014: 201) defends Arendt by interpreting very generously what she meant by the inability to think and to put oneself in other people's shoes. He writes:

> Eichmann's failure to think was a failure of imagination, a failure to see humanity in others, and a failure to see outside his own blinkered worldview. His thoughtlessness made Eichmann blind to the basic human fact of plurality.

Yet, is this interpretation not merely an admission that, for true believers like Eichmann, National Socialism became a political religion? As with all religions, certain aspects are taken for granted as incontestable. Given one's belief system, then, one can commit acts that seem justified to those who share that belief system, but which are immoral to those who do not. Thus, political religion makes it easier for people to commit "evil" acts than banality does.

CRITIQUE OF MILGRAM

Milgram (1963, 1974) was inspired by Arendt and he wanted to see if ordinary Americans would be willing to torture people if they were told their actions were contributing to science. In the experiments he conducted to test this, participants were told to give electric shocks to a "learner" in another room whom they could see through a window when that person gave the wrong answer to a question. The shocks would allegedly help the learner to learn better. Moreover, participants were told it would help the learner if they gradually increased the level of the shocks. In reality, the learner was an actor and he did not receive any shocks. Some of the participants were willing to increase the shocks to levels that would have been fatal had they been real. It turned out that a high proportion of people would fully obey such instructions, albeit reluctantly.

Psychologists who criticize Milgram point to the differences between the logic behind the Milgram experiments and that behind the Nazi reality. For example, participants in the experiments were assured that the shocks would not be hazardous and would not harm the learner. They became disobedient when they started to doubt that the learner was not being harmed (Blass 1993: 34). In fact, other experiments have shown that, when participants are told the learner is in danger of suffering harm, none of them are obedient to the scientist.

Fenigstein (1997) points out that, in contrast to Eichmann and many others who took part in the Holocaust, almost all of the participants in Milgram's experiments experienced great tension, distress and inner conflict while punishing the learner. Many of them suffered because they believed they had acted against their moral values. Eichmann, on the other hand, faced no psychological barriers to carrying out his orders.

One argument against the claim that the perpetrators were ideologically motivated comes from Browning's (1992/2001) study of members of Reserve Police Battalion 101, which engaged in mass executions on the eastern front during the war. The vast majority agreed to participate in the shootings, even though they would not have been punished if they had refused and requested a transfer. This supports the idea that they were motivated by obedience. In addition, some did suffer psychologically from their actions. In fact, one of the main reasons behind the decision to establish death camps using poison gas was that the psychological costs were so high among those who had to shoot the victims.

As Fenigstein (1997) notes, however, Browning admitted that those who quit cited physical revulsion rather than any ethnical principles as their reason for so doing. Neither did they show any regret in their testimony at the postwar trials, even though the trials took place in a democratic country where a display of remorse would have mitigated their guilt and reduced the severity of their punishment. Their testimony showed, namely, that their psychological problems did not result from a bad conscience, but rather from the revulsion they felt at experiencing the gruesome events (Zukier 1994: 435 and Vetlesen 2005: 210 also make this point).

SOCIAL-PSYCHOLOGICAL APPROACHES TO EVILNESS

Recent studies on evilness have emphasized the importance of social-psychological factors, such as the need to create an outside "other" or outgroup, to create a sense of outside threat and so on. I support this approach, but it is not enough in itself. We need to know why regimes would want to resort to such tactics in the first place. My approach, then, accepts the importance of such social-psychological factors but connects them with the issue of state-building and legitimacy.

Citing the Holocaust and Serbia's ethnic cleansing as examples, Vetlesen (2005) claims that large groups commit evil acts when leaders instill *existential fear* among the people they rule, giving them the feeling they must wipe out another group to save themselves. He notes it is easiest to create fear of an existential threat from an enemy if the leaders can point to an historical defeat. Hitler argued that Jews in the German military had betrayed the country and were responsible both for the defeat in WWI and for the signing of the Versailles Treaty. However, this type of argument cannot explain why only some regimes try to use genocide/mass murder as a weapon. After all, almost every country in the world can claim to have suffered injustice at some point in its history. However, what Hitler and Milosevic had in common was that they were both trying to build new states. In Hitler's case, Germany had only been united a little more than 60 years before he came to power; moreover, this new state had lost a lot of territory due to its defeat in WWI. The imperial regime had lost its legitimacy when it lost the war; and the Weimar Republic for its part was never able—during its existence of a little more than two decades—to gain legitimacy among civil servants, among some of the main political parties and among a large part of the population at large. This made it possible for Hitler to gain widespread legitimacy by calling for the unification of all ethnic Germans in a new German state that would include Austrian Germans, Sudeten Germans, and Germans living in the territories that the country had lost as a result of WWI (interestingly, though, Hitler did not press any claim on the German-speaking part of Switzerland). Leaders like Hitler try to create existential fears among the population *because* they consider it useful for the state-building process; moreover, they feel they need a legitimizing ideology—which can take on a totalitarian character—in order to hold the state together. The population in turn, is quite receptive to such arguments under these conditions, because as citizens of a new state—or denizens of a territory in the process of becoming a new state—they feel more vulnerable and less secure than do the inhabitants of states that have existed for hundreds of years.

Meanwhile, Waller (2007) claims that cultural factors, the psychological construction of the "Other" as the "outgroup" and the social construction of cruelty induce people to behave in an evil way. As many scholars have pointed out, once rulers choose an outgroup, they find it necessary to start dehumanizing its members. Then, when members of the ingroup no longer see members of the outgroup as human, they find it much easier to commit "evil" acts against them (Berger 1993; Blass 1993; Browning 1992/2001; Grodin and Annas 2007; Hinton 2005; Mann 2005; Midlarsky 2005; Vetlesen 2005; Welzer 2005). Thus, Germans (and Austrians) were more willing to murder Jews during WWII than they had been in 1932 before the Nazis came to power because Jews had been subjected to a process of increasing dehumanization during the intervening years. This process included a long period during which the general population underwent indoctrination against the Jews and a succession of measures deprived Jews of their rights and made them more and more impoverished and less and less dignified-looking. And when members of a given group look less human, it is easier to think of them as being subhuman.

Again, however, this social-psychological approach does not give any reason why regimes would *want* people to behave in an evil manner. The state-building hypothesis, however, does offer a plausible explanation: yes, totalitarian regimes are more likely to arise in countries with a more authoritarian culture, but the state-building process encourages leaders to induce a collective feeling to gain the loyalty of the population; therefore, such leaders have an incentive to create an outgroup against which society can unite in loyalty to the new state. The mere act of creating a united Germany, for example, made it necessary to decide who was a German and who was not. The same need arose when Spain became one country. In Germany, the outgroups were identified by their ethnicity, in Spain by their religion.

Moreover, the "story" the rulers tell to legitimize their regime also influences the previously existing culture. If a portion of the population believes in the legitimacy of the regime, then many of these believers will be willing to commit "evil" acts in support of the regime, as they do not define such actions as evil but rather as necessary to remove an existential threat. This can explain, for example, why Eichmann, who claimed only to be following orders, was willing to disobey Himmler's orders to stop the

Holocaust. In his view, Himmler's orders were not legitimate, for Himmler was trying to save himself and to negotiate a separate peace with the Western allies, which required him to abandon the regime's ideology of anti-Semitism. The legitimate thing to do, as Eichmann saw it, was to try to finish his task of eliminating the Jewish "enemy."

As will be discussed in Chap. 6, the situation in Sweden was different from that in Germany in one crucial regard. That is to say, even if anti-Semitism was widespread in the former country during the first decade of the twentieth century, Swedes never saw Jews as an existential threat. In addition, the Swedish state had no reason to search for a scapegoat to frame as an existential threat, because it had existed for many centuries and enjoyed great legitimacy. It had no need to find an outgroup against which to mobilize the population in order to gain legitimacy. Moreover, since public administrators in Sweden traditionally enjoyed great autonomy, and since in contrast to their German counterparts they were chosen on the basis of merit rather than of loyalty, it is doubtful that many of them would have supported a totalitarian regime that wanted them to carry out "evil" acts. This combination of great autonomy with a lack of blind loyalty encouraged Swedish bureaucrats to take greater moral responsibility than their counterparts in Germany. For example, civil servants at the Swedish foreign office decided on their own to start helping Jews escape from Nazi-held territories, even though the government never made a decision to change its previously strict immigration policy.

This also fits well with the Spanish case. As Chap. 5 will show Spain was a newly created state that needed legitimacy. There was some existential fear among the general population, due to the disorder that had existed before Ferdinand came to power. In addition, Jews who had converted to Catholicism, so-called *conversos*, were starting to threaten the aristocracy's legitimacy, as the nobility based itself on the notion that it had better blood than the peasants. Wealthy *conversos*, namely, were marrying into aristocratic families, so it was becoming more and more difficult for the nobility to claim it had better blood than the peasantry. Jews also represented a threat as they could induce *conversos* to revert to Judaism, which would threaten the Catholic ideology on which the regime based itself. Meanwhile, Muslims—including those who had converted to Christianity—also represented a potential threat, as the rulers saw them as a possible "fifth" column that might cooperate with invading Muslim forces from the Ottoman Empire or from Morocco.

France, by contrast, was a relatively well-established country, so its rulers did not have to worry so much about who belonged, and its population
did not feel the same kind of existential threats (although wars with
England later did, of course, pose problems). As Chap. 4 will show converted Jews in France did not pose the same kinds of threat as they did in
Spain, both because they were much smaller in number and because the
French aristocracy was not based on blood. So once again, the type of
state-building matters here, as does the issue of whether the country in
question was well-established or had only recently come into being.

Culture and Killing

Among authors who take a cultural approach, many have emphasized the
emergence of racial anti-Semitism in Germany in the nineteenth century
(e.g., Weiss 1996). The most provocative and hotly debated of these contributions is undoubtedly Goldhagen's (1996) *Hitler's Willing
Executioners*. Whereas much previous literature plays down individual
responsibility for the Holocaust and emphasized such issues as group pressure (Browning 1992/2001) or the desire to do one's duty (Arendt
1963/2005), Goldhagen's starting point is that the henchmen may actually have thought they were doing something good and that Jews should
be killed. He gives many examples throughout his book of Nazi killers'
going well beyond just following orders, and he discusses in great detail
how some of them showed great sadism far beyond what would have been
necessary if they had only been following orders. He also criticizes the
group-pressure theory, pointing out that the police who did the shootings
in Poland were given the choice of opting out if they did not want to kill
people (and some of them did in fact refuse). None of those refusing were
ever punished for this. Goldhagen's main argument is that a special "eliminationist" brand of anti-Semitism had emerged in Germany in the 1800s;
that most of the population believed in it; and that, given this belief, many
Germans were willing to take part in mass killings of Jews when Hitler
came to power and made it possible for them to do so. However, even if
it is true that many of the perpetrators probably thought what they were
doing were justified, critics have brought up several problems with the
eliminationist argument.

First, Goldhagen gives an overly static view of anti-Semitism (e.g.,
Hillberg 1997; Moses 1998; Rosenfeld 1999). From the early 1800s to
1945, in fact, the degree of anti-Semitism in Germany varied, growing

stronger and becoming weaker at various times. Goldhagen's critics also note that, when the Nazis came to power, they were able to use their propaganda to increase support for anti-Semitism. Furthermore, anti-Semitism grew worse as a result of the German defeat in WWI, which the Nazis blamed on the Jews. As Weiss (1999) points out, even though racial anti-Semitism developed in the 1880s, anti-Semitic parties never got more than 1–3 percent of the vote until 1928. Moreover, by the time the Holocaust began, Germans had been bombarded with anti-Semitic propaganda from the state over nearly a decade, which also probably influenced their views.

Second, Goldhagen provides no evidence that German anti-Semitism was any more eliminationist than the Russian, French or other variants of the doctrine. So far no serious study has systematically compared the degree of eliminationist anti-Semitism across European countries, but Chap. 7 will discuss evidence showing that it was strong in France as well (even if it is difficult to determine which country had the greatest problem with eliminationist anti-Semitism). Moreover, German perpetrators were also willing to kill members of other groups, such as Roma, homosexuals, the mentally disabled and so on, so their behavior was not based only on eliminationist anti-Semitism.

Third, as Weiss (1996) notes, not all Germans believed in eliminationist anti-Semitism. As mentioned, for one thing, anti-Semitic parties rarely polled well before 1928; for another, the Social Democrats were usually the largest party in the country, and they were strongly against any kind of anti-Semitism. As will be discussed in Chap. 6, this was not the case in Sweden, where there was a tradition of some anti-Semitism within the Social Democratic Party, although it faded away by the 1930s. In other words, rather than speaking of one culture in a country, we should recognize that there are several different cultures in each country and that not all groups are equally influenced by the same cultural traditions.

Finally, although Goldhagen accepts Browning's (1992) assertion that the police (*Ordnungspolizei*) who did the killings in Poland were "ordinary people," this assertion is disputable. In any country, those who choose to be police are likely to have more authoritarian personalities than the population in general. Moreover, as will be discussed in Chap. 7, even regular police were under Himmler's control and had been indoctrinated in Nazi racial propaganda. Furthermore, as Mann (2004, 2005) shows, the Nazis recruited most of their perpetrators from areas where the inhabitants were more likely to be anti-Semitic and nationalist. Refugees from territories lost as a result of WWI figured prominently here, as did people living in border areas (who felt more threatened).

My state-building approach allows for a much more dynamic model than Goldhagen's cultural argument. My starting point is that the state-building process made ethnicity a more central question, since the new rulers had to decide exactly who was a German and who was not, and they had to decide whether the new state would be a state for ethnic Germans from all over the world or a state for all of the people living on its territory. The unification project always had a strong ethno-nationalist element. After the Austro-Hungarian Empire collapsed at the end of WWI, the newly founded Austrian state faced similar existential issues. Was it simply a shrunken version of the old empire? Had a new Austrian people emerged? Were Austrians simply Germans, who ought therefore to join up with Germany? In fact, Mann (2005) argues that Austrians were more likely than Germans to engage in mass murder because they were influenced by the expansionist "greater Germany" perspective, whereas Germans were more influenced by the "little Germany" approach that had led to unification under Protestant-Prussian rather than Catholic-Austrian rule.

From this perspective, it is not necessary to accept Goldhagen's thesis that eliminationist anti-Semitism was stronger in Germany than in other countries. Instead, it is enough to argue that a large number of Germans and Austrians—not all of them—basically accepted the legitimacy of the Hitler regime. Their main motive may not have been anti-Semitism, but rather the belief that Hitler could unite Germans and make them strong again after the humiliation of defeat and the resulting Versailles treaty, as well as the suffering caused by hyperinflation and the Great Depression. However, given the fact that the Nazis blamed Jews for many of these problems, and given the constant propaganda against Jews as well as their progressive dehumanization, some Germans came to accept the basic anti-Semitic argument that the Jews presented an existential threat—that they were responsible for the country's defeat in WWI, for the Versailles Treaty which had punished Germany for the war, and even for hyperinflation and high unemployment. Such persons might also blame "Jewish liberalism" for the breakdown of the party system and for the divisiveness which party competition had brought about. However, one major reason why many Germans assented to these arguments and accepted the legitimacy of the Nazi regime was that they saw it as building a strong state that would unite the Germans of Germany, Austria and the Sudetenland. They also approved of its having put an end to the unstable governments of the Weimar Republic. Taken together, these factors rendered the population more susceptible to the Nazis' arguments in other spheres, such as in connection with anti-Semitism.

Of course, both overt and latent anti-Semitism undoubtedly existed in Germany. As will be discussed in later chapters, Catholics and Lutherans had promoted anti-Semitism throughout Europe. I will argue it is wrong, furthermore, to assume that this was limited to religious anti-Semitism (in contrast to "modern" racial anti-Semitism). According to myths which were widespread well before the nineteenth century, namely, Jews belonged to a different species, and thus they remained dangerous even after converting to Christianity. In addition, Spain enacted purity-of-blood laws in the fifteenth and sixteenth centuries, which excluded "New Christians"—that is, Christians with Jewish ancestry—from public offices and many professions. Thus, anyone living in Europe grew up against a cultural backdrop that included anti-Semitic elements. In support of Goldhagen, this book will also show that, while eliminationist anti-Semitism existed in Germany, it was virtually unknown in Sweden, despite the existence of widespread racial prejudice against Jews in the latter country. Yet, as already noted, it seems that eliminationist anti-Semitism *did* exist in other countries, such as France. In any case, given Germany's long history of anti-Semitism, which made such ideas acceptable or at least familiar to large portions of the population, the Nazis were able to play on such latent beliefs. They were then able to add other elements to the witch's brew besides, derived from the humiliation that Germans felt in connection with military defeat and the reparations required by Versailles, as well as from the *existential fear* which the onslaught of the Great Depression called forth. Under these circumstances, it was easier for the Nazis to gain support for their attempts to portray Jews as the dangerous "outgroup." Moreover, as theorists of political religions have pointed out, people find it easier to commit evil acts if the regime under which they live is widely seen as legitimate—even they do not completely accept its ideology.

Summary

Thus, my argument is not that Germans were necessarily more anti-Semitic culturally than other Europeans, but rather that, as long as they had some basic belief in the regime's legitimacy as the "true" representative of Germans, they were likely to believe that committing atrocities in the name of this regime was legitimate and perhaps even necessary. The regime, in turn, had an incentive to present the Jewish outgroup as an existential threat in order to mobilize support. The state was rather new, having been created in the 1870s. Yet, the Kaiser's regime lost legitimacy when it lost WWI and the Weimer Republic had trouble gaining legitimacy as a replacement. The Weimar Republic had been weak and unstable. Consequently, part of the Nazis' legitimizing strategy was to project themselves as the saviors of the new state, who could make it strong enough to fight the existential threats it faced. It is true that the country had a long cultural history of dehumanizing Jews, and some of its ideologists had propagated an eliminationist anti-Semitism, but these things could not have led to the Holocaust by themselves. However, the new Nazi regime had gained a lot of legitimacy; it had created a political religion that indoctrinated the population into believing in its ideology, and it had carried out a step-by-step process of dehumanizing the Jewish outgroup. Under these conditions, the regime was able to convince those who already had the most authoritarian and anti-Semitic tendencies to commit atrocities. In fact, as several scholars have noted, the perpetrators saw themselves as moral beings carrying out their duty when they killed Jews and others. Even though they were willing to commit mass murder against groups that allegedly posed an existential threat, they refused to commit other acts which they considered to be immoral, or at least they claimed they would not be willing to commit such acts (e.g., Burleigh 2011; Welzer 2005).

The other totalitarian country in this study, Spain during the Inquisition, also induced people to carry out evil acts. As Mann (2005) points out, the Spanish Inquisition carried out "evil" acts against ethnic Jews, even if did not carry out a Holocaust. Although Mann himself does not use the term "evil," he writes that (p. 48):

> This was no holocaust, since the only deaths were incurred after rigorous (if often dubious) trials or during armed resistance. But it was total religious cleansing, becoming more ethnic as it proceeded.

Arguing much as I do in this book, Mann (2005: 45–6) depicts the ethnic cleansing surrounding the Inquisition as part of a state-building process. In his words:

The process of unification had increased the power of Spanish churchmen and lessened papal control. Catholicism expressed both Spanish unity and its means of defense. In 1481 the powers of the Inquisition of Aragon were extended to the whole kingdom in a bid to enhance doctrinal purity.

Thus, my model of how totalitarian states are able to induce people to commit "evil" acts is as follows: Totalitarianism arises as a new regime comes to power in order to create a new state. The rulers of the new state then have to decide which people belong to the new state and which do not. This gives them an incentive to find an outgroup. In addition, they can gain legitimacy and support for their regime by dehumanizing the outgroup and claiming that it poses an existential threat to the population. This, in turn, encourages the population to unite behind the regime in defense against the alleged threat.

REFERENCES

Arendt, H. (1948/1973). *The Origins of Totalitarianism.* San Diego: Harvest.

Arendt, H. (1963/2005). *Eichmann and the Holocaust.* London: Penguin.

Arendt, H. (1971). Thinking and Moral Considerations. *Social Research,* 38(3), 417–446.

Baehr, P. (2010). Banality and Cleverness: Eichmann in Jerusalem Revisited. In R. Roger Berkowitz, J. Katz, & T. Keenan (Eds.), *Thinking in Dark Times: Hannah Arendt on Ethics and Politics.* New York: Fordham University Press.

Bauman, Z. (1991). *Modernity and the Holocaust.* Oxford: John Wiley & Sons.

Berger, R. J. (1993). The "Banality of Evil" Reframed: The Social Construction of the "Final Solution" to the "Jewish Problem". *Sociological Quarterly,* 34(4), 597–618.

Berkowitz, R. (2014). Did Eichmann Think? A Review of Eichmann Before Jerusalem: The Unexamined Life of a Mass Murderer by Bettina Stangneth. *The Good Society, 23*(2), 193–205.

Bernstein, R. J. (2008). Are Arendt's Reflections on Evil Still Relevant? *The Review of Politics, 70*(1), 64–76.

Blass, T. (1993). Psychological Perspectives on the Perpetrators of the Holocaust: The Role of Situational Pressures, Personal Dispositions, and Their Interactions. *Holocaust and Genocide Studies, 7*(1), 30–50.

Browning, C. R. (1992/2001). *Ordinary Men.* New York: Harper Collins.

Burleigh, M. (2000). *The Third Reich: A New History.* London: Macmillan.

Burleigh, M. (2011). *Moral Combat: Good and Evil in World War II.* New York: HarperCollins.

Cesarani, D. (2005). *Eichmann: His Life and Crimes.* London: Vintage.

Clarke, B. (1980). Beyond 'The Banality of Evil'. *British Journal of Political Science, 10*, 417–439.

Culbert, J. L. (2010). Judging the Events of Our Time. In R. Berkowitz, J. Katz, & T. Keenan (Eds.), *Thinking in Dark Times: Hannah Arendt on Ethics and Politics* (pp. 145–150). New York: Fordham University Press.

Ezrahi, Y. (2010). Arendt's Banality of Evil Thesis and the Arab-Israeli Conflict. In R. Berkowitz, J. Katz, & T. Keenan (Eds.), *Thinking in Dark Times: Hannah Arendt on Ethics and Politics* (pp. 153–157). New York: Fordham University Press.

Fenigstein, A. (1997). Reconceptualizing the Psychology of the Perpetrators. In D. Shilling (Ed.), *Lessons and Legacies* (Vol. II). Evanston, IL: Northwestern University Press.

Gerlach, C. (2001). The Eichmann Interrogations in Holocaust Historiography. *Holocaust and Genocide Studies, 15*(3, Winter), 428–452.

Goldhagen, D. J. (1996). *Hitler's Willing Executioners.* London: Little Brown Group.

Grodin, M., & Annas, G. (2007). Physicians and Torture: Lessons from the Nazi Doctors. *International Review of the Red Cross, 89*(867), 635–654.

Hillberg, R. (1997). The Goldhagen Phenomenon. *Critical Inquiry, 23*(4), 721–728.

Hinton, A. L. (2005). *Why Did They Kill? Cambodia in the Shadow of Genocide.* Berkeley: University of California Press.

Kohn, J. (2002). Arendt's Concept and Description of Totalitarianism. *Social Research, 69*(2), 621–656.

von Lang, J. (1986). *Das Eichmann-Protokoll: Tonbandaufzeichnungen der israelischen Verhöre.* Berlin: Quadriga.

LeBor, A., & Boyes, R. (2005). *Seduced by Hitler: The Choices of a Nation and the Ethics of Survival.* New York: Barnes & Nobel.

Lozowick, Y. (2000). *Hitler's Bureaucrats (London: Continuum). Maccoby, Hyam (2006) Antisemitism and Modernity: Innovation and Continuity.* London: Routledge.

Lozowick, Y. (2001). Malicious Clerks: The Nazi Security Police and the Banality of Evil. In S. E. Ashheim (Ed.), *Hannah Arendt in Jerusalem* (pp. 214–223). Berkeley: University of California Press.

Mann, M. (2004). *Fascists.* Cambridge: Cambridge University Press.

Mann, M. (2005). *The Dark Side of Democracy: Explaining Ethnic Cleansing.* Cambridge: Cambridge University Press.

Marrus, M. R. (2001). Eichmann in Jerusalem: Justice and History. In S. E. Ashheim (Ed.), *Hannah Arendt in Jerusalem* (pp. 205–213). Berkeley: University of California Press.

Midlarsky, M. I. (2005). *The Killing Trap Genocide in the Twentieth Century.* Cambridge: Cambridge University Press.

Milgram, S. (1963). Behavioral Study of Obedience. *Journal of Abnormal and Social Psychology, 67*, 371–378.

Milgram, S. (1974). *Obedience to Authority: An Experimental View*. New York: Harper & Row.

Miller, S. (1998). A Note on the Banality of Evil. *Wilson Quarterly, 22*(Autumn), 54–59.

Mommsen, H. (2001). Hannah Arendt's Interpretation of the Holocaust as a Challenge to Human Existence: The Intellectual Background. In S. E. Ashheim (Ed.), *Hannah Arendt in Jerusalem* (pp. 224–231). Berkeley: University of California Press.

Moses, A. D. (1998). Structure and Agency in the Holocaust. *History and Theory, 37*(2), 194–219.

Rosenfeld, G. D. (1999). The Controversy that Isn't. *Contemporary European History, 8*(2), 249–273.

Safrian, H. (1993/2010 English translation). *Eichmann's Men*. Cambridge: Cambridge University Press.

Stangneth, B. (2014). *Eichmann vor Jerusalem: Das unbehelligte Leben eines Massenmörders*. Hamburg: Rowohlt Taschenbruch Verlag.

Stangneth, B. (2016). *Eichmann Before Jerusalem: The Unexamined Life of a Mass Murderer* (R. Martin, Trans.). London: Vintage.

Vetlesen, A. J. (2005). *Evil and Human Agency*. Cambridge University Press.

Waller, J. E. (2007). *Becoming Evil* (2nd ed.). Oxford: Oxford University Press.

Weiss, J. (1996). *Ideology of Death: Why the Holocaust Happened in Germany*. Chicago: Ivan R. Dee.

Weiss, J. (1999). Daniel Jonah Goldhagen, Hitler's Willing Executioners: An Historian's View. *Journal of Genocide Research, 1*(2), 257–272.

Welzer, H. (2005). *Täter. Wieausganznormalen Menschen Massenmörderwerden*. Frankfurt/Main: Fischer

Zukier, H. (1994). The Twisted Road to Genocide: On The Psychological Development of Evil During the Holocaust. *Social Research, 61*(2), 435.

CHAPTER 4

France and the Non-Totalitarian Inquisition

France makes for a good starting point for this book, since the first Catholic inquisitions were held in that country. Moreover, these inquisitions laid the basis for the more totalitarian Spanish Inquisition, which in turn seems to have influenced "modern" totalitarian regimes. As one observer notes, the inquisition became "one of the most effective means of thought control that Europe has ever known" (cited in Martin 2005: 105). Another scholar claims: "Modern totalitarian governments have made few innovations; they have simply been more efficient."[1] Yet this book will show that in France, unlike in Spain, the inquisition did not lead to totalitarian rule.

This chapter begins with a brief background on the development of France as a country. All countries change constantly over time, but France was one of the most established countries in the region during the time of the papal inquisition there. According to Poplin (2006: 1), France is "the oldest nation of Europe." As Bartlett (1993: 42) points out, by the time the inquisition began, France had risen to "the dominant political position [in Europe]… which it had attained under the Capetian kings of the thirteenth century." Consequently, the inquisition was not part of a state-building strategy; in fact, the crown did not even support the inquisition at first. This section will also show why the French monarchy did not see the same kind of existential threat in *conversos* that the Catholic monarchs in Spain did. Next, this chapter will give some background on the development of the inquisition as an institution. Finally, it will show how the

© The Author(s) 2019   79
S. Saxonberg, *Pre-Modernity, Totalitarianism and the Non-Banality of Evil*, https://doi.org/10.1007/978-3-030-28195-3_4

inquisition met with great resistance throughout French society—including sections of the Church—which prevented the country from becoming totalitarian. In addition, it will show that crown-Church relations were complicated and in flux, with the crown sometimes supporting the pope and the inquisition, and sometimes opposing them. Thus, while the Spanish Inquisition helped unify the newly created country of Spain, the papal inquisition in France helped divide an already established country.

THE DEVELOPMENT OF FRANCE

Even though France had not yet become a modern state with a modern bureaucracy, and even though some of the king's vassals enjoyed great autonomy, it was one of the most established "royal states" (Potter 2003: 4) or "dynastic states" (Collins 1997) in medieval Europe. As Elias (1939) observes, the French kingdom was not static; rather, it developed over time. This "traditional state" (Hastings 1997) began to take shape in the middle of the tenth century (Bergin 2015: 3f.; cf. Ertman 1997: 35) with the emergence of the Capetian monarchs (Armstrong 1982: 155ff.; Naus 2016: 15ff.). In Llobera's (1994: 356) words:

> The Capetian monarchy was critical to creating the idea of France and extending it, from an initial nucleus (*l'île de* France) to an ever wider geographical circle. It would appear that in France at least, the state preceded and created the nation, although once the latter was in existence a kind of feedback would operate.

Cabannes (2007: 98) notes that, already in 481, King Clovis I (481–511) gained the title *rex Francorum* (king of the Franks), while in 1165 Philip II became the first to use the phrase *rex Franciae* (king of the French).

Beaune (1991: 283) claims that, after the Treaty of Verdun in 843, "people finally began to speak of 'France.'" She gives an earlier date for official usage of the term, noting that, already in 1083, King Philip I had signed a diploma as "Philip reigning in France" (p. 284). She also remarks that "[a]round 1100 the *Song of Roland* portrayed Roland remembering *douce France*—sweet France...." (p. 285).

Duby (1993: 129) places the date between the two Philips, noting that Louis VI had described himself as "king of France" over 40 years before Philip II used the term. He adds that, with this change in concept in 1119, "[t]he shift in terminology from 'kingdom of the Franks' to 'kingdom of

France' marked the arrival of France as a political entity" (p. 130). For purposes of this book, the difference between a country as a kingdom and a country as a state is not so important; what does matter is that France had already existed as an entity for many centuries before Philip II used the expression "Kingdom of France." Duby (p. 182) notes, "[t]he concept of the State became increasingly widespread and accepted [in France] during the twelfth century."

According to Collins (1997: 606),

> this replacement of the concrete (the Franks) by the abstract (France) marked a dramatic shift in the nature of the monarchy and heralded the development of a national consciousness, because the monarchy sought to get agreement on the very existence of an entity over which it ruled. Louis VI simultaneously described himself, in a charter issued to the Cluniac order, as charged with the "public defense" of the kingdom; that is, the king defended not his personal interests, but those of the commonwealth.

Cabannes (2007: 98) adds that, while the first Frankish kings had been elected by the lords, the King's son was the designated heir after 987. Thus,

> [t]he Capetians were firmly rooted in the land of France. The origin of the accession to the throne was no longer the acclamation, but only the link between Capetians and France....The link between the King and the accession to the Crown was no longer the Lords, but rather the land of France... and God. Thus the kings became monarchs only by divine right.[2]

When the Capetian kings first came to power in the tenth century, the country was "a patchwork of innumerable nearly independent lordships"; but even then, as Fawtier (1960: 60) concludes:

> ...no lord, however powerful, refused to recognise the king's theoretical supremacy. The name "France" came to mean only a narrow belt of territory around Paris; but the kingdom of France, the ancient *regnum Francorum*, survived not only in theory but even to some extent in practice. The king might be feeble. He might be weaker than some of his great vassals. Nevertheless, the great vassals owed him homage, and it is significant that they performed it.

Similarly, Duby (1993: 30) notes that, even before the country was known as France, under Capetian rule "[t]here were many kingdoms in Gaul, but only one king, the king of the Franks, who owed his incontestable pre-eminence to the unction of his coronation."

Nevertheless, Elias (1939: 38) claims, some vassals enjoyed great inde-pendence from the crown at the beginning of the twelfth century. French state-building was a process whereby the king progressively gained power as the number of powerful local lords steadily decreased, due to competi-tion between them. This competition between nobles led to a natural monopoly of power in the hands of the king, as stronger lords beat out weaker ones until the king emerged as the most powerful figure.

Elias' analysis does not contradict Fawtier's (1960) claim that the vas-sals still acknowledged the king as their ruler. In fact, as Reynolds (1997: 278) asserts, even if some powerful French noblemen, such as Count William V of Poitou (ruler of the French province of Aquitaine 990–1030) were considered to be like kings, they still were only *like* kings—everyone accepted the French king as the true king. She also points out that French lawyers had begun speaking of a "common law" by the thirteenth century (p. 43). Petit-Dutaillis (1936: 14f.) notes that, even though some counts and dukes enjoyed relatively high levels of autonomy in the eleventh cen-tury, "the great barons considered themselves as the kings' 'men'." Reynolds (1997: 280) adds that the idea that vassals belonged to France proper was so strong that, during the eleventh century, even "Normans in England were referred to as *Franci.*" In addition, "[a]lthough the govern-ment of Normandy and England was for a while quite closely integrated and wars with the king of France were frequent, Normandy continued to be considered in some sense part of the kingdom of France" (p. 280). Duby (1993: 123) gives another example of how the king of France had powers overriding those of his vassals. He notes that, although the count of Flanders was under the tutelage of the king of England in the early twelfth century, "he was bound to serve Henry of England only if the king of France was not involved"—the reason being that "[t]he claims of the French king, as his liege lord, were overriding." Duby notes too that King Louis VII had such power in the 1160s and 1170s that he was able to keep the peace throughout the kingdom. When he visited unruly areas under the rule of his vassals, "[a]ll lawlessness ceased at the mere approach of his army" (p. 188).

Beaune (1991: 6) points out that France was "one of the largest king-doms of the time and one of the best organized." In addition, by the late 1100s, it "boasted great numbers of royal officials; its central institutions (the Chambre de comptes, the Parlement) were precociously effective" (ibid.).

It is difficult to know what kind of national feelings peasants and serfs had, but Heer (1961: 281) maintains that, although the monarchy was still weak in the early twelfth century, those living in the center of the kingdom had "deeply-rooted national feelings." This could be seen, for example, in the "vigor" of their resistance to the German invasion in 1124. Heer also asserts that kings such as "Philip August (1180–1223), Louis IX (St. Louis) (1226–1270) and Philip the Fair (1285–1314)....all consciously fostered popular confidence in kingship...." (p. 282). He adds (p. 283) that, by the final quarter of the thirteenth century, France had become a "modern state," for the concept of sovereignty had replaced the idea of the state as the private possession of the king. "[N]ow, however, royal authority was seen as something abstract and impersonal." Even though France did not become a modern state until the last part of the thirteenth century, Heer admits that it had previously been a state—just not a "modern" one. Beaune (1991: 299) concurs, noting that people felt devoted to the French "fatherland" by the early twelfth century, even if the term was not used at the time. Starting in 1124, rulers began using the term "the defense of the realm" to induce inhabitants to take up arms and defend the country. Petit-Dutaillis (1936: 8) too states that the first Capetian kings were rather weak. Their weakness does not mean, however, that the country they ruled did not exist. Thus "we can admit that there was a kingdom of France not only in the formulas of chanceries but in the opinions and speech of the people." Furthermore, in the eleventh century "[t]here was also a strong popular tradition along all the main pilgrim routes and around the holy places where crowds gathered and a common tradition, a national life, was being built up; poets, inside the Church and without, were singing the praises of 'Gentle France' and her former glories and of the time when Charlemagne had conquered all the West."

According to Finer (1974: 97), by the time the inquisition began in France in the thirteenth century, the country had become much more unified and centralized. Royal law had also started to replace feudal law, enabling subjects to bypass local lords and to appeal directly to the crown. Reynolds (1997: 178) notes that "[f]rom the reign of Philip Augustus onward the monarchy steadily extended its authority over towns all through the kingdom." Collins (1997: 609) describes how kings progressively increased their power over their vassals: "By 1300, the French polity had accepted important principles of central state building." Finer (1974:

99) calculates that in 1328 the country had 19–21 million inhabitants, compared to only 4.5–6 million in England.

Even though France established itself as a country and a state relatively quickly, it took longer for its population to perceive it as a nation-state. In the traditional type of society that it was, most people had contact with their local lords rather than with the central authorities. As Hastings (1997: 29) notes, France was a traditional state rather than a modern one: that is, compared with its modern counterpart, the central government in that period imposed lower taxes, exercised less control over formal education, enforced universal standards to a lesser extent, and intruded less often into the lives of ordinary people (except in times of crisis). Nevertheless, the state became progressively more prominent, and by the thirteenth century the kings had amassed a relatively large amount of centralized power in their hands. As already noted in Chap. 2, royal law had begun to replace feudal law, serfdom had been virtually abolished and many tasks were carried out paid by professional officials rather by than local lords. Thus, when the crown gained control over a province, "the king preserved its customs and its institutions, but the customs were enforced and the institutions were staffed by men sent out from the royal court at Paris" (Strayer 1969: 5). By the beginning of the thirteenth century, the kings were relying on paid professionals (known as *baillis* and *sénéchaux*) to rule the country (Finer 1974: 101). These local administrators were normally outsiders without any roots in the region, so the king could trust them (Strayer 1969: 5). Needless to say, public-opinion surveys from the period are not available, so it is hard to know when the country's inhabitants started seeing themselves as part of a nation instead of just subjects of a certain ruling family; but some scholars have argued that, by the beginning of the fourteenth century, the people of the kingdom felt they formed a nation (cited in Llobera's (1994: 352)).

Since France was and still is a collection of regions, with diverse languages, the crown could not base the kingdom on linguistic criteria (Collins 1997: 604; Finer 1974). As James (1982: 4) notes, "[a]s late as 1863 a quarter of the population of France did not speak French, and perhaps another quarter used it as their second language." Beaune (1991: 266) claims that language did not cause a problem for French rulers in the eleventh to thirteenth centuries, as most nations were multilingual in the medieval era. In fact, some French intellectuals, such as Etienne de Conti, even saw the country's multilingualism as an advantage and as proof of its superiority over England, which only had one language (p. 272).[3]

At the beginning of the twelfth century, the crown only had direct control over a relatively small territory, but the kingdom was still one of the most stable in Europe, due to the uninterrupted reign of the Capetian dynasty between 987 and 1316 (Acharya and Lee 2015; Field and Gaposchkin 2014; Lewis 1981). Nevertheless, on account of (rather autonomous) vassals under him, the French king still reigned over a relatively large territory. In subsequent centuries the monarchs greatly expanded the territory under their direct control and reduced the power of their vassals. Consequently, they were able to acquire several large and important territories in areas such as Toulouse (1271) and Champagne (1314). Thus, the country had become more centralized than the type of system seen under traditional feudalism. Strayer (1969: 11) notes that, precisely because the country was a collection of diverse regions, the kings had to build up loyalty based on the country rather than on their person, because only those in the oldest domains would have felt loyalty to the king personally. In the newer territories, "regnum" (kingdom) and "patria" (fatherland) appealed more to the reason and emotions of the populations than did personal loyalty to the king. Therefore, no matter how independent the lords might have felt in their daily life, they agreed to send troops to defend the king of France when the country was threatened. For "the King of France was a suzerain entitled to the service of all his vassals but it is interesting to note that he could count on it in fact if the kingdom was threatened and that there remained some feelings of unity" (Petit-Dutaillis 1936: 85). As an example, Petit-Dutaillis cites the general mobilization of 1124, against the threat of an attack by the Holy Roman Empire. Moreover, as Duby (1993: 231) points out, even though southern France had been rather autonomous before being incorporated into the royal domain, accused heretics in the inquisition "acknowledged themselves French subjects" in the court proceedings. This indicates there was a strong awareness among the people that they belonged to a country called "France."

Spruyt (1994: 92) notes that, in contrast to the situation prevailing under traditional feudalism, towns played a major role in late medieval France. Since the towns wanted to become as independent as possible, they strove to bypass local lords and to become direct vassals of the king. Consequently, compared to their counterparts in the more feudal German territories, the kings of France gained more power over the lords, as they based their power to some extent on the support of the burghers. In addition, the towns wanted a more rationalized and centralized administration than was possible under the traditional decentralized feudal system centered on local lords. This helped the kings gradually centralize the country. Spruyt (ibid.) adds:

> The idea of personal bondage disappeared within the walls of the towns; the innumerable relationships of dependence in the countryside-in short, the feudal ordering of society-were broken and subdued. This was the burghers' doing, and it laid the basis for their subsequent designation of the proper relationship of the individual to this state as "citizen of the state, not a subject."

In addition, according to Spruyt (1994: 95), the system in France differed from traditional feudal arrangements in a second important respect: the crown demanded monetary payment for specific services, rather than allowing vassals to send soldiers to the royal army. Under traditional feudalism, the overlord grants land, titles and shares in the spoils of war to vassals in return for their military help. However, once kings gave away land as a reward, they lost control over their vassals. In contrast, the French kings developed a centralized administration, enabling them to pay people in money rather than to give them land: "The royal administration thus became an attractive source of employment for the middle- and lower-range aristocrats. They performed administrative, judicial, military, and financial tasks. But they did this on the basis of payment rather than exchange military service for land." In addition, "the King's standardization of tax procedures benefited the commercial interests of the burghers." The kings centralized their power further by appointing bailiffs, who were responsible for checking the abuses of provosts and making sure the king received the revenues due him. This further strengthened the royal administration, making the crown stronger in the French system than was characteristic under traditional feudalism (ibid.: 100).

The result was a state that was more centralized than a traditional feudal kingdom, with weaker lords and stronger and more influential burghers. The state was thus fairly strong, even though the country over which it ruled encompassed many regions with different dialects and languages. As Spruyt (1994: 109) observes, this path of development differed radically from Germany's:

> In France the king allied with the burghers, made side payments to the aristocracy, and established a considerable measure of centralized and

hierarchical control. The German king, by contrast, favored the lords at the expense of the towns. Forced to fend for themselves, the towns formed city-leagues to protect their interests against the lords. The result was that Germany's future, after the middle of the thirteenth century, was determined by a combination of lordships, independent towns, and city-leagues. Under the nominal authority of the emperor, lords and towns vied for real control....In contrast to the French king, the German king, who was also the Holy Roman Emperor, opted for a policy against the towns. Instead he sought support from the dukes and ecclesiastical lords, in order to pursue imperial control of Italy, and granted them control over the towns. This strategy proved to be a failure. The German king gradually lost all real authority to the German lords. The ensuing history of Germany is therefore one of weak kings and strong feudal lords. The dukes and counts struggled in turn with towns that sought independence. The explanation of German political development revolves around this axis of lord-town opposition.

These differences help explain why France was one of the most successful countries in establishing itself, while Germany was not able to unite into one country until 1871. The French kingdom differed so much from the traditional feudal model that serfdom was becoming rare by the twelfth century. As Beech (1964: 107) notes in his study of medieval French peasants: "Finally the heavy obligation of Carolingian peasants to work several days a week farming their lord's *domaine* was either restricted or nonexistent in the eleventh and twelfth centuries."[4] Interestingly, the one exception within the area of France that Beech studied was the Church: the monks of l'Absie demanded that their tenants do unpaid labor for them. Thus, Heper (1985:99) claims, France developed a "bastard" form of feudalism. Bergin (2015: 54) maintains that French administration in the early 1300s was "probably the most advanced in Europe."

THE EMERGENCE OF THE INQUISITION IN FRANCE

This section discusses why the inquisition was set up in France, before going on to discuss how it functioned.

Deciding to Have an Inquisition

In 1177, the Lateran II council met and devised a rationale for holding inquisitions. The council agreed on the need to fight heresy, especially the Cathar heresy in the French areas of Albi and Toulouse (i.e., the Languedoc region) (Moore 2012: 204–5). In 1199 Pope Innocent III issued the *Vergentis in senium* decree, which associated heresy with treason. Thus, for the first time, spiritual sin was linked to secular law. Heresy had now become a legal crime. "After 1199, those convicted of heresy were to have their goods confiscated and their children subjected to perpetual deprivation; the consequences of heresy were now juridically regulated and historically enduring" (Deane 2011: 89).

The main target group, the Cathars, believed in celibacy and vegetarianism They claimed that there are two gods: one good and one evil (e.g., Barber 2000; Martin 2005; Moore 2012; Wakefield 1974). At that time, "the doctrine of the church was not fully developed" (Wakefield 1974: 16). Since it was in the process of developing parts of its doctrine, the Church felt threatened by the spread of alternative interpretations of the Bible that was taking place. There was a common belief that, if the Church points out the truth and a given group denies it, then such people are not only evil—they also threaten to infect the community and to bring God's wrath down upon it (Wakefield 1974: 7). Consequently, the Church made fighting heresy a top priority. However, as will be discussed below, the French crown was very lukewarm to the idea at first; and it turned out that the Vatican could only carry out the inquisition with support from the monarchy, as the Pope lacked the military means for enforcing his unpopular institution on the population.

The fact that the Vatican could eventually gain the support of the crown shows that the relationship between Church and state was fluid and changeable. Papal thinking itself was in flux about the role of the Church in this era. In 494, Pope Gelasius developed the doctrine of "the two swords," according to which rightful power over sacred and religious matters belonged to the Church, while rightful power over secular and political matters belonged to the emperor (Gomes 2017: 201). However, after the death of Charlemagne in 814, the papacy started to claim temporal supremacy as well. Now the emperor "had also to acknowledge that his imperial power came from the pope" (Knowles 1967: 9–10). Ertman (1997: 419) concurs in this assessment, adding that "the Carolingians seemed to be prepared to acknowledge for the first time the papal claims to independent moral authority set down in 494 in Gelasius's doctrine of the two swords, and they saw in the protection and propagation of the faith their highest duties as emperors."

By now the Church was firmly involved in secular as well as sacred issues. Dumont (1985: 113) remarks: "The Church now pretends to rule, directly or indirectly, the world, which means that the Christian individual is now committed to the world to an unprecedented degree." Théry-Astruc (2017: 223) argues that the Church had in practice become a "papal monarchy," which held itself superior to all secular rulers since it offered universal salvation. This stance brought the popes into conflict with the emperors. Starting in the twelfth century, therefore, popes often took refuge in France, which as the strongest regional power could offer them protection. However, despite the French monarchy's support for the Church, the latter had less influence in France than it did in the Holy Roman Empire. Whereas the Holy Roman emperors allowed bishops and other clergy to hold high political positions, such as dukedoms (Elias 1939: 259), the crown in France used the clergy for administrative duties instead. The clergy in France reduced the power of the aristocracy, such as by monitoring local counts on behalf of the king (Ertman 1997: 43f.). This led to a situation where the king was stronger against both the Church and the nobility than was the Holy Roman emperor, who was more dependent on both groups.

Moreover, although the monarchy claimed to be defending the Church, it also claimed to be defending the common good of society (Dunbabin 2002: 43). Sometimes these two ideals came into conflict in the eyes of the rulers. Thus, as the discussion below will show, Church-state relations were constantly in flux both in France and in Spain during the period under study. This was true not only of the relationship between the kings and the popes but also of that between the local churches, the kings and the popes. Elias (1939: 259f.) notes that the French kings were more powerful vis-à-vis the Church than the emperors were.

> The Church in the western Frankish area never attained major secular power as it did in the empire. Archbishops did not here become dukes. The ecclesiastical peers remained by and large outside the system of competing territorial lords....The church therefore desired a central rule, a king who had enough power to protect her against secular violence.

Thus, as rulers of the strongest kingdom, the French kings could at times afford to stand up to the popes. One of the most extreme examples of tension between Church and state can be seen in the squabbles between King Philip the Fair and Pope Boniface (see, e.g., Brown 2012). The king and the pope were fighting over the state's right to tax Church properties in France. Philip claimed he needed more money to finance his treasury (e.g., Fawtier 1960: 92). The pope argued that states could only tax their local churches if the pope approved; however, the French and English kings were strong enough to resist this (Tierney 1964: 173 and 1999: 287–90). Thus, Philip decided to tax the Church lands in France (Denton 1997). In 1294, when Philip imposed new taxes on the Church in order to finance his invasion of English-held Aquitaine, the pope excommunicated him (Spruyt 1994: 97f.). Eventually, the pope gave in, though, for the French monasteries, bishoprics and parishes were more dependent for their survival on the king of France then they were on the pope. Then, in 1302, the king had Bishop Bernard Saisset arrested for treason, blasphemy and *lèse-majesté*. This meant the king was claiming jurisdiction over the clergy. In response, the pope summoned the French prelates to Rome; however, Philip forbade them from to go. Half of the prelates did defy Philip and come to Rome, but the pope was angered that the other half had disobeyed him. As (Spruyt 1994: 98) reflects:

> The pope's solution to the Gelasian theory of the two swords was thus not a reconciliation of the two but a clear advancement of supremacy of the church over ecclesiastical and temporal matters. In short, sovereign authority and universalist claims clashed head-on.

The conflict went so far that Philip's councilor, Guillaume de Nogaret, had the pope indicted for heresy (Dunbabin 2002; Théry-Astruc 2017: 222). Nogaret persuaded Philip to call an ecumenical council to judge the pope. The pope had planned to retaliate by excommunicating Philip, but Nogaret had the pope arrested and brought before a general council of the Church (Théry-Astruc 2017: 246f.). The pope was released after a brief detention, but he died 2 weeks later—allegedly from the shock of having been arrested (Spruyt 1994: 98).

Thus, even though the inquisition in France was "papal," the popes and the French kings often came into conflict. The monarchy tried to assert its power over the clergy and the Church was dependent on the Crown for carrying out the inquisition. Nevertheless, in contrast to the case with the Spanish Inquisition, the pope took the initiative in demanding a crusade against heretics and then—once the Cathars had been defeated militarily—the establishment of an inquisition for weeding out heresy. As such, the inquisition in France was officially under the Holy Office. Yet even this is a simplification, as the original initiative to take action against heretics had come from a local ruler, Count Raymond V of Toulouse, who had attacked the Cathar sect in 1178. He tried to get the French king to support him, but he failed, so he turned to the Holy See (Wakefield 1974: 83ff.; cf. Duby 1993: 240). Even though the Vatican supported the idea, for the pope to be able to carry out the crusade against the Cathars, he needed the French king to send soldiers; however, as will be discussed below, the king obliged only reluctantly and only in certain periods. Moreover, when the crusade finally succeeded in subduing the Languedoc region, the pope lacked the means to introduce the inquisition without the support of the French king:

> The only thing that remained was the Inquisition for which Saint Louis was directly responsible. It was thanks to his active support that the popes Gregory IX and Innocent IV were able to establish the Inquisition in France at a time when, in most European countries, the secular clergy refused the co-operation of the Dominicans and rejected the terrible means they had been led to crush the heroic resistance of the 'Perfects'—secret trial, repeated and captious questioning, torture to enforce a confession and the name of accomplices....[Moreover] Louis IX and his mother paid the expenses of the Inquisitors and gave them a guard responsible for their protection. (Petit-Dutaillis 1936: 283)

Thus, we have a situation in which local rulers and clergy interacted with both the crown and the papacy in a complicated relationship.

Setting up the Inquisition

This section gives a brief overview of how the papal inquisition was set up. Given (1989: 339) points out that, in 1231, Pope Gregory IX codified the existing papal legislation concerning heresy, thereby institutionalizing the inquisition. No single centralized institution was established; rather,

> a number of inquisitorial tribunals, some run by Franciscans or Dominicans, others by local bishops, were scattered across Europe. In the Middle Ages, these were never integrated into one unified organization....

In addition,

> [d]espite the lack of institutional definition and coordination, all medieval inquisitorial tribunals shared certain characteristics. They possessed an extraordinary jurisdiction. Tribunals staffed by members of the mendicant

orders were usually exempt from ordinary episcopal control and were immediately subject to the pope. The inquisitors proceeded against suspected
heretics ex officio, by virtue of their office, without having to wait for a
formal accusation to be brought against a suspect. Those who appeared
before the inquisitors were made to take an oath and testify against themselves under pain of prosecution for either contumacy or perjury. All proceedings were secret. Moreover, the accused were denied the assistance of
attorneys or notaries. They were not told the names of those who had testi-
fied against them. Depositions against suspects were also accepted from
types of witnesses normally barred by canon law from giving testimony:
children, convicted criminals, accomplices, and other heretics. Finally, a condemned prisoner had no right of appeal from the decisions of the inquisitors.

Martin (2005: 108–9) describes how the agents of the inquisition behaved
when they came to a village:

> When the Inquisition came to a town or a village, the first thing its agents
> would do was to talk to the clergy, in order to brief them on their procedure.
> The inquisitors were then allowed to give a sermon in the church, in which
> they demanded a profession of faith from all males over the age of 14 and all
> females over 12. Those who did not or could not profess were automatically
> suspect and would be the first to be questioned. The congregation was
> obliged to swear an oath against heresy and ordered to go to confession
> three times a year. The Inquisitors then asked them to think about their past
> actions and make confidential statements the following week, either confess-
> ing to their own sins, or denouncing their neighbour. Cathars who volun-
> tarily confessed were resettled in areas where no heresy was known, and had
> to wear two yellow crosses sewn onto their clothes, which identified them as
> former heretics. Known or suspected heretics who hadn't confessed volun-
> tarily within the first week were issued a summons to appear before the
> Inquisitors immediately.

When appearing before the inquisition, one had to be very careful. Not
only could one be convicted of a previously committed "crime," one could
also be convicted for making a sloppy statement—leading to a further
conviction for a new "crime" (Stork 1999: 253).

Given (1989: 344) adds that, in the first years of the inquisition in
France, torture was rarely used to extract confessions. Instead, the inquisitors would lock up the accused for long periods, until they realized the
futility of insisting on their innocence. For example, Guillem Salavert of
Albi was arrested in 1300, but the trial against him was not concluded

until 19 years later. Davis (1948: 18) notes that word reached Pope Clement V in 1310 and 1313 that ten citizens of Albi had been held in prison for 8 years or more, under suspicion of heresy. Yet, they had neither been tried nor convicted. Given (1989: 345) concludes that the accused often confessed whether they were guilty or innocent because they feared that their associates would eventually break down and confess. If they were denounced by their associates, namely, their sentence would be harsher, so they often thought it better to confess before they were denounced. Another way of extracting confessions was to keep the accused in chains and to restrict their food (ibid.: 345). Thus, when Clement V complained about the excesses of the inquisition, he did not focus on the overuse of torture, but rather on the terrible conditions in the prisons (Davis 1948: 35).

The mere fact that the pope could complain about the excesses that occurred, and that he took measures to curb them, shows that the inquisition did not become as totalitarian in France as it did in Spain. In addition, as Shannon (1985) notes, it was quite common for people to appeal to the pope against the verdicts of the inquisition. In the 1240s, "a flood of appeals against inquisitorial sentences flowed to Rome, and Innocent IV granted many of them. Indeed he suspended, April 21, 1245, the imposing of the most serious penalties, except for manifest heretics...." (p. 94). According to Shannon (p. 95f.), the Dominican friars got so frustrated with the pope's interference in their decisions that they refused during much of the 1250s to continue with the inquisition in France. Nevertheless, the inquisition began operating again toward the end of the decade. This unevenness indicates that the inquisition did not provoke as widespread fear in France as it did in Spain. Another obstacle to the spread of fear in France was the small number of inquisitors. Normally there were two each for the southern provinces of Languedoc and Dauphiné and Provence, and four to six for the rest of the country (p. 72).

Even though the French inquisition was not as far-reaching as the Spanish, "impertinent heretics" could still be sentenced to be burnt at the stake (Haskins 1902: 646–49). In these cases, the Church handed the victims over to the secular authorities (the Church was not allowed to kill people). Other punishments included being buried alive, having one's head shaved, being forced to wear crosses, having one's home destroyed and having one's property confiscated. Furthermore, even when former heretics were not sent to prison, they were still socially isolated (Given 1989: 353):

Penitent heretics were not reintegrated into the society of the faithful but were carefully marked out and set apart from everyone else, a separation made manifest by the physical symbols that most had to wear. Almost all convicted heretics not kept in prison were required to wear yellow crosses sewn on their clothing, the arms of the crosses two-and-a-half fingers in breadth, two-and-a-half palms in height, and two palms in width. One cross was to be worn on the chest and one on the back.

Guilt was hereditary: the Papal statutes of 1231 prohibited sons and grandsons of heretics from holding ecclesiastical offices or benefices. As to the frequency of punishments, Wakefield (1974: 185) estimates that, for every person sentenced to be burnt at the stake, 10–11 were sentenced to prison. Nevertheless, fear of being burnt at the stake or spending one's life in prison gave victims a strong incentive to confess to crimes they had not committed, even if they had not been tortured.

The most obvious case—and one of the most extreme—was the decision of Philip the Fair to crush the Templar Knights in order to be able to write off his debts to them. The Templars were charged with heresy and given the choice of confessing to acts they obviously had not committed (such as engaging in demon worship) or being burnt at the stake. First, they were interrogated by royal agents and made to learn their lines by heart (a tactic that communist secret services used during show trials against communist leaders in the early 1950s). The charges included absurd accusations about what their commander had made them do when joining the organization: For example, to renounce Christ and spit on a cross or to get naked and kiss the commander on the base of the spine, on the navel and on the mouth (Field 2016a: 48). The Templars were only allowed to alter their confessions very slightly from the predetermined form that had been prepared for them. For example, the Templar Tomas was allowed to claim he had only spat on the cross once, rather than the three times on which his interrogators insisted (ibid.: 49). Then after learning their lines, the Templars were handed over to the ecclesiastical inquisitors. At last the pope sent commissioners to investigate the affair, whereupon many of the Templars took back their confessions, claiming they had made false statements under torture. Those who had taken back their confessions were burnt at the stake, as relapsed heretics (Field 2016a, b; Givens 1989: 351ff.). Despite the widespread claim that the inquisition in France was "papal," the king could not have carried out his aim of destroying the Templars without the active cooperation of the head inquisitor. As Field (2017: 60) concludes:

For Philip IV to accuse an entire order of heresy, he needed unhesitating cooperation from an inquisitor who was absolutely his man and completely in his confidence. The convergence of royal confessor/papal inquisitor by early 1306 provided this possibility for the first time [that is, the first time that the king's royal confessor was also the head inquisitor].[5] Without this crucial element, it is hard to see how Philip could ever have hoped to put his plans for the Templars into effect.

Théry-Astruc (2017: 249) argues that Philip's approach was also a way of "decisively demonstrating the King's superiority over the papacy." Thus, the French crown fought against the notion that the pope was the ultimate authority.

As in many of the more "normal" cases where the inquisition used torture, fear and deprivation to get false confessions, the destruction of the Templars shows how little interest the inquisition often had in any objective investigation of those charged with heresy. This lack of regard for the truth contradicts Kelly's depiction (1989: 450) of the inquisition as a "brilliant and much-needed innovation in trial procedure" which laid the foundations for modern criminal procedure. To be sure, Lea (1888: 124) gives an example of the type of person who on rare occasions could succeed in getting released from the inquisition without punishment. In this case, the accused was a well-connected person, who was not just able to gain the support of a bishop; he was also wealthy enough to be able to pay a bribe. Even this man, however, had to appeal to the pope to get released. Finally, it should be noted that, even if scholars enumerate many cases where people were falsely accused, Davis (1948: 41) concludes that those sentenced in the Albi trials of 1299–1300 probably really were "guilty" of heresy.

INQUISITION AND RESISTANCE

As already noted, it would be a simplification to claim that the inquisition in France was completely different from the one in Spain. While it is true that the former was "papal" and the latter was under the crown, this does not mean the two institutions were completely different. Even though the crown's influence over the inquisition was much weaker in France, the inquisition in that country was still dependent on royal support: the crown paid the inquisitors' salaries (in Spain they were financed through confiscations), and the pope needed the crown's military support in order to carry out the inquisition. In contrast to the Inquisition in Spain, which was all-encompassing, the inquisition in France was mostly confined to the areas where the Cathar heresy was strong (i.e., in the south), although it also operated in other parts of the country (Haskins 1902: 631). Lea (1888: 117) notes the inquisitors' lack of interest in the northern regions of France: "Heretics throughout the North were comparatively few and scattered; the chroniclers of the period take no note of their discovery and punishment, nor even of the establishment of the Inquisition itself. That a few friars should be deputed to the duty of hunting heretics was too unimpressive a fact to be worthy of record." The French kings generally supported the inquisition because confiscating the property of heretics fattened the royal treasury (ibid.: 649). Furthermore, since the king considered Jews "a significant source of income, [he] jealously guarded his rights over them, and for this reason, he restrained the inquisitors on several occasions from intervening in Jewish affairs" (Yerushalmi 1970: 320–1). In other words, the king concluded that taking property from alleged heretics would increase his income while repressing Jews would deny him the substantial income that he received from their business and banking activities. Yerushalmi (1970: 320) sums up the relationship between the monarchy and the inquisition in France as follows: "The king cooperated with the inquisitors when it suited him or, as in his suppression of the Templars, when he needed them. However, when he felt that his own interests were in jeopardy, Philip did not hesitate to assert himself and to curb the inquisitors' activities."

Given (1989: 356) describes a relationship between the inquisition and the crown in France which does not differ very much from that in Spain. He notes that, like their counterparts in Spain, inquisitors in France could only operate with help from the secular authorities. They were also economically dependent on the latter, which paid them out of the proceeds of property confiscated from condemned heretics. Finally, they relied on royal or seigneurial officials for "hunting down and arresting fugitive heretics. Although the inquisitors had the right to excommunicate anyone who refused to assist them, they often found secular authorities, perturbed by local hostility to the inquisitors, less than enthusiastic partners."

Thus, the relationship between the monarchy and the Church was complicated in both countries, in view of the inquisitors' dependence on the pope for approval and on the crown for financing. However, there is one important difference: in France, the inquisition did not form part of a state-building strategy, so it was not used to homogenize the country around a legitimizing ideology.

In fact, whereas the Inquisition in Spain helped unify the country, in France it met with great resistance and served to divide the country. In Spain, it was easy to rally the population against the outgroups in question, as the main ones—those of Jewish and Muslim origin—comprised separate groups with "bloodlines" different from those of other inhabitants. In France, by contrast, the Cathars, who were the target of the inquisition, were considered to be of the same "blood" as that of other French; and the areas where they predominated—subject as they were to the control of vassals rather than being under direct royal rule—did not influence the core of the kingdom. In addition, the Cathars not only enjoyed the support of large portions of the population in the Languedoc region; they also enjoyed the respect of many nobles and public officials, who did not necessarily share their religious beliefs. Consequently, in order to subdue the Cathars, it was first necessary to use military force in the Albigensian Crusades, after which the Church could begin its inquisition. Yet, these military actions often met with stiff opposition, and they did not always have the full support of the crown. The crusaders had trouble winning battles when they did not have royal troops at their side. Often they suffered military defeats and only rebounded when the king sent troops to aid them.

In 1204, for example, Pope Innocent wanted King Philip Augustus to launch a crusade against the count of Toulouse, but the king refused (Moore 2012: 92; Duby 1993: 241; Sumption 1978: 70). In 1205 and 1207 the pope tried again to gain the king's support, but in vain (Sumption 1978: 70ff.; cf. Petit-Dutaillis 1936: 277ff.). Some French soldiers did take part in the crusade but without the king's backing. In 1208, the pope asked Philip Augustus if he could at least co-finance the crusade, but the king turned him down once again (p. 80). In 1222, when Count Raymond VI of Toulouse died and his son Raymond VII took over, papal legates again called for help. Again Philip Augustus resisted, but his son (the future Louis VIII) agreed and laid siege to Toulouse; however, he returned home once the 40 days he had vowed to devote to the crusade had ended (Moore 2012: 267). The fact that he returned after 40 days indicates a lack of enthusiastic support. However, upon succeeding his father in 1223, Louis VIII took a tougher stance against the Cathars. In 1224 he launched a new crusade, which he led personally. Since the king had more resources than anyone else in society, and since his soldiers were both more numerous and better trained, this crusade was more powerful than previous ones (Sumption 1978: 209ff.). After decades of fighting, a peace deal was finally reached in Paris in 1229. However, the war did not end because the forces of Raymond VII were defeated militarily, but because the count could no longer finance the war; moreover, he realized he could never completely defeat the French army, which could always return (ibid.: 268; Wakefield 1974: 127). Sumption (1978: 223) adds that the inhabitants of the region were becoming "increasingly war-weary and mutinous."

The Church's anti-Semitism was on prominent display in this case, as one of the conditions for the truce was that Raymond VII fire all the Jews working under him (Wakefield 1974: 128). Another requirement of the peace agreement was that the inquisition be allowed into the area. Yet, the inquisition met with stiff resistance. Thus, in Toulouse in 1235,

> after opening proceedings against a dozen such people as believers [in the Cathar heresy], the inquisitors were run out of town, "seized by the heads and feet and carried through the gate by force." Soon afterwards, the con-suls [i.e., local government officials] ordered a boycott of the Dominicans, who were blockaded in their convent for three weeks, living on what food their supporters could throw over the wall at night. (Moore 2012: 293)

Even after the truce, the inquisition met great resistance in Toulouse. In 1235, for example, suspects accused of heresy refused to appear before the tribunal after having received citations and they received the support of the count. The townspeople demanded that the inquisition drop its proceedings and that the inquisitor, Friar William Arnold, leave town. The town consuls then forcibly expelled him. The consuls also decided to expel all the Dominicans from the convent, whereupon a crowd gathered and forced them out, save for one elderly friar and seven sick ones (Wakefield 1974: 147; cf. Shannon 1985: 87; Sumption 1978: 231). Martin (2005: 112) reports that the mob threw stones and excrement at the inquisitors as they were leaving.

Resistance was also strong in Narbonne, where the population thought the inquisitor, Friar Ferrier, too severe. After protests, the royal seneschal rescinded many of the confiscations there and punished only a few citizens for the deaths that had resulted when the population attacked the inquisi-tors (Moore 2012: 293). Meanwhile, in Albi the royal officials were the more oppressive ones: they wanted to maximize the amount of property seized from heretics, while the bishop and the inquisitors wished to show greater leniency, to prevent families from becoming impoverished (Martin 2005: 123). This example shows two things: first, the inquisition and the crown had to cooperate in order to wipe out heresy successfully; and second, the conflict that sometimes arose between them did not always occur because the Church wanted to be tougher than the crown—at times it was the other way round.

The dependence of the papal inquisition on royal cooperation can also be seen in a case at *La Charité*, where, according to Haskins (1902: 651), the inquisitor, Friar Robert, performed his duties

> with the King's aid and under his authority. The king's offices carry out the friar's sentences, the King's soldiers accompany him as a guard, the King and Queen themselves take a personal, and it must be said a merciful, interest in his proceedings and the fate of his victims.

Haskins adds that the royal treasury paid for the expenses of the inquisition. Later, in the 1290s, King Philip IV,

> confronted with widespread anti-inquisitorial agitation in Languedoc and involved in disputes with the papacy, for several years lent some assistance to the inquisitors' opponents. Moved by their complaints, he instructed his seneschal of Carcassonne in the early 1290s to assist the inquisitors in arresting suspected heretics only following consultation with the judges of the royal court and only when convinced, either by a suspect's confession, public report, or the testimony of credible witnesses, that the person in question was indeed a heretic. (Given 1989: 357)

Thus, although the inquisition needed royal support to be able to operate, it also came into conflict at times with the crown, as the latter tried to curb its activities.

Martin describes the opposition the inquisition met in Albi:

> Despite the power they wielded, the Inquisition met fierce—and frequently violent—resistance. In Albi, the Inquisitor Arnold Catalan's assistants were too frightened to enter the cemetery to dig up the body of a woman who had been posthumously accused of heresy. (Martin 2005: 110; see also Barber 2000: 151)

Furthermore, "a mob set upon Arnold and nearly beat him to death" (Martin 2005: 111; see also Barber 2000: 151).

Portions of the clergy also opposed the inquisition. In Carcassonne, the Dominican friars were in charge of the inquisition, but they met resistance from the Franciscans (Ames 2011; Friedlander 2000). Consequently, in 1291, Philip the Fair gave his seneschal of Carcassone an order to restrain the power and prerogatives of the inquisitors. The king admitted that the region was suffering from the excesses of the Inquisition (Friedlander 2000: 21). The population, however, still was not satisfied; and in 1295 and 1296, the town's burghers protested violently against the inquisitor and the Dominican friars. Mobs attacked the friars, and the townsmen "shut them out of the churches of the Burg." The inquisitor, Nicolas d'Abbeville, responded by excommunicating the town (ibid.: 30). The Franciscans even helped the population battle against the Dominicans and their sergeants, who had come to attack the convent of the Franciscan friars in the Burg. Thus, divisions between the two Catholic orders had become violent.

A Franciscan friar, Bernard Délicieux, emerged as leader of the movement against the inquisition. Interestingly, Louis IX had already introduced the position of *enquêteur-réformateur* in the 1240s. Persons appointed to this position were charged with investigating and correcting governmental abuses. This shows the crown did not have totalitarian ambitions (Friedlander 2000: 69f.). In the *vidame* of Amiens, the *enquêteur*, Jean de Picquigny, supported the population against the inquisition and cooperated with Délicieux. De Picquigny concluded that the inquisition was provoking popular discontent, which could cause instability in the country.

In 1301, with de Picquigny's support, Délicieux helped Albi's citizens appeal directly to King Philip IV:

[However,] Philip's subsequent restrictions on the bishop and the inquisitors, including a suspension of inquisitor Foulques de Saint-Georges, did not prevent further violence. Townspeople cursed and attacked local Dominicans, forcibly ejecting them from Albi's churches in 1302. (Ames 2011: 49)

One of the reasons the inquisition in France encountered such opposition is that the population saw its actions as contrary to the norms of behavior and standards of justice that were traditional in the country. Thus, Wakefield writes,

there were conspiracies of witnesses to keep silent, either out of self-interest or in fear of retaliation from those whom they might incriminate; there were also agreements to give false evidence....Nothing causes more public disgust and resentment than the sight of exhumed corpses dragged through the streets to the fire. Toulouse was full of complaints against the inquisitors by the end of the summer of 1234 and the agitations were egged on by a number of individuals who had so far successfully delayed the pilgrimages to which they had been sentenced by Cardinal Romanus in 1229. (Wakefield 1974: 142)

This widespread feeling—that the inquisition violated traditional norms of proper behavior—did not escape the attention of Guillaume Pelhisson, who was appointed inquisitor in Albi in 1234. Pelhisson admitted that the activities of the inquisition disturbed the local population (Ames 2011: 117).

The lack of popular support for the inquisition in France made it difficult for it to become as totalitarian as the later Spanish one. Wakefield notes, "The situation was dangerous for heretics but not intolerable. There was no reign of terror and heretics could count on protectors, even among *baillis* of the count of Toulouse, but the halcyon days of freedom were gone, and caution became their rule" (Wakefield 1974: 133). In general, the Inquisition took place "in the face of hostile communities and uncooperative [sic] secular rulers" (Barber 2000: 36)—hardly a totalitarian atmosphere, despite the repression from which the population suffered.

Another factor hindering society from becoming totalitarian was the sympathy or at least respect that many aristocrats had for the Cathars. Although it does not seem many aristocrats actually became Cathars, many of them respected people of this faith and protected them. For example, Aimery, who held the lordships of Laurac and Montréal, allowed the Cathars to live openly there. Even though the chroniclers never claimed he was a heretic, "[m]any, perhaps most, of his knights and their families respected the [Cathar] *perfecti* and their teaching" (Barber 2000: 36). The chronicler William of Tudela gives yet another example of an aristocrat who was not a Cathar but who protected them nonetheless. He wrote that, although Lord Raymond Roger Trencavel himself was not a heretic, his knights and vassals let the heretics stay in their towers and castles (ibid.: 52).

Finally, it should be noted that one reason why much of the population in southern France sympathized with the Cathars is that they saw the Catholic Church as corrupt and exploitative. In his studies of the French village Montaillou in the south of the country, Ladurie (1978) shows that, although serfdom had basically disappeared throughout the region, the Church continued to extract tithes (one-tenth of the yield) from those working its lands. Thus, the Church was seen as a bigger exploiter than the nobility. Ladurie gives the example of the local nobleman Roger-Bernard, the old *Comte de Foix*, who successfully protected the population against Church demands that the peasants hand over one-tenth of their sheep to the organization.[6] However, the *Comte* had to be careful not to oppose the Church too strongly, as the king might always send troops to defend it. The strong anti-Church sentiment in the area was summed up by the statement of a local provost (*bayle*), who exclaimed that "[m]y only enemies...are the priest and the vicaire. I know no others" (p. 22). Thus, Ladurie links the resistance to the Church to the conflict over tithes.

The local clergy were also perceived to be very corrupt. The most powerful family in Montaillou was the Clergue family. The father was a Cathar; one of the sons was a Catholic priest. The priest often helped the Cathars, even giving them some of the money from the tithes. Yet, he also cooperated with the inquisition. One peasant asked the priest why he now persecuted the "good Christians" (i.e., the Cathars) although he used to be fond of them. He replied:

> I have not changed....I still am very fond of the good Christians. But I want to be revenged on the peasants of Montaillou, who have done me harm, and I will avenge myself in every possible way. I shall know how to settle up with God. (p. 57)

Given this combination of corruption and economic exploitation, it is not surprising that many people of all classes had sympathy for the Cathars, even if they were not all active members in the sect. As Strayer argues (excerpt published in Chalk and Jonassohn 1990: 117–8), many lost faith in the Church because of the cruelty of the inquisition and they saw that institution as a way for the Church to seize the property of innocent people. Even if they did not believe in the Cathar doctrine, "...the citizens of Béziers refused flatly to betray their unorthodox brethren. As was to be shown again and again during the following decades, the Occitanians felt that the argument between Catholic and heretic was their own private affair and that the real enemy was the French intruder" (ibid.: 118). Ruthven (excerpt published in Chalk and Jonassohn 1990: 126) adds that "[t]he majority of the population of the towns as well as their town leaders supported the rebellion [in southern France]. Catholics supported the heretics as they thought the Crusades threatened their economic and commercial life."

ANTI-SEMITISM IN MEDIEVAL FRANCE

Throughout Europe in the medieval era, anti-Semitism was spreading. Trachtenberg (1943) documents how Jews across Europe were being portrayed as nonhuman or subhuman. He notes the totalitarian nature of Church doctrine in that period:

> Medieval Christendom was so firmly convinced of the incontestable truth of its own tradition and teaching that it could conceive of no rival truth. Curious as this may seem, there is overwhelming evidence that the Catholic world believed that the Jew himself recognized the truth of Christian doctrine! (1943: 15)

Thus, if the truth of the Church's doctrine is so obvious, then it must be equally obvious to Jews; but they are so evil and in such close collusion with the devil that they pretend all the same not to believe it.

Another common argument was that the Jews were indeed being honest in rejecting Church doctrine, but that this was because they were not human at all. Trachtenberg (1943: 18) cites Peter the Venerable of Cluny, who wrote: "Really I doubt whether a Jew can be human for he will neither yield to human reasoning nor find satisfaction in authoritative utterances, alike divine and Jewish." Jews, it was claimed, spread the plague by poisoning wells. Rumors of blood sacrifice spread, as Jews were accused of killing Christian children to use their blood in religious rituals (1943: 135). Jews were seen as devilish and alien; they might even have horns, or at least smell different. They posed an existential threat to the Christian civilization which they allegedly wanted to destroy.

In such a situation, it was not difficult to develop an anti-Semitism based on "race" rather than religion (although the term "race" was not yet in use). Yet, only the Spanish Inquisition embraced the notion that "blood" matters. In France, when anti-Semitic riots broke out in this period, one of the goals was often to get Jews to convert—and "blood" was not an issue in that connection. In 1321, for example, panic broke out after a leper said to the inquisition that he had poisoned the wells after a rich Jew had promised him money for poisoning the wells (Barber 1981a). This led to pogroms against Jews; many were burnt alive. The royal authorities do not seem to have offered Jews any protection. According to a report from Nangis, for example, 160 Jews in that town were burnt to death in a large pit, and mothers threw their children into the pit to prevent them from being baptized. Attacks took place in Paris as well—to the enrichment of the king, who was able to confiscate the incomes and assets of the victims.

A year earlier, a peasant uprising known as the *Pastoureaux* (Shepherds' Crusade) had taken place. Peasants attacked and plundered Jews along their route from Paris to the south of France. For example, in 1322 they "burned a royal tower at Saintes in which the Jews had taken refuge and massacred them, probably with the help of some of the local inhabitants" (Barber 1981b: 147). The attackers did not focus solely on Jews; they also robbed and attacked clergy. They were able to attack so freely due to support from the local population and even at times from town councils. They were eventually captured by the royal authorities. Yerushalmi (1970: 328) writes that when 24 cartloads of captured *Pastoureaux* were brought into Narbonne Fort in Toulouse, a crowd of bystanders set them free and, together with the *Pastoureaux*, attacked the Jewish quarter. They forced any Jews they encountered there to convert or to face death. The uprising was soon subdued, however, and it did not lead to the kind of mass conversions seen in Aragon and Castile before Spain's unification.

In this highly Catholic country, Jews faced various stereotypes and prejudices and there were many professions they were not allowed to enter. Many Jews made themselves unpopular, moreover, because moneylending was one of the few occupations in which they could engage. In this setting it was common to blame Jews for calamities such as epidemics. As already noted, French nobles never feared Christians with Jewish blood, because their position was not based on blood to the same extent as their Spanish counterparts' was. Furthermore, since *conversos* were far fewer in France than in Spain, there were fewer cases where Christians of Jewish ancestry married into aristocratic families. Thus, people of Jewish ancestry represented much less of an existential threat to the ruling aristocracy, and the crown felt confident enough in its rule over a well-established country that it did not feel the need to look for a scapegoat in order to unite the country. Yet, since Jews were not popular, given the common prejudices and the negative view of them which the Church and the burghers took; as a result, the crown was willing to expel Jews (among other things, as we saw in Chap. 2, in order to get support for introducing new taxes).

Even though popular prejudices against Jews in France were similar to those in Spain and the rest of Europe, and even though the crown operated in a cultural setting that allowed for actions against Jews and those of Jewish ancestry, the manner in which French state-building developed helps explain why the crown did not consider Jews and *conversos* to pose the kind of existential threat which the crown in Spain believed they did. First, there were not nearly as many Jews in France; nor were there many *conversos* as Jews felt less pressure in France than in Spain to convert to Catholicism. In contrast to their counterparts in Spain, Jews in France did not face mass riots in which their only choice was to convert to Catholicism *en masse* or to face the sword (Yerushalmi 1970: 334–5). Nevertheless, as mentioned earlier, there were some riots where the perpetrators tried to force Jews to convert, but these events were not comparable to the mass riots that took place in Spain.

Second, in contrast to the situation in Spain, ethnic diversity and religious heterogeneity were not an issue in France. Some of the wealthier *conversos* might marry into the nobility, but this was not seen as a threat to the prevailing order since noble status in France was not based as strictly on "blood." In contrast to the situation in Spain, for example, *it was quite common for burghers to be granted noble status in France* (Bergin 2015: 7). Starting in the twelfth century, burghers could purchase a noble fief (Bien 1989: 445–86; Lucas 1977: 239). Parks reports: "As noble status was usually confirmed on the mere oral evidence of witnesses, who could vouch for the lifestyle or military prowess of the family concerned, it was often only necessary to live like a noble to become one. Three generations of officeholding also sufficed..." (Parker 1996: 137). Thus, "true" French aristocrats rarely intermarried with Jews or Catholics of Jewish descent, and membership in the aristocracy was not based nearly as much on "blood." It was much less likely, therefore, for "blood" to become an issue in French politics.

It is true that King Philip the Fair expelled the Jewish population from France in 1306; however, he did so because the crown needed additional resources to finance its wars. Expelling the Jews enabled Philip to confiscate their property, and at the same time to gain the burghers' acceptance of the need to pay taxes to contribute to the state treasury (see the discussion below).

Meanwhile, King Louis X announced that Jews would be able to return temporarily (although two-thirds of the debts that others owed them, upon being collected, would need to be turned over to the crown). The

Jews were then expelled by a third king, Charles IV, in 1322, but were permitted to return in 1359 (e.g., Yerushalmi 1970: 320ff.).[7]

Whereas the expulsions in totalitarian Spain had an ideological basis—the need to preserve the new country's Catholic character and to prevent Jews from tempting *conversos* to revert to Judaism—the reasons for the expulsions in France lay in the crown's need for more resources to fight its many wars (Barkey and Katznelson 2011). The crown, Barkey and Katznelson forcefully argue, had previously financed itself to a large extent through Jewish financiers, but this source did not provide enough to meet the monarchy's needs when its budget greatly expanded. In order to gain the support of the burghers (who espoused anti-Semitic views) and to get them to accept the need to pay regular taxes, the crown agreed to expel the Jews. Barkey and Katznelson note that military victories enabled Philip to quadruple the size of French territory, resulting in a still greater need for additional resources to finance his administration (ibid.: 492). They describe the logic of the expulsions as follows:

> This period also saw the rise of local anti-Jewish mobilization and local expulsions. As groups were assailed by growing taxes, among them the clergy, they became less tolerant of the Jews in their midst. Charged with an expulsion tax, Jews were expelled from different regions, among them, in 1290, Saint-Pierre-sur-Dives and Nevers. Further, the example of the English expulsion that year demonstrated both to the crown and to political society that Jewish extrusion was possible and that profits could be made. (ibid.: 497)

Thus, the king could profit both from the increased willingness of the towns and burghers to pay taxes, and from the property which he confiscated from the Jews.

In addition to yielding financial gains for the crown, the expulsions seem to have been quite popular. Even though Jews and *conversos* did not represent the same kind of existential threat as they did in Spain, the expulsions appear to have helped the king gain greater support from society (Chazan 2010: 94):

> As reflected in Rigord's enthusiastic account [Rigord was the king's clerical biographer] of the royal anti-Jewish steps, various elements in the subject population approved of the moves, especially of the expulsion of Jews. Rigord's catalogue of Jewish misdeeds suggests that many in the Christian population would have seen Philip Augustus's edict of expulsion as remov-

ing a Jewish threat to physical safety (the killing of Christian youngsters), a Jewish threat to the economic well-being of the Christian populace (the suffering engendered by Jewish moneylending), and a Jewish threat to the religious purity of Christian society (the religious backsliding encouraged by Jews). For a young and embattled monarch, such popular approbation was no small matter....It is clear that Philip Augustus's anti-Jewish actions resonated positively for Rigord, who regularly designates Philip "the most Christian king" throughout his account of these anti-Jewish moves.

CONCLUSION

In contrast to the Spanish Inquisition, the French inquisition did not lead to a totalitarian society. As it did not form part of a state-building process in which rulers sought to homogenize society around a Catholic ideology, it did not have the full backing of the crown. Nor did it have the support of the population. The crown did not need the inquisition to justify its rule, and the population did not perceive the Cathars as a threatening outgroup. While the Muslims and Jews in Spain—including those who had converted to Catholicism—were widely seen as belonging to a separate bloodline, the Cathars did not represent a different bloodline from that of other French. In addition, they enjoyed the sympathy and protection of many nobles and public officials in the Languedoc region.

Since the French inquisition faced much more opposition than the Spanish one, and since it was specifically established to fight a single Christian sect, it was largely confined to one area in southern France. By contrast, the Spanish Inquisition encompassed the entire country. The French inquisition, furthermore, did not create the same atmosphere of terror as its Spanish counterpart. It did not engage in mass mobilizations through *autos de fe*. In contrast to the more totalitarian Spanish Inquisition, finally, it was not interested in past acts of heresy, such as statements one might have made over 20 years earlier; rather, it was concerned with fighting people who in fact were active heretics (of the Cathar sect).

NOTES

1. Excerpt from Strayer, published in Chalk and Jonassohn (1990: 117).
2. Petit-Dutaillis (1936: 8) has a similar view.
3. Nevertheless, Beaune (1991: 273) concludes that "as early as 1300, the French language had become one of the distinguishing characteristics of the nation."

4. As Moore (1966: 41–2) writes: "At quite an early date the peasant had managed to escape from personal servitude, mainly by capitalizing on the demand for labor in the countryside that increased as the growing towns presented the possibility of another way of making a living. By the time of the Revolution, peasants possessed close to *de facto* property rights."
5. Field and Gaposchkin (2014: 574) note that William of Paris, the main inquisitor for northern France, became Philip IV's personal confessor in 1305.
6. When the *Comte* died, however, the Church once again demanded the payments (p. 12).
7. According to Brown (1991), Charles did not actually expel the Jews in 1322; instead they had to leave the country in 1327, because their 15-year-long permission to stay in the country ended in that year.

References

Acharya, A., & Lee, A. (2015). *Medieval State Building and Contemporary European Development Evidence from a Natural Experiment*. Retrieved from http://www.rochester.edu/college/faculty/alexander_lee/wp-content/uploads/2015/04/europe10.pdf.

Ames, C. C. (2011). *Righteous Persecution: Inquisition, Dominicans, and Christianity in the Middle Ages*. Philadelphia: University of Pennsylvania Press.

Armstrong, J. A. (1982). *Nations before Nationalism*. Chapel Hill: University of North Carolina Press.

Barber, M. (1981a). Lepers, Jews and Moslems: The Plot to Overthrow Christendom. *Journal of Ecclesiastical History, 66*(216), 1–17.

Barber, M. (1981b). The Pastoureaux 1321. *History, 32*(2), 143–166.

Barber, M. (2000). *The Cathars: Dualist Heretics in Languedoc in the High Middle Ages*. Abingdon: Routledge.

Barkey, K., & Katznelson, I. (2011). States, Regimes, and Decisions: Why Jews were Expelled from Medieval England and France. *Theory and Society, 4*(5), 475–503.

Bartlett, R. (1993). *The Making of Europe: Conquest, Colonization and Cultural Change 950–1350*. London: Penguin.

Beaune, C. (1991). *The Birth of an Ideology: Myths and Symbols of Nation in Late-Medieval France* (S. R. Huston, Trans. & F. L. Cheyette, Ed.). Berkeley: University of California Press.

Beech, G. T. (1964). *A Rural Society in Medieval France: The Gâtine of Poitou in the Eleventh and Twelfth Centuries*. Baltimore: John Hopkins Press.

Bergin, J. (2015). *A History of France*. London: Palgrave.

Bien, D. D. (1989). Manufacturing Nobles: The Chancelleries in France to 1789. *The Journal of Modern History, 61*(3), 445–486.

Brown, E. A. R. (1991). Charles IV, and the Jews of France: The Alleged Expulsion of 1322. *Spectrum, 66*(2), 294–329.

Brown, E. A. R. (2012). Moral Imperatives and Conundrums of Conscience: Reflections on Philip the Fair of France. *Speculum, 87*(1), 1–36.

Cabannes, X. (2007). A Subtle Difference: King of France or King of the French? An Informal Historical Reflection on the Relationship between the Sovereign, the Power and the Country. *Political Science, 59*(2), 97–103.

Chalk, F., & Jonassohn, K. (1990). *The History and Sociology of Genocide: Analyses ad Case Studies*. New Haven: Yale University Press.

Chazan, R. (2010). *Reassessing Jewish Life in Medieval Europe*. Cambridge: Cambridge University Press.

Collins, J. B. (1997). State Building in Early-Modern Europe: The Case of France. *Modern Asian Studies, 31*(3), 603–633.

Davis, G. W. (1948). *The Inquisition at Albi 1299–1300*. New York: Columbia University Press.

Deane, J. K. (2011). *A History of Medieval Heresy and Inquisition*. Plymouth: Rowman & Littlefield.

Denton, J. H. (1997). Taxation and the Conflict between Philip the Fair and Boniface VIII. *French History, 11*(3), 241–264.

Duby, G. (1993). *France in the Middle Ages 987–1460* (J. Vale, Trans.). Oxford: Blackwell.

Dumont, L. (1985). A Modified View of Our Origins: The Christian Beginnings of Modern Individualism. In M. Carrithers, S. Collins, & S. Lukes (Eds.), *The Category of the Person: Anthropology, Philosophy, History*. Cambridge: Cambridge University Press.

Dunbabin, J. (2002). The Political World of France, c. 1200–c. 1336. In D. Potter (Ed.), *France in the Later Middle Ages 1200–1500*. Oxford: Oxford University Press.

Elias, N. (1939/1997). *Über den Prozess der Zivilisation. Soziogenetische und psychogenetische Untersuchungen, volume 2*. Frankfurt: Suhrkamp Verlag.

Ertman, T. (1997). *Birth of the Leviathan*. Cambridge: Cambridge University Press.

Fawtier, R. (1960). *The Capetian Kings of France: Monarchy & Nation (987–1328)* (L. Butler & R. J. Adam, Trans.). Basingstoke: Macmillan Education Ltd.

Field, S. L. (2016a). Royal Agents and Templar Confessions in the Bailliage of Rouen. *French Historical Studies, 39*(1), 35–71.

Field, S. L. (2016b). Torture and Confession in the Templar Interrogations at Caen, 28–29 October 1307. *Speculum, 91*(2), 297–327.

Field, S. L. (2017). King/Confessor/Inquisitor: A Capetian-Dominican Convergence. In W. C. Jordan & J. R. Phillips (Eds.), *The Capetian Century, 1214–1314*. Turnhout, Belgium: Brepols.

Field, S. L., & Gaposchkin, M. C. (2014). Questioning the Capetians, 1180–1328. *History Compass, 12*(7), 567–585.

Finer, S. E. (1974). State-building, State Boundaries and Border Control: An Essay on Certain Aspects of the First Phase of State-building in Western Europe Considered in the Light of the Rokkan-Hirschman Model. *Social Science Information, 13*(4/5), 79–126.

Friedlander, A. (2000). *The Hammer of the Inquisitors: Brother Bernard Délicieux & the Struggle Against the Inquisition in Fourteenth-Century France.* Leiden: Brill.

Given, J. (1989). The Inquisitors of Languedoc and the Medieval Technology of Power. *The American Historical Review, 94*(2), 336–359.

Gomes, F. E. X. (2017). Church-State Relations from a Catholic Perspective: General Considerations on Nicolas Sarkozy's New Concept of Laïcité Positive. *Journal of Catholic Legal Studies, 48*(2), 201–217.

Haskins, C. H. (1902). Robert Le Bougre and the Beginnings of the Inquisition in Northern France. *The American Historical Review, 7*(4), 631–652.

Hastings, A. (1997). *The Construction of Nationhood: Ethnicity, Religion and Nationalism.* Cambridge: Cambridge University Press.

Heer, F. (1961/1990). *The Medieval World: Europe from 1100–1350* (J. Sondheimer, Trans.). London: Weidenfeld and Nicolson.

Heper, M. (1985). The State and Public Bureaucracies: A Comparative and Historical Perspective. *Comparative Studies in Society and History, 27*(1), 86–110.

James, E. (1982). *The Origins of France: From Clovis to the Capetians 500–1000.* Basingstoke: Macmillan.

Kelly, H. A. (1989). Inquisition and the Prosecution of Heresy: Misconceptions and Abuses. *Church History, 58*(4), 439–451.

Knowles, D. (1967). Church and State in Christian History. *Journal of Contemporary History, 2*(4), 3–15.

Ladurie, E. L. (1978). *Montaillou: Cathars and Catholics in a French Village 1294–1324* (B. Bray, Trans.). Middlesex: Penguin.

Lea, H. C. (1888). *A History of the Inquisition of the Middle Ages: Volume 2.* London: Sampson Low, Marston, Searle, & Rivington.

Lewis, A. W. (1981). *Royal Succession in Capetian France: Studies on Familial Order and the State.* Cambridge, MA: Harvard University Press.

Llobera, J. R. (1994). State and Nation in Medieval France. *Journal of Historical Sociology, 7*(3), 343–362.

Lucas, R. H. (1977). Ennoblement in Late Medieval France. *Mediaeval Studies, 39*, 239–260.

Martin, S. (2005). *The Cathars.* Harpenden, Herts: Pocket Essentials.

Moore, B. (1966). *Social Origins of Dictatorship and Democracy.* Boston: Beacon Press.

Moore, R. I. (2012). *The War on Heresy.* Cambridge, MA: Belknap Press.

Naus, V. (2016). *Constructing Kingship: The Capetian Monarchs of France and the Early Crusades.* Manchester: Manchester University Press.

Parker, D. (1996). *Class and State in Early Modern France: The Road to Modernity*. London: Routledge.

Petit-Dutaillis, C. (1936/1964). *The Feudal Monarchy in France and England, From the Tenth to the Thirteenth Century*. New York: Harper & Row.

Poplin, J. D. (2006). *A History of Modern France* (3rd ed.). Upper Saddle River, NJ: Pearson/Prentice Hall.

Potter, D. (2003). Introduction. In D. Potter (Ed.), *France in the Later Middle Ages 1200–1500*. Oxford: Oxford University Press.

Reynolds, S. (1997). *Kingdoms and Communities in Western Europe, 900–1300* (2nd ed.). Oxford: Clarendon Press.

Shannon, A. C. (1985). *The Medieval Inquisition* (2nd ed.). Collegeville, MN: Liturgical Press.

Spruyt, H. (1994). *The Sovereign State and Its Competitors: An Analysis of Systems Change*. Princeton: Princeton University Press.

Stork, N. P. (1999). Cathar and Jewish Confessions to the Inquisition at Pamiers, France 1318–1325. *Multilingua, 18*(2/3), 251–265.

Strayer, J. R. (1969). Normandy and Languedoc. *Speculum, 44*(1), 1–12.

Sumption, J. (1978/1999). *The Albigensian Crusade*. London: Faber and Faber.

Théry-Astruc, J. (2017). The Pioneer of Royal Theocracy: Guillaume de Nogaret and the Conflicts between Philip the Fair and the Papacy. In W. C. Jordan & J. R. Phillips (Eds.), *The Capetian Century, 1214–1314*. Turnhout, Belgium: Brepols.

Tierney, B. (1964). *The Crisis of Church & State, 1050–1300*. Englewood Cliffs, NJ: Prentice-Hall.

Tierney, B. (1999). *The Middle Ages*. New York: Cornell University.

Trachtenberg, J. (1943). *The Devil and the Jews: The Medieval Conception of the Jew and Its Relation to Modern Antisemitism*. New Haven: Yale University Press/Varda Books 2001.

Wakefield, W. L. (1974). *Heresy, Crusade and Inquisition in Southern France 1100–1250*. Berkeley: University of California Press.

Yerushalmi, Y. H. (1970). The Inquisition and the Jews of France in the Time of Bernard Gui. *Harvard Theological Review, 63*(3), 317–376.

CHAPTER 5

Spain: Pre-Modern Totalitarianism

Despite the vast amount of literature linking totalitarianism to modernity, Chap. 2 shows that it is reasonable to consider Spain during the first decades of the Inquisition to have come rather close to the totalitarian ideal-type. Thus, the question arises as to why the country became totalitarian. Here I show how the process of state-building gave the crown an incentive to pursue such policies.

This chapter proceeds by first discussing the state-building process and its link to legitimacy. Then, it considers the interaction between state-building, legitimacy and evilness. Previous studies have reached interesting conclusions to the effect that governments can get their population to engage in evil acts if they are able to define an outgroup as an existential threat. However, this book shows how state-building gives leaders a stronger incentive to find an outgroup to frame as an existential threat. Next, the chapter discusses the rise of anti-Semitism, which played a key role for the founding of the Inquisition. After this, the chapter shows how the Inquisition was set up. Finally, this chapter analyzes the reasons why some people in Spain were willing to commit evil acts against people of Jewish or Muslim heritage.

Spanish Totalitarianism as a State-Building Process

With the marriage of Isabella of Castile and Ferdinand of Aragon, the two most important Iberian kingdoms united. Then, with the victory over Grenada in 1492, the *Reconquista* drive succeeded in uniting all of the

© The Author(s) 2019   113
S. Saxonberg, *Pre-Modernity, Totalitarianism and the Non-Banality of Evil*, https://doi.org/10.1007/978-3-030-28195-3_5

territories of Spain into one country. This meant the new country now had a large Muslim population in the south, as well as relatively influential *converso* communities of Jewish converts in some urban areas in the north. As Nathans (2004) shows in his study of citizenship policy in Germany after its unification, the process of uniting territories into a new state requires its rulers to discuss what kind of state it will be, who belongs to it and who represents a threat to the new order. Now the Spanish crown had to develop a strategy to gain legitimacy among a population which until recently had lived under different kingdoms, had different religions and even spoke different languages. Ferdinand and Isabella decided to follow a strategy of homogenizing society around Catholicism (Gómez 1995; Payne 1973). They styled themselves the "Catholic Monarchs" (Nader 1979; Roth 1995), who would defend the faith against the Muslim threat that the Ottoman Empire posed in Europe, while also spreading the faith throughout Spain's colonial territories in Latin America. Plaidy (1959: 86) concludes that "[t]he Catholic Sovereigns were determined to have a united country, and they did not believe this ambition could be achieved unless all their subjects accepted one religion." Along the same lines, Alvarez (2002: 15) maintains that a Spanish identity developed after unification based on loyalty to the monarchy and adherence to the "true" religion. Atkinson (1934: 81) sums up Isabella's thinking on the importance of Catholic hegemony: "One God, one King, one Law"—which comes surprisingly close to Hitler's "One People, one Führer." This legitimizing strategy involved giving Spain a mission to spread the "true" doctrine throughout the world. This has some parallels with the ideological basis of Soviet expansionist dreams. Thus, Columbus conducted his expedition to America that same year, and Spain began to establish itself as a world power.

To legitimize their rule over the new country, the rulers did not necessarily have to attempt to create a homogenized Catholic society marked by both religious and lifestyle-cultural uniformity. In theory, they could have allowed religious freedom. After all, as many authors have pointed out, Catholics, Muslims and Jews had been living in the area for centuries with a relatively high degree of tolerance for each other (e.g., Roth 1995: 9ff.; Mann 2005: 45). This does not mean their relations were problem-free: anti-Semitism did exist, and Muslims did not grant equal status to Jews and Catholics living in Moorish territory; neither did Jews and Muslims enjoy equal status with Christians in territories ruled by Catholic monarchs (e.g., Pérez 2004: 2ff.). Sometimes anti-Jewish riots broke in Catholic areas—during outbreaks of plague and other diseases—as parts of the population blamed the Jews for such calamities. Nevertheless, relations were on the whole tolerant by the standards of the time, and Jews reached high positions in society. Until the fifteenth century, moreover, they were basically free to live where they wanted.

Even if the crown could have chosen a different legitimizing strategy, certain structural factors gave the rulers an incentive to base their new country on a homogenizing Catholicism. These include:

1. The reconquest of Spain from the Muslim Moors, framed as a religious crusade
2. The lack of order in Castile before the Catholic monarchs came to power
3. The large number of "New Catholics" (i.e., *conversos*), who had Jewish ancestry

Concerning the first point, *the desire to reconquer the peninsula* dates back to the toppling of the Visigothic kingdom in 711 by a group of Muslim Arabs and Moroccan Berbers. This meant that much of the area was now under Islamic control. The Umayyad Caliphate of Córdoba ruled over a large part of the Iberian Peninsula until it collapsed in 1031. Several Catholic kingdoms emerged, which fought against the Muslim-controlled states, leading to the notion of *reconquista*. O'Callaghan (2004: 3) points out that the goal of *reconquista* was not merely to defeat the Muslim armies, but to eject Muslims from Spain. The Catholic rulers, namely, saw the Muslims as intruders, who occupied Spanish territory, which rightfully belonged to Christians. "In time, the kings of Asturias-Leon-Castile, as the self-proclaimed heirs of the Visigoths, came to believe that it was their responsibility to recover all the land that had once belonged to the Visigothic kingdom."

O'Callaghan also notes (p. 209) that the popes actively supported this mission by giving financial support and promising participants in the expedition absolution for their sins. In 1212, for example, Pope Innocent III urged European rulers to aid the Iberian kings in the holy task of reconquering the area. He also pleaded with the Iberian kings to cooperate in this endeavor, and he granted indulgence to the participants (Bishko 1975: 422). The fact that the pope took such an interest in the reconquest increased Isabella and Ferdinand's bargaining power vis-à-vis the Vatican when they finally succeeded in conquering the remaining Muslim territory. Lea (1906: 14) asserts that Isabella and Ferdinand further increased their domination over society by claiming that "whatever might be the papal rights in other countries, in Spain the patronage of all benefices belonged to the crown because they and their predecessors had wrested the land from the infidel." With this argument, they were able to gain control over the inquisition that they wanted to initiate.

The second point is *the lack of order and security that people felt in Castile*, which encouraged the crown to push for more authority in order to bring order to society. Lea (1906: 18) writes that, before the Catholic monarchs came to power,

> [t]he fabric of society seemed about to fall in ruins. To evolve order out of this chaos of passion and lawlessness was a task to test to the uttermost the nerve and capacity of the most resolute and sagacious.

In addition (ibid.: 1–2),

> [i]t were [sic] *difficult to exaggerate the disorder pervading the Castilian kingdoms*, when the Spanish monarchy found its origin in the union of Isabella of Castile and Ferdinand of Aragon....The struggles of the reconquest from the Saracen, continued at intervals through seven hundred years and varied by constant civil broils, had bred a race of fierce and turbulent nobles as eager to attack a neighbor or their sovereign as the Moor...So fragile was the feudal bond that a *ricohome* or noble could at any moment renounce allegiance by a simple message sent to the king through a hidalgo. The necessity of attracting population and organizing conquered frontiers, which subsequently became inland, led to granting improvidently liberal franchises to settlers, which weakened the powers of the monarchy, without building up, as in France, a powerful Third Estate to serve as a counterpoise to the nobles and eventually to undermine feudalism. In Spain the business of the Castilian was war....No flourishing centres of industrious and independent burghers arose out of whom the kings could mould a body that should lend them efficient support in their struggles with their powerful vassals. The attempt, indeed, was made; the Córtes [parliaments], whose co-operation was required in the enactment of laws, consisted of representatives from seventeen cities, who while serving enjoyed personal inviolability, but so little did the cities prize this privilege that, under Henry IV, they complained of the expense of sending deputies. The crown, eager to find some new sources of influence, agreed to pay them and thus obtained an excuse for controlling their election, and although this came too late for Henry to benefit by it, it paved the way for the assumption of absolute domination by Ferdinand and Isabella....

Similarly, Bishko (1975: 440) observes that "[b]etween Peter 1 (1350–1369) and Henry IV (1454–1474) a dismal succession of minorities regencies, weak rulers, and spreading intra-aristocratic and anti-royal strife kept Castilian society in a state of constant civil violence and disorder, drastically weakening the monarchy's traditional authority, leadership, and ability to mobilize its military and financial resources or stir the popular enthusiasm necessary for the Granadan struggle." Roth (1995: 51) claims one cause of the civil violence was the desire of the nobility to increase its power:

> Throughout the fifteenth century the nobility was taking control of the cities—legally where possible, by force if necessary. Obviously, the conversos were the single most powerful element standing in their way. Members of that group were already solidly entrenched in government positions precisely in the cities.

To bring order to the newly created country in this unstable situation, the Catholic monarchs had an incentive to centralize power and to act more and more autocratically. Religion was a tool for legitimizing this vastly increased power, while establishing the Inquisition and taking action against the *conversos* helped placate the nobility (cf. Pérez 2002).

The third issue was the large number of Jews living in the country, and the even larger number of New Christians (i.e., Christians of Jewish ancestry). The most important events in this regard were the riots of 1391, which started when local clergy roused the populace against the Jews in Seville. These riots spread throughout the area causing a wave of mass conversions to Catholicism among the Jewish population (Carrete 1992: 19–20; Friedman 1987: 7; Kamen 1985: 7; Nirenberg 2002: 6; Pérez 2004: 8; Roth 1995: 11ff.). A second wave of mass conversions came about when St. Vincent Ferrer, with support from the papal court in Avignon and the crowns of Aragon and Castile, traveled around the Spanish territories. While doing so he held sermons aimed at getting Jews to convert (Nirenberg 2002: 11; Pérez 2004: 9; Roth 1995: 49). Then, in 1492, when Jews were given the choice of converting or leaving the country, more Jews converted in order to avoid having to leave.

Since a large number of Jews had converted, it is not surprising that some individuals among them had gained influence in society. According to some estimates, there were as many as one million *conversos* by 1492, although other historians claim the number was actually around 250,000.

In either case, the number of Jews and *conversos* was quite high (Friedman 1987: 8). Roth (1995: 9) asserts that more Jews lived in medieval Spain than in all other European countries combined. As New Christians did not face the same restrictions to begin with as Jews, some were able to rise in society and to marry into aristocratic families. This posed a great dilemma for the aristocracy, which based its right to rule on family background. Nobles saw themselves as coming from the best and most capable families with the best "blood." Yet, their "blood" was now becoming tainted by Jewish-*converso* "blood." Suddenly, low-status peasants could claim they had purer "blood" than the aristocracy, posing an existential threat to the aristocracy's right to rule (Kamen 1985: 23 and 115). In addition, as Yerushalmi (1982: 19) points out, the mass conversions caused fear among much of the population, because it was difficult to know who had "Jewish" blood, so people were not sure about how to protect themselves from the alleged threat. "When, as happened in both [Medieval Spain and united Germany], assimilation had become a sufficient reality (Catholic orthodoxy in the Iberian Peninsula; acculturation and the erosion of Jewish religious identity in Germany), the old religious definition of Jewry became a palpable anachronism and yielded increasingly to a racial one." Thus, as in Nazi Germany, having Jewish ancestry became seen as a threat to the social order.

The fear also arose that, with so many people having converted within such a short period, many of the "New Christians" would not be true believers. As will be discussed below, this fear played a major role in the decision to introduce the Inquisition. In addition, the presence of Jewish communities in the country was perceived as a threat, as it could tempt *conversos* to return to their previous non-Christian beliefs. It was, therefore, logical to expel the Jews, so that they could not tempt *conversos*. In fact, some *conversos* supported the expulsion of Jews, so that their fellow *conversos* would not be tempted (e.g., Giordano 2010).

Yet, even after the expulsions the *conversos* still represented a threat to the aristocracy, given the role that ancestry played in the latter's legitimacy. Consequently, even if the Inquisition might originally have been about enforcing a unitary belief system, it soon became about "blood" as well. Already decades before the Inquisition was instituted, religious organizations, universities and local governments began introducing *limpieza* (pure-blood) rules, which banned *conversos* from public office or from joining their organizations (Roth 1995: 230). Then, in 1484, the Grand Inquisitor Torquemada tried to introduce the "pure-blood" laws in the entire country. Yet, the Inquisition did not get the support of the crown on this issue until 1556, when King Philip approved the *limpieza* rules, thus making them official policy (Kamen 1985: 120). However, the king was not completely consistent: for example, he introduced the purity statue for the city of Toledo, but he opposed it for the University of Salamanca (Kamen 1997: 84). Nevertheless, as a way of homogenizing and thereby uniting the country, the crown started using racial purity in addition to the Catholic faith (Povedano 1980: 145f.). Silverblatt (2011: 136) concludes that, "[b]y the 16th century, reigning (but not universal) learned and popular beliefs held that a Spaniard's spiritual core was, in fact, biologic in origin and that a true and legitimate Spaniard could only have pure blood coursing through his veins."

These three points can be summed up in terms of neo-institutional theory. When the Catholic monarchs Isabella of Castile and Ferdinand of Aragon united the country through their marriage and their conquest of Granada, they found themselves at a "critical juncture" (Collier and Collier 1991), in which they could have chosen different paths for the newly cre-ated country. Given their Catholic values and given the several hundred years of religious wars against the Moors, it was "logically appropriate" for them to legitimize their rule on the basis of the notion that they were great Catholics, who had been able to unite the country by winning a great victory for Christianity through defeating another religion (Islam) that was threatening the Catholic world. In addition, given the great divi-sions and disorder in Castile and given their desire to unite the country, it was logically appropriate to introduce a more autocratic type of rule. Finally, given their Catholic values and their decision to use Catholicism to legitimize their rule, it made sense to take repressive measures against those with Jewish heritage. Jews represented a threat because they could tempt new converts to revert to Judaism, while those who did convert represented a danger, as they still might secretly harbor Jewish values. Thus, the Inquisition could help combat such tendencies. Furthermore, given the fact that the nobility in Spain based its right to rule on blood to a much greater extent than its counterpart in France, it made logical sense to try to eliminate persons of Jewish ancestry from public life, as the ability of some of them to gain wealth and to intermarry with aristocratic families made it hard for nobles to legitimize their rule on the basis of their alleg-edly superior blood. Then, once the Inquisition was in place and was enforcing ideological purity, it also made sense for it to expand its tasks to rooting out all forms of blasphemy and heresy.

This endeavor to control people's minds so that they would blindly accept Catholicism and the rule of the monarchy seems to have succeeded to a large extent. Of course totalitarianism is only an ideal-type, and total mind control is never possible in reality. Alvarez (2002: 16) notes that

> [t]here were some "ethnic" components in that identity, since it was referred to as a "people" or "nation" that allegedly had existed for millennia, whose members were all supposed to have the *same religious beliefs and psychological traits* [my emphasis] and whose extraordinary exploits were attributed to their spiritual cohesion.

In other words, the Catholic monarchs succeeded in legitimizing the newly united country of Spain, but to be Spanish one had to have the "correct" beliefs *and* the "correct" ancestry.

Legitimizing Evilness

Previous theorists have pointed out that governments are able to get parts of the population to engage in evil acts when they succeed in defining an outgroup as an existential threat. In the case of Spain this included Jews and Muslims, as well as Jews and Muslims who had converted to Catholicism. Bloxham (2008: 208) adds that systemic actions against groups of people are more likely if they "had previously been the subject of suspicion, stereotype, or persecution." This was obviously the case with Jews (including those who had converted to Catholicism), although it also pertained somewhat to Muslims. This book goes one step further, in showing the link between state-building and evilness. That is, in order to legitimize a new state, rulers often find it useful to use the outgroup(s) as a way of unifying the country and endowing their power with legitimacy.

In the Spanish case, crusading in the name of the "true" religion (Alvarez 2002: 15) and imposing the "correct" belief system became part of the legitimizing strategy. The Church and the Inquisition helped impose the "correct" beliefs on the population as Isabella and Ferdinand legitimized themselves as the defenders of Christianity against the Muslim threat. A few decades later, King Philip II promoted the

> family myth which sacralized his dynasty: the role of the Habsburgs as guardians of the Blessed Sacrament. He also cultivated a royal vision with popular roots, which you can still see embodied on the main façade of his foundation of El Escorial. The kings carved there are not kings of Spain but

of ancient Israel, leading a chosen people through trials of faith, just as Philip tried to do in a life of unremitting and ultimately unrewarding duty. (Fernández-Armesto 2000: 123)

Basing legitimacy on uniting the country around Catholicism necessitated pointing out certain outgroups as the "others," who posed an existential threat to the existence of the new state. Thus, rather than implementing an inclusive strategy, the Catholic monarchs carried out an exclusive strategy based on uniting the country against the Muslim, Jewish and *converso* threats. As discussed in Chap. 3, people are more likely to commit evil acts if a state is able to convince them they face an existential threat. This occurs most often after a national trauma, such defeat in a war. In the case of Spain, this feeling of facing an existential threat greatly increased when Spain had won a war—that is, when it had reconquered all the territories from the Muslim Moors and Isabella and Ferdinand had united the country into a single state.

When attacking Muslim Grenada, the Catholic monarchs could portray the Moors as a threat and justify reconquering the Muslim areas of Spain on the grounds that doing so was part of a holy war—the Crusades—against Islam (Lomax 1978: 61). Linking the *reconquista* to the Crusades gave it ideological legitimacy, while linking the Muslim population to the Ottoman-Turkish threat made it easier to rally the population behind the newly united state. The threat seemed more acute after the fall of Constantinople and the Turkish invasion of Italy (Housley 2002; Meyerson 1995: 64f.). Thus, the Catholic monarchs could question whether their Moorish subjects would really be loyal to the new Spanish state during a war with the Ottoman Empire. As Hess observes, the Spanish regime "charged, in effect, that the Moors in Spain made up a fifth column that aided both the Ottoman advance in North Africa and the Protestant cause in Europe" (Hess 1968: 5–6). Meanwhile, the pope pressured Ferdinand and Isabella to conquer Granada as part of the Crusades against Islam. Thus, the unification of the country was linked to a fight against a perceived existential Muslim threat to the newly united Spanish state. This fear, combined with the strong Catholic ideological commitment of the crown and the belief that Christianity was superior to Islam encouraged Ferdinand and Isabel to ban Islam within the country, and to use Catholicism as a unifying and legitimizing force for their rule as the "Catholic Monarchs" (Pérez 2002: 367–8). Thus, like the Jews, Muslims faced the choice of either converting or leaving the country. Eventually, however, even converted Muslims (*Moriscos*) were expelled.

The expulsion of the Muslims took place in stages. First, from 1502 to 1526, they were forced to convert and became known as *Moriscos* (Pérez 2004: 44ff.). As with the Jews, they had to give up their traditions completely, including their clothing and their use of the Arabic language. Under totalitarianism, giving up one's lifestyle is as important as giving up one's religion. Pérez (2004: 48) concludes that "what opposed the Old Christians and the Moriscos was not religion, but their respective civilisations and lifestyles." Three years after defeating a revolt which had broken out in the Moorish quarter of Granada in 1568, Philip II ordered the expulsion of the *moriscos*. There were some delays, so the official expulsion decree was issued on April 4, 1609 (Kamen 1985: 111).

In other words, throughout history the Inquisition evolved and changed its focus. At first *conversos* were the main enemy, then *moriscos*, Lutherans and other "heretics." In order to gain more complete control over the countryside, moreover, the Inquisition expanded to include the fight against blasphemy and superstition, so that the peasants would become fully indoctrinated. As will be discussed later in this chapter, these repressive acts during the Inquisition not only helped to make the new state totalitarian, they fit this book's definition of "evil."

In conclusion, in order to unite the population behind the new Spanish state, the crown decided that Catholicism would provide a homogenizing ideology for legitimizing the regime and gaining the loyalty of its main subjects. Similar to secular totalitarian regimes that create a political religion in which only the regime has the right to interpret Truth for the population, the Crown, Church and Inquisition in Spain combined in this era to promote a Catholic ideology under which no alternative interpretations, beliefs or lifestyles were allowed. Even the slightest deviation in lifestyle, such as washing one's hands after using the toilet, was enough for somebody to be persecuted. In carrying out these repressive policies, moreover, the crown seems to have gained the support of the population.

In the next section, I will explain in more detail why Spanish monarchs depicted Jews and *conversos* as an existential threat.

THE ROOTS OF RACIAL ANTI-SEMITISM

Since anti-Semitism played such a central role for state formation in general and for the Inquisition in particular, this section will discuss the roots of Spanish anti-Semitism before presenting the actual set-up of the Inquisition, which as an institution originally committed most of its "evil" acts against those of Jewish ancestry. First, as already noted in Chap. 4, Trachtenberg (1943) documents how Jews were portrayed throughout medieval Europe as nonhuman or subhuman. Thomas (2010: 1745) too analyzes how it became increasingly common in medieval Europe to see Jews as a different species. He notes that

> they were seen to be "the possessors of diseased and debased bodies"….
> [having] defective bodies and inferior blood-lines…The Jewish Other was everything unclean and incomplete, while Christians were equated with having a healthy, White body.

If Jews were a different species, then they could not become "true" Christians even if they converted. Yet, Jews still faced pressures to convert to Catholicism. These pressures were especially great during the riots of 1391, which began in Castile when the archdeacon Ferrand Martínez incited the crowds in Seville (Roth 1995: 33). These riots spread throughout the area and took on a popular character (Carrete 1992: 19–20). Friedman (1987: 8) notes that the "widespread anti-Jewish rioting in 1391 led to renewed massacres and often to the forced conversion of many Jews as they learned that death might be avoided through baptism." Nirenberg (2002: 9) notes that thousands or even tens of thousands of Jews were killed. Consequently, a large group of *conversos* emerged, and this group was gaining influence in society. Nirenberg (2002: 11ff.) adds that, with the support of the papal court in Avignon and the crowns of Aragon and Castile, a friar by the name of St. Vincent Ferrer played an important role in a second wave of mass conversions. Between 1412 and 1415, Ferrer he went through the country engaging in mandatory disputations with rabbis, which members of the Jewish community were forced to attend. Pérez (2004: 12) reports that "[b]etween 1391 and 1415 more than half of the Jews in Spain are said to have been baptised, among them many rabbis and figures of note." When rabbis converted, this encouraged more Jews to convert. At the time of the expulsions, only around 100,000 Jews remained.

Second, anti-Semitic outbursts tended to take place when people felt existentially threatened, either by economic crises or by outbreaks of disease. In both cases, Jews and *conversos* made useful scapegoats. One problem for Jews was that, given restrictions on which professions they could undertake, some engaged in unpopular occupations like tax tax-collecting or money-lending (e.g., Gómez 1995). Thomas (2010: 1744) analyzes the predicament that Jews faced: "They were relegated to usury because they were prohibited from other economic spheres. Yet because of this, they were vilified by Christian society." When the Jews were expelled, many of the professions in which they had typically engaged were taken over by *conversos*, since they had knowledge of these fields and Old Christians did not want to do such work (e.g., Díaz-Plaja 1996: 59; Gómez 1995: 38–9). Even though anti-Semitic clergy, such as Bernáldez (a chronicler of the Catholic Monarchs), claimed that "all" *conversos* were merchants or tax collectors or officials, and that "none" of them worked the land, both Jews and *conversos* worked in a variety of professions (Roth 1995: 82). Thus, Roth (ibid.: 83–4) explains that sources from Toledo show that *conversos* there were bakers, tailors, shoemakers, farm owners, soap store workers, and scribes of the city or of the king. Until their expulsion, Jews played an important role in bookbinding and bookselling. Afterward they were replaced by *conversos*. Jews and *conversos* were also disproportionately represented among physicians. Kamen (1985: 21) reports on a survey of 1641 *conversos* in Toledo who were accused by the Inquisition in 1495. It shows that "the majority were in modest occupations, but there were a significant number of jewellers and silversmiths (59), traders (38), taxfarmers (15) and money-changers (12)." Nevertheless, Jews and *conversos* were associated in the popular mind with tax-collecting, and Jews with money-lending. This made them vulnerable to attack when people's livelihoods were threatened.

Pérez (2004: 5) maintains that, until the fourteenth century, the population was relatively tolerant toward those of the Mosaic faith. As long as the economy was growing, both Jews and Christians benefited. Consequently,

> the militant anti-Judaism of the Church and the monks had found few supporters. But the social, economic and political upheavals of the fourteenth century, and the wars and natural catastrophes that preceded and followed the Black Death, created a new situation. They ushered in a phase of recession, hardship and tensions when, for both Christians and Jews, everything changed.

Similarly, MacKay (1977: 186) writes that poor harvests, chronic shortages of grain, the plague and inflation all combined to lead to increased attacks on Jews and *conversos*. From 1400 to 1445 prices were rather stable, but inflation started to increase in 1445 and it became especially high in the 1460s and 1470s. During the crisis of 1469–1473, "the prices of grain and other foodstuffs, especially in Andalusia, reached catastrophic heights. These were the years of endemic urban unrest which led up to the pogroms of 1473." When prices rose so did the price of tax farms, leading to an increase in taxes, which Jews and *conversos* were responsible for collecting.

> The pogrom of 1449 in Toledo, for example, was sparked off by an additional and heavy tax levied by the Crown. The tax-farmer was a *converso*, Alonso Cota, and his house was the first target of the enraged populace. But Cota, like so many other *conversos*, was something more than a mere tax-farmer: he was a merchant and treasurer of the town council—in other words, he was one of a "subversive" group who raised prices and, by controlling municipal government, condoned the unfair distribution of royal taxation as well as profiting from local maladministration. The attempts to exclude *conversos* permanently from office in such towns as Toledo and Córdoba, therefore, were the logical consequences of the "moral" objectives of urban uprisings.

Even though, in the period before the country was unified, kings had usually tried to protect the Jewish population against anti-Semitic mobs, fanatical clergy were increasingly using anti-Semitism as a way to mobilize the population against their rule (e.g., Contreras 1996: 74–5). Pérez (2004: 7) gives the example of Henry of Trastámara. Henry led a rebellion against his half-brother, Peter I, the king of Castile. He accused Peter "of surrounding himself with infidels (Moors and Jews) and favoring them over Christians." Henry's rebels massacred Jews in Toledo in 1355 and, together with French mercenaries, attacked the Jewish quarter in Burgos as well. Taking the Jews prisoner and demanding a large ransom, they announced that those who could not pay it would be sold into slavery. Henry eventually defeated his half-brother and became king.

The most infamous riots against Jews took place in 1391. Pérez (2004: 7) argues these riots were caused by fanatical monks, who riled up the populace against Jews and blamed them for recent inflation and declining living standards.

> The idea that all Jews were money-lenders took a general hold. From there it was but one step to believing that the Jewish usurers were responsible for, and benefited from, the poverty of the Christian people....

Pérez adds (pp. 10–11) that the mass conversions after the riots damaged Spanish Jewry more than the massacres did. Until then, only a small number of wealthy or well-educated Jews had converted. However, from 1391 to 1415 a large number converted—especially because in 1412, Queen Catherine (who was regent of Castile until John II came of age) decided to force the Jews to live in ghettos. She also forced them to dress differently—to have long beards and to wear red discs sewn on to their clothing. In addition, she prohibited Jews from working as "doctors, chemists, drug-sellers, blacksmiths, carpenters, tailors, butchers, cobblers, traders, tax-collectors." In 1415, Aragon also enacted these regulations.

This increase in repression, combined with attacks against Jews, led to an increase in conversions. Friedman (1987: 8) concludes that, "[a]s a result, in the century between 1391 and 1492, New Christians came to exert great influence in Spain's economic, institutional, and cultural life, and played a significant role in the urban *communero* movement" (ibid.).

As Christians, these *conversos* had many new opportunities. Some became public officials, others got involved in commerce. The success of some New Christians led to resentment as well as growing intolerance (e.g., Gómez 1995; Vozmediano 2005). For example, in 1449 the mayor of Toledo, Pero Sarmiento, led an attack against *conversos*. He blamed them for a new tax the crown had imposed upon the inhabitants of the city, although the real reason for his disdain was that some of the local *conversos* had supported his competitor in local power struggles. He tried to use the uprising to threaten the king; thus, the rising anti-Semitism also posed a threat to the royal family, and it led to civil war in Castile (cf. Kamen 1985: 25; MacKay 1977: 187; Pérez 2004: 14; Rawlings 2006: 51ff.; Roth 1995: 89). In order to regain support in the city, King Juan II accepted the local council's decision to prohibit *conversos* from holding office (Roth 1995: 101). Thus, the initiative for the blood laws that later became national policy started at the local level, after which local supporters of restrictions on *conversos* pressured the national rulers into making concessions.

Another example comes from Córdoba, where widespread looting broke out in 1473. Harvests in the area had been poor for several years, leading to food shortages followed by plague epidemics. This led to anger against the wealthy, who were protected from these calamities. The main targets of the looting were *converso* homes (Pérez 2004: 15). The riots spread to Montoro, Adamuz, Bujalance, La Rambla and Santaella. They became so extreme that the Constable of Castile, Miguel Lucas de Iranzo, was murdered in the town of Jaén because he tried to protect the *conversos*. His family fled and hid in a castle to avoid being further terrorized (Roth 1995: 104–5). Friedman (1987: 11) also lists anti-*converso* riots that took place in 1435 in Majorca, in 1473 in Valladolid and in 1474 in Segovia.

However, MacKay (1977: 187) points out, "[t]he monarchy regained the initiative…when it set up the Inquisition in 1478, for the urban populace now witnessed the official persecution of many of those who had previously been the targets of popular insurrection. The inquisition was, in a different sense, a 'popular' institution and Isabella the Catholic was a 'popular' monarch."

Finally, the *conversos* presented an existential threat to the regime, because its legitimacy was also based on blood. In contrast to the situation in France, where many commoners got ennobled, ennoblement was rare in Spain. Spanish aristocrats emphasized their claim to come from the best and most capable families—the families with the best blood—as the basis for their right to rule. However, some wealthy *conversos* were able to marry into aristocratic families, who had the right family names but were lacking in funds. These aristocratic families were happy to gain the wealth of the *conversos*. This represented a great dilemma for the aristocracy, however, as low-status peasants could now claim they had purer blood than the aristocracy. This posed an existential threat to the latter's right to rule.

Kamen (1985: 23) sums up the quandary:

On the one hand the nobility was claiming for itself a privileged position in return for its long services to the crown, and on the other it was being morally undermined by a racial dilution which tended to bring it into contempt. If the nobles were no longer truly Old Christians, then they had no right to true nobility. The dangerous point was obviously approaching at which membership of the nobility was in itself grounds for suspicion of debased blood, and only membership of non-noble classes provided any guarantee against Jewish descent.

Furthermore, Kamen (1985: 115) adds:

By the fifteenth century it was felt by many that the honour of one's faith and nation could be preserved only by ensuring that one's lineage was preserved free of contamination by Jews and Muslims. Yet what if the highest ranks of the nobility had been penetrated by Jewish blood? It was notorious that the principal families of Aragon and Castile, and even the royal family, could trace their descent through conversos. Old Christian Spain would collapse if this process went on. A few zealous souls therefore considered that now was the time to stop the Jewish fifth column. With this we have the beginnings of a new stress on racial purity and the consequent rise of the cult of *limpieza de sangre* (purity of blood).

Thus, as in Nazi Germany, Jewish blood came to be seen as a threat to the social order. Of course, other aspects were also important, such as the fear that the "New Christians" would not be true believers, since their mass conversion had been based on threats and pressure. This in turn threatened the project of unifying the country as a Catholic nation. In addition, the existence of Jewish communities in the country could tempt the *conversos* to go back to their old "evil ways." This labeling of Jews and even *conversos* as an "outgroup" posing an existential threat to the new Catholic state gave the regime the impetus to expel the Jews and to repress the *conversos*. As already noted, even before the Inquisition was instituted, local governments began introducing *limpieza* (pure-blood) rules banning *conversos* from public office and other organizations[1] (cf. Roth 1995: 230); in the 1500s, however, these rules became the official policy of the national regime. Thus, not only did the crown use the Inquisition to homogenize the faith and unite the country around a Catholic ideology (e.g., Povedano 1980: 145f.); it also eventually united the country around the notion of racial purity.

Interestingly, although the blood laws pertained to Spain itself, they did not always apply to its colonies. According to Kamen (1988: 47), the crown continued to allow Jews to live in its African colonies, where they would not corrupt the thoughts of Spaniards in Spain. This shows that the crown differentiated somewhat between the country and its colonies, although it did institute an inquisition in its Latin American colonies and imposed blood laws there as well (Silverblatt 2011).

In summary, the decision to introduce the Inquisition helped unite the country and make it more homogeneous. Through the Inquisition, the crown used Catholicism to legitimize its rule. Even though the decision came from the top, it was not merely a top-down process; it was bottom-up too. Hostility to both Jews and *conversos* was increasing in the country, as many people were suffering periodically from inflation, epidemics and lack of food. Local clergy and nobles used these ill feelings to start riots and to demand the exclusion of people with Jewish blood from society. In a period of political instability and civil war, rebel leaders used anti-Semitism to threaten the rulers. When Isabella and Ferdinand united the country, therefore, they could use the Inquisition to coopt these forces, bring stability to the country and gain acceptance for their rule. Next this chapter discusses the establishment of the Inquisition, which as an institution led to the "evil" persecution of many innocent people, who were forced to confess to crimes that they often did not commit; and even in those cases where they really did commit "crimes," an open society would not consider their acts to have been crimes at all.

SETTING UP THE INQUISITION

In 1475, the friar Alonso de Hojeda, prior of the Dominicans of Seville, reported to the queen that many *conversos* had become Christians only to get access to public offices; in private, however, they still practiced Judaism, circumcised their sons and celebrated Jewish holidays (Kamen 1985: 29; Pérez 2004: 19). In 1477–1478, the monarchs visited Extremadura and Andalusia to get a first-hand view of the situation. The queen was not convinced that action was needed. Her confessor, Friar Hernando de Talavera, took the same view, as did the archbishop of Seville, Cardinal Mendoza. Ferdinand, however, became convinced of the need for action. Consequently, Ferdinand and Isabella asked Pope Sixtus IV to authorize them to appoint inquisitors. In response, the pope issued a Bull in 1478, and the Spanish Inquisition began its activities two years later (Kamen 1985: 30; see also Díez 1997; Hossain 2007: 1281)

The crown was able to gain a high degree of control over the Inquisition because the king nominated the grand inquisitor, although the pope confirmed his choice (Gómez 1995: 43). Lynn (2013: 18) observes that this format "…mirrored the privilege of appointment of bishops and archbishops that Spanish kings had likewise acquired from the papacy." Thus, the monarchy had great influence over the Catholic Church in Spain, although the Inquisition did manage to gain some autonomy from the crown, as it sometimes prosecuted people whom the kings wanted to protect. For example, in 1559 King Philip II eventually yielded to the Church and handed over his personal confessor, de Carranza, to the Inquisition after the pope had threatened the king with excommunication (Atkinson 1934: 104). Sometimes tensions arose when a pope tried to stop excesses on the part of the Inquisition. By the eighteenth century, the Inquisition had gained great autonomy from the monarchy, although the crown struggled to regain control over it and finally reached an accommodation with it (Marín 1997: 234–5).

Concerning squabbles between the papacy and the crown, Kamen (1985: 34–5) notes that Pope Sixtus IV claimed the Inquisition was motivated by lust for wealth, as it confiscated the possessions of the accused. The proceeds went to the crown, which returned much of it to the Inquisition to finance its costs. He claimed that many true Christians had been punished based on false testimony without real proof. Therefore, the pope ordered a suspension of the Inquisition in 1482, but in May of that year, Ferdinand wrote to the pope complaining that this amounted to a general pardon and in October, the pope gave in and allowed the Inquisition to continue. Nevertheless, throughout the next 50 years popes often tried to intervene on behalf of unfairly condemned *conversos*.

Another example is the battle over naming the grand inquisitor. Although the crown managed to secure this privilege, in 1522 the newly elected pope, Adrian VI, claimed that the privilege of nominating the grand inquisitor has been granted to Ferdinand personally. Thus, now that Ferdinand no longer lived, the right reverted to the pope. Charles V refused to give up this privilege, and the pope gave in. However, this does not mean the king had total power over the Inquisition. Even though the king nominated the grand inquisitor, he could not fire him, although he could marginalize him or pressure him to resign. Pérez (2004: 103) observes that Alonso Manrique was the only grand inquisitor whom a king ever marginalized, but there were five cases of forced resignation. Thus, despite tensions with popes and inquisitors, the kings were able to use the Inquisition as a way to increase their power over the local and international Church (Benassar et al. 1981: 322–3). As a result, society identified the Inquisition as representing state power (Carrete 1992: 328).

Although *conversos* were the main target at first, the Inquisition fought all forms of alleged heresy. Once it had thoroughly repressed the *conversos*, it moved on to other targets: former Muslims who had converted, Lutherans, followers of Erasmus and so on. It also expanded its efforts to wipe out "superstition" and improper Catholic practices in the countryside, where the population was less schooled in Catholic ideology. Another focus was on censoring and prohibiting texts it found to be "heretical." Kamen (1985: 62) sees the shift toward fighting Lutheranism as leading to greater repression of intellectual freedom. He notes that Philip II was so concerned about the possibility of bad "foreign" (i.e., Lutheran) influences on Spaniards that, in 1559, he ordered all Castilians studying abroad to return to Spain (Kamen 1997: 81).

Manning (2009) describes the development of censorship during the Inquisition. In 1502, Fernando and Isabel demanded that licenses be secured both for books printed in Castile and for imported ones. "The law designated particular Archbishops and certain presidents of the Chancellerías (High Courts) as censors" (p. 21). Books were not so widespread back then, so the crown did not pay much attention to the issue until Protestant influence began to grow. Therefore, in 1558, the monarchy issued more detailed requirements for printers to seek licenses from the Council of Castile and from local bishops. It also restricted the import of books into Castile, and "mandated that booksellers keep a copy of the Index of Prohibited Books." Then Inquisition officials began patrolling ports to prevent the import of banned books, and they helped compile the Index of Prohibited Books (p. 22).

To get around the censorship, people distributed handwritten copies among a small circle of readers. So, it was a bit similar to the *samizdat* form spreading unapproved literature in the Soviet Union. Nevertheless, some unpublished manuscripts too made their way into the Index of Prohibited Books (p. 26). By 1540, the Inquisition had started patrolling book vendors to ensure they did not sell any prohibited books (p. 55). The main work in this regard was carried out by *familiares* (lay servants of the Holy Office who could bear arms to protect the inquisitors). Kamen (1985: 88) gives the example of Seville, where in 1566 the local inquisitor ordered a thorough check on booksellers. At a certain hour *familiares* occupied all the bookshops in the city, so that the sellers had no chance to warn each other or to hide any books.

By 1629, the Inquisition had greatly intensified its oversight of booksellers. New regulations threatened excommunication and a fine of 20 ducats. Booksellers had to keep lists of all their texts, to be presented to the Inquisition for inspection (Manning 2009: 63). Similar to the authorities in Nazi Germany, the Inquisition engaged in book burnings. For example, in the fifteenth century it burned books several times from the library of the University of Salamanca, and in the sixteenth century it burnt heretical books by such authors as Erasmus. However, not all confiscated books were thrown on to the pyre (pp. 86–7).

The main form of control was fear. Authors learned to avoid punishment through self-censorship (Manning 2009: 109). However, even though the Inquisition exercised "a great deal of control over the general populace, vehement disagreements over matters of doctrine among the

educated elites were quite common during the period" (p. 111). The idea
was that members of the elite could carry on disputes in Latin as long as
their ideas are not heard on the street (p. 112). In conclusion, it seems the
Inquisition had totalitarian aspirations for censoring literature, but it
lacked the resources to do as it would have liked. Moreover, while the
Inquisition deemed it important to stop the spread of "heretical" ideas, it
did allow for some discussion within the elite. This corresponds somewhat
to Lenin's later idea of "democratic centralism," according to which members of the ruling elite could debate among themselves, but none could
call a doctrinal position into question once it had been decided upon.

It should also be noted that, even if some discussion was allowed among
members of the elite, they still had to be on their guard. Kamen (1985:
69–70) gives many examples of their being persecuted. For example,
Mateo Pascual, who had been professor at the University of Alcalá, was
accused of doubting the doctrine of purgatory in 1530. The Inquisition
found him guilty and confiscated all his goods, sending him to exile in
Rome where he spent the rest of his life. Another example is Pedro de
Lerma, who had been chancellor of the University of Alcalá and was canon
of the Burgos cathedral. Because he publicized some of Erasmus' sermons,
the Inquisition imprisoned him in 1537. For his punishment, he had to
abjure his ideas publicly in the towns where he had preached. Then he
moved to Paris and resumed a position he had held earlier—that of dean
of the theology faculty at the Sorbonne. The fact that he was allowed to
work in France once again shows that that country was less totalitarian
than Spain. After the prosecution of de Lerma, people in Burgos became
so afraid that they immediately recalled sons of theirs who were studying
abroad. The atmosphere was so tense that, in December 1533, even the
son of the grand inquisitor wrote in a private letter to a friend in Paris that
one could not possess any culture in Spain without being suspected of
heresy. The Inquisition even wanted to ban the study of Greek at the
University of Alcalá (pp. 71–2). As noted in Chap. 2, some observers
claimed that priests were even afraid to preach, because they might say
something to incur the wrath of the Inquisition.

Kamen (1985: 45) describes the atmosphere of terror. He cites the
Jesuit monk, Juan de Mariana, who wrote in the sixteenth century that
even though the Inquisition had become popular, it had seemed very
oppressive to Spaniards at first, because children were being punished for
their parents' crimes. Furthermore, people could not talk freely because
there were informants in all of the cities, towns and villages.

And what was most serious was that because of these secret investigations they were deprived of the liberty to listen and talk freely, since in all the cities, towns and villages there were persons placed to give information of what went on. This was considered by some to be the most wretched slavery and equal to death.

Of course, the greatest fear in a society based on fear was to be brought before the Inquisition. As noted in Chap. 2, the Spanish Inquisition was very theatrical. On a Sunday, inquisitors would arrive in a town or village and read an "edict of faith" after the mass. All of the area's inhabitants had to attend, and to swear an oath of allegiance to the Holy Inquisition. They were then asked to admit their own sins and to denounce their family, friends and neighbors. There was a 30–40-day grace period during which one could confess without being penalized. Those who had been denounced and had not admitted their ill deeds voluntarily before the end of the grace period were brought before the Inquisition.

The demand that one denounce one's family was so great that one could be punished for not having denounced one's parents several decades beforehand when one was still a child. Haliczer (1990: 216) describes the case of a Valencian draper, who was condemned to be burnt at the stake because 35 to 40 years earlier, when he was between 12 and 15 years old and living with his parents, his family had celebrated some Jewish holidays. He did not even seem to know that these were Jewish practices. He realized one of them was Jewish when the inquisitor asked him if he had ever observed a fast in honor of Queen Esther. The fact that he had not engaged in any Jewish practices as an adult did not matter. He had failed to mention these celebrations when he had made his confessions during the period of grace when inquisitors had visited his town in 1491. Consequently, he was condemned 27 years later, in 1518, for not having confessed completely. It is typical of totalitarian regimes that one is supposed to place the state above one's own family and to be willing to denounce one's own parents. Yet, even for totalitarian regimes it is unusual to punish people for not having denounced their parents several decades earlier.

While local inquisitors were responsible to the grand inquisitor, the grand inquisitor in turn was officially overseen by the *Suprema*. This Council had four councilors (six by the end of the sixteenth century), as well as one secretary for Castile and another for Aragon (Pérez 2004: 108). The grand inquisitor recommended three candidates for each position, and then the king chose between them. The *Suprema* did not have clearly defined areas of competence, and its role expanded in periods when the grand inquisitor was absorbed in other functions, as when Cisneros, on two separate occasions, was required to govern Castile, as regent, or when the grand inquisitor had lost the confidence of the sovereign, as happened to Manrique from 1529 to 1538. In his *Grand Memorandum* of 1624, Olivares, who was well versed in the institutions of the monarch, represents the *Suprema* as essentially required to examine appeals against judgements given by provincial courts. (Pérez 2004: 109)

Pérez (2004: 112ff.) notes that there were normally two inquisitors for each court, aided by two secretaries, a public prosecutor (*fiscal*), a police officer (*alguacil*), a receiver, a nuncio, a porter, a magistrate who was responsible for administering confiscated property, and a physician for making sure victims survived their torture. The pope wanted the inquisitors to be bishops or priests who were at least 40 years old. In spite of this, the first grand inquisitor, Torquemada, changed the rules so that one only needed to be a university graduate. Even though most inquisitors did not belong to a holy order, they had to be celibate. If they got married, they had to resign their post. In 1595, Philip II ruled that all future inquisitors and procurators had to be ordained; however, Philip III did not specify this in his instructions from 1608. As a result, it was not until 1632 that the *Suprema* ruled that anyone not ordained had to resign. Of 45 grand inquisitors, 6 were Dominicans, 1 was a Franciscan, and the rest were secular clergy (i.e., they were priests for an area, not monks or members of an order). Most of the lower inquisitors were jurists who specialized in canon law. Pérez (2004: 119) notes that inquisitors got advice from theologians such as Dominican, Franciscan and Jesuit monks.

As Nalle (1987: 559) remarks, the personnel of the local tribunals were too few in number to generate the type of presence in the countryside that was necessary if the Inquisition was to promote the Tridentine reforms among the entire population. These reforms comprised measures demanded by the Vatican for fighting Lutheranism.

For this reason, during the 1550s, the *Suprema* took measures to create effective networks of non-salaried officials who would extend the Inquisition's presence into the countryside on a permanent basis. These officials were the familiars, *comisiarios, notarios,* and *alguaciles,* all of whom had been known to the pre-Valdesian Inquisition. Under [General Inquisitor] Valdes, however, the Inquisition carefully began to recruit, place, and control these officials so that they could be reliably used as aids to the inquisitors. The most important of these officials were the comisarios and the familiars.

When the Inquisition changed its focus from repressing *conversos* to fighting blasphemy, the general level of repression in society increased, in that even the most ignorant peasants now had reason to fear persecution. Flynn (1995: 32) gives many examples, such as that of an adolescent boy from Naples in 1526, who had come to work as a servant in Toledo. He was surprised at being arrested for having uttered a profanity when he was angered. He noted that it was common back in Italy for people to make such statements when they felt frustrated, but there was little tolerance in Spain for such things. This contradicts Kamen's (1985: 99) claim that, despite the repression of the Inquisition, political debate in Spain was among the freest in Europe at the time. Perhaps political discussions that did not include any mention of religion or theology were relatively open, but in those days religion played a role in most political discussions. In any case, Flynn (1995: 32–3) claims that blasphemy was the number-one cause for punishment by the Inquisition. Such cases outnumbered prosecutions for Judaizing, Lutheranism, Illuminism, sexual immorality or witchcraft. Flynn cites one study showing that, in Toledo in the sixteenth century, half of all trials "concerned errors of language or palabras against the faith." Another study she cites shows that, in Toledo between 1531 and 1565, only ten cases dealt with heresy, compared to 161 which dealt with blasphemy and profanity (p. 33 fn). Several authors have pointed out that people often uttered blasphemous words while drunk, or in a fit of anger at losing money in gambling (e.g., Edwards 1988: 14; Flynn 1995), or the like—again indicating that the society of the time was quite totalitarian, because all it took for one's life to be destroyed forever was to lose one's temper a single time.

Consequently, the Inquisition increased its ability to control all of society, and not just the areas on which it was concentrating at any particular moment. Nalle (1987: 559) claims the *comisarios* were the most important of the non-salaried officials. They were responsible for taking denunciations and sending them to the inquisitional tribunal. They also collected testimony from denouncers and prepared most of the evidence for the judges. Meanwhile, the *familiares* assisted the inquisitors by delivering messages and capturing prisoners (ibid.). They became a supplementary police force, tasked with keeping the population under surveillance, encouraging denunciations and helping to arrest heretics (Pérez 2004: 121). They bore arms in order to protect the inquisitors (Kamen 1985: 143).

As noted in Chap. 2, the Inquisition culminated in local areas in the *auto de fé*—a mass public spectacle which the entire local population was obliged to witness. The condemned were paraded around in special clothing, and unrepentant heretics were then given over to secular guards to be burnt alive later that day. These events offered the kind of salvation central not only to Catholicism, but to totalitarian political religions as well (Flynn 1991). In Spain it was a question of a politicized religion, where the monarchy used religion as a way to legitimize its rule and thereby gain totalitarian control over society.

DOING EVIL FOR THE INQUISITION

So far, this chapter has argued that Spain during the first century or so of the Inquisition had become totalitarian, in large part due to the state-building process that was taking place in the country as the Catholic monarchs sought to unite the country behind one religion and one homogenized culture. In its efforts to develop a politicized religious regime that would legitimize its rule over the newly created state, the Spanish crown used the Inquisition as a tool for taking control. Its expulsion of large groups of people because of their religious-ethnic background amounted to an "evil" act, as did its attempt to wipe out all cultural traits among converts from Islam and Judaism, as well as its persecution of many who did not even commit the "crimes" with which they were charged.

As defined in Chap. 1, evil acts are "deliberate harm inflicted against a defenseless and helpless group targeted by a political, social, or religious authority..." (Waller 2007: 14). Jews, Muslims and people of Jewish and Muslim ancestry constituted defenseless groups, who were obviously harmed by the crown's actions. Even "Old Catholics" suffered, as they were often charged unfairly and forced—by means of long imprisonment, torture, or the threat of torture—to confess to "crimes" they had not committed. Previous theorists have linked the commission of state-sponsored evil acts to the ability of leaders to convince the population that the "outgroup" presents an existential threat.

This book contributes to the discourse by showing that *leaders of a newly created state have a greater incentive to create the feeling that such a threat exists, as it helps them consolidate their power and unite the country.* Thus, this book links evilness to the issue of legitimacy, as well as arguing that people are more likely to commit evil acts if they consider them to be legitimate. Regimes in newly created states have a special incentive to focus on persecuting an outgroup, because doing so helps them to legiti-mize their rule and to unite the population. It has to do with the needs of state-building: having an enemy makes it easier to unite the population. Creating a new state or country also brings up the question of who belongs. By contrast, an already existing state does not face so much pres-sure to decide that issue, since it already has legitimacy developed over the centuries.

This section will first argue that the acts were indeed "evil." Then it will claim that, in contrast to its counterpart in France, the Inquisition in Spain enjoyed a high level of popular support. However, not everyone who commits an evil act under a totalitarian regime does so just for reasons of ideology. Some might do so sooner for personal gain. Nevertheless, as theorists of political religion argue, the creation of a political religion (or politicized religion) to support the regime legitimizes such acts and makes it easier for people to commit them, even when they do not fully believe in the ideology.

Evil Acts

Just the expulsion of large groups of people because of their religious beliefs or ethnic background may be considered evil. Pérez (2004: 50) estimates that around 300,000 *Moriscos*—slightly less than 5 percent of the total population—were deported. Over 120,000 in the Valencia region were expelled, as were more than 60,000 in Aragon. Fernández-Armesto (2000: 133) puts the overall number of *Moriscos* expelled at a slightly less than 275,000—a bit lower, but still a rather similar total. As noted above, there were around 100,000 Jews in the country when the Inquisition started, and they had to leave. Therefore, combining the number of Jews and the number of *Moriscos*, we find that around 400,000 people were forced out of the country.

There are various estimates as to how many of the people who con-verted and stayed in the country were persecuted. For example, Pérez (2004: 34) reports that, between 1450 and 1500, over 2000 Judaizers were killed by the Inquisition. He also notes (p. 151) that, according to the chronicler Bernáldez, approximately 5000 people were sentenced to life imprisonment in the year 1488 (or thereabouts). Nonetheless, due to a lack of space they were set free after four years. He further notes (p. 173) that Jaime Contreras and Gustav Henningsen calculated that the Inquisition arrested 49,092 people between 1540 and 1700. Around

125,000 trials took place in that period. However, Llorente concludes that three times as many people were arrested. The most common reasons for trying a person were unseemly talk and blasphemy (27 percent of all charged), Judaism (10 percent), Lutheranism (8 percent) and superstition (including witchcraft) (8 percent). Contreras and Henningsen estimate that the death penalty was imposed in 3.5 percent of all cases in this period, but that only 1.8 percent of the condemned persons were actually executed, with the rest being burnt in effigy. "So it is reasonable to suppose that, in the course of its history, the Inquisition was responsible for fewer than 10,000 death sentences followed by execution." Meanwhile, Kamen (1985: 32) writes, during the first eight years of the Inquisition in Seville, over 700 people were burnt at the stake and over 5000 were punished in other ways. In comparison, even if the inquisition in France hurt many people, it did not involve harm on such a large scale. It did not focus on ethnic groups either, but rather on members of a sect that had broken away from Catholicism.

The manner in which accused persons were tried can also be considered evil, as the purpose was not to find out the truth; on the contrary, the starting point was that the Church is always correct, so the accused must be coerced into confessing. In this sense, the Inquisition had a philosophy similar to that of the communist secret police, which took as its starting point that the Party can never be wrong.

Pérez (2004: 145) describes how the Inquisition operated to get the results it wanted. First, when accused persons were brought before the judges, they were questioned about their background; then they were "tested to see if [they] knew the principal prayers of Catholicism and the catechism, and [they were] required to say where and when and to whom [they had] last made [their] confession." In terms of domination and mind control, this was more totalitarian than the Nazis or the Communist regimes in the Stalinist era, as one had to prove that one really believed in the ideology and had memorized certain texts. In conclusion, Pérez writes, since the detainee was presumed to be guilty, the whole procedure was geared toward getting them to confess: "[I]t was essential that the accused acknowledge his guilt and that he do so publicly, just as he was expected to express his repentance in public: this was one of the purposes of an auto da fé." Also, as noted in Chap. 2, the same procedure was used in the Soviet Union: suspects were not even told what the charges were, so they had to guess exactly what crime they were supposed to have committed.

The accused people had the right to a lawyer, but their attorney could not be alone with them—an inquisitor always had to be present. Only very rarely, moreover, were accused persons allowed to choose their lawyers. Furthermore, the task of lawyers was not to defend accused persons but rather to persuade them to confess (p. 146). Finally, the inquisitors never wanted to acquit anyone "unless there really was no way of avoiding this….The single objective of the whole procedure and instruction of the trial was to persuade the accused to recognise his guilt" (p. 148). In the worst case,

> [i]f a conviction really seemed too hard to justify, the court declared an adjournment (*suspensión*), which made it possible to reopen the case at any time….a verdict should never state that the accused was innocent; it was better simply to say that nothing had been proven against him, thereby leaving open the possibility of bringing new charges if new facts came to light. Even when an adjournment was declared, it was accompanied by a minor penalty, for example an official warning. Why such severity? Because it was essential that the Holy Office was never seen to be in the wrong. Above all, no one should ever be able to claim that it had wronged the innocent. (p. 149)

These procedures are reminiscent of the Communist regimes in the Stalin era, in which the starting point was that the Communist Party can *never* be wrong. Even if one is innocent, then, one should confess one's guilt in order to support the system. In contrast to the case under the Communist regimes, though, it was essential in Spain to prove that one truly believed in the ideology, even if one admitted to having committed what Orwell would have called "thought crimes." If one confessed *and repented*, then one could avoid being burnt alive at the stake. Even if one refused to repent at the trial, one could still avoid the worst fate by repenting at a later stage. (That is, the executioner would behead the condemned person before tying him or her to the stake, thereby sparing the latter the enormous pain of being burnt alive.) Neither the Nazi regime nor the Communist ones demanded that their victims prove they believed in the ideology before being executed.

Along these lines, Roth (1995: 217) observes that almost all of the charges against *conversos* for following Jewish customs were the ones that the Inquisition's manuals described. This resembles the pattern of Stalin's secret police, the victims of which had to figure out exactly what "crimes" they were to confess to having committed. "Never do we find, in fact, charges of observing less hazardous and less public religious practices which are not mentioned in the manuals but were no less important in Jewish life." In addition, the accusations were usually about incidents that had allegedly taken place many years or even decades before the Inquisition opened the case. Furthermore, there was rarely more than one witness to the alleged crime. Some *conversos* were even charged with building a sukkah, even though the whole town would have seen it had they done so. Such an accusation was highly illogical, since "by the late 1480s, condemned 'heretics' were being burned in large numbers all over Castile. Surely only an insane person could have imagined that it would be possible to practice openly and in public such notorious Jewish religious customs."

Since the Inquisition was not about finding out the truth, its victims had to develop strategies for confessing in the "correct" manner rather than simply telling the truth. Gitlitz's (2000: 56) study of such confessions explains the strategies that accused persons applied. First, "the confession had to appear comprehensive and complete, for obvious gaps invited the Inquisitors to use torture to elicit a fuller confession." Second, the victim had to focus the confession strategically so as to highlight virtuous acts, "admitting to just enough sin so as to leave Inquisitors satisfied with the results of their inquiry and without whetting their appetites for more, and omitting incriminating details without seeming to do so." Third, the accused should try to shift responsibility as much as possible to other people, "either to someone they did not care about very much, or to loved ones who were already safely dead or emigrated."

Gitlitz (2000: 59) describes the terror the population felt because of the Inquisition:

> The mere presence of the Inquisition, and the very real possibility that one might be called to account completely for the particulars of one's life, made every living soul a potential autobiographer. From 1480 through the next two hundred or so years, Spaniards, and particularly Spanish conversos, who were suspect by nature of their lineage, had to keep a mental notebook of everything they had done, and when, and with whom; they had to keep a mental log of the events they had witnessed, and what they might mean; of the conversations—first hand, second hand, third hand—to which they had been party. Moreover, it was imperative to keep running mental track of the implications of all of these events for their own life, and be attentive to how others might interpret their actions or their spiritual development.

Consequently, similar to people living under the communist-led regimes, Spaniards under the Inquisition had to lead double lives. In Gitlitz's (2000: 59–60) words:

> Mentally, then, people kept at least two sets of books: the book of their life as they perceived it, and as they hoped the all-seeing divine judge would view it, and the book of their life as they hoped the temporal judges might read it, the temporal judges being the neighbors and servants, the business acquaintances and clergy—those people whom Ferlinghetti called the 'priests and other patrolmen'—who might at any moment narrate their life to the Inquisition.

Of course, this does not mean all converts believed wholeheartedly in Catholic theology. If hundreds of thousands of people are pressured to give up their religion and lifestyles and to convert to a different religion and take up different lifestyles, one cannot expect that each and every one of them will really believe completely in the new religion; some might well have converted in order to avoid deportation. Views vary widely on how often converts secretly maintained their previous beliefs. For example, Friedman (1987: 13f.) claims that most Jewish converts to Catholicism were sincere about their conversion. Similarly, Roth (1995: 114) states that Christian sources show that the "overwhelming majority" of conversions were genuine. Netanyahu (1995) argues that almost all *conversos* became true believers. In contrast, others have claimed that relatively large numbers of *conversos* did in fact continue to harbor Jewish beliefs secretly (e.g., Comella 1998: 54ff.; Gómez 1995; Krow-Lucal 1997; Pérez 2004). It is likely that at least *some* of those charged with heresy or blasphemy really had committed the acts of which they were accused. The point, however, is that the Inquisition was not set up to evaluate the evidence for or against a suspect honestly; rather, it was set up to terrorize Spaniards into accepting Catholic ideology submissively, and to show them that the regime-Church is always right.

Reasons for Committing Evil Acts

Scholars of the Inquisition all seem to agree that the Inquisition in Spain eventually enjoyed great popularity. So the question is: why would people be willing to denounce, arrest and torture the innocent? The answer probably lies in a combination of two factors: (a) belief in the legitimacy of the regime, and (b) incentives of a personal and egoistic kind. As theorists of political religions/politicized religions have pointed out, totalitarian regimes use ideology to justify their acts. In addition, as theorists of evil have pointed out, people are more likely to commit evil acts if the regime can find outgroups it can label as presenting an existential threat. Many perpetrators carry out their acts because they truly believe in the ideology and think they are doing good deeds. However, it is not necessary for all perpetrators to believe in the ideology: for some of them, it may be enough that they think they can gain something from their acts. The ideology may simply offer them convenient justification for their selfishly motivated acts.

Of course, it is difficult to ascertain exactly how much individual perpetrators believed in the ideology; nevertheless, scholars are in agreement that the Inquisition was genuinely popular (e.g., Díaz-Plaja 1996). Thus, the perpetrators could destroy the lives of *conversos*, and later of converts from Islam and other groups charged with thought crimes, because they knew they had the support of much of society. Even the evil act of torture was unproblematic, as it was a common practice in medieval times; indeed, the torture used in the ordinary justice system in Spain was probably worse than that used in the Inquisition (Benassar et al. 1981: 96ff.).

Consequently, Pérez (2004: 158) remarks, by the mid-sixteenth century accounts of *autos da fé* "became so popular that booksellers would provide special catalogues of them for their clients." The account of the *auto da fé* in Logrono in 1610 was in such high demand that it was reprinted up until the beginning of the nineteenth century! Painters began publicizing the *autos da fé* as well. For example, a painting of it by Pedro Berruguete can be seen at the Prado Museum (p. 159).

Similarly, Kamen (1985: 59) concludes that by 1533

[n]ot only did the existence of the Inquisition become almost wholly unquestioned, but toleration of its attendant abuses became more widespread and pronounced. As papal and royal favour confirmed it in its position as one of the key institutions of the realm, it grew to overwhelm all opposition and criticism.

The spectacle of the *auto de fé* was also popular in mobilizing support for the regime and the Inquisition: large audiences filled the largest square of the town in question, with visitors from outlying districts attending as well (Kamen 1985: 190).

This is not to deny that some people protested against the excesses of the Inquisition. For example, Rawlings (2006: 61) notes that, in the 1530s in Monzón,

> deputies protested that inquisitors were taking the definition of heresy beyond its natural limits. Repeated complaints of unfair practice were raised over the course of the first half of the sixteenth century in both kingdoms, but to no avail. The Inquisition, despite its opponents, was fast becoming a vital institution, protected by both the Crown and the papacy, and tacitly supported by the vast majority of the Old Christian community whose values it reinforced.

Moreover, those protests that did take place generally occurred in the first years of the Inquisition, before society had gotten used to the institution. In addition, when towns opposed the Inquisition, it was usually because of *converso* influence. For example, in Teruel in October 1484, the magistrates refused to give the inquisitors permission to enter the city. The inquisitors then went to the neighboring town of Cella, where they declared the magistrates of Teruel to be excommunicated. However, the clergy of Teruel obtained papal letters relieving the city of the excommunication. King Ferdinand responded to this in February 1485 by ordering his officials in Aragon to help the inquisitors militarily; but they did not raise enough support, so Ferdinand called in troops from Castile, who were able to subdue the city. According to Kamen (1985: 38), "[t]he reasons for Teruel's resistance seem to have lain almost exclusively in the great influence exercised there by conversos..."

This contrasts greatly with the situation in France, where the inquisition met great opposition and even led to wars that continued for decades. In Spain, by contrast, people in the towns and villages usually did not sympathize with condemned persons (unless the local leaders happened to be *conversos*, who had good egoistic reasons for fearing the Inquisition). Moreover, while some Spanish nobles were critical of the Inquisition for disrupting the economy, they did not support condemned persons in the way their French counterparts did. The Inquisition in France sharply divided the country; in Spain it helped unite it.

Even when carrying out the most brutal tortures, perpetrators could have a clear conscience, since their actions were legitimized by the regime's ideology. Silverblatt (2011: 135–6) describes the logic as follows:

State abstractions seem to remove these acts from the realm of accountability, and they do so by dismembering humanness; abuse is splintered into columns of an account ledger, torture is fragmented into events and responses, horror is objectified into smaller and smaller components, and then acts are legitimized by following the rules….Torture, then, was party to both state control over violence and to state control over ruthfulness. The history of modernity, in its institutional origins and pretensions to global dominance, reveals how bureaucratic language and practice could write away the horrors of torture, could legitimize torture, make it civil, and even make it necessary for civilization.

Thus, although the Inquisition began in the late medieval period, Silverblatt sees it as a step that helped usher in modernity.

Even though there were ideological reasons for supporting the Inquisition—as one could see it as an important institution that was unifying the country and preventing subversive behavior which threatened the moral fabric of society—personal and egoistic motives certainly also played a role to some extent. On the ideological side, Lynn (2013: 11) notes, inquisitors were motivated by "the accumulation of practical experience, religious belief, and the hope of salvation." On the practical side, however, they were often motivated by a desire to advance in the Church hierarchy and to become bishops (p. 4).

Familiares and notaries—who played the most important role in gathering evidence and in organizing local inquisitions—had little economic incentive to take part, as they were not paid for their endeavors. However, they were exempted from taxes and from communal obligations (Bethencourt 1995: 165). They also gained socially, since their task was a prestigious one; moreover, it offered protection from prosecution (e.g., Comella 1998: 133). They could also use their position to prove they had "purity of blood," enabling them to marry people of higher social status (Ortiz 2010: 150). Pérez (2004: 122) too argues that familiars often saw their position as a way to advance socially. He notes that familiars in Aragon came mostly from the popular or middle strata, and could use their position to climb the social ladder.

Not everyone was motivated by a desire to advance, as some already held high positions in society. For example, Pérez (ibid.) reports that, in Valencia, the percentage of aristocrats, ecclesiastics and rich wholesalers among familiars was 5.6 percent, 2.5 percent and 6.5 percent. Nevertheless, the largest group comprised those who might want to use their position as a familiar to advance socially: 44.2 percent were laborers (well-to-do peasants who labored on the land) and 31 percent were artisans. Similarly, *comissarios* were not highly paid, and they did not receive a fixed salary; instead they received certain jurisdictional privileges, such as a different legal status and preferential places in churches and public areas (Cruz 1997: 159–66). The fact that they saw such value in having a preferential place in churches shows how important it was for their social prestige to be seen as good Catholics.

Secretaries were paid a salary, but it was quite low. This led to some corruption, as secretaries tried to pad their income by charging the Inquisitional authorities for tasks they did not carry out (Torquemada 1997: 67–75).

Thus, the main motivating factors for perpetrators committing evil acts for the Inquisition seem to have been a combination of two things: ideological belief in a legitimized action, together with social prestige.

An additional incentive in this totalitarian society based on fear lay in the immunity that one gained from prosecution by the Inquisition (Cruz 2000). As Pérez (2004) explains, the Holy Office considered it to be in its best interests to cover up even the most reprehensible acts committed by its officials. It usually gave such culprits no more than a few words of blame and remonstrance, because it feared any public scandals would hurt its reputation.

As noted in Chap. 2, almost all denunciations came from neighbors rather than from Inquisition officials. It is hard to know the motives for such denunciations. Surely some reflected adherence to Catholic ideology, as well as a belief that those guilty of heresy or blasphemy were a threat to society. Neighbors could also have personal-egoistic reasons for denouncing somebody, such as a desire for revenge, an interest in removing an economic or political competitor and so on. As already noted, in a totalitarian system it is not necessary that everyone believe in the system completely. However, the system legitimizes evil acts committed in compliance with it, even if those who commit such acts do so for alternative reasons. The result, in any case, is that all lived in fear of their neighbors. When the Inquisition came to their area, they had to consider who their enemies were, and whether anyone would denounce them. In fact, it was more beneficial to confess immediately to ideological "crimes" that one did not actually commit (thereby only having to do penance) rather than to risk one's life and the confiscation of one's goods because of the false accusations of a neighbor. Rawlings (2006: 30) summarizes the situation:

The fear of being exposed to public scrutiny by their neighbours (rather than fear of the Inquisition *per se*) prompted many false confessions of guilt. The collaboration of ordinary people was thus fundamental to the Inquisition's work on the ground and particularly so in areas where social discord was rife.

In other words, in a situation where the entire population had an incentive to commit evil acts and to persecute the innocent, the innocent had an incentive to lie—to claim they had committed "thought crimes" even when they never had.

CONCLUSION

In contrast to its counterpart in France, the Inquisition in Spain helped set the country on a totalitarian path of development. By the standards of the time, France was already an established country, so the inquisition there was not part of any state-building strategy. To be sure, the country was generally expanding, but that is not the same as creating a new state or country. In contrast, when Isabel and Ferdinand got married, their marriage united the kingdoms of Castile and Aragon, creating a new country. When they succeeded a few years later in defeating the last Moorish enclave in Spain (in Granada), Spain became one country. They decided that the best way to hold it together was by homogenizing society around one religion. They called themselves the "Catholic monarchs," and legitimized their power on the basis of their victory over the Moors. They also used this victory to demand that the pope give them control over the Inquisition, so that it would be national and not papal. At various times in history, Spanish monarchs also had colonies in Latin America and Africa, as well as controlling the Netherlands, Portugal and parts of Italy: but these were not considered part of Spain proper, so the policies pursued there fall outside the scope of this study.

The policies in question—to introduce the Inquisition and to expel the Jews—were not merely top-down. They gained resonance easily because anti-Semitism had a long tradition in the country, and it was gaining in popularity besides. Moreover, since large numbers of Jews had been pressured into converting, local clergy and noblemen riled up the population against these *conversos*, whom they claimed were secretly keeping their Jewish customs and whom they claimed were posing a threat toward society. Riots started breaking out against the monarchy as well as against *conversos*. The very idea of setting up an inquisition had come from the same local clergy that was propagating against the *conversos*. Thus, the crown was able to coopt this grassroots movement by leading the fight against *conversos*. Since there were animosities against Jews, the decision to expel them was an easy one. As numerous authors have pointed out, though, Ferdinand and Isabella did not have harbor any personal animosity toward Jews. On the contrary, they had many Jewish friends and many Jews and *conversos* worked for them (e.g., Kamen 1985; Pérez 2004; Roth 1995). Expelling the Jews, however, helped them to gain support and to consolidate their power, since it enabled them to coopt the local clergy and nobles who had been using anti-*converso* sentiment to lead rebellions against the monarchy. The Catholic monarchs also seemed to be genuinely concerned that the existence of the Jewish population within the country posed a threat to the Christian faith of the *conversos*, who might be tempted to revert to Judaism. So, even if they did not necessarily espouse a biologically based anti-Semitism, they did believe strongly in the Catholic ideology that they were using to unite the country.

Interestingly, Roth (1995) argues against the view that Isabella and Ferdinand used the Inquisition and the expulsion of the Jews as a way of unifying the country. Instead, he claims, they were concerned about the safety of the Jewish population. They had reason to fear that the Jews would be massacred if they did not leave the country. This argument, however, is not compelling. If the Catholic monarchs had been concerned about the well-being of the Jews, they would not have force them to leave the country; instead they would have given them protection and offered them the choice of staying or leaving. Furthermore, the idea that rulers will repress a group out of concern for its safety is less than persuasive. Such arguments bring to mind the claim that the Nazis used during the *Kristallnacht* pogroms—that they were arresting Jews in order to place them in "protective custody." In any case, even though it is difficult to know exactly what Isabella and Ferdinand were thinking deep inside, it is clear that the Inquisition *did* help to unite the country, to give the regime legitimacy and to increase the power of the crown.

Even if Isabella and Ferdinand did not espouse any biologically based anti-Semitism, and even if they were probably concerned about the possibility that *conversos* would revert to Judaism or practice that religion secretly, the perception of Jews as a biological group was strong in Spanish society. Thus, the impetus for the "purity-of-blood" laws came from below. Local governments in places like Toledo implemented them even before the time of Isabella and Ferdinand. After the Catholic monarchs had passed, moreover, "purity of blood" eventually became official state policy. Moreover, the Catholic monarchs agreed it was important for converts to give up their previous lifestyle and cultural practices completely, even when they had nothing to do with religion. Spain was to be a homogenized country with a homogenized culture.

In contrast to the situation in France, where the Inquisition divided the country, the Inquisition in Spain united it. France already existed as a country, so it did not need to be united in the same way. Moreover, the inquisition there was not aimed at outside groups of different "blood," but rather at people considered to have the same "blood." The inquisition in France was more like a family feud. Everyone belonged to the same French-Christian family, but many were dissatisfied with the Church—which they perceived as corrupt and exploitative—so they supported the Cathar movement or at least sympathized with it. Thus, there was violent opposition to the Inquisition in many areas of France. In Spain, on the other hand, the Inquisition was generally welcomed, as much of the population looked upon *conversos* (as well as *Moriscos*) with disdain.

Even though the Inquisition became an effective tool for controlling thought and creating an atmosphere of fear, it was popular precisely because the regime was able to label the *conversos* and *Moriscos* as outgroups that posed an existential threat. Moreover, people still remembered the instability and civil wars of the pre-unification period, so it was fairly easy to awaken their sense of threat. The *Moriscos* were a threat because they had recently been defeated in a centuries-long war, and they could be expected to support future Muslim invasions from the Ottoman Empire or by Berbers and Arabs. The *conversos* were a threat to aristocratic bloodlines, through their intermarriage with Christians of high status; and they endangered Catholic hegemony in the country with their possible secret retention of the Jewish faith. The obsessive concern with people's private beliefs shows how totalitarian the society had become. In addition, the *conversos* were an existential threat because they carried the wrong "blood" and belonged to another species, so they could never "really" become Christians/Spaniards. Finally, they were blamed for their allegedly great economic power and for causing the spread of epidemics and disease.

The Inquisition made heavy use of totalitarian methods to gain public support, such as forced confessions. This made it seem as if the accused persons had admitted to their "crimes," when in fact they had only confessed to avoid punishment (torture, lengthy imprisonment, etc.). With the *auto da fé*, the Inquisition conducted great public spectacles viewed by the entire local population, including people from nearby villages. Since those who participated in the Inquisition believed in the legitimacy of the regime and of the ideology behind it, it was easy for them to carry out their task of persecuting large numbers of people. The fact that one of the egoistic benefits of taking part was privileged seating in the local church shows that those involved either truly believed in the religious ideology, or that they at least understood the social prestige tied to supporting Catholicism. They also had less ideological reasons for supporting the evil persecution of innocents. One was to advance socially. Another was to gain immunity from being prosecuted themselves—an important privilege in a totalitarian society based on fear where even the strongest believers can be persecuted.

We cannot know how much twentieth-century totalitarian leaders were directly or indirectly inspired by the Spanish Inquisition, but it is clear that they adopted many of its methods. This includes the practice of not telling suspects what crimes they were charged with, and telling them that if they cooperated and confessed all their "crimes" they could go free. Stalin's secret police, for example, made heavy use of these methods. Forcing victims to confess according to a certain predetermined script was also a method used in show trials in the Soviet Union and Eastern Europe in the early 1950s. Some similarities with Nazi racial policies are also evident (even if the notion of race biology had not yet emerged): for example, the classification of Jews as different in "blood" than others, and the act of excluding "blood Jews" (i.e., Jews who had converted to Christianity) from public life. The Inquisition also resorted to burning books, as the Nazis did; and it made use of public spectacles reminiscent of those conducted by the Nazi and communist regimes. Of course, the events in Spain took place in the pre-modern era, so the mass mobilizations there took a different form than they did under twentieth-century totalitarianism; but the *auto da fé* was a striking case of mass mobilization nonetheless.

NOTE

1. This eventually led to their being banned even from universities and Catholic orders such as the Jesuits, even though the Jesuits had been founded by *conversos* (e.g., Friedman 1987: 23).

References

Alvarez, J. (2002). The Formation of Spanish Identity and Its Adaptation to the Age of Nations. *History & Memory, 14*(1/2), 13–36.

Atkinson, W. C. (1934). *Spain: A Brief History*. London: Methuen.

Benassar, B., et al. (1981). *Inquisición Española: Poder Político y Control Social*. Barcelona: Editorial Crítica.

Bethencourt, F. (1995). *The Inquisition: A Global History, 1478–1834* (J. Birrell, Trans.). Cambridge: Cambridge University Press.

Bishko. (1975). The Spanish and Portuguese Reconquest, 1095–1492. In H. W. Hazard (Ed.), *A History of the Crusades, vol. 3: The Fourteenth and Fifteenth Centuries*. Madison: University of Wisconsin Press.

Bloxham, D. (2008). Organized Mass Murder: Structure, Participation, and Motivation in Comparative Perspective. *Holocaust and Genocide Studies, 22*(2), 203–245.

Carrete, C. (1992). *El Judaísmo Español y la Inquisición*. Madrid: Editorial Mapfre.

Collier, D., & Collier, R. B. (1991). The Comparative Method: Two Decades of Change. In A. Rustow & K. P. Erickson (Eds.), *Comparative Political Dynamics: Global Research Perspectives*. New York: Harper Collins.

Comella, B. (1998). *La Inquisición Española*. Madrid: Rialp.

Contreras, J. (1996). Domínguez Ortiz y la Historiografía sobre Judeoconverson. *Manuscrits, 14*, 59–80.

Cruz, G. C. (1997). Los Comisarios de la Inquisición de Sevilla en el Siglo XVIII. In E. G. Fernández (Ed.), *El Centinela de la Fe*. Sevilla: Universidad de Sevilla.

Cruz, G. C. (2000). *Los Familiares de la Inquisición*. Valladolid: Junta de Castilla y León, 2000 Library of Diputacion Alava.

Díaz-Plaja, F. (1996). *La Vida Cotidiana en la España de la Inquisición*. Madrid: EDAF.

Díez, G. M. (1997). *Bulario de la Inquisición Española*. Madrid: Editorial Complutense.

Edwards, J. (1988). Religious Faith and Doubt in Late Medieval Spain: Soria circa 1450–1500. *Past & Present, 120*, 3–25.

Fernández-Armesto, F. (2000). The Improbable Empire. In R. Carr (Ed.), *Spain: A History*. Oxford: Oxford University Press.

Flynn, M. (1991). Mimesis of the Last Judgment: The Spanish Auto de fe. *The Sixteenth Century Journal, 22*(2), 281–297.

Flynn, M. (1995). Blasphemy and the Play of Anger in Sixteenth-Century Spain. *Past & Present, 149*, 29–56.

Friedman, J. (1987). Jewish Conversion, the Spanish Pure Blood Laws and Reformation: A Revisionist View of Racial and Religious Antisemitism. *The Sixteenth Century Journal, 18*(1), 3–30.

Giordano, M. L. (2010). 'La Ciudad de Nuestra Conciencia': Los Conversos y la Construcción de la Identidad Judeocristiana (1449–1556). *Hispania Sacra, 62*(125), 43–91.

Gitlitz, D. (2000). Inquisition Confessions and Lazarillo de Tormes. *Hispanic Review, 68*(1), 53–74.

Gómez, D. L. (1995). *Hechicería, Brujería e Inquisición en el Nuevo Reino de Granada: Un Duelo de Imaginarios.* Bogotá: Editorial Universidad Nacional.

Haliczer, S. (1990). *Inquisition and Society in the Kingdom of Valencia, 1478–1834.* Berkeley, Los Angeles and Oxford: University of California Press.

Hess, A. C. (1968). The Moriscos: An Ottoman Fifth Column in Sixteenth-Century Spain. *The American Historical Review, 74*(1), 5–6.

Hossain, K. L. (2007). Unraveling the Spanish Inquisition: Inquisitorial Studies in the Twenty-First Century. *History Compass, 5*(4), 1280–1293.

Housley, N. (2002). *Religious Warfare in Europe, 1400–1536.* Oxford: Oxford University Press.

Kamen, H. (1985). *Inquisition and Society in Spain in the Sixteenth and Seventeenth Centuries.* Bloomington: Indiana University Press.

Kamen, H. (1988). The Mediterranean and the Expulsion of Spanish Jews in 1492. *Past & Present, 119*, 30–55.

Kamen, H. (1997). *Philip of Spain.* New Haven: Yale University Press.

Krow-Lucal, M. G. (1997). Marginalizing History: Observations on the Origins of the Inquisition in Fifteenth-century Spain by B. Netanyahu. *Judaism, 46*(1), 47–62.

Lea, H. C. (1906). *A History of the Inquisition of Spain.* London: Macmillan.

Lomax, D. W. (1978). *The Reconquest of Spain.* London and New York: Longman.

Lynn, K. (2013). *Between Court and Confessional: The Politics of Spanish Inquisitors.* New York: Cambridge University Press.

MacKay, A. (1977). *Spain in the Middle Ages: From Frontier to Empire, 1000–1500.* Basingstoke: Palgrave.

Mann, M. (2005). *The Dark Side of Democracy: Explaining Ethnic Cleansing.* Cambridge: Cambridge University Press.

Manning, P. (2009). *Voicing Dissent in Seventeenth-Century Spain: Inquisition, Social Criticism and Theology in the Case of El Criticón.* Leiden: Brill.

Marín, J. M. G. (1997). Judaísmo entre el Poder y la Envidia: El Caso Ávila ante la Inquisición. In E. G. Fernández (Ed.), *El Centinela de la Fe.* Sevilla: Universidad de Sevilla.

Meyerson, M. D. (1995). Religious Change, Regionalism, and Royal Power in the Spain of Fernando and Isabel. In L. J. Simon (Ed.), *Iberia and the Mediterranean World of the Middle Ages: Studies in Honor of Robert I. Burns.* New York: E.J. Brill.

Nader, H. (1979). *The Mendoza Family in the Spanish Renaissance 1350–1550*. Rutgers University Press. The Library of Iberian Resources Online. Retrieved from http://libro.uca.edu/mendoza/mendoza.htm.

Nalle, S. T. (1987). Inquisitors, Priests, and the People during the Catholic Reformation in Spain. *The Sixteenth Century Journal, 18*(4), 557–587.

Nathans, E. (2004). *The Politics of Citizenship in Germany*. Oxford: Berg.

Netanyahu, B. (1995). *The Origins of the Inquisition in Fifteenth Century Spain*. New York: Random House.

Nirenberg, D. (2002). Mass Conversion and Genealogical Mentalities: Jews and Christians in Fifteenth-Century Spain. *Past & Present, 174*, 3–41.

O'Callaghan, J. F. (2004). *Reconquest and Crusade in Medieval Spain*. Philadelphia: University of Pennsylvania Press.

Ortiz, A. D. (2010). *Estudios de la Inquisición Española*. Granada: Editorial Comares.

Payne, S. G. (1973). *A History of Spain and Portugal, Volume One: Antiquity to the Seventeenth Century*. Madison: University of Wisconsin Press.

Pérez, J. (2002). *Crónica de la Inquisición Española*. Barcelona: Martínez Roca.

Pérez, J. (2004). *The Spanish Inquisition: A History* (J. Lloyd, Trans.). London: Profile.

Plaidy, J. (1959). *The Spanish Inquisition*. New York: Barnes and Noble.

Povedano, J. M. R. (1980). Las 'Conversiones' de Sinagogas a Raíz del Decreto de Expulsión (1492). *Miscelánea de Estudios Árabes y Hebraicos, 29*, 143–162.

Rawlings, H. (2006). *The Spanish Inquisition*. Oxford: Blackwell.

Roth, N. (1995/2002). *Conversos, Inquisition, and the Expulsion of the Jews from Spain*. Madison: University of Wisconsin.

Silverblatt, I. (2011). Colonial Peru and the Inquisition: Race-Thinking, Torture, and the Making of the Modern World. *Transforming Anthropology, 19*(2), 132–138.

Thomas, J. M. (2010). The Racial Formation of Medieval Jews: A Challenge to the Field. *Ethnic and Racial Studies, 33*(10), 1737–1755.

Torquemada, M. J. (1997). Los Secretarios o Notarios del Secreto en Sevilla desde Comienzos del Siglo XVIII. In E. G. Fernández (Ed.), *El Centinela de la Fe*. Sevilla: Universidad de Sevilla.

Trachtenberg, J. (1943). *The Devil and the Jews: The Medieval Conception of the Jew and Its Relation to Modern Antisemitism*. New Haven: Yale University Press/Varda Books 2001.

Vozmediano, M. F. G. (2005). El Silencio de los Inocentes; Ecos Inquisitoriales en Madrid y su Tierra durante el Epígono Trastámara. Una Aproximación Prosopográfica. *Cuadernos de Historia Moderna, 30*, 41–62.

Waller, J. E. (2007). *Becoming Evil* (2nd ed.). Oxford: Oxford University Press.

Yerushalmi, Y. H. (1982). Assimilation and Racial Anti-Semitism: The Iberian and the German Models. In *Leo Baeck Memorial Lecture*. New York: Leo Baeck Institute.

CHAPTER 6

Sweden

Among the modern totalitarian countries, this book focuses on Nazi Germany, but compares it to Sweden, which is the topic of this chapter. Sweden provides an interesting comparison, because like Germany it was a "Germanic" country, where a political consensus existed on the need for research on race biology; myths were strong about a glorious past where pre-Christian Germanic gods ruled the planet; and there was a strong belief in the need for racial purity. In fact, the State Institute for Race Biology at Uppsala University, which was created with wide support across the political spectrum, became one of the most important centers for research on race biology in the world. Yet, an important difference existed: Sweden had already been a country for hundreds of years; therefore, it enjoyed a high level of legitimacy. Consequently, its rulers did not need to take any special measures to recruit a loyal bureaucracy, as they could count on the bureaucracy's already being loyal to this well-established state; nor did they have to take any special actions to gain legitimacy among the population or political parties. In addition, despite racist tendencies, the Swedish state did not have any pressing need to determine who qualified as a true Swede. The German state was created quickly in the 1870s, when Bismarck succeeded in uniting the German kingdoms after Prussian victories on the battlefield; and it quickly dissolved in a revolution after defeat in WWI. The Swedish state, by contrast, was strong and stable. In fact, the transition from a monarchy to democracy (based on a constitutional monarchy) went smoothly and without great

© The Author(s) 2019   153
S. Saxonberg, *Pre-Modernity, Totalitarianism and the Non-Banality of Evil*, https://doi.org/10.1007/978-3-030-28195-3_6

disruptions, as the country developed a "policy legacy" (Skocpol 1985) of cooperation and consensus, rather than opposition and strife. Being a strong state with a long tradition, it was also able to adapt well to the pressing issues of the Great Depression, the rise of fascism and the onset of WWII. The fact that Sweden had a policy legacy of consensus and cooperation made it easier to reach a consensus on the transition to democracy, to which the monarchy and all major political parties could agree. Therefore, in contrast to its fragile counterpart in Germany, the democratic regime in Sweden enjoyed great legitimacy and was basically accepted by the vast majority of people in all sectors of society.

The manner in which the state developed also influenced the transition. In Sweden the landowning peasants had a relatively large influence on politics, as the king often aligned with them against the nobility. They also formed one of the estates in the Swedish parliament, giving them a say in lawmaking. When the country democratized, peasants soon formed two parties of their own, which eventually merged into one. Thus, Swedish peasants supported the democratically oriented Farmers' Party when the Great Depression struck. This contrasted greatly with the situation in Germany during the Weimar Republic, where the peasants did not feel their interests were represented by the mainstream parties. In this period, Bavaria was the only German province to have a peasant party. Because of this lack of alternatives, German peasants outside of Bavaria often turned to the Nazis, while Swedish peasants tended to support the Peasant Party. To be sure, this Swedish party did have some nationalist and racist traditions. However, since it was a democratic party that accepted the legitimacy of the system, the social democrats were able to coopt it into taking responsibility for building up the country's famed welfare state. Consequently, this party and its peasant supporters were kept within the democratic political sphere.

Another important aspect of the Swedish path of state-building concerns the way the bureaucracy developed. The Swedish bureaucracy gained a great deal of autonomy and influence on policymaking—a rather unusual development. Since it kept its privileged position, and since it was not—in contrast to its German counterpart under Bismarck—recruited on the basis of political criteria, it accepted the legitimacy of the democratic regime and worked with the government. Swedish bureaucrats were not political, and they enjoyed relative autonomy. This encouraged them to act in a more moral manner than German bureaucrats, whose combination of conservatism and anti-Republicanism led many of them to oppose the Weimar Republic and to cooperate with the Nazis in carrying out "evil" acts of repression. In contrast, Swedish bureaucrats at times took the initiative to fight evilness.

Finally, there is the issue of racism. Although widespread anti-Semitism existed and there was a consensus on the value of studying race biology, Sweden never developed an "eliminationist" anti-Semitism. This is *not* to claim that Goldhagen (1996) was necessarily correct to emphasize eliminationist anti-Semitism as a reason for German support for Hitler and the Holocaust. As will be discussed in the next chapter, there is evidence that eliminationist anti-Semitism was just as strong in several of Germany's neighbors, such as France. Rather, the point is that, given the absence of such a discourse in Sweden, it was less likely for a racist regime with genocidal ambitions to come to power in that country, and it was also more likely that Swedish bureaucrats would take measures to help victims of genocide. Furthermore, whereas nationalists in Germany succeeded in monopolizing the term *Volk*, social democrats were able to appropriate the corresponding Swedish term (*folk*), and to use it to promote democratic values.

This chapter begins with a discussion of the stability of Sweden's state-building process. Then it analyzes the policy legacy of consensus and compromise that came from this state-building process, and shows how this helped create a smooth transition to democracy. Next, the chapter shows how this state-building process helped incorporate peasants into the democratic process and made them less liable to join totalitarian movements. The next step is to show how the state-building process led to a relatively autonomous bureaucracy that accepted the legitimacy of the democratic regime, and which was willing at times to take actions to help victims of genocide *despite* the anti-Semitic values of many bureaucrats. Finally, this chapter shows why racism, anti-Semitism and support for research on race biology did not translate into support for any kind of eliminationist-genocidal ideology.

SWEDISH STABILITY

It is hard to say exactly when Sweden became a country. Elias (1976) argues that kingdoms in Europe developed as part of a long-term process. According to Bägerfeldt (2004: 19), Sweden was already described as an organized country in the year 98, when the Roman Tacitus wrote about the Germans. Starting in the late 900s, a kingdom based on the Christian model started to emerge, with Olof Skötkonung as the first king who sought to introduce Christianity in a serious manner. He set up the Skara diocese, but was overthrown in 1019, probably because he did not want to participate in the *riksblot* (the national sacrificial feast) (Bägerfeldt 2003: 26). The Christian type of kingdom became fully established in the 1200s. As Harrison (2002: 56ff.) notes, a Swedish ethnicity did not exist from the beginning; instead it developed over time, promoted by successive kings and their representatives. Ertman claims that Sweden was already a "durable polity of the western type" by the mid-1100s (Ertman 1997: 312). Bägerfeldt (2003: 28ff., 2004: 13ff.) puts the date a century later (1247), when the king defeated the *folkungar* at Sparrsäter. The *folkungar* favored a decentralized system, with decisive power in the hands of regional magnates. The remaining opponents of monarchical rule were executed after the battle at Härvadsbro in 1251, whereupon Roman law was introduced. The king was thereby forbidden to own land, which instead belonged to the state. This was an important step in the transformation of Sweden from a kingdom into a full-fledged state. Another important step was the decision in 1247 to force peasants in Uppland to begin paying a yearly tax, after the navy (*ledungsflotta*) was eliminated (Bägerfeldt 2003, 2004; Harrison 2009). Previously, they had sent people from each community to the fleet, rather than paying taxes. This was a further step toward a more modern type of state, in which the crown financed its operations through taxes. In 1290, Magnus established a system whereby nobles were placed under the king, thereby depriving the magnates of the equality with royalty which they had previously enjoyed. The royal council, the *riksråd*, then became the prime decision-making organ, instead of the regional assemblies under the control of local magnates. The *riksråd* consisted of 14–20 young aristocrats. In the beginning they were loyal to the king and always voted in his favor. For the first time, then, there was now an authority that stood above the magnates and their assemblies. This authority could judge people for treason, and in case of conviction could confiscate their property and condemn them to death.

For a monarchy, Sweden's system was relatively democratic in its first years, as the king was elected. Lindkvist (2007: 83) notes that, in 1319, a 3-year-old boy became king. He was in the hands of leading representatives of the aristocracy. This led to greater limits on royal power and on arbitrary taxation. Four peasants from each district (*härad*) participated in the vote for the king. Thus, as will be discussed below, in contrast to their

German counterparts Swedish peasants were long able to participate in and to influence politics. Lindkvist (2007: 92) adds that, even though the king was elected, the rule since the mid-1300s was to choose him from the existing royal dynasty if possible. Sweden also had a written constitution. Known as "the Land Law of Magnus Eriksson," it was formalized in the 1350s. It stated that there was a united kingdom called "Sweden," and that the kingship was elective rather than hereditary. The royal office was also contractual, as the king had to exchange oaths with his subjects upon being elected (Roberts 1968: 40; Upton 1998: 1). Thus, royal powers were limited.

By the standards of the time, moreover, the country was fairly tolerant. For example, Harrison (2002: 145) observes, that it was extremely unusual in medieval Sweden for people to be accused of heresy. In 1311, however, some cases of persecution against heretics did take place. For instance, a peasant from Gottröra was executed for relapsing and denying Christ. The most famous case was in 1520, when King Kristian II judged a person for heresy in order to justify the Stockholm Bloodbath. Nothing like the Inquisition emerged, although in 1523 Bishop Hans Brask suggested setting up an inquisition to campaign against Lutheranism.

A further factor favoring stable development was the absence of sharp ethnic tensions. Parts of today's Finland started to become incorporated into Sweden in the 1100s, but the language question was not important in medieval times, so little ethnic tension between Swedes and Finns resulted (p. 238). Finland remained part of Sweden until 1809, when Russia took it over after having defeated Sweden. (This was the last time that Sweden took part in a war.) Furthermore, Jansson (1995: 33) points out, Finnish children living in the Swedish part of the country were not punished if they spoke Finnish.

In 1397, Sweden joined a union with Denmark and Norway, which lasted until 1523 (Böhme 1994; Lindqvist 1992: 325; and Gustafsson 2000). Yet, this was never a true union, as the three national councils were kept separate: they never shared resources or followed any common agenda (Harrison 2002: 318). Sweden then dropped out of this tripartite arrangement under Danish rule, and re-established full independence under Gustav Vasa. The kingship was made hereditary in 1544. Now, rather than being elected, the king would be chosen by the grace of God (Upton 1998: 5). This led eventually to the development of a more absolutist type of rule (Upton 1998, especially Chap. 3). After the death of

Karl XII in 1718, however, the country underwent liberalization, and parliament was able once more—during the period known as the "Age of Liberty"—to exert some influence over policymaking (Ertman 1997: 314). By the end of the 1400s, according to Premfors (1993: 20–1), Sweden already had clear borders, a distinct national identity and cohesive laws holding the country together. By the standards of the time, moreover, broad strata of the population were able—due to the peasantry's representation in the Swedish parliament (*riksdag*)—to take part in politics.

Parliament consisted of four estates (nobles, clergy, burghers and peasants). Thus, as will be discussed below, peasants had much more influence in Sweden than they did in the German kingdoms. Another important issue is that guilds were powerful and were represented in parliament. Starting in the 1770s, however, the board of trade (*Kommerskollegium*) worked to loosen guild rules and to reduce market restrictions; and after 1820 it advocated the abolition of the guild system altogether (Kyle 1989: 328ff.). The board of trade served as a transactional channel for some groups that were not represented in the estates, thus adding to the inclusiveness of the political system.

Similar to Spain during its Inquisition, Sweden had only one legal religion: Catholicism. In 1527, however, Gustav Vasa broke with Rome and made the church subordinate to the state on all earthly questions, thereby transforming it into a power resource and a source of norms that the king could utilize (Holm 2007: 48). In 1593 the state church officially became Lutheran. In contrast to its predecessor, this body was under government control. Nevertheless, while the country now had its own national religion, the crown did not base its legitimacy thereon, as many of the peasants were skeptical of the new religion. Instead the king concentrated on legitimizing his actions by reference to law and tradition. Above all, taxation depended on Gustav's claim to be protecting his subjects from external enemies. Military protection in exchange for taxes became the ideological foundation of the Vasa state (Hallenberg et al. 2008: 253). Gustafsson (2008) argues that the decision to break with Rome and to create a Swedish state church advanced the state-building process, by helping to differentiate Swedish culture from that in other countries.

Similar to France and different than Spain, Sweden had an aristocracy that was not based solely on blood. It was common for kings to reward people by ennobling them. In addition, many nobles came from other countries, so they could not have the same "blood." In part this was due to the small size of the country, since there were not enough nobles to fill all the government posts (Böhme 1994). So even if ideas of race biology became popular in Sweden in the early twentieth century, the mixing of blood did not represent the same kind of existential threat to Swedish nobles that it did to their Spanish counterparts. In addition, since there were very few Jews or others of non-Swedish ethnic ancestry in the country, the nobility did not have many opportunities to intermarry with ethnic minorities. The one ethnic minority that was relatively numerous were the Sami; but they lived in the north, were mostly poor, and did not mingle much with the aristocracy. Finns comprised another ethnic minority even after Finland separated from Sweden, but once again, they did not intermarry with the Swedish nobility.

In contrast to Germany, moreover, Sweden had no need to decide who "belonged," because it was already an established country. Like almost all countries, to be sure, Sweden did see changes in its borders over time, with corresponding changes in its ethnic composition. Most of what today is Finland was part of Sweden until 1809. Norway was under Swedish rule from 1814 until 1905, although it enjoyed a very high degree of autonomy on most issues other than foreign policy. In this sense, Sweden was ethnically purer when WWI broke out than it had been before. Even earlier, however—when the country was larger—it had no sharp ethnic divisions. Before 1809, as Edgren (2010: 10) points out, "Sweden" could mean the western part of the kingdom (today's Sweden), or it could mean Sweden *and* Finland. "As the king's subjects and as Lutherans, and thus in the eyes of neighboring powers, all were 'Swedes.'" Edgren adds that the main division in those days was not between Sweden and Finland, but rather between on the one hand a core area consisting of Götaland, Svealand and western Finland, and on the other various peripheral areas (whether Swedish- or Finnish-speaking), such as Småland, Dalarna, Västerbotten, Österbotten, Savolax, Karelen and Skåne.[1] Similarly, Premfors (1993: 7) maintains that Sweden became a unified nation at a very early stage, with little in the way of ethnic, linguistic or regional conflicts.

As a stable country that had existed for many centuries, then, Sweden did not face the same problem that Germany confronted in the 1880s, when its government sought to gain legitimacy for the newly unified country; or that Spain faced in the 1480s, when the "Catholic monarchs" undertook to do the same. As this chapter will show, this stability helped ease the transition to democracy in Sweden, and helped make the new democratic system to get consolidated more quickly and completely.

POLICY LEGACY OF CONSENSUS AND COMPROMISE

This section has two parts. The first part discusses how the policy legacy of consensus and compromise made it easier to democratize the political system in Sweden, giving the democratic regime much greater legitimacy than that enjoyed by the Weimer Republic in Germany. The second part examines how this tradition of consensus helped the social democrats to coopt the term *folk*, rather than leaving it to right-wing extremists as in Germany. In addition, the period in question saw the emergence of popular movements. These were usually politically neutral, but they still helped create a democratic and consensus-oriented atmosphere.

Consensus and Democratization

The country's stability can also be seen in the manner in which the monarchy transformed itself into a parliamentary democracy. In Germany, the political system was democratized through a divisive revolution that overthrew the monarchy of the young state after its humiliating loss in WWI. Sweden, by contrast, stayed out of the war, and the evolution to a democratic system took place on the basis of the country's long tradition of compromise and consensus. In contrast to their counterparts in Germany, conservative monarchists in Sweden could support the democratic transition, as the king remained head of state (Lewin 1992, Chap. 4; Thulstrup 1968: 101ff.).

In fact, the social democrats could use the argument that an evolutionary transition to a parliamentary democracy was necessary if a worker-led revolution like that seen in Germany was to be avoided. The Swedish economist Bo Södersten (1975) once wrote a book using the "Swedish turtle" as a metaphor for the Swedish model, with its basis in compromise and evolutionary change. This tradition goes back to medieval days, when kings often had to compromise with peasants and other groups.

In support of the notion that Sweden has a policy legacy based on cooperation and consensus, Hallenberg et al. (2008: 249) remark that late sixteenth-century sources describe the political culture of Early Modern Sweden as being based on bargaining and mutual interaction between rulers and subjects. Hallenberg observes that, in 1619, the king tried leasing out land to wealthy people who then collected the taxes for themselves and paid the king a certain fee per year. They leased the land for several years. This led to protests among peasants, because the leasers had an incentive to increase demands on the peasants, who would have to pay more than when they rented from the king. Due to peasant resistance, the experiment was discontinued after 15 years. "From that time on, the kings and aristocrats who ruled the Swedish realm would have to acknowledge the need for legitimacy and dialogue, which made direct bargaining with the peasantry the most important task of government" (Hallenberg 2009: 266). Österberg (1989) also claims that a political culture of consensus emerged already in the 1500s, as the monarchy decided it was important to make compromises with the peasants and keep them satisfied. She points out that the state budget was highly dependent on peasants, so the king had an incentive to place the peasants.

Kyle (1989: 337) writes that, already in the nineteenth century, a tradition of cooperation existed among the decision-makers and the state bureaucracy. Furthermore, the system of state reports (*utredningsväsendet*) provided a channel for people outside the government—such as peasants, industrialists and tradesmen—to make their voices heard, as by the 1800s experts from the technical and business spheres could participate in drawing up these reports. An additional arena for influence by social forces was in government committees, where "politically unrepresented or under-represented bourgeois interests from industry and commerce were noted from the beginning" Kyle (1989: 353).

A tolerant atmosphere also emerged because of the country's relatively free press, which helped make the political atmosphere more inclusive than that found in pre-WWI Germany. von Vegesack (1995: 34) claims that "in 1766 Sweden passed a regulation on press freedom, which for its time was the most liberal in the world."

This combination of tolerance, relative openness and a policy legacy based on cooperation and consensus helped pave the way for Sweden's transition to democracy after WWI, in which all of the political parties and even the monarchy approved of the democratic reforms.

Di Palma (1980: 170) provides the helpful concept of backward legitimacy for explaining Sweden's path toward democracy and democratic consolidation. He develops this notion in analyzing the democratization of Spain. In the 1970s in that country, the king and the ruling political group decided that, rather than fight the democratic parties, they would promote democracy. In so doing they supplemented their backward legitimacy, which derived from the past, with "forward" legitimacy oriented to the future. Thus, when democratization enjoys support from the old regime, which transforms itself, the transition is more likely to be stable than when democratization comes about as a complete break with the past.

In a similar vein, Lipset (1959) contends that, when democracy comes about through a revolution against a monarchy—as in France—it tends to be less stable, because the right wing (clerics, aristocrats, etc.) do not view the new regime as legitimate.

Olsson (2000) builds on these insights from di Palma and Lipset. One reason why the transition to democracy was much smoother in Sweden than in Germany, he argues, was that it took place in Germany through a revolution, while it came about in Sweden through compromise and consensus. In the former country, therefore, the conservative parties never accepted the legitimacy of the new constitution; whereas in the latter country all of the major political groups supported the new regime. According to Olsson, an ideology based on the need for cooperation dominated Sweden during the nineteenth century. Despite their original fear of democracy, Swedish conservatives worked since at least the end of the 1800s for national unity, which they thought was in the national interest (p. 35). According to Higley (cited in Olsson 2000: 36), a consensual elite had emerged already in 1809, after the coup against Gustav IV Adolf.

Throughout 1917, there were demonstrations across the country as the food situation got worse. The unions planned a mass demonstration in Stockholm, so there were fears that the protests would turn violent. However, in contrast to their German counterparts—who saw social democrats as subversive traitors and a threat to the country—Swedish conservatives trusted the social democrats to keep the peace. Accordingly, they decided against using the *skyddskår* (paramilitary force) to patrol the demonstration. It was clear that the conservative head of government, Swartz, wanted to cooperate with the social democrats (Olsson 2000: 80).

In 1917 the king agreed to let the social democrats join a coalition government, which gave them increased legitimacy. Then in 1918 when it was clear that Germany would lose the war, the worsening economic situation, together with their fear of revolution after the events in Germany and Russia, convinced the conservatives of the need to cooperate with the liberals and social democrats in reforming the constitution. Even though many conservative leaders did not like this government's proposal for how to reform the electoral system, they agreed on the need for some kind of universal voting rights and for female suffrage.

Nevertheless, there were some important differences between the conservatives on the one hand and the liberals and social democrats on the other. Since the members of the first chamber were chosen by the municipal governments, which in turn were elected according to a graduated voting system that gave the most votes to those with the most money, the conservatives enjoyed a majority in that chamber, enabling them to block any reforms. The social democrats warned that strikes and demonstrations would result if the conservatives used their control of the first chamber to block constitutional reform (Olsson 2000: 143ff.). Swartz, the former conservative prime minister, wrote in his diary that a governmental crisis, a nationwide strike and perhaps even a civil war might ensue if the system was not reformed. Meanwhile the king supported the leftist government, and he let the conservatives know he would not appoint a right-wing government if the proposed reform failed to go through. In addition, the directors of the largest companies supported the reform, especially because they saw that Great Britain was going to win the war and therefore, would decide the rules over international trade. Consequently, much of the business community began to orient itself toward Britain. In contrast to their German counterparts, they were not reactionary; instead they had liberal sympathies. Some business leaders even had good contacts with the social democrats, so they were not so scared of a social democratic government. Consequently, conservatives agreed to the larger part of the government's proposal.

The remaining question was whether persons who paid no taxes would be able to vote in elections for the first chamber. A committee was set up to work out a compromise, with two people from the left (including the social democratic leader, Hjalmar Branting) and two from the right. The first chamber accepted the compromise by a large majority (Olsson 2000: 147). Even though the social democrats wanted the voting age to be 21 for the second chamber, the conservatives got support for their demand that the voting age be raised to 23 for the second chamber. In addition, they gained support for their demand that the voting age be 27 for the "Landsting" (the provisional governments that in turn elected members to the first chamber of parliament). Furthermore, the electoral term would be lengthened to eight years for the first chamber, while for the second chamber it was four. The final proposal passed in the first chamber without a vote, and in the second chamber by a majority of 122 to 37 (pp. 156–7).

Olsson (2000) shows that, each time the conservatives compromised, they saw the need for consensus as more important than any rational calculus about how to maximize their own power. In neo-institutional terms, one could say that the Swedish policy legacy meant that policymakers gave the highest priority to reaching a consensus when major reforms were discussed.

Premfors (1993: 7–8) agrees there was a desire among the political parties to compromise on how to implement universal voting rights. He adds that Sweden had already developed a strong tradition of legality, liberalism and constitutionalism. Of course, this came about because of the long state-building process where the king's powers were rather limited, and he needed the support of social groups such as peasants and nobles. The result was a relatively consensual model of development. After the reforms of 1918, accordingly, political democracy was taken for granted by all of the political parties

Since Sweden had a strong and stable state, with a tradition of compromise and consensus, it was easier for parties to reach pragmatic compromises and to form stable coalition governments once the country had democratized. Thus, when the Great Depression struck in the 1930s, the social democrats were able to form a coalition government with the Farmers' Party, which kept the nationalist tendencies of the latter party in check. The leader of the Farmers' Party had some anti-Semitic and authoritarian tendencies, but the party's participation in the coalition pressured it into following a democratic path.[2] Then, after the German invasion of Denmark and Norway, the social democrats were able to put together a unity government that included all of the democratic parties—that is, all of the parties in parliament except the communists (cf. Hägglöf 1972; Wahlbäck 1972).

The social democrats feared an outcome similar to that in Norway, where the social democrats were unable to keep the country unified. Vidkun Quisling, who had been a minister (having been suggested by the Farmers' Party), established a fascist party that was willing to collaborate with the Nazis. Quisling's name later became synonymous with "traitor." The Farmers' Party did not openly support Quisling or become a fascist party, but it did enter into negotiations with Quisling's party to form a national front. Moreover, although it reached agreements with the social democrats on some crisis packages, it never formed a coalition government with them. Nor was a unity government with all of the democratic parties ever formed in Norway (for a discussion of this, see, e.g., Lindström 1983).

Rather than supporting revolutionary change, Per Albin Hansson, the social democratic prime minister, played upon the consensual policy legacy. The country would benefit most, he claimed, if the different parties cooperated with one another. Lewin (1998: 22–3) observes that, when Hansson became prime minister, he defended his *kohandel* (bargaining) with the Farmers' Party on the grounds that the bargaining had led to a better outcome, thereby representing a truer expression of parliament's real preferences than would have been the case had the social democrats simply pushed through their policies without compromising. He went so far as to say that he would prefer it if all of the parties except the communists joined a coalition government—as in fact they later did, during the war (1940–1944). He did not want the bourgeois parties to be in perpetual opposition, as that would not be a healthy political situation. In his view, it would be better to bring all of the parties into the government, because democracy would be healthier if they cooperated. Hansson also believed the quality of political debate would improve if the different parties cooperated, because they would be able in that case to hold relaxed discussions rather than all blaming each other.

In emphasizing the neo-institutional concept of policy legacies, my approach may seem rather structural. However, these structures/institutions simply encourage certain paths of development; they do not determine them.

Creating Consensus and Coopting the Term Folk

As part of their strategy for creating a consensual society, the Swedish social democrats were able to coopt the term *folk*. The corresponding term in German is *Volk* (pronounced "folk"). It is hard to render either *folk* or *Volk* fully in English, but the idea of *Volk* was central to the ideology of the Nazis. They talked about their "*Volk* comrades," and they considered their ideology to be *völkisch*. In Germany, the extreme right claimed to represent the German *Volk* (i.e., ethnic Germans). In Sweden, by contrast, the social democrats used the term *folk* to mean the common people, who would be united in building a better and more just society. Thus Per Albin Hansson, who was prime minister from 1932 to 1946, laid the foundations for the modern Swedish welfare state on the basis of the image of the *folkhem* (people's home). The idea was that Sweden would become one big home, where people from all backgrounds lived together in harmony. In addition, the social democrats helped to set up *folkets hus*— literally "houses of the people"—in all of Sweden's larger towns; these are buildings that hold cultural events. Finally, they helped to establish *folkparker* ("people's parks"), where outdoor cultural events like dances are held in the summer (cf. Hall 2000: 260). This exemplifies the role of actors: the term *folk* existed and was popular and the social democrats were able to take the initiative to appropriate this term to support their policies. In many other countries, such as Germany, right-wing groups used this term for exclusionary nationalist causes; in Sweden, by contrast, the social democrats used this term to develop a culture of solidarity. Some post-structuralist theorists have portrayed politics as a battle over the interpretation and reinterpretation of words (e.g., Laclau and Mouffe 1985). One might accordingly say that, while the right in Germany won the battle over the interpretation of *Volk*, the left in Sweden won the battle over the interpretation of *folk*. Moreover, Swedish social democrats interpreted the idea in a highly inclusive manner, so as to include even wealthy persons who voted for right-wing parties. This was a conscious strategy, but the idea behind it was facilitated by the country's policy legacy of consensus and cooperation.

In addition to the institutionalization of "folk organizations" by the social democrats, a tradition developed of "folk movements." This latter term is often rendered in English as "associational life." These were popular movements, such as the temperance movement and the cooperative movement. They were officially politically neutral, but their leaders were often social democrats or liberals. Edquist (2016: 103) maintains that, although it was common in the 1950s to see these folk movements as schools of citizenship which trained people to become good democrats, researchers nowadays often take a more critical view, portraying them as organizations that reproduced society's structures and fought against views seen as undesirable. Moreover, even if these movements did in fact help to further democratic ideals, it is not clear they had greater influence than did their counterparts in Germany, which had a vigorous civil society under the Weimar Republic.

Yet it is interesting to note that, in contrast to their counterparts in Germany, folk movements in Sweden often cooperated with the state in promoting democracy. In 1912, for example, the state started supporting study circles (groups that meet once a week in the evening to discuss a topic about which they have read). It did so by giving subsidies to local libraries to buy the books these groups used. Then, in 1920, the state allocated funds to educate the public on democratic principles, so that citizens could make more informed choices when voting (Edquist 2016: 104–5). Yet, Edquist (2016: 111) concludes that, despite the good intentions, these policies did not have much impact as expected: instead of the hoped-for 1000, only some 125 study circles were conducted per year. Östberg (1990: 49ff.) summarizes authors with a more positive view of folk movements and folk education. According to this view, the Swedish folk movements played a decisive role in supporting dialogue over confrontation. Through them, people from different classes learned to cooperate with each other. The folk movements used the liberal ideology of participation to legitimize their political actions. Along these lines, members of free churches, temperance lodges and worker associations took the initiative to organize election meetings and influence political opinion. Östberg also notes that many activists from these movements got involved in party politics. These organizations were neutral, but many of their members joined political parties to influence their nominating processes. In 1911, according to Östberg (p. 54), 62 percent of the members of the second chamber were teetotalers, including 21.5 percent of the conservatives, 73 percent of the liberals and 87.5 percent of the social democrats.

It is difficult to ascertain how much influence these folk movements actually had over the process of consolidating the democratic system and rendering it immune to totalitarian movements. After all, Germany had many of the same kinds of movements. In fact, almost all European countries had temperance and cooperative movements. What is clear is that the "folk movement" ideology fit in well with the "folk home" ideology that the social democrats developed. This supports the idea that "folk" does not have to be used in a nationalist way, as it was done in Germany, but can instead be used to promote social solidarity.

STATE-BUILDING AND THE INCORPORATION OF PEASANTS INTO THE DEMOCRATIC PROCESS

One reason why the political system developed differently in Sweden than how it did in Germany is that, in the former country, the state-building process relied much more on peasant support. This made the peasants much more influential than they were in Germany, where a strong Junker class emerged. Whereas the German kingdoms were very feudalistic, serfdom in Sweden was abolished as early as in 1335 (Bägerfeldt 2003: 18). As Roberts (1968: 38) underlines, moreover, the monarchy in Sweden was poor compared to the nobility and the Church, and it also held far less land than the peasants. In 1523, around 52 percent of the land belonged to tax-paying peasants, 21 percent belonged to the Church, slightly less than the latter figure belonged to the nobility and only a bit more than 5 percent belonged to the crown.

Aware of their relative strength, peasants were not afraid to rebel; furthermore, kings often relied on them for support against the nobility. In the words of Heclo and Madsen (1987: 9), "[King] Vasa broke the power of the aristocracy by siding periodically with an independent peasantry and rising merchant class and by assimilating nobles into the national military and civil service." Thus, to placate the peasants and restore the legitimacy of his regime, Vasa told the peasants after the Dacke peasant rebellion of 1542 to send their complaints against local officeholders directly to him. Those who appealed to the king had a realistic chance of succeeding, as bailiffs and other local representatives were regularly removed and often prosecuted for mistreating the peasantry (Hallenberg et al. 2008: 253). Vasa was dependent on peasant support, as he had won the crown by persuading peasants from the province of Dalarna to rebel against the three-crown arrangement under which the Danes were ruling Sweden. Thus, the peasantry was central to national politics from the very beginning of the new regime.

> The peasant militia was an independent power resource that could only be countered by substantial numbers of experienced soldiers. Consequently, the King did not have the military resources to clamp down on local protest, so he had to bargain with the peasants in order to collect the necessary contributions. The peasantry was accordingly represented in the Swedish diet, a direct consequence of King Gustav's need for an effective interest aggregation. While their political clout there may have been inferior to that of the King and the nobility, the fact that the peasants could bargain with their superiors at the central political arena as well as in the local district courts opened up new possibilities for political initiative from below. Meanwhile, the new tax-system that was introduced meant that the peasants now acquired a position to bargain over their individual taxes. They would use this position most frequently to question earlier tax assessments, demanding new surveys of their lands and a more equitable distribution of burdens. (ibid.)

Even though Swedish peasants had much more power than their German neighbors, their power should not be exaggerated. For example, Bengtsson (2019: 8ff.) notes that even though peasants formed the fourth estate, they were still subordinate to the other three estates. In contrast to the other estates, they were not even able to choose their speaker in parliament, as the king took this responsibility upon himself. Nonetheless, the relative strength of the Swedish peasantry helped curb authoritarian and absolutist tendencies and made the transition to democracy easier. In contrast to their counterparts in Germany, Swedish peasants were well-organized, and they created their own party already in 1913 and they started a second one in 1915. Thus, they had their own parties even before the introduction of universal suffrage. As will be discussed in the next chapter, many German peasants voted for the Nazis at least in part because no other parties supported their interests. (In Bavaria, on the other hand, a peasant party existed as an alternative, and peasants in that state were much more likely to support it than to turn to the Nazis.)

Notwithstanding the Farmers' Party's acceptance of democracy, however, it did have some racist and authoritarian tendencies. The other center-right parties, by contrast, rejected anti-Semitism. In 1939, for example, the Conservative leader Gösta Bagge criticized an anti-Semitic speaker in parliament as follows: "Anti-Semitism," he said, "is a misfortune [*olycka*] for a country. It is a spiritual pestilence against which people in a healthy country must fight" (Valentin 1964: 178). To be sure, there were individual racists in each party—otherwise Bagge would not have needed to issue his condemnation of anti-Semitism; but only the Farmers' Party had racism in its program (Åmark 2011: 360). There were two peasant parties originally: *Jordbrukarnas riksförbund* (the National Farmers' Union) and the *Bondeförbund* (Farmers' Association). Eventually, the former party joined the latter one. According to Nilsson (2000: 67), there was deep-seated anti-Semitism in *Jordbrukarnas riksförbund*. Its platform for the 1920 elections, for example, included a plank stressing the importance of race biology. When it joined the *Bondeförbund* in 1921, furthermore, it succeeded in pushing through its racist platform. The discussion of race disappeared from the *Bondeförbund*'s program at the end of the decade, but it reappeared in the party's basic program in 1933 (Mohlin 1988: 95). It is "a national task," the program proclaimed, to "protect the [continued purity] of the Swedish popular stock (*folkstam*) against the mixing of inferior race elements, as well as to fight against the immigration into Sweden of undesired strangers. The continuation and strengthening of the popular material (*folkmaterialet*) is of greatest importance for our national development."

Anti-Semitic statements were made by leaders of the Farmers' Party, as well as by its newspapers. To give some examples: In 1921, CG Björk, a substitute member of parliament, spoke of how the healthy peasant class was losing influence in society as the racially inferior industrial working class was gaining in influence. Economics, moreover, was a false doctrine, and it led to a situation where a great amount of wealth came into a few hands—mostly those of immigrant Jews (Mohlin 1988: 97). A decade later, the head of the Farmers' Party in Stockholm County, Adolf Anderson, claimed it was the fault of the Jews that Swedish agriculture was in crisis in the 1930s. According to Mohlin (p. 98), Farmers' Party MP Otto Wallén agreed with the Nazis that Jews were the cause of all evil in the world. In 1938, conservative MP Gunnar Heckscher (son of Eli Heckscher, the famous liberal Jewish economist), wrote negatively about the leader of the Farmers' Party in an article, whereupon the youth organization of that party counterattacked in an anti-Semitic manner: "The Swedish peasant class does not love…Jews…it may soon be time for expulsion measures against undesirable elements" (Åmark 2011: 382). The Farmers' Party justice minister, Karl Gustaf Westman, made many anti-Semitic comments in his diaries, although he did not give voice to such sentiments in public (e.g., ibid.: 380). Peasant newspapers such as *Landsbygden* criticized film, jazz music and the secularization of society—all allegedly inspired by Jews and produced by them. It also claimed that socialism was a Jewish invention, as were modern ideas like freedom, equality, brotherhood and individualism (Catomeris 2004: 127).

Even though the Farmers' Party had clear racist and anti-Semitic tendencies, its anti-Semitism was not eliminationist, or anywhere near as vicious as that of the Nazis. For example, when the government set aside money in 1939 to support refugees who had come to the country, the party argued that the money should go instead to educate small farmers who had lost their land due to rationalization. In the second chamber, Wallén made it clear that he thought the funds would go to Jews and especially Jewish doctors, which he strongly opposed. This "Asian tribe," he declared, "does not suit our decent Swedish stock (*folkstam*).…Let us show humanitarian feelings by sending the money abroad and sending Jews abroad, but let's keep work in Sweden for Swedes" (Mohlin 1988: 97). It is hard to imagine Nazi leaders harboring "humanitarian feelings" or suggesting to send money abroad to help Jews.

Probably the most extreme anti-Semite with roots in the peasant movement was Elof Eriksson, whose views became radical after he left the Farmers' Party. What should be done with the Jews? he asked in 1935. He suggested that they be completely separated from non-Jews; however, he only reached this conclusion after having rejected bodily elimination—because it would be technically impossible and would make Jews into martyrs (Catomeris 2004: 128). This is about the closest anyone in the Swedish mainstream came to eliminationist anti-Semitism. Even this man, however, opposed elimination—although for practical rather than moral reasons.

According to Broberg and Tydén (2005: 54), the cooptation of the Farmers' Party by the social democrats was a major reason for the failure of Nazi organizations to gain support in Sweden. They emphasize the success of the two-party coalition agreement in 1933, which alleviated the suffering which the depression had caused through investments in new housing and a generous social policy. The economy also started picking up, and unemployment was falling. The Farmers' Party remained in government throughout the decade, although once WWII began in 1939, the other non-socialist parties joined them and the social democrats in a grand coalition government. They add that the mild anti-Semitism of the Farmers' Party was enough to pick up votes from anti-Semites. In other words, the policy legacy of cooperation and consensus won out in the end over the impulses toward anti-Semitism and racism from within that party. Moreover, the anti-Semitism that had existed was far from the violent, eliminationist variant that the Nazis promoted in Germany.

Developing a Relatively Autonomous Bureaucracy

Finally, since parliamentary democracy came to Sweden in an evolutionary manner and on the basis of a solid consensus among all of the political parties, the democratic regime did not face strong opposition from the state bureaucracy. To be sure, bureaucrats in Sweden had a conservative bias; however, in contrast to their counterparts in the Weimar Republic, they considered the democratic government to be legitimate. After all, the transition to democracy had gained the support of all of the major political parties, and indeed of the monarchy itself. In contrast to their German counterparts, moreover, Swedish bureaucrats were not politicized, and they did not need to display "loyalty" to the monarchy or to have conservative values in order to get their positions. The Swedish bureaucracy also had an advantage over the German one in that it was much more autonomous and its members were more accepting of the notion that they had a moral responsibility to society. This section examines the relative professionalism of Swedish bureaucrats, and then discusses their autonomy and their ability to take moral judgments into account.

One key point is that the Swedish social democrats, in contrast to their German counterparts, did not face conservative bureaucrats who questioned the government's legitimacy. To be sure, these bureaucrats lacked enthusiasm in certain areas, such as school reform. Nonetheless, the social democrats got around this problem, either by passing detailed regulations (as they did for school reform) or by creating new institutions to carry out their core programs (as they did for their labor-market policies) (Rothstein 1986). As a result, they were able to make substantial changes even in the area of education, in a manner which still eludes the German social democrats in the twenty-first century; and they were able to transform the labor market by implementing the world-famous Swedish model of labor-market policy (a subject which, however, is beyond the scope of this book).

Creating a Professionalized Bureaucracy

As Rothstein (1998: 292–3) points out, positions in the Swedish bureaucracy were previously reserved for nobles. However, the Act of Union and Security stipulated in 1789 that, while the "highest and most distinguished" offices would continue to be reserved for nobles, the estate to which applicants belonged would not otherwise be relevant. Then, in 1809, Sweden lost Finland in a war with Russia, which led to a coup that removed the king. Those behind the coup blamed the military and a lack of efficient state organization for the loss, leading them to propose changes in public administration. As a result, the "new Constitution of 1809 removed almost all preferential treatment of nobles within public administration." However, "[t]he last statute to uphold noble priorities, stipulating that half of the members of the Supreme Court must belong to the House of the Nobility, did not disappear until 1845" (Rothstein 1998: 293). Another important reform forbade bureaucrats from selling their positions. That system had been based on the idea that the money gained from selling one's position would act as a pension; accordingly, a pension system for public administrators was now introduced (Rothstein 1998: 294). When the bureaucracy was based on noble status, civil servants did not need any special training; their authority as aristocrats was deemed sufficient. Therefore, if a modern bureaucracy was to be created, educational demands would have to be introduced. As a result of the reforms, the most important qualification for a position in public administration was a degree in law from a university (Rothstein 1998: 296). In 1855, moreover, the state started abolishing the system of in-kind payments, in favor of salaries (Rothstein 1998: 300). "The civil service needed to be seen as legitimate by the people, which required recruitment based on merit and service based on impartiality as essential ingredients" (Rothstein and Teorell 2015: 246).

As a result, the Swedish bureaucracy became more merit-based than the one in Prussia. In the latter country, the civil service was completely dominated well into the 1800s by conservative Junkers, whose position was based on their ties with the Kaiser. It is true that by choosing these Junkers the Kaiser became less dependent on the upper nobility. However, the point here is that loyalty to the Kaiser was more important than competence, which hindered the Prussian bureaucracy from modernizing as much as in Sweden. In Sweden, by contrast, "a new breed of bureaucrats more attuned to the specialized needs of an industrialized society arose, [and] professionalization ceased to be a cause of division in the bureaucracy and became a source of a new kind of consensus based less on traditional corporate concepts such as honor and pride than on expertness and efficiency" (Rothstein 1998: 302).

Ironically, then, the loss of much of its territory in a major war actually helped Sweden to modernize and to create a more efficient bureaucracy. Rather than blaming an ethnic group like the Jews, as German nationalists did, the political elite blamed the inefficient organization of the state and moved to reform it. One obvious reason for this is that there were very few Jews in the country. Furthermore, those few were not yet emancipated, so they could not join the military or hold any public positions. Naturally, this made it hard to blame them for Sweden's defeat in the war. Similarly, the Sami (Lapps) lived mostly in the north, isolated from other groups, and they were not involved in the country's politics or its military endeavors. In theory, Swedish leaders could have blamed the Finns (for not fighting better),[3] but it would have been contradictory both to blame the Finns and to feel sorrow for losing them. Since they had no ethnic scapegoat they could easily blame, then, Swedish leaders were forced to respond to the loss of Finland in a more rational way, such as by blaming the organization of the military and the general inefficiency of the state bureaucracy. Thus, as Teorell and Rothstein (2015: 230) argue,

The most direct outcome of the loss of Finland was the great overhaul of the entire constitution and political system, bringing a new constitution that balanced the power of the king and the diet, and a new king from abroad. This constitutional reform in itself had important implications for the structure of the public administration, both in terms of further reforms of the Supreme Court, which only now was granted secure independence, as well as decreased influence by the nobility and the ensuing rise in meritocratic recruitment. But the point is not simply that the war of 1808–9 led to the loss of Finland, which was apparently far less "traumatizing" than previous historians have thought, but that it produced a generally held insight among the Swedish political and military elite that the very existence of Sweden as a sovereign nation had been under severe threat. The officers who took the initiative to the revolution of 1809 were convinced that Napoleon and the Tsar had decided to divide the country, incorporating the southern half with Denmark and giving the northern part to Russia. During the first months of 1808, large French, Spanish and Dutch forces joined the Danish army in order to attack the south of Sweden which, moreover, was ill-defended. Had these forces attacked, they would have outnumbered the part of the Swedish army stationed in Scania (Skåne) at a 6:1 ratio and the future of Sweden as a sovereign nation-state would have been severely threatened.

Sweden's bureaucracy was becoming increasingly professionalized, with recruitment to it being based more on merit. Since the Swedish state, in contrast to the German state after unification, already had a high level of legitimacy, there was no need to base employment on perceived loyalty to the state or on the conservatism of candidates.

The Relatively Autonomous Bureaucracy

Anton et al. (1971: 628) describe the unusual power and autonomy of the Swedish bureaucracy, and link it to the manner in which Gustav Vasa developed the Swedish state:

> Swedish administrators constitute an exceptionally powerful force in Swedish politics.…The centralized state created by Gustav Vasa in the sixteenth century was built upon an elite cadre of officials who, over time, earned both noble rank and special political privileges through services performed for the king. The national legislative body developed later, and when it did, royal administrators were guaranteed representation—a guarantee that permitted administrators to control the activities of the Riksdag for long periods of time. This situation no longer exists, of course, but administrators continue

to sit in the Riksdag, and continue to enjoy the high status conferred by the Swedish historical experience.

The next steps toward creating an autonomous, professionalized bureaucracy came under Gustav II Adolf and Queen Kristina in the early seventeenth century. Axel Oxenstierna, who was their Lord High Chancellor, took such steps as introducing collegial decision-making and a division of labor within the administration (Nilsson 1996: 181). While Oxenstierna was Chancellor, Johan Skytte donated money to Uppsala University to set up the world's first professorship in political science (actually it was called political science and rhetoric) in order to train the administrators.

Anton et al. note (p. 629) that Sweden has developed a unique system, with departments (similar to ministries) and administrative boards. A cabinet minister heads each department. The departments are rather small, usually with fewer than 100 employees, and they concentrate on proposing budgets, drafting legislation and engaging in long-term planning. The administrative boards, which are responsible for the daily work, are directly responsible to the cabinet as a whole rather than to a specific minister. Thus, no specific minister has authority over the boards, which are headed by general directors who are also largely independent of the ministries.

Again, this system of relative independence has its roots in the late medieval era. A state report (Statens offentliga utredningar 1968: 19) notes that the 1634 governmental reform led to the creation of national boards which developed into the administrative boards (*centrala ämbetsverken*), which are independent of each other and of the ministerial departments. Premfors (1993: 28) adds that this system of small departments and larger, independent administrative boards was established already in the 1720s. After the coup of 1809, the new constitution envisaged the public administration as an organization that could balance between the king and the political representatives of the public (*folkrepresentation*); accordingly, it made the bureaucracy into a mediating but independent organ (Statens offentliga utredningar 1968: 19). Administrators were to make their decisions according to the laws and regulations, and their responsibility was to be legally binding. The report further notes (p. 25) that administrative agencies in Sweden have tried to preserve their independence, on the grounds that decisions should be made on the level at which responsibility lies.

Consequently, civil servants in Sweden enjoyed much greater autonomy than their counterparts in Germany after unification. While I argue in this book against Arendt's idea of the "banality of evil"—according to which German bureaucrats simply did their duty and took no moral responsibility for their actions—it is true that the Swedish bureaucracy was more professionalized, less dependent on political appointments and less based on an ethos of obedience and loyalty. The Swedish model encouraged greater initiative on the part of civil servants, giving them greater scope to follow their conscience in developing and implementing policies. This can be seen clearly in the changes in Swedish refugee policies toward Jews during the Nazi era.

Tydén (2007: 123) reports that, despite awareness of the repression against Jews in Germany and Austria, Sweden only let in about 3000 Jewish refugee before the outbreak of war in September 1939. Most of these refugees were allowed into the country because of family connections. Levine (2002: 217) asserts that "key officials in Sweden's Foreign Office displayed clear anti-semitic attitudes" on the refugee issue. In fact these attitudes were so strong that, at the beginning of the war, restrictions on Jewish immigration were so strict that a doctor was turned back at the border even though she planned to fly to England, where she had a job waiting for her! (Hagberg 1966: 243). Tage Erlander, who was then at the interior ministry and who later became prime minister, writes in his memoirs—without any evident regret—that the government did not wish to allow Jewish immigration for fear that it would cause "far-reaching changes in Swedish society" (Erlander 1973: 110).

Tydén (2007: 123ff.) notes that the restrictive policy loosened up first in 1941, after the Nazis had introduced a prohibition for Jews to emigrate from Nazi-controlled areas. Until 1944 Sweden made no serious attempt to help non-Nordic Jews. However, despite censorship, many newspapers criticized Nazi Germany. Beginning in 1942, several newspapers started reporting details of the Holocaust. Because of this, a variety of individuals and private organizations worked hard to support Jewish refugees. Some businessmen risked their lives in 1940–1942 to smuggle out information on the Holocaust from Poland. Seven were arrested by the Gestapo and interned until 1944. During the last years of the war, moreover, people at the foreign office sought to help Jews and their families by trying to show they had Swedish connections, or by naturalizing them as Swedish citizens. The border with Norway was opened in 1942 to let Jews escape before deportations began, and in October 1943 Danish Jews found a safe refuge in Sweden. In Budapest, the Swedish delegation and Raoul Wallenberg worked to save as many Hungarian Jews as possible by giving them protected Swedish status. In the spring of 1945, Swedish "white busses" took in 18,000 people from German camps, of whom 4000–7000 were Jews. According to some estimates, around 45,000 Jews received help from Sweden. Some claim this policy was opportunistic—that Sweden waited until Germany began losing, at which point it started helping Jews in order to cultivate goodwill among the Allies. (Alternatively, some argue that Sweden was cowardly, because it did not help Jews when Germany was winning.) However, one reason for the increased willingness to help at the later stages was that Swedes learned more about the Jews' desperate situation as time went on. Furthermore, German troops remained in Sweden's Nordic neighbors until the end of the war and the German threat to Sweden did not recede much until the summer of 1943 at the earliest. Thus, Sweden took in Norwegian and Danish Jews *before* Germany started losing the war.

The cause for the shift in policy seems to have been the horror that some civil servants felt about the Holocaust. It was first Jews from Norway and Denmark who were given help to come to Sweden, since they were from fellow Nordic countries and so were not seen as "alien." According to Tydén (2007: 130), attitudes among the population started changing in 1941, out of outrage over the government's decision to allow Germany to transport soldiers through the country to Norway. Then, in 1942, some bureaucrats in the foreign ministry changed the direction of policy because they were becoming increasingly aware of the extraordinary events taking place on the continent. There was also increased pressure from the Swedish population. After the Norwegian Jews came in 1942, people wrote debate articles and held opinion meetings, and the Church demanded that "something be done" (p. 131). This major policy change did *not* come from the cabinet, but rather from civil servants, who felt the call of conscience and who therefore took courageous decisions. Information about the Holocaust started reaching ministry officials as early as 1941, from reliable first-hand informers who told of the mass execution of Jewish civilians taking place in German-occupied areas of the Soviet Union (Tydén 2007: 141).

Levine (2002: 219–20) observes that Under-Secretary Gösta Engzell was a key player, both in developing the Foreign Office's restrictive immigration policy during the 1930s and in formulating the change in policy once he received information about the Holocaust. Although he had previously held anti-Semitic views,

> Engzell seems to have been inclined to believe that what the Germans were doing to the Jews on the Continent was terrible, unprecedented and now, for him, confirmed. Indeed, years later he told two separate interviewers that by the late summer of 1942 he and other UD [foreign office] officials were convinced of the Germans' policy of extermination. Critically, in addition to possessing large amounts of credible information (again, as did his counterparts in the American and British governments), Engzell believed his information. And, as events were shortly to prove, he was psychologically prepared to allow this information to affect his actions, motivating him to make different choices than he had previously with regard to matters concerning Jews. (p. 223)

Even though Engzell had previously thought the fate of the Jews was not Sweden's concern, he took a different view once he found out about the Holocaust:

> [T]o his profound credit, once he did adopt a new attitude towards the issue of helping Jews, he did not allow Sweden's increasingly positive response to be constrained either geographically or ethnically. With one important exception, from the autumn of 1942 until the end of the war Engzell used his position to effect aid, relief and even the rescue of, eventually, tens of thousands of Jews. (p. 224)

Thus, the foreign office took action to help Jewish refugees at the same time that Christian Günter, the foreign minister, made it clear he harbored no sympathy for Jews and wanted Sweden to conduct a more pro-German foreign policy. Günter, who did not belong to any party, but had been nominated to his position by the conservatives (*Allmänna valmansförbundet*), assumed that Germany would win the war. Consequently, rather than staying neutral, he argued, Sweden should support Germany in order to be on good terms with the country after its victory (Krantz 1977: 248–9; Yahil 1967: 279). When a member of the cabinet complained about the Holocaust, Günter replied that his colleague had lost his balance because of his "Jewish blood" (Catomeris 2004: 141). The prime minister, for his part, seems to have been indifferent and to have taken no interest in the Holocaust (Tydén 2007: 137). Yet Under-Secretary Engzell at the foreign office—who had himself harbored anti-Semitic feelings earlier, and who had tried to restrict Jewish immigration rigorously—became morally repulsed by the Holocaust and, in opposition to the foreign minister, took action to help European Jews.

This is not to say that all governmental officials wanted to help Jewish refugees. Some were willing to collaborate with the Nazis. Tydén (2007: 141) reports that, after the *Kristallnacht* pogroms in Germany in 1938, Swedish authorities at the *Socialstyrelse* (National Board of Health and Welfare) began registering the racial background of foreigners. One of the employees at the *Socialstyrelse*'s bureau for foreigners was found guilty of forwarding the register to Nazi Germany. This man was an anti-Semite, and he hated communists. Such views were not thought especially unusual at the time for officials working there. This shows that the relatively autonomy enjoyed by the Swedish bureaucracy created an atmosphere where employees enjoyed some amount of leeway to make decisions they thought were morally correct, without having to worry about being "loyal" to the state in the unquestioning way that German bureaucrats were expected to do. However, this does not mean these bureaucrats all used their autonomy the same way. When following their conscience, some chose the "good" path of helping refugees; others took the "evil" path of supporting their persecution.

In conclusion, the Swedish bureaucracy differed from the Weberian ideal-type of a rational-legal bureaucracy, where the government passes detailed laws and civil servants have little autonomy in making decisions (cf. Rothstein 1992). Instead, Swedish public administrators enjoyed relative independence from the government. A tradition had developed whereby public servants were to follow the general policies of the government, but then to figure out the best ways of implementing them in individual cases (cf. Rothstein 1986). In addition, Swedish civil servants have traditionally had great influence in developing policies in the first place. In contrast to their German counterparts during the Bismarck era or under the Nazis, they were not chosen on the basis of their political ideology or their loyalty to the state. Instead they had a greater degree of professionalism, as the state already enjoyed so much legitimacy that the crown did not doubt their loyalty. This does not mean Swedish civil servants all had progressive views. Many were conservative, and it was common for those responsible for refugee issues to harbor anti-Semitic sentiments. Nevertheless, given the fact that they enjoyed great autonomy and did not feel the same pressure to be loyal to the government as their counterparts in Germany, they were able to follow their conscience when confronted with the horrors of the Holocaust. The result was that, although during the grand coalition government the conservative-leaning foreign minister[4] opposed increased Jewish immigration, and although the social democratic prime minister took no interest in the issue, these bureaucrats were able to change Sweden's policy and to foster the immigration of tens of thousands of Jewish refugees. Far from being banally evil robots who merely followed orders, they took initiative and showed moral courage.

RACISM SWEDISH-STYLE

As Sweden became a great power in the 1600s following its liberation from the Kalmar Union, its mythology surrounding its origins grew. Olof Rudbeck, professor of medicine at Uppsala University, played a central role here. In the late 1600s he wrote *Atlantica*, in which he claimed that Sweden was the sunken Atlantis about which Plato had written. It was the fatherland of the Gothic warriors and the mother of all civilization. Rudbeck noted the similarity in name between the Swedish *götar* (Geats) and the Goths (Hall 2000: 7ff.). Other Swedish authors elaborated this ideology further, but Gothicism as an idea was already present in the 1400s; thus, Rudbeck popularized ideas that existed already. According to this ideology, Magog Japhetson had come to Sweden 88 years after the Biblical flood and established the Gothic culture. Then, 871 years after the flood, Berik and his people sailed to the south and conquered Eastern Europe, driven by their inborn lust for battle. Meanwhile, the Geat amazons (female Geats) grew tired of staying at home, so they became warriors and conquered Asia (ibid.: 24ff.). Thus, Swedes were the most civilized people and had the highest culture.

This way of thinking gained popular support in the early twentieth century, as intellectuals began to think of Swedes as a "Germanic" people. Rudolf Kjellén, professor of political science at Uppsala University, was famous for his research on geopolitics, and he inspired Nazi geographers such as Haushofer (Hall 2000: 207). In 1903, Otto Sjögren claimed that Swedes and Norwegians were the closest of all peoples to their Germanic roots, being the least watered down by foreign influence. A few years later, in 1914, Henrik Schück, the rector of Uppsala University, wrote that a Germanic nationality had emerged during the Stone Age, consisting of people with long skulls who were superior to non-Germanic people, who had broad skulls. Schück's description was close to the Gothicist tradition and to Rudbeck. He went so far as to claim that Indo-Europeans came not from India but from the coast of the Baltic Sea, and that the Danes had come from Uppland (Hall 2000: 183–4).

With the advent of social Darwinism, this kind of thinking led to support for race biology. Scientists interested in this topic founded two organizations: the Swedish Society for Race Hygiene (*Svenska sällskapet för rashygien*), in Stockholm in 1909; and the Mendel Society (*Mendelska sällskapet*), in Lund in 1910. These organizations have two main goals: to set up a research institute for the study of race biology and to get support for a campaign to sterilize persons born with mental handicaps (Björkman 2012: 38; Broberg and Tydén 2005: 9; cf. Lindquist 1997). Many of the scientists involved were right-wing nationalists; however, some of the board members of the Swedish Society for Race Hygiene were left-leaning liberals with a strong commitment to social reform, such as Johan Vilhelm Hultkrantz, a medical professor from Uppsala University (Björkman and Widmalm 2010: 382).

Swedish researchers were also very active in promoting race biology internationally. For example, 46 of the 290 members of the *Internationale Gesellschaft für Rassenhygiene* (International Association for Race Hygiene) were Swedish, making the contingent from Sweden almost as big as that from Germany, a much larger country. The Swedish committee board for the *Internationale Gesellschaft für Rassenhygiene* included such notables as the founder of Swedish criminology, Olof Kinberg, and the Nobel Prize winner Svante Arrhenius (Broberg and Tydén 2005: 32). German race biologists also lobbied for the creation of an institute for the study of race biology in Sweden. In 1920, for example, Erwin Baur, professor of heredity at the agricultural college in Berlin, gave a lecture that was published in *Svenska läkartidningen* (Swedish Medical Magazine), calling on Sweden to contribute to human culture by establishing an institute of this kind. Germany, he noted, could not afford to set up such an institute, as it could barely maintain its existing ones (Hagerman 2015: 179).

Support from political leaders was just as strong for the creation of such an institute. Some of Sweden's most influential politicians were on board, among them Hjalmar Branting and Arvid Lindman, leader of the social democrats and conservative former prime minister respectively. The parliamentary committee dealing with the issue supported the motion unanimously (Broberg and Tydén 2005: 38). The proposal then passed in both chambers with little opposition (Björkman and Widmalm 2010: 386). Consequently, in 1922, the government established the first institute for research on race biology in the world: the State Institute for Race Biology (*Statens institut för rasbiologi*), based at Uppsala University (Björkman and Widmalm 2010: 379; Blomqvist 2006: Chap. 3; Broberg 2002, Broberg and Tydén 2005; Hagerman 2006; and Höjer 2012). Other prominent people, such as Hjalmar Hammarskjöld—former prime minister and father of Dag Hammarskjöld (Broberg and Tydén 2005: 42)—were on the Institute's board (*styrelse*). As the first such institute in the world, the State Institute for Race Biology had great influence on the development of the field.

According to Björkman and Widmalm (2010: 380):

> Not all early supporters of eugenics in Sweden subscribed to the radical ideas that we associate with these scientists, but the fact that some of its most influential promoters did—not least the director of the race-biological institute—would in effect make Swedish eugenics in the 1920s an important contributor to the right-wing flank of "mainline" or "orthodox" eugenics that would eventually become a pillar of Third Reich biopolitics. The Swedish race-biological institute was in fact the model for the corresponding Kaiser Wilhelm Institute founded in 1927 with Fritz Lenz as Director; after 1933 the Swedes Herman Nilsson-Ehle, Herman Lundborg and Torsten Sjögren would support Nazi interests in international organizations such as the International Federation of Eugenic Organisations.

The director of the Institute, Herman Lundborg, became famous for his studies of the Sami (Lapps) and of Baltic people (which in his view included Finns). He measured skulls in these studies, in an effort to develop theories linking human behavior to the shape and size of the skull. Lundborg sympathized with the Nazis, as did some of the members on the Institute's governing board (Björkman and Widmalm 2010: 387). Their research also influenced Nazi race biologists, and members of the Institute kept close contact with their German colleagues. Hence Hans F. Günther, the future Nazi race ideologist, lectured at the institute and took part in its activities. One prominent visitor in 1924 was Eugen Fischer, who later became rector of Berlin University and head of Berlin's Institute for Race Hygiene. In 1925, the author of the standard work in the field, Fritz Lenz from Munich, graced the Institute with his presence. Other well-known Nazi race biologists who gave lectures at the Institute were Hermann Muckermann, Walter Scheidt, Ernst Kretschmer and Egon von Eickstedt. Researchers from the other Nordic countries also visited the Institute.

With their public lectures, these various visitors provided important propaganda for the Institute (Broberg and Tydén 2005: 45). Lundborg privately shared the anti-Semitism of his German colleagues and he clearly sympathized with the Nazi regime. He felt, however, that he could not make these views public. Doing so, he believed, would endanger the funding which the Institute got from parliament. In fact, he always felt the Institute was underfinanced, so he was worried about its survival. Since he believed the Jews controlled the mass media, he thought the Institute would come under public attack if his true views became known, and then parliament might reduce its funding (Björkman and Widmalm 2010: 387). Thus, when the Swedish Nazi newspaper *Nationalsocialisten* was founded in 1924, its editor Sigurd Furugård, together with his brother Birger, wrote to Lundborg asking for his public support, since they got many of their race arguments from the Institute. Lundborg replied in a letter that he could not support them openly, although he sympathized with their views, because it would lead to press campaigns against him and the Institute would lose its public funding (Hagerman 2015: 241–2). The fact that Lundborg had to keep his views secret for tactical reasons shows that, even if there was widespread anti-Semitism in Sweden, it was nowhere near as radical or as openly embraced as in Germany.

Rather than stamping any group as an existential threat to society, race researchers such as Lundborg focused more on the alleged problems arising from racial mixture, and the consequent need to keep the Swedish "race" pure. Lundborg (1914: 58) wrote, for example, that "[i]t is not advisable for Swedes to mix with Finns or Lapps who have Mongolian origins. For the same reason, mixing with Slavic peoples, Russian Jews and such races should be avoided." Another issue, which was more important for the political discourse, was the perceived need to improve the "popular stock" (*folkstam*) through sterilization policies, thereby preventing mentally weak persons from reproducing, and to promulgate policies encouraging people with the best genes to have the most children (e.g., Hansson 1994: 22; Lindquist 1997: 48).

However, the Institute started to lose influence when the Nazis came to power, as many Swedish politicians began to grow skeptical of research on race biology when they saw how the Nazis were using it. Only the Farmers' Party called in its platform for measures to preserve the Swedish "race." The youth section of the conservative party also began to sympathize with the Nazis. As a result, however, it was thrown out of the party, prompting its members to create their own party with their three MPs, who had been elected as conservatives. In the next election, in 1936, the new party failed to get into parliament.

Another reason for the Institute's loss of influence had to do with Lundborg's character. He gained a reputation as a person with whom it was hard to cooperate (e.g., Broberg 2002: 36–7; Hagerman 2015: 315). Consequently, of the seven people who were employed at the institute from the beginning, by 1930 only his Austrian-Jewish assistant Krauss was left. The vice head, Linders, openly criticized Lundborg for not giving him enough freedom to do his own research, and claimed it was difficult to work with him (Hagerman 2015: 315). In addition, Lundborg's racism seemed less credible when it became known that his long-time assistant was an Austrian Jew (Åmark 2011: 364). Even more damaging were the many love affairs he was alleged to have had with Sami women. In fact, he had a child with a woman whom he considered to be of "mixed" Sami and Baltic blood and eventually married her (e.g., Hagerman 2015; Svensson 2015).

When Lundborg retired, a big battle over his successor ensued. He preferred another racist, Torsten Sjörgren; but several top social democrats, such as the political scientist Herbert Tingsten and the economist Gunnar Myrdal, lobbied the government successfully to choose an anti-racist, Gunnar Dahlberg. Dahlberg then led the Institute more in the direction of medical research on genetics (Åmark 2011: 365; Hagerman 2015: 328ff.; Lindquist 1997: 131).

Despite the widespread initial support for research on race biology in Sweden, it did not lead to the kind of extreme racism that developed in Germany. Lundborg studied the Sami, but they mostly lived in the isolated north of the country, so it was hard to argue that they controlled the economy or the press or that they were involved in any kind of international conspiracy. Neither were they active in political parties. Therefore, it was hard to portray them as an existential threat to society, in the way that German racists portrayed the Jews. As for the Jews themselves, they were perceived as much less of a threat in Sweden than they were in Germany, partly because there were far fewer of them, and partly they had lived in the country for a much shorter period. Since Sweden was a long-established, stable and secure state that enjoyed a high level of legitimacy, leaders found no need to search for an outgroup to persecute in order to gain legitimacy.

In contrast to the German states, in many of which Jews had been living ever since medieval times, Sweden did not allow Jews to immigrate until Gustav III became king (Catomeris 2004: 113; Runblom 1995: 93). Valentin (1964: 47ff.) reviews the history. In 1774, Aaron Isaac became the first Jew to be permitted to move permanently to Sweden without converting to Christianity. The responsible authorities had in fact ruled that he could only remain in the country if he converted to Christianity, but King Gustav III decreed in 1775 that he could stay without doing so, together with his brother and a companion. Isaac also received permission from the governor (*överståtshållare*) to bring in at least ten men for 13 years (ten being the quorum for holding religious services). He also got permission for a rabbi and a Jewish cemetery. The first Jewish congregation was thereupon founded in Stockholm. Then, in 1777, three Jews got the right to work as stone carvers (*stensnidare*) and seal engravers (*sigillgravörer*). The authorities had initially turned them down, as the government did not want engravers but rather merchants. Members of the political elite were more tolerant than Swedes in general, who tended to be suspicious of Jews and to believe in tenacious myths about them. Thus, when Isaac, as the first Jew, received the right to live in Stockholm, he dared not go out in public during the first two weeks, because the atmosphere toward Jews was so negative, including in the press.

The guilds in particular were against Jewish immigration, fearing increased competition. Over subsequent decades, laws and regulations were gradually loosened up to allow for increased immigration by Jews. The old estates and guilds opposed these developments. As Valentin states, "[t]he burghers and the guilds saw Jews as intruders who threatened their living standards." By contrast, Valentin points out, "the bureaucracy— including the government, the provincial administrations (*länsstyrelser*) and the magistrates—sought to loosen economic regulations" (p. 62). In this regard, the situation in Sweden was different than that in the German states, where bureaucrats tended to hold negative views about Jews. In 1812, the Board of Trade declared that Jews in Sweden had benefited the general public through their industry and entrepreneurialism, and suggested measures to encourage the immigration of wealthy Jews. Carl David Skogman played an important role in this connection. As under-secretary in charge of trade and finance from 1821 to 1838, and as president of the Board of Trade from 1833, he laid the basis for the liquidation of the guilds. During his last months as under-secretary, moreover, he prepared—with the support of the king—the suspension of the rules regarding Jews.

Such moves met with opposition, for the commoner estates were overwhelmingly anti-Jewish, as were many of the craftsmen, traders and entrepreneurs. Yet, during this period, most of Europe was getting rid of laws that discriminated against Jews. "The more the laws regarding Jews seemed to be an anachronism, the less motivated the authorities became to treat Jews who were born in Sweden and who spoke Swedish as strangers; accordingly, the government started exempting Jews from the exclusionary rules which had separated them from other inhabitants" (Valentin 1964: 74–5). However, none of the leading newspapers supported Jewish emancipation, except for *Göteborgs Handels och Sjöfartstidning*.

Popular opposition to Jewish emancipation was so great that, on August 30, 1838, there were fears that a pogrom would take place. Accordingly, those who felt threatened asked the authorities for protection for their life and property. The military got involved and was able to keep order. On September 10, however, mobs broke the windows of many Jewish and even some non-Jewish homes. These riots met with general disapproval and they were not repeated. Even so, the government responded to them by withdrawing its resolution to grant Jews the right to live wherever in the country they wished (Catomeris 2004: 115; Valentin 1964: 79–80).

By 1851, not only had most of Europe introduced Jewish emancipation, that year even Norway decided on full emancipation, making it even harder for Sweden to oppose it. The bourgeoisie, which had been the strongest opponents previously, now supported emancipation enthusiastically. The upper estates were no longer showing any animosity toward Jews at this point, although the lower strata in the cities were still very negative. The trend among peasants was positive, because increased *folkupplysning* (public awareness, education) was making them less susceptible to anti-Jewish portrayals. Moreover, since every change in the constitution required the support of all four estates, the abolition of the four-estate system of representation in 1866 was a great victory for emancipation, because it reduced the importance of representatives from the church. In the four-estate system, the clerical chamber had been able to block reforms. Now, however, there were only two parliamentary chambers, neither of which was estate based; as a result, MPs hailing from the church were too few in number to be able to block reforms (Valentin 1964: 98ff.). Finally, in 1870, both chambers voted to grant Jews full emancipation (Catomeris

2004: 118). Valentin (1964: 107) remarks: "Both liberals and conservative[s]…greeted the reform with enthusiasm." At the same time, the number of Jews in the country was too small to prompt the kind of debates seen in Germany about the alleged economic power of the Jews. In 1843 the Jewish congregation had about 400 members, of whom 80–90 had converted (p. 119).

Another important difference from the situation in Germany was that Jews were not associated with the socialist parties in Sweden. In Germany, many of the leading socialist theorists and leaders—among them Marx, Kautsky, Bernstein and Luxemburg—were of Jewish descent. Consequently, the German social democrats fought against anti-Semitism continuously, and racists claimed the party was controlled by Jews. According to Brustein and King (2004), moreover, anti-Semitic political movements were stronger in countries where leftist parties were alleged to be under Jewish influence.

In Sweden, by contrast, the social democrats did not have any prominent Jewish leaders, and the party itself had a tradition of anti-Semitism (although such views were never generally accepted as party policy). Already before the party was founded, in fact, the socialist newspaper *Folkets Röst* had been attacking Jewish merchants and factory owners (Blomqvist 2006: 261). Atterdag Wermelin, who introduced Marx to Swedish socialists, gave a speech at a meeting of the Social Democratic Association in 1886 in which he warned about the desire of rich Jews to get 40 percent in profit while people were starving. His speech was printed as a brochure (pp. 274–5). The newspaper *Proletären*, put out by the socialist workers' club in Norrköping, trafficked in stereotypes about Jews during the late 1880s and early 1890s, equating them with capitalist oppression and imputing certain racial properties to them. By the turn of the century, however, such anti-Semitic formulations were less and less frequent (pp. 277–8).[5]

Anti-Semitism, then, became less common within the social democratic party. Yet, it did not disappear. In 1907, for example, the Social Democratic Youth Club in Luleå circulated a petition against dirty literature in which they complained that the country was owned by "usurious Jews" (Blomqvist 2006: 302). In 1921, the social democratic newspaper *Arbetet*, based in southern Sweden, warned of the deleterious effects of racial mixture and averred that Judaism was a parasite on society. The newspaper's editor, the aforementioned Arthur Engberg, contended that the Bolshevik danger was Jewish and not Russian (Blomqvist 2006: 20–25). Engberg penned such articles between 1917 and 1924. They did not lead to any reactions and they did not prevent him from holding high posts within the party. In other words, while the party did not promote anti-Semitism, and while it never had racism in its party program (in contrast to the Farmers' Party), it still tolerated racist and anti-Semitic views until the early 1930s. In 1924, Engberg became the chief editor of *Social-Demokraten*, the main party organ. In 1932 he was appointed minister for education and religion (by which time, however, he had renounced anti-Semitism and become an active anti-Nazi) (Catomeris 2004: 127).

Meanwhile, the first professor[6] to join the social democrats, Bengt Lidforss, defended Strindberg's anti-Semitism, arguing that the author's critics lacked an "Aryan soul" (Catomeris 2004: 130). In 1908, Lidforss claimed that mixing with lower races was fatal and that racial mixture had undermined the different races. He relied in this regard on *Die Grundlagen des neunzehnten Jahrhunderts*, a highly racist and anti-Semitic book by H.S. Chamberlain which would have great influence on the Nazis (p. 176). By the late 1920s, though, anti-Semitism was dying out within the party, and its association with the Nazis in Germany—whom the social democrats saw as ideological enemies—made it much less palatable. In any case, given the lack of Jewish leaders in the party, and given the element of anti-Semitism found within it, the social democrats in Sweden could not be plausibly portrayed as under the control of Jews.

Moreover, to the extent anti-Semitism existed within the social democratic movement, it did not have any eliminationist tendencies. To be sure, anti-Semitism was hegemonic in Swedish society during the first three decades of the twentieth century. It was seen to a great extent as obvious and natural (Blomqvist 2006: 254). It did not, however, take the extreme form that it did in Germany. Furthermore, the mainstream of the party never embraced anti-Semitism. In fact the first leader of the party, Hjalmar Branting, "was an outspoken opponent of the antisemitic movement in Germany" (Blomqvist 2017: 330).

While it is true that, unlike their German comrades, the Swedish social democrats were not linked in the public mind with Jews, the Bolsheviks in Russia *were*. Blomqvist (2013: 87) gives many examples of this. Warning of a "Jewish invasion from the east to Berlin," the newspaper *Stockholms Dagblad* referred darkly to "doubtful elements, mostly Jews who were moving into the city and engaging in usury under the protection of radical groups, who opposed measures against Jews…" In 1923, P.A. Norstedt & Söner published Viktor Malmberg's eyewitness account of the Soviet

Union, *Några år i Lenins paradis*. Malmberg, who had worked in a Soviet hospital, claimed that Jews were the "secret hand" behind the revolution (p. 112). Similarly, the labor liberal[7] Anton Nyström wrote that, in 1919, 80 percent of the Soviet regime's commissioners were Jews, and that Jews dominated the Spartacus League in Germany as well. He added that he had heard the Bolshevik movement had been founded by Jews in New York many years before. Furthermore, Jews directed all of the departments in the Soviet regime, from defense to the commission for Polish affairs (p. 89). Blomqvist concludes that the claim that "Bolshevik power to some extent went together with Jews and Jewishness was nearly trivial [i.e., was seen as obvious] in the academic literature as well as in the broader popular representations published by well-respected publishers" (p. 195). However, the Swedish communist party remained small and was not thought to be infiltrated by Jews; thus, while the presumed link between Jews and the Soviet regime led to increased support in Sweden for Nazi Germany in WWII, it did not lead to greater support for national socialist parties within the country, or to greater support for any eliminationist type of anti-Semitism.

Yet, anti-Semitism was widespread in Sweden, even if support for racist political parties was weak, and even if the kind of eliminationist anti-Semitism of which Goldhagen writes never developed. For example, a running theme in Swedish films during the 1930s was the impossibility of Jews' ever becoming Swedish (Wright 1998).

Catomeris (2004: 121) remarks that humor magazines, such as *Söndags-Nisse*, *Strix*, *Naggen*, *Karbasen* and *Figaro*, made jokes about Jews. Together, these magazines had around 700,000 readers per week in the 1890–1920 period. Inspired by the German press, they told hundreds of anti-Semitic jokes—even though they were mostly liberal or leftist (see also Andersson 2000: 473–85). Again, however, this type of anti-Semitism was not eliminationist. Similarly, one of the key figures in anti-Semitic campaigns in Sweden was Pehr Emanuel Lithander, a wholesaler and conservative MP. Lithander made public statements against Jews, yet he called the pogroms in Russia "barbaric" (although he also claimed they were caused by "Jewish exploitation") (p. 125). Lithander's anti-Semitism, then, was not eliminationist, since he condemned the pogroms in no uncertain terms.

Some of the "free churches" (i.e., Protestant churches not belonging to the state church) showed some sympathy with the Nazis when they came to power; but even these groups found Germany's anti-Jewish policies too extreme to be palatable. Thörn (2006) has studied their magazines. He reports that *Missions-Barnet*, a publication of the Örebro Evangelical church, praised Hitler for fighting against anti-Christian communism and low morals in society (p. 19). Nevertheless, it criticized the bloody violence of the regime and its persecution of the Jews, the people with whom God had made a covenant in the Old Testament. It also criticized the regime for confusing the human level with that of the divine. After the beginning of 1933, the magazine ceased all praise for the Nazi regime (p. 20). *Bibliskt Månadshäfte*, a magazine for biblical study, took a harsher view of Jews and spread stereotypes about them, including the idea that they were trying to take over the world. It claimed they were behind communism and that they had chosen Russia for their experiment. It also described Jews as greedy. Yet, it claimed too that God loves Jews, having made them His chosen people; Christians, therefore, could not be hateful toward Jews (pp. 24–25). Neither did all free-church publications hold anti-Semitic or pro-Nazi views. *Veckoposten*, a magazine put out by the Swedish Baptist Mission, criticized Nazism from the beginning, claiming it had nothing to do with Christianity and was a dangerous national-pagan doctrine (p. 22). Finally, none of these Christian magazines—whatever their views otherwise about either Jews or Nazis—shared the eliminationist anti-Semitism of the latter.

Sweden's upper classes were another possible source of anti-Semitism, given the good relations they had traditionally maintained with Germany. This pro-German sentiment did result initially in some sympathy for the Nazis. For example, it was a tradition for the king to marry a German. Moreover, King Gustaf V congratulated Hitler on his invasion of the Soviet Union. However, the king's support was based on anti-Bolshevism, not anti-Semitism. Bojerud (2010: 45) reports that, in the spring of 1933, Gustaf V visited Berlin and met Hitler, who became very angry when the king urged him to stop the repression of the Jews. Nevertheless, the king sympathized with Hitler's foreign policy, expressing his "warm thanks to the Führer" when Germany invaded the Soviet Union, and praising the dictator for his decision to wipe out "the Bolshevik epidemic" (Uhlin 1972: 36–7).

According to Åmark (2011: 376ff.), a large number of Swedes harbored anti-Semitic prejudices during this period, but rejected national socialism at the same time. It was common in the 1930s to weigh the Jews' good sides against their bad sides and to take a "balanced" position based on "facts," leading to an ambivalent attitude (p. 389). Åmark notes that many of those who rejected Nazism still thought that a wave of Jewish immigration would threaten "Swedish culture" and the "Swedish race." Moreover, even those who rejected anti-Semitism often argued that the solution would be the assimilation of Jews or their conversion to Christianity. It was rare to argue for a generous immigration policy toward Jews in the 1930s. Some debaters displayed everyday anti-Semitism and accepted certain stereotypes about Jews, but rejected the increasingly violent Nazi policies toward them. Furthermore, when they saw how things were turning out in Germany, many renounced their previous negative attitudes toward Jews. Even Sven Hedin, the pro-Nazi author—who gave vent to deep anti-Semitism in his diaries and letters—wrote in 1937 that the Nazis' violence against Jews was "regrettable." So, even if anti-Semitism was widespread in Sweden, it was not an anti-Semitism of the eliminationist kind. Most Swedes opposed the extreme type of anti-Semitism that the Nazis were implementing. Thus, after the *Kristallnacht* pogroms in Germany in 1938, the conservative magazine *Svensk Tidskrift* reacted angrily, calling them "barbaric" (Åmark 2011: 386).

Not surprisingly, the only groups in Sweden to espouse eliminationist anti-Semitism in some measure were the various Nazi parties that emerged during the 1920s, and that largely disappeared when WWII ended. However, these parties were all rather small. They failed to get into parliament, they fought constantly among themselves, and they split repeatedly (e.g., Åmark 2011; Bojerud 2010). During the 1930s, openly Nazi parties gained 15,000–25,000 votes, or well under one percent (Åmark 2011: 292).

Interestingly, even though the Swedish Nazi parties were anti-Semitic, even they at times had trouble with Hitler's eliminationist policies. One of the country's most infamous Nazi leaders was Sven Olov Lindholm. Despite his support for dictatorship, Lindholm started to find Hitler's anti-Semitism too extreme. He grew disillusioned with Hitler, so he decided in 1938 to change his party's name from *Sveriges nationalsocialistiska arbetarparti* (Sweden's National Socialist Workers' Party) to *Svensk socialistisk samling* (League of Swedish Socialists). He also removed the swastika as its symbol. To justify this move, he wrote: "If we are honest, we must certainly admit that Germany's policies toward the Jews are not the correct ones. We don't hate the Jew because he is a Jew, but rather for the policies he carries out" (Nilsson 2000: 72). Nilsson (2000: 95) claims that many national socialist activists began to rethink their views in reaction to the persecution of the Jews. However, one Nazi organization—the

New Swedish Movement—did not change its views even when the extermination camps became known.

The most successful pro-Nazi organization was *Sveriges Nationella Ungdomsförbund* (Sweden's National Youth League; Swedish acronym: SNU). The SNU started out in 1915 as an independent organization (Larsmo 2007: 94; Nilsson 2000: 83), but it soon became the youth league of the conservative party. At the end of the 1920s it started moving closer to Nazism. In 1934, the conservative party reacted to this development by repudiating the SNU and starting its own youth organization, whereupon the SNU became a party: *Sveriges Nationella Förbund* (Sweden's National League; Swedish acronym: SNF). Three of the organization's leading members—who had been sitting in parliament as conservatives—then started their own legislative fraction, but it did poorly in the 1936 elections. In 1940, finally, the group completed its evolution from a right-wing extremist party into a more purely Nazi organization (e.g., Åmark 2011: 289; Bojerud 2010: 30ff.). Its clear anti-Semitic stance was evident in its program, which read in part: "We want to destroy Jewish influence, because it is a danger to the nation—but without turning innocent people's lives into tragedies" (Bojerud 2010: 31).

Berg (2016) has surveyed the motions made by the SNF's members of parliament. She notes that, in 1935, they made a motion on the population issue, in which they argued that immigration by non-Scandinavians would be inappropriate from a race-biological viewpoint (p. 28, Motion AK 1935 no. 3, p. 7). They also wanted to make "kin hygiene" an obligatory course in school (pp. 37–8, Motion AK 1936 no. 622, pp. 3–5). They believed, namely, that a family's survival would be seriously threatened if persons with poor genes were allowed to marry into it. People with good genes should be encouraged to reproduce more, people with bad genes to reproduce less. They also called for the immigration law to be changed, so that physicians would check those wishing to move to Sweden to ensure they did not have physical or psychological ailments that might be heritable or contagious. They also thought it important that immigrants be as much like Swedes as possible in ethnic terms, so that minority problems could be avoided. They gave Jews as an example of a group that, being too different from Europeans, would give rise to such problems. Ernst Hage, a social democratic MP, pointed out that Jews were the obvious target of the motion, and he expressed satisfaction that the conservative party did not support it; thus, the SNF stood alone (p. 44, Motion AK 1936 no. 603, pp. 1–11).

The fact that national socialist and fascist parties did not gain much support does not mean that no Swedes would have been willing to collaborate with a Nazi occupation regime. Rather it means that, without a military occupation of the country, it is extremely unlikely that a totalitarian regime could have been established. The military and the police merit particular attention here. These sectors may be expected to have harbored a disproportionately large number of Nazi sympathizers, inasmuch as officers and police tend to have more authoritarian personalities than people in general. Of tradition, moreover, ties with Germany were strong within industrial, aristocratic and military circles in Sweden. Officers, finally, often had great respect for Germany's military might.

A police commission set up by the security services looked into the issue of extremists among the police. Its investigators interviewed 420 police out of 2700 in the three largest cities. They did not find any communists. Nineteen police were members of *Svensk socialistisk samling*, which was the only Nazi party at the time (1942). Fifty-nine had previously been a member of a Nazi organization but were no longer. Another 23 were members of a relatively new pro-Nazi organization, *Svensk Opposition* (Swedish Opposition), which was not a political party. A further 20–30 sympathized with Nazism but were not members of any Nazi organization. Around 120 police, then, were active Nazis or had been (Åmark 2011: 295).

Where the military is concerned, Bojerud (2010: 49) cites a study by the Swedish intelligence service which calculated that, in 1940, 162 officers had Nazi sympathies. However, these figures only included registered members of pro-Nazi organizations, so other officers may have been sympathizers without being members (p. 50). Most of these officers, however, were members of the Sweden-Germany National Association (*Riksföreningen Sverige-Tyskland*), rather than of any openly national socialist organization. In 1942, the commander-in-chief of the Swedish military (*överbefälhavare*) ordered a study of Nazis and communists within the defense establishment. The study concluded that 18 officers, 17 warrant officers and 43 noncommissioned officers had Nazi sympathies, as did 341 draftees. Around 20–25 noncommissioned officers (*underbefäl*) were communists, as were 3000–3500 draftees. These figures are doubtful, however, because only one year earlier the Navy had 30 officers who were members of the pro-Nazi *Svensk Opposition*. At the infantry school in Rosersberg, moreover, 17 officers were members of that organization (p. 51).[8]

Even if only a small minority of officers sympathized openly with the Nazis, German diplomats at any rate seem to have been under the impression that the bulk of the Swedish officer corps supported Germany in the war. According to Gunnar Hägglöf, head of the foreign trade section at the foreign ministry, the German envoy Schnurre reported to the German foreign office in July 1944 that 90 percent of Sweden's officers supported Swedish participation in the war against Russia. The military attaché, General Major von Uthman, repeated this to Hägglöf, who denied it was true; but von Uthman claimed he had heard it from high-level Swedish officers (Nilsson 2000: 52). Whether true or not, this shows at least that well-placed German diplomats thought Germany would be able to count on help from Swedish officers.

Another example comes from Helge Jung, head of the Swedish military from 1944 to 1951. Jung wrote in his diary that, in 1945, an officer by the name of C.A. Ehrensvärd spoke of the perception held among members of the German delegation in Sweden. In 1941, that is to say, members of said delegation had suggested that Swedish officers would work on Germany's behalf, by openly aiding Finland in its war against the Soviet Union. Ehrensvärd had been chief of staff in the Swedish Volunteer Corps during the Winter War in Finland in 1940; thus, he had been involved personally in the fight against the Soviet Union. Another officer, Axel Rappe, had also sought Swedish entry into the war on Finland's side; accordingly, he wanted Ehrensvärd to be chief of staff while he himself would be *kårchef* (head of the military unit). Ehrensvärd refused, however, to appoint Rappe to the latter position, so Rappe wanted someone else to be chief of staff. Rappe wanted to go much further than just taking Finland's side against Russia. In fact, he spoke of recruiting Swedish officers to assist German units on the eastern front. Berlin, however, rejected this idea, showing that German military headquarters took a different view than the German delegation in Stockholm (Nilsson 2000: 52).

Several officers wrote in their memoirs that there had even been talk of a military coup. For example, Stig H:son Ericson mentioned in his memoirs that, at an official dinner in March 1940, Rappe asked him if he would support a coup. In *Per Albin och kriget*, Alf W. Johansson wrote that Colonel Axel Gyllenkrok spoke openly with his colleagues about a military coup. Johansson also reported that Charles de Champs, a retired admiral, discussed the idea of setting up a new government with the king, whereupon the king replied that Hansson, the social democratic prime minister, would be the one setting up the government (cited in Nilsson 2000: 57). Among top military leaders, Nilsson concludes (p. 65), "there was a deep seated anti-communism. They expected Germany to win the war, so it was important to be on the winning side." They were motivated more from anti-communism and a pro-German stance than from any kind of eliminationist anti-Semitism.

Why was Swedish anti-Semitism less hateful than the German variant? Again, part of the answer has to do with state-building. The Swedish state was strong and stable and had existed for centuries, so there was no need to unite the country by stigmatizing an outgroup. It was also hard to claim that Jews posed an existential threat. It was especially difficult to make such a claim since there were very few Jews in the country and few Swedes had ever had any contact with Jews. Furthermore, while Swedish researchers on race biology tended to have Nazi sympathies, their studies were focused mainly on the Sami ("Lapps"), most of whom lived in the north of Sweden. This ethnic group lived largely separate lives from the other inhabitants of the country. Since they mostly lived in the poorer north, they did not play much of a role in the country's economic, cultural or political life. This made it difficult to mobilize society by portraying them as some kind of existential threat.

Nor did the loss of Norway in 1905 lead to the kind of pro-fascist nationalism seen in Austria after the break-up of the Austro-Hungarian Empire as the departure of Norway did not alter the Swedish sense of nationhood. It should be noted that even during the union period, Norway had its own constitution and government. Norway enjoyed great independence from Sweden concerning domestic policies, but the king was Swedish and Sweden determined foreign policy. Thus, Norway was never integrated into Sweden the way, for example, the Czech lands were integrated into the Austro-Hungarian Empire. Moreover, Swedish nationalists saw Norwegians as belonging to the same Germanic ethnicity as Swedes (Hall 2000: 103), so the dissolution of the union did not result in any change in the country's ethnic make-up. In addition, few Norwegians had moved to Sweden during the period of the union, because Norway was the more industrialized of the two countries at the time. Instead, it was more common for Swedes to move to Norway (Runblom 1995: 93). Consequently, Sweden never had any issue of how to deal with a Norwegian minority within Sweden itself. In Austria, by contrast, the loss of the empire meant that areas with large Hungarian and Slavic populations were now lost, leaving just a small rump state of almost exclusively German ethnic composition. This bred pro-German feelings and support for *Anslußß*.

Conclusion

Even though Sweden is a Germanic country that had a history of anti-Semitism, support for race biology and myths about its alleged superiority over other peoples and countries, it did not follow Germany's totalitarian path; neither did it support "evilness" on a mass scale. This chapter shows that Sweden's state-building process encouraged a more tolerant, democratic path of development. In contrast to Germany, which only recently had become a state, Sweden had existed for many centuries by the time that fascist movements emerged across Europe. As a strong state that enjoyed a high level of legitimacy, the country's leaders had no need to find an outgroup to stigmatize and present as an existential threat in order to unite the country. In addition, no outgroup presented a credible existential threat. Furthermore, despite widespread anti-Semitism, little support for the "eliminationist" variant arose, as even some pro-Nazi leaders opposed the Holocaust.

In further contrast to Germany, Sweden developed in a manner, which encouraged consensus and cooperation. Historically, Swedish peasants had a relatively high level of influence, as the kings often relied on their support against the nobles. Consequently, peasants formed one of the four estates that comprised the Swedish parliament until electoral reforms took place in the nineteenth century. Thus, traditionally the Swedish monarchy had to reach compromises with groups in society outside of the aristocracy. Even the transition to democracy was based on consensus and compromise, as all the political parties supported democratization as did the king. Since the crown supported the reforms the system enjoyed great "backward legitimacy" and conservatives had little reason to oppose these changes. This contrasts greatly to Germany where none of the political parties in parliament at the time of the revolution—including the social democrats—wanted to overthrow the old regime and dispose of the monarchy. This caused a legitimacy crisis for the Weimar Republic in Germany.

Since the peasants in Sweden were well-organized, they formed a political party that represented their interests when the country democratized. This again contrasts to Germany, where outside of Bavaria, peasants did not have their own party; therefore, many of them turned to the Nazis. Many peasants in Sweden did display some authoritarian and racists tendencies, as did the Farmers' Party itself. Yet, since the party accepted democracy and formed a coalition government with the social democrats for much of the 1930s, the party had to downplay its racism and support the creation of a modern welfare state. As a result, peasants with mildly anti-Semitic attitudes got coopted into the democratic system.

Another important difference to Germany concerns the bureaucracy. Since Germany was a newly created state, the rulers feared that civil servants might not be loyal to the new state, so they purposely recruited people with conservative, authoritarian values, whom could be trusted to be faithful to the Kaiser. Thus, when Germany democratized through a revolution, the democratic regime met great resistance from the public administrators. In Sweden, by contrast, the state was so well-established and uncontested that loyalty to the state was never an issue. Therefore, qualifications rather than political views became more important for recruiting public servants in Sweden than in Germany. Consequently, the rulers could trust the bureaucrats to do a good job, so they granted them much more autonomy than in Germany. In addition, since the transition to democracy was peaceful and based on a consensus and enjoyed the blessing of the king, bureaucrats had little reason to oppose the democratic state. It is certainly possible that if Sweden's democratization had come about through a revolution, then some public employees would have been critical of the new regime, but it is unlikely that their opposition would have been anything like the opposition to the new regime in Germany, because in contrast to Germany, having conservative, anti-democratic values was not a condition for recruitment to the bureaucracy in Sweden. Since they were used to having autonomy and were not pressured to be blindly loyal to the state, it was also easier for Swedish bureaucrats than for German bureaucrats to take the initiative in committing "good" acts, such as saving Jewish lives and it would have been easier for Swedish civil servants to refuse to carry out "evil" acts of repression than it was for their German counterparts.

Even though the state-building process played the most important role in preventing a turn toward totalitarianism, the choices of actors was important. For example, the social democrats followed a conscious strategy of appropriating the term "folk" to use it for supporting solidarity projects that would increase public support for them, while in Germany the anti-democratic right was able to appropriate the term for supporting racist-nationalist policies. In addition, the social democrats in Sweden consciously chose to invite the Farmers' Party into the governing coalition in order to coopt peasants and get them to support the democratic welfare state rather than go in an authoritarian direction.

Of course, *if* Nazi Germany had invaded Sweden, it would have found willing collaborators as many officers and policemen sympathized with them. However, the point is that Nazi parties fared poorly and had little chance of coming to power without outside intervention. In addition, even if they had invaded and even if they would have found collaborators, they would have likely met stiff resistance from portions of the bureaucracy, which did not share their authoritarian values and which enjoyed a tradition of having autonomy and taking responsible for their decisions.

NOTES

1. Skåne was previously a part of Denmark and was conquered by Sweden in the seventeenth century and then underwent a process of becoming culturally Swedish.
2. On the party leader's anti-Semitism, see, for example, Hall (2000: 265).
3. In fact, some did put the blame on Swedish speaking Finnish officers (see a discussion in Edgren 2010), but that is not the same as blaming the Finns in general. Moreover, these generals were ethnic Swedes, which made it even more difficult to blame Finns as an ethnic group.
4. Again, the foreign minister did not belong to any party, but the conservatives proposed him for the position. In fact, they even threatened to resign from the coalition if Günther were fired from his position. Many social democrats opposed the foreign minister's pro-German stance and wanted him removed from office, but the prime minister thought it was more important to keep the coalition together than to fire Günther.
5. For a discussion in English, see Blomqvist (2017).
6. Note: in the Swedish system until recently, most departments only had one professor. Thus, the title was much more prestigious than it has been at American universities.
7. "Labor Liberal" was a term that was common in the late 1800s and early 1900s, to denote liberals who supported the labor movement in Sweden.
8. Åmark (2011: 297) gives slightly different statistics. According to him, the security service reported that, in April 1940, 162 out of some 4800 active officers were suspected of being Nazis or Nazi sympathizers. However, this figure included retired and reserve officers. A new study, done in 1942, found only 18 registered Nazis among officers. Moreover, all one had to do to end up on the list was to subscribe to a Nazi newspaper or to requisition some Nazi materials. The Sweden-Germany National Association was not openly Nazi; but it was pro-German, and it took an understanding attitude toward German Nazism. Three-hundred and nine members of the organization had officer titles; but here too, retired and reserve officers were

included. Eight were generals, 2 were admirals, and 25 were colonels (*över-
star*). *Svensk Opposition* had 221 officers as members, of whom 46 were in
the group's national organization (*riksförening*).

REFERENCES

Åmark, K. (2011). *Att bo granne med ondskan: Sveriges förhållande till nazismen,
Nazityskland och Förintelsen* (5th ed.). Pössneck: Bonniers.
Andersson, L. M. (2000). *En jude är en jude är en jude: representationer av "juden"
i svensk skämtpress omkring 1900–1930*. Lund: Nordic Academic Press.
Anton, T. L., Linde, C., & Mellbourn, A. (1971). Bureaucrats in Politics: A Profile
of the Swedish Administrative Elite. *Canadian Public Administration,
16*(4), 627–651.
Bägerfeldt, L. (2003). *När Sverige blev till: En annorlunda teori om Svea rikes
vagga*. Falköping: Lars Bägerfeldts förlag.
Bägerfeldt, L. (2004). *När Sverige blev en stat: Övergången från rike to stat i bör-
jan av medeltiden*. Falköping: Lars Bägerfeldts förlag.
Bengtsson, E. (2019). The Swedish Sonderweg in Question: Democratization and
Inequality in Comparative Perspective, c.1750–1920. gtz010, https://doi.
org/10.1093/pastj/gtz010.
Berg, S. (2016). *Ökända fascister eller goda högermän? En studie av Sveriges natio-
nella förbunds riksdagspolitik åren 1933–1936*. BA thesis, Umeå University,
Liberal-Arts and Social Science Program.
Björkman, M. (2012). Från rasbiologi till ärftlighetsskräck. Nils von Hofsten, nät-
verket och steriliserings-verksamheten. *Socialmedicinsk tidskrift, 1*, 35–43.
Björkman, M., & Widmalm, S. (2010). Selling Eugenics: The Case of Sweden.
Notes and Records of the Royal Society of London, 64(4), 379–400.
Blomqvist, H. (2006). *Nation, ras och civilisation i svensk arbetarrörelse före nazis-
men*. Stockholm: Carlsson.
Blomqvist, H. (2013). *Myten om judesbolsjevismen: Antisemitism och kontrarevolu-
tion*. Stockholm: Carlsson.
Blomqvist, H. (2017). Socialist Patriotism, Racism and Antisemitism in the Early
Swedish Labour Movement. *Patterns of Prejudice, 51*(3–4), 318–334.
Böhme, K.-R. (1994). Building a Baltic Empire: Aspects of Swedish Expansion,
1560–1660. In G. Rystand, K.-r. Böhme, & W. M. Carlgren (Eds.), *In Quest
of Trade and Security: The Baltic in Power Politics 1500–1990. Volume I 1500–
1890* (pp. 177–220). Lund: Lund University Press.
Bojerud, S. (2010). *Nazism i Sverige 1924–1945*. Estonia: Sivart.
Broberg, G. (2002). *Statlig rasforskning: en historik över rasbiologiska institutet*.
Lund: Ugglan.
Broberg, G., & Tydén, M. (2005). *Oönskade i folkhemmet* (2nd ed.). Stockholm:
Dialogos förlag.

Brustein, W. I., & King, R. D. (2004). Anti-semitism in Europe Before the Holocaust. *International Political Science Review, 25*(1), 35–53.

Catomeris, C. (2004). *Det ohyggliga arvet.* Stockholm: Ordfront.

Di Palma, G. (1980). Founding Coalitions in Southern Europe: Legitimacy and Hegemony. *Government and Opposition, 15*(2), 162–189.

Edgren, H. (2010). Traumakonstruktionen: svensk historieskrivning om rikssprängningen 1809. *Scandia, 76*(1), 9–39.

Edquist, S. (2016). Staten, folkbildningen och demokratifostran – ett exempel från 1920-talet. In U. Claesson & D. Åhman (Eds.), *Kulturell reproduktion i skola och nation: En vänbok till Lars Petterson.* Möklinta: Gidlunds förlag.

Elias, N. (1976). *Über den Prozess der Zivilisation. Soziogenetische und psychogenetische Untersuchungen.* Frankfurt: Suhrkamp Verlag.

Erlander, T. (1973). *1940–1944.* Stockholm: Tidens förlag.

Ertman, T. (1997). *Birth of Leviathan.* Cambridge: Cambridge University Press.

Goldhagen, D. J. (1996). *Hitler's Willing Executioners.* London: Little Brown Group.

Gustafsson, H. (2000). *Gamla riken, nya stater: Statsbildning, politisk kultur och identiteter under Kalmarunions upplösningsskede.* Stockholm: Atlantis.

Gustafsson, H. (2008). Statsbildning och territoriell integration linjer i nyare forskning, en nordisk ansats samt ett bidrag till 1500-talets svenska politiska geografi. Retrieved from www.scandia.hist.lu.se.

Hagberg, H. (1966). *Röd bok om svart tid.* Staffanstorp: Cavefors.

Hagerman, M. (2006). *Det rena landet: om konsten att uppfinna sina förfäder.* Stockholm: Norstedts.

Hagerman, M. (2015). *Käraste Herman: Rasbiologen Herman Lundborgs gåta.* Stockholm: Norstedts.

Hägglöf, G. (1972). *Samtide vittne.* Stockholm: Nordstedt.

Hall, P. (2000). *Den svenskaste historien: Nationalism i Sverige under sex sekler.* Stockholm: Carlsson.

Hallenberg, M. (2009). Peasants and Tax-farmers in Seventeenth-Century Sweden: Local Conflict and Institutional Change. In W. Blockmans, A. Holenstein, and J. Mathieu, in collaboration with D. Schläppi (Eds.), *Empwoering Interactions: Political Culture and the Emergence of the State in Europe 1300–1900.* London: Routledge.

Hallenberg, M., Holm, J., & Johansson, D. (2008). Organization, Legitimation, Participation. *Scandinavian Journal of History, 33*(3), 247–268.

Hansson, H. (1994). *Alkemi, romantik och rasvetenskap.* Falun: Nya doxa.

Harrison, D. (2002). *Sveriges historia medeltiden.* Stockholm: Liber.

Harrison, D. (2009). *Sveriges Historia: 600–1350.* Stockholm: Norstedts.

Heclo, H., & Madsen, H. (1987). *Policy and Politics in Sweden: Principled Pragmatism.* Philadelphia: Temple University Press.

Höjer, H. (2012). En meningslös sortering av människor. *Forskning & framsteg*, 8(September 7). Retrieved from http://fof.se/tidning/2012/8/en-meningslos-sortering-av-manniskor.

Holm, J. (2007). *Konstruktionen av en Stormakt: Kungamakt, skattebänder och statsbildning 1595 till 1640*. Stocholm: Stockhoms University, Acta Universersitatis Stockholmiensis Studies in History 90, doctoral dissertation in History.

Jansson, T. (1995). Från stormakt till smånation. En väv av ekonomisk-politiska och socio-kulturella trådar. In S. Dahlgren, T. Jansson, & H. Norman (Eds.), *Från stormakt till smånation* (pp. 23–34). Stockholm: Tiden.

Krantz, L. (1977). *Hur tyskarna flög i luften*. Uddevall, Sweden: Bohusläningens AB.

Kyle, J. (1989). Formeringen av ett Liberalt Samfund: Statsmakt och samhällsorganisation i Sverige 1810–70. *Historisk tidskrift, 3*, 321–353.

Laclau, E., & Mouffe, C. (1985/1993). *Hegemony and Socialist Strategy*. New York: Verso.

Larsmo, O. (2007). 'Bollhusmötet' 1939 – konstruktionen av en rasistisk opinion. In L. M. Andersson & M. Tydén (Eds.), *Sverige och Nasaityskland: Skuldfrågor och moraldebatt* (pp. 193–228). Stockholm: Dialogos Förlag.

Levine, P. A. (2002). Attitudes and Action: Comparing the Responses of Mid-level Bureaucrats to the Holocaust. In D. Cesarani & P. A. Levine (Eds.), *"Bystanders" to the Holocaust: A Re-evaluation*. London: Routledge.

Lewin, L. (1992). *Ideologi och strategi: Svensk politik under 100 år* (4th ed.). Stockholm: Norstedt.

Lewin, L. (1998). *Bråka inte: Om vår tids demokratisyn*. Stockholm: SNS.

Lindkvist, T. (2007). Att skapa ett kungarike: Maktlegitimering, regional variation och framväxten av ett kristet kungadöme i Sverige. *Saga och sed. Kungl. Gustav Adolfs Akademiens årsbok, 2006*, 83–98.

Lindquist, B. (1997). *Förädlade Svenskar: drömmen om att skapa en bättre människa* (2nd ed.). Falun: Alfabeta.

Lindqvist, H. (1992). *Historien om Sverige: Från islossning till kungarike*. Stockholm: Nordstedt.

Lindström, U. (1983). *Fascism in Scandinavia 1920–40*. Doctoral Dissertation, Department of Political Science, University of Umeå, Umeå.

Lipset, S. M. (1959). Some Social Requisites of Democracy: Economic Development and Political Legitimacy. *The American Political Science Review, 53*(1), 69–105.

Lundborg, H. (1914). *Rasbiologi och rashygien: små populärvetenskapliga skisser*. Stockholm: P.A. Norstedt & Söners förlag.

Mohlin, Y. (1988). *Konflikten land-stad och aktiv rasbiologi: Två viktiga faktorer i mellankrigstidens bondeaktivism*. Umeå: Umeå University Research Report, Statsvetenskapliga institutionen, 8.

Nilsson, S. A. (1996). Gustav II Adolf och Axel Oxenstierna: En studie i maktdelning och dess alternativ. *Scandia, 62*(2), 169–194.

Nilsson, K. N. A. (2000). *Svensk överklass och högerextremism under 1900-talet.* Stockholm: Federativs.

Olsson, S. (2000). *Den svenska högerns anpassning till demokratin.* Doctoral Dissertation, Uppsala University, Uppsala.

Östberg, K. (1990). *Byråkrati och reformism: En studie av svensk socialdemokratis politiska och sociala integrering fram till första världskriget.* Doctoral Dissertation, Lund University, Arkiv avhandlingsserie 34.

Österberg, E. (1989). Bönder och centralmakt i det tidigmoderna Sverige. Konflikt – kompromiss – politisk kultur. *Scandia, 55*(1), 73–95.

Premfors, R. (1993). *Sveriges demokratisering: Ett historiskt-institutionalistiskt perspektiv.* SCORE Rapportserie 3, Stockholms universitet.

Roberts, M. (1968). *The Early Vasas: A History of Sweden, 1523–1611.* Cambridge: Cambridge University Press.

Rothstein, B. (1986). *Den socialdemokratiska staten: Reformer och förvaltning inom svensk arbetsmarknads- och skolpolitik.* Lund: Arkiv förlag.

Rothstein, B. (1992). *Den korporative staten.* Stockholm: Norstedts.

Rothstein, B. (1998). State Building and Capitalism: The Rise of the Swedish Bureaucracy. *Scandinavian Political Studies, 21*(4), 287–306.

Rothstein, B., & Teorell, J. (2015). Getting to Sweden, Part II: Breaking with Corruption in the Nineteenth Century. *Scandinavian Political Studies, 38*(3), 238–254.

Runblom, H. (1995). Det öppna och det slutna Sverige. Ett perspektiv på invandringen. In S. Dahlgren, T. Jansson, & H. Norman (Eds.), *Från stormakt till smånation* (pp. 88–104). Stockholm: Tiden.

Skocpol, T. (1985). Bringing the State Back In: Strategies of Analysis in Current Research. In P. B. Evans, D. Rueschemeyer, & T. Skocpol (Eds.), *Bringing the State Back In.* Cambridge: Cambridge University Press.

Södersten, B. (1975). *Den svenska sköldpaddan.* Falköping: Raben & Sjogren.

Statens offentliga utredningar 1968:47 *Förvaltning och folkstyre.* Stockholm: Kommunikationsdepartementet.

Svensson, P. (2015, September 20). Den romantiske rasbiologen. *Sydsvenskan.* Retrieved from https://www.sydsvenskan.se/2015-09-20/den-romantiske-rasbiologen.

Teorell, J., & Rothstein, B. (2015). Getting to Sweden, Part I: War and Malfeasance, 1720–1850. *Scandinavian Political Studies, 38*(3), 217–237.

Thörn, A. (2006). *I gränslandet mellan svensk frikyrka och tysk nazism Frikyrkans förhållningssätt till nazismen i Vecko-Posten, Missions-Baneret och Bibliskt Månadshäfte 1933, 1938, 1939 och 1945 ur ett sociologiskt perspektiv.* BA thesis in History, Örebro University.

Thulstrup, Å. (1968). *Svensk politik 1905–1939: Från unionsupplösningen till andra världskriget.* Stockholm: Bionniers.

Tydén, M. (2007). Att inte lägga sig i: Till frågan om Sveriges moraliska skuld till Förintelsen. In L. M. Andersson & M. Tydén (Eds.), *Sverige och Nazityskland: Skuldfrågor och moraldebatt* (pp. 123–147). Stockholm: Dialogos Förlag.

Uhlin, Å. (1972). *Februari Krisen 1942*. Stockholm: Allmanna Förlaget.

Upton, A. F. (1998). *Charles XI and Swedish Absolutism*. Cambridge: Cambridge University Press.

Valentin, H. (1964). *Judarna i Sverige*. Stockholm: Bonniers.

von Vegesack, T. (1995). *Smak för frihet: Opinionsbildningen i Sverige 1755–1830*. Stockholm: Natur och Kultur.

Wahlbäck, K. (1972). *Regeringen och kriget*. Stockholm: Prisma.

Wright, R. (1998). *The Visible Wall: Jews and Other Ethnic Outsiders in Swedish Film*. Uppsala: Uppsala University.

Yahil, L. (1967). *Et demokrati på prøve. Jøderne i Danmark under besættelsen*. Gyldendal.

CHAPTER 7

Nazi Germany and Non-Banal Evilness

In contrast to Sweden, which was a well-established state that had existed for centuries, Germany did not unite into one country until 1871 under Bismarck. A new state, such as Germany, faces a question which an old state such as Sweden does not: how is the state to be defined—that is, who belongs to it and who is an "outsider"? The need to answer this question encouraged an anti-Semitic discourse, as the new rulers did not think that Jews (or Poles, French and others) would be loyal to the new state. As in Spain, the rulers had to decide what to base their state on. In the beginning, there was a certain trend toward basing it on Lutheranism but Bismarck realized he needed the support of Catholics to keep the country stable. The rulers could have based the new state on language—those who speak German are German—but the problem was that many German-speakers lived outside of Germany (especially in Austria and Switzerland). As Sheehan (1989: 4) points out, it is not even clear which dialects are truly "German" and which are not:

> The lines between the speakers of Dutch and *Plattdeutsch* are hard to draw; the distance between the dialects of Hamburg and Swabia is surely no less significant. Like the drawing of national borders, the defining of a national language is essentially a political process which creates more than it reflects 'natural' entities.

Of course, the classic civic-nationalist idea would have been to base belongingness on territory: whoever lives in the country of Germany is

© The Author(s) 2019   205
S. Saxonberg, *Pre-Modernity, Totalitarianism and the Non-Banality of Evil*, https://doi.org/10.1007/978-3-030-28195-3_7

German. However, as already noted, the rulers were fearful that nonethnic Germans would not be loyal to the new state. This opened the path eventually for the Nazis to base German belongingness on ethnicity understood in racial terms (according to which Jews, among others, could not be Germans).

The imperial state does seem to have enjoyed some legitimacy eventually. After all, a large part of the population was eager to go off to battle in WWI, and even the social democrats voted for war appropriations, thereby abandoning their international solidarity with the workers of the world. Mommsen (2009: 1) reports that bourgeois intellectuals saw the war as a way to unite the country and bring about national rejuvenation. Nevertheless, the mere fact that proponents of the war saw it as a way to unite the country implies that before the war the country was not completely united and that not all citizens believed in the new state's legitimacy. Moreover, the imperial German state lost its legitimacy when it lost the war. This humiliating defeat led to the Kaiser's abdication and to revolution. However, it was a revolution that none of the major parties wanted. Even though the social democrats became the leaders of the revolution and the first rulers under the new regime, their top officials were actually against the idea of a revolution and would have preferred to see the monarchy continue. As a result, a new regime emerged that nobody wanted. While the Swedish state benefited from its "backward legitimacy," in which the conservative parties and the monarchy could claim to have supported the democratic transition, the Weimar Republic was seen as illegitimate by large sectors of society and several of the important parties in parliament. A further factor reducing the legitimacy of the new republic was the fact that its leaders were pressured into signing the Versailles Treaty, which punished Germany harshly and forced it to pay huge war reparations that led to hyperinflation.

As leaders of a new state, Germany's rulers also had to try to ensure the loyalty of civil servants to the new state. Accordingly, they decided to require recruits to show they were loyal to the Kaiser and had conservative values. The Swedish state, by contrast, already enjoyed almost unquestioned legitimacy, so the regime in that country based recruitment more on merit than the German state did. Moreover, since administrators in Germany were chosen for their values, they tended to be more conservative and authoritarian than their counterparts in Sweden. As a result, most of them opposed the democratic Weimar Republic. On the other hand, they had little difficulty adjusting to the autocratic Nazi regime. These factors—the emphasis on loyalty and the organization of the bureaucracy along strictly legal-rational lines—encouraged German civil servants to support the shift to totalitarianism under the National Socialists. In Sweden, by contrast, the bureaucracy was traditionally strong and independent, which encouraged civil servants to take greater moral responsibility and to try to counter "evil" acts.

Another important factor in the development of the German state was the role of the nobility. In contrast to the pattern seen in France (where the crown based itself on the support of the burghers) and that seen in Sweden (where the crown kept the aristocracy in check by cultivating the support of the peasants), the Holy Roman emperors based their power on the support of the aristocracy, so they gave the nobility great autonomy in running their states, rather than trying to create a unitary state. This kept the German states very divided and hindered them from uniting to form one country. Thus, by the time Germany became a united country, France and Sweden had each been united for hundreds of years. The German form of state development also kept the peasants very weak. So, in contrast to their Swedish counterparts, who organized a strong peasant party to defend their interests, German peasants were unrepresented and without much political influence during the Weimar Republic. Consequently, they were more easily drawn into a totalitarian movement than their brethren in Sweden.

Thus, even though the pattern of state-building is not enough by itself to explain the Nazi rise to power, the factors mentioned made it easier for them to come to power, as well as making it easier for them to install a totalitarian regime once they were in power. This is not to say their rise to power was inevitable. If the Great Depression had not taken place, or if certain actors like Hindenburg had made different choices, then perhaps the Nazis would have not come to power. And even if they had come to power, they may not have been able—if the state had enjoyed greater legitimacy and the bureaucracy had been more willing to oppose totalitarian measures—to carry out the policies that they did. However, the way in which the state had developed historically—with a conservative, antidemocratic bureaucracy—made it much easier for an authoritarian party to carry out totalitarian measures.

Finally, there is the issue of the banality of evil. Many historical studies have now cast doubt on the banality-of-evil thesis. They have shown that the perpetrators were not nonideological bureaucrats who were merely doing their duty; rather, they were people who took great initiative in carrying out horrendous acts because they believed in what they were doing. Even if the German bureaucracy emphasized loyalty more than the Swedish one did, and even if it had a less independent tradition, the bureaucrats serving the Nazi regime still took a lot of initiative in developing and pursuing genocidal policies. This may seem to support Goldhagen's argument that the perpetrators believed in what they were doing because an eliminationist anti-Semitism was widespread in Germany. However, this book argues instead that these people were willing to commit such acts because they considered the regime to be legitimate; therefore, they considered its policies to be legitimate.

This chapter proceeds by first discussing the state-building process in Germany. Then it discusses the development of the bureaucracy in that country, after which it discusses which social groups supported the Nazis and why the state-building process gave the peasants an incentive to support the Nazis. Next, it discusses how civil society actually worked to undermine the democratic Weimar regime. It supports Berman's (1997) claim that, when the state is weak and not well-institutionalized, civil society can fill the gap—but that it does so by opposing democracy. Thus, the type of state-building process also influences civil society. In Sweden, where the state was firmly established, civil society tended to support democracy, and the social democrats were able to coopt the term *folk* to gain support for building the welfare state. In Germany, where the state was weak and newly created, militarist-nationalist associations used the corresponding term (*Volk*) to gain support for an antidemocratic *völkisch* ideology that opposed the liberal democratic Weimar Republic. Then I analyze the development of German anti-Semitism and discuss whether the "eliminationist" hypothesis can explain the Holocaust. Finally, I discuss the reasons why so many people were willing to commit evil acts and to support genocide.

German State-Building

While Sweden and France started developing as countries already before the second millennium and became relatively stable states early on, Germany did not become a country until Bismarck united its many kingdoms and principalities in 1871. To be sure, there were the Holy Roman emperors in the earlier period; however, as Sheehan (1989: 14) points out, the Holy Roman Empire "was not a nation or a state, nor was it an international organization." There was no real organized entity called

"Germany." In addition, the Holy Roman Empire "was not really a German polity," as it included many non-Germans, such as Flemings, Walloons, Italians, Czechs, Slovenes and so on (p. 15; c.f. Dann 1996: 45). As discussed in Chap. 4, the Holy Roman emperors allied themselves with the nobility, thereby preventing the different German principalities from uniting and forming a country. Instead, separate kingdoms, duchies and states developed within the Empire. The leaders of these duchies and states successfully blocked attempts at building a German state (Dann 1996: 42). Thus, Panayi (2001: 4) observes, "[u]nlike Britain and France, which had existed as monarchies since the medieval period...no unitary German state, with executive control over all German areas of Europe, had ever existed." In France, the monarchy granted considerable power to the burghers in order to counterbalance the nobles. Since the emperors, by contrast, relied on the landed nobility, the burghers remained weak and the towns without influence. Moore (1966: 418) asserts that the "weakness of the towns has been a constant feature in German history...." Moreover, the emperor was Austrian much of the time (Hastings 1997: 107), although Austria did not end up belonging to the German state that was eventually created. In addition, the Austrian Empire included many non-German peoples and territories. This decision to base the Holy Roman Empire on an alliance with nobles contrasts with the approach taken by the French crown, which looked to the burghers for support against the nobility. By keeping the nobility weak, the French king was able to unite the country under his rule. By contrast, when the different German states and kingdoms united in 1871, strong regional identities still existed, which made it more difficult for the Kaiser to acquire legitimacy and to gain the full support of the population in general and of civil servants in particular.

Germany was so split that, when the Thirty Years' War ended in 1648, it consisted of 2000 sovereign territories with around 360 principalities (Kühnl 1996: 14). The number diminished over time, but there still were 50 dynastic German states when the country united in 1871 (Sheehan 1989: 30). As late as 1773, a German author wrote: "The German nation is not really a nation, but rather an aggregation of many nations" (Dann 1996: 51). Grebing (1986: 86) argues that the German nationalist movement did not start until different German groups united to fight Napoleon. Moreover, although nationalist feelings began to emerge at that point, 60 local historical societies established themselves in the various German territories after the defeat of Napoleon (Green 2001: 103). These historical societies had a local patriotic orientation: their focus was on studying the history of their own state (Saxony, Hanover, Württemberg, etc.). Yet, as of 1850, "there was not as yet a single society dedicated to the study of the greater German Fatherland. Whatever their political beliefs, in practice the Germans remained interested in local not national history." In fact, as Grebing (1986: 89f.) notes, even among German nationalists there was great sympathy for a "third Germany" that would include Baden, Bavaria, Saxony and Württemberg as a counterbalance to Austria and Prussia.

Thus, Confino (1993: 48) concludes,

> German history…[was] not the single story of a fixed entity…[but] many different histories that coexisted. Before 1871 there was a history of the Germans and German history, but no history of Germany; only thereafter did German history proceed as a single development. The unification of 1871, therefore, joining the German nation, German society and a German state within a single territory, redefined the spatial and historical dimensions of the nation and the ways Germans remembered their pasts. To be sure, Germans had national recollections before 1871, but the foundation of the nation state conditioned a reevaluation of old memories as never before. To suppose otherwise is to view German history and German national memory as predetermined: before the Prussian-Austrian war in 1866, however, the exclusion of Austrian history, the hegemony of Prussian history and the superiority of Protestant to Catholic memories, to mention only a few notable examples, were not inevitable for German nationhood. The beginning of modern German national memory, therefore, was 1871.

Confino (ibid.) adds that the united country adopted a federal system based on a "patchwork" of regions and states with different histories and cultural heritages. Furthermore,

> the regional states maintained their pre-unification structure including a head of state, symbols, a Landtag, a government, a bureaucracy and peculiar laws. Apart from losing their sovereignty, German regions remained after 1871 virtual states. This high level of regional fragmentation reflected the diversity of regional identities and their autonomy with respect to national identity.

Green (2001: 320) describes the strong regional identities that persisted after unification, with many regional governments still headed by their own monarch. Before unification, the *Mittelstaaten* in the center of the country had built strong regional state (or *Land*) identities, although these were anchored within a larger framework of national German cultural identity (p. 281). Due to these strong regional identities, it was difficult to centralize the country, which therefore ended up being much more federalized than France and many other contemporary nations. The nation-building project under the Kaiser was incomplete and contested because any unifying and coherent set of values or symbols would provoke opposition from one or another regional or political group (p. 285). Wehler (1995: 129) adds that it took almost 30 years—until the late 1890s—to consolidate the new German state.

It was not clear to all of the German states that they should belong to a Prussian-dominated Germany. As Ziblatt (2006: 42) observes, "[m]ost leading figures in Bavarian state politics before 1866 were explicitly pro-Austrian and anti-Prussian....Some...wanted to preserve Bavarian autonomy; others were conservative and pro-Hapsburg." Interestingly, some of the original leaders of the German National Socialist Workers' Party supported Bavarian independence as late as the early 1920s, but they met stiff opposition from Hitler (Reuth 2009). Jacob (1963: 91) notes that, during the Weimar Republic, national leaders decided they had to compromise with Bavaria, fearing it might otherwise secede from the federation.

Wehler (1995: 122) notes that a German nationalism did not emerge among the individual German states until the 1780s and that even then there was no consensus on which states a unified Germany should include. During the civil war of 1866, the most important states in the north German customs union actually supported Austria over Prussia (p. 128). Sheehan (1989: 907) concurs: "[I]t is worth noting that almost every important German state lined up on the Austrian side in 1866." Langewiesche (1995: 140) reports that even Prussian conservatives feared that a unified Germany under Prussian control would have negative consequences—that the old Prussian state would be destroyed, as it would have to give up its identity in order to support the national idea. These conservatives did not accept the new German state until the 1870s when Bismarck ended the liberal reform era and took Germany in a conservative direction.

Green (2001: 298–9) argues that the Franco-Prussian war in 1870 induced a stronger feeling of national community among those living in the various German states. Yet, when the united country held elections, only 51 percent of eligible voters bothered to vote (showing their apathy toward the new country), while another quarter voted for parties which were critical of the new nation-state or at best lukewarm. Thus, only about one-fourth of the male population showed support for the new country. When a new state is created—even a federal one like Germany—it is necessary to decide what to base it on. According to Hastings (1997: 107), language became the most important bond for the new country, because the latter was fragmented politically and divided religiously between Catholics and Protestants. Yet, it did not base itself only on language at first. As Wehler (1970: 122) notes:

> The legitimacy of the young Reich had no generally accepted basis nor was it founded upon a generally accepted code of basic political convictions.... Bismarck had to cover up the social and political differences in the tension-ridden class society of his new Germany, and to this end he relied on a technique of negative integration. His method was to inflame the conflicts between those groups which were allegedly hostile to the Reich, *Reichsfeinde*, like the Socialists and Catholics, left-wing Liberals and Jews on the one hand, and those groups which were allegedly loyal to the Reich, the *Reichsfreunde*. It was thanks to the permanent conflict between these in- and out- groups that he was able to achieve variously composed majorities for his policies. The Chancellor was thus under constant pressure to provide rallying points for his *Reichspolitik*, and to legitimate his system by periodically producing fresh political successes.

Thus, Bismarck and the bureaucracy tried to hinder Jews from becoming citizens even though they spoke German. Interestingly, despite this anti-Jewish stance on naturalization, Bismarck basically argued that those Jews who were already citizens should not have to encounter any obstacles except exclusion from the public sector. The reasoning behind this exclusion was that Germany is a Christian society, so non-Christians should not be able to work for the Christian state (Jöhlinger 1921). Nathans (2004: 8) maintains, German officials generally refused to naturalize foreign Poles and Jews starting in the 1880s, out of fear that they would not be loyal to the new German state. However, policies in this regard differed among the states: for example, Bavaria forbade the naturalization of foreign Jews; Baden permitted it, but prohibited Jews from moving to communities without Jewish residents. (Since there were no Jews in 90 percent of the communities in Baden, it was difficult for Jews to move to that state) (p. 68). In 1885, in his capacity as Prussian minister-president, Bismarck ordered the expulsion of all foreign Jews and Poles living in the eastern provinces of Prussia; accordingly, 10,000 foreign Jews had to leave the country (p. 111). This discrimination against Jews continued after Bismarck. Nathans (p. 128) notes that "by the early 1890s at the upper levels of the Prussian civil service, officials reasoned that Polish and Jewish immigrants would not be able to become loyal to the German state." Then, in 1911, an internal document at the Interior Ministry argued against naturalizing foreign Jews, on account of the presumably negative traits arising from their racial origins—traits which would not disappear if they converted. In 1913, for example, the Ministry rejected an application for naturalization by a man who had converted to Protestantism and had lived in Germany for 30 years. This discrimination continued under the Weimar Republic, for although the social democratic interior minister of the state of Prussia changed the rules to end discrimination against any ethnic groups in naturalization cases, he left office in 1920. Moreover, most of the Ministry's officials opposed his policy, so he was not able to influence the naturalization process. It is ironic that bureaucrats and poli- cymakers doubted the Jews' loyalty because evidence indicates that most Jews were extremely loyal to the German state. The fear was based solely on prejudice.

As Maccoby (2006: 25) states, "Jews, in fact, always tended to be enthusiastically loyal to any state that showed them kindness; but this very enthusiasm aroused resentment in antisemites who saw it as one more impudent disguise of the essentially alien Jew." Weiss (1996: 73) under- lines this lack of trust in Jews, noting that, even though Jews were loyal to the Prussian crown and fought against the French in the Napoleonic wars, "they were no longer allowed to join the military or to be teachers, judges, or civil servants." This only changed in 1914, on the brink of the world war. In the minds of much of the state bureaucracy, Jews could not become Germans. Germany was to be a country based on ethnicity.

In addition, Bismarck did, in fact, try at first to base the country on religion, as he conducted a *Kulturkampf* ("cultural struggle") against Catholicism in the first years of his rule. This followed the *kleindeutsch* strategy of basing Germany on Protestant Prussia rather than Catholic Austria. According to Kühnl (1996: 40f.), this tactic led to the formation of a national consciousness based on the norms of obedience derived from the Prussian military caste. This type of militaristic consciousness sup- ported an antidemocratic, racist national identity. Eventually, as the newly founded Catholic *Zentrum* party gained strength in parliament, Bismarck gave up his *Kulturkampf*, realizing it was better to try to integrate Catholics into the new state rather than to repress them (e.g., Nathans

2004: 114; Reagin 2004: 286; Weiss 1996: 86). Bismarck abandoned the *Kulturkampf,* however, in such a way as to stigmatize the Jews still further:

> Bismarck encouraged the press, including papers he illegally subsidized with secret funds, to blame the Jews in the Reichstag for the persecution of the church. By betraying his allies, Bismarck encouraged the Catholic press to claim that the *Kulturkampf* was orchestrated by Jews to cover up their frauds during the crash. They ignored the fact that many Jewish leaders... opposed the conflict. (Weiss 1996: 86)

Interestingly, the national liberals were one of the main groups to oppose Catholicism. This is quite striking, inasmuch as one might assume liberals would be in favor of religious tolerance. Ping (2012: 609) remarks that Gustav Freytag, a leading national-liberal politician, feared that Bismarck's territorial annexations would reduce Prussia to the status of a Protestant province within a mainly Catholic empire. However, once Catholicism was accepted, a more ethnic definition of Germaneness won out, which in the eyes of the bureaucracy excluded groups such as Jews, Poles and French, even if they lived in German territory.

The new state seems to have been gaining legitimacy, as indicated by the enthusiastic support of much of the population for participating in WWI (e.g., Mommsen 2009: 13). Yet, this does not necessarily mean that the regime really enjoyed much legitimacy. Several scholars have argued (e.g., Wehler 1985: 177ff.) that, precisely because the regime was lacking in support and facing problems in overcoming the many conflicts between classes and groups, the Kaiser embarked on an imperialist strategy in order to unite the country behind him. In other words, just because much of the population became enthusiastic about the war does not mean they were supportive of the regime before the war started. Dann (1996: 220) claims that, when the war broke out, it was the first time people experienced a feeling of unity behind the imperial regime. In any case, regardless of how much or how little legitimacy the regime might have enjoyed before the war started, it soon lost its legitimacy after the humiliating German defeat in the war. This led to an uprising and to the decision of the Kaiser to abdicate. However, this was largely an unwanted revolution, as even the social democrats (who became the leaders of the revolution) wanted piecemeal reform rather than revolution, and actually would have preferred to keep the monarchy (e.g., Grotkopp 1992: 12; Hürten 1988: 81f.; Wirsching 2008). The social democrats, the liberals and the Catholic *Zentrum* supported the new republic (even if they would have preferred a constitutional monarchy). However, conservative groups openly opposed it. For example, the leader of the German National People's Party (*Deutschnationale Volkspartei*), Kuno Graf von Westarp, said in January 1920 that the republic was illegitimate and that he hoped for a quick end to it (Gerwarth 2008: 19). The liberal-conservative German National Party also opposed the revolution and the establishment of a parliamentary democracy (Brustein 1996: 34). Meanwhile, more radical socialists, such as the independent socialists and the Spartacus League, thought the revolution did not go far enough.[1] They sought the establishment of a socialist state (e.g., Hürten 1988; Kühnl 1996). During the revolution that established the Weimar Republic, workers rebelled and set up workers' councils in many cities and provinces. The independent social democrats (USPD) favored a republic based on these councils rather than on a parliamentary system (Grebing 1986: 145; Mommsen 2009: Chap. 2). Thus, no major political group was satisfied with the parliamentary republic that emerged: the right opposed democracy; the liberals and the social democrats wanted a parliamentary system based on a constitutional monarchy, and the independent socialists and communists wanted a socialist republic based on workers' councils.

As the revolution threatened to turn into a socialist revolution, the government used paramilitary units (the *Freikorps*) to crush workers' uprisings throughout Germany (Jones 1987). Since the interior minister who ordered the crackdown was a social democrat, this led to a bitter split on the left between revolutionaries and reformists. Soon after, the main revolutionary group—the Spartacus League—become the German Communist Party. Because of the violence which the social democratic-led government employed against the revolutionaries, the split between communists and social democrats became much more bitter in Germany than in Sweden. Furthermore, the newly created Weimar Republic represented a new type of state—one that lacked legitimacy among conservative groups and much of the bureaucracy. The newly founded republic was also pressured into signing the Versailles Treaty, which demanded reparations that brought about hyperinflation in the country. In Panayi's (2001) words, "[a]part from the recovery period of 1924–29, when the world economy emerged from the postwar slump…the Weimar period is characterized by economic stagnation, collapse and disaster, the memory held by Nazi voters about the whole period 1919–33." Panayi adds that, when the Nazis came to power, "they got rid of a regime unloved by virtually all sections of society" (p. 10).

In addition to these events, which much of the population saw as humiliating (e.g., Sturmer 1981: 27), the political system was unstable, with coalition governments often only lasting a short period before collapsing. The legitimacy of the Weimar Republic was further reduced by the rapid increase in unemployment during the Great Depression. These factors enabled the Nazis to present themselves as a group that would finally unite Germans around a functioning state, under the motto: "one Führer, one country!" An example of this belief in Hitler's legitimacy can be seen in the words of the poet Gottfried Benns, who wrote when Hitler came to power that it was "the last attempt to regenerate the people" (*Volk*). He added: "I do not know if the methods being used are correct, I even doubt this; but an admirable willpower is there nevertheless" (Mommsen 1999: 49). In other words, not everyone was a believing National Socialist in 1933; in fact, the majority had voted against the Nazis. But there was a widespread hope that this new legitimate leader would regenerate a people who had suffered under the Weimer Republic, which many considered to have been an illegitimate bastard of the recently created German state.

This contrasts greatly with the situation in Sweden, where even the monarchy supported the transition to democracy. This gave the democratic regime in Sweden much greater legitimacy than that enjoyed by the republic in Germany. All of the parties in Sweden supported the democratic regime, except for the small Communist Party. In addition, since the transition in Sweden came about peacefully through compromise, there were no socialist revolts which might have caused a rancorous split on the left between communists and social democrats. The Swedish communists were too small to be of much importance; but in any case, they did not hate social democrats the way their German comrades did, as they had not been violently attacked by any Swedish equivalent of the *Freikorps*. This split between communists and social democrats in Germany also played into the Nazis' hands, as the communists refused to support any governments led by the social democrats, whom they reviled as "social fascists." As for supporters of the right, those from the middle class has less reason to turn to antisystem parties in Sweden, since the regime in that country enjoyed a high level of legitimacy. By contrast, many of their counterparts in Germany did not believe in the regime and were hoping for systemic change. Moreover, in contrast to the situation in Germany, where the antidemocratic right could portray the Weimar Republic as "Jewish" and as contrary to German *Volk* traditions, in Sweden, the social democrats were able to coopt the term *folk* and to use it to their advantage. In addition, governments in Sweden were able—given the peaceful transition to democracy in that country, with the support it enjoyed from all major political parties—to propagate democratic values by supporting "folk movements" such as the cooperative and temperance movements.

BUREAUCRACY AND LEGITIMACY

When Bismarck united Germany in the 1870s, he had to create a German identity among a population that had previously belonged to several different states with separate bureaucracies and strong regional identities. Under these conditions, it was not clear that administrators around the country would be loyal to the newly created state dominated by Prussia. Esping-Andersen (1990), a well-known expert on social policy, argues that Bismarck introduced his social-insurance system first for the state officials (*Beamte*) precisely because he wanted to gain their support for the new order.

In Germany, creating loyalty to the new regime was a particularly important issue. It was even more important than in Italy, because virtually the entire Italian-speaking world was part of the new Italian state, whereas a large number of German-speakers lived outside of Germany (particularly in Austria and Switzerland). In Germany, a real problem arose in convincing inhabitants (including bureaucrats) of long-standing independent states to give their allegiance all of a sudden to the new German state. Creating a new German identity also made it necessary to determine who was German. In Prussia, for example, there were large areas where the majority of the population was Polish; in the west, there were areas where parts of the population spoke French. After unification, two questions, therefore, arose: First, would it be best to regard these ethnic groups as German? Second, could the rather militaristic new German state count on the *loyalty* of these ethnic groups if it went to war with its neighbors? Accordingly, the rulers of the new state made loyalty the most important criterion for recruiting people to the civil service. This led to the development of a very conservative bureaucracy with pro-Kaiser and antidemocratic sympathies. The German bureaucracy based itself on "the ideal of complete and unreflective obedience to an institution over and above class and individual..." (Moore 1966: 436).

Thus, if we look at the German bureaucracy in terms of state-building and legitimacy, we can understand better why it often obstructed the Weimar Republic and why it was so willing to cooperate with the Nazis. For example, Goldhagen (1996) denies that Germany's bureaucracy was loyal since it often opposed the Weimar Republic. However, when uniting the country, Bismarck consciously applied a recruiting strategy aimed at hiring *conservative* administrators, who would be loyal to the Wilhelmian dynasty. Brandt (1976: 75ff.) notes that the goal of the recruitment policy was to ensure that bureaucrats would have conservative values and so would limit the process of democratization. Social democrats were therefore excluded, as were Catholic supporters of the *Zentrum* party.

This recruitment policy continued until the fall of the monarchy at the end of WWI. Mann (1983: 84) describes a conservative homogenization of the German bureaucracy in this period (see also Bracher 1957: Chap. 7). Before the Weimar Republic, democratically minded citizens had little chance of finding employment in the state administration. Social democrats were excluded and Catholics could only get a position if they were known to be more conservative than the Catholic *Zentrum* party (Wunder 1986: 91–2). Jews also found it difficult to get a job in the state bureaucracy (Wunder 1986: 122); therefore, when the Nazis came to power, the public administration was composed largely of people who had previously had little contact with Jews. Finally, once Bismarck had abandoned his cooperation with the national liberals, liberals too found it difficult to land a position within the administration (see, e.g., Witt 1983: 142). Conservative dominance of the bureaucracy went in the other direction as well: the conservative parties in the German parliament were dominated by civil servants (Pollmann 1983: 65).

Wunder (1986: 94) concludes that the aim of the imperial regime's personnel policy was to achieve and maintain conservative homogeneity in the public administration. Consequently, the bureaucracy had little reason to feel loyalty to the subsequent Weimar Republic. Most public officials seem to have been very critical of it and to have seen it as illegitimate, both because they were skeptical of democracy and because they saw the Versailles Treaty as a betrayal and a selling-out of German interests. Consequently, the vast majority of upper-level public officials rejected the Weimar Republic (Wunder 1986: 117; cf. Brandt 1976: 90). On the other hand, the bureaucracy was loyal to the regimes it considered legitimate: that is, the Kaiser's and then Hitler's.

Jacob (1963: 12) summarizes the situation of the bureaucracy under the imperial regime:

During most of the 19th century the Prussian bureaucracy was autocratic, designed to support the Hohenzollern monarchy through administrative efficiency and political loyalty. Prime Minister Baron von Stein decided to appoint laymen to honorific positions in the bureaucracy in order to nurture Prussian patriotism. Prime Minister Prince von Hardenberg later replaced him and emphasized bureaucratic over collegial organization to maximize efficiency.

He also notes (p. 24) that it was difficult at first to gain the loyalty of bureaucrats from other German states:

...many of the most influential politicians and bureaucrats in the smaller states looked with dread on the unification, fearing complete submergence into a Greater Prussia. Their suspicions were based not only on parochial patriotism. Religious, cultural, and linguistic differences emphasized and reinforced their apprehensions. In the context of the federal structure in which the new Reich operated, the fears and jealousies of non-Prussian governments constantly threatened to obstruct responsive field administration of national mandates.

Eventually, it seems Bismarck succeeded in gaining the loyalty of the bureaucracy to the Kaiser through his recruitment policies. However, this also meant that large portions of the bureaucracy were critical of the Weimar Republic, which they regarded as illegitimate. This lack of loyalty to the regime can be seen in how the legal system operated. There were almost 400 political murders between 1919 and 1922, of which 354 were committed by rightists and only 22 by leftists. Yet 17 of the 22 leftist killings led to stiff sentences, including 10 death penalties. Meanwhile, of 354 rightist murders, 326 went altogether unpunished. While the average sentence for leftist murders was 15 years, for rightists it was only 4 months (Jones 1987: 228).[2] Of course, the most infamous example was the light sentence that Hitler received for his attempted putsch, which allowed him to leave prison after serving only 9 months. While Hitler received a light sentence for trying to overthrow the government, Felix Fechenbach received an 11-year sentence for giving an author a telegram from 1914. In this telegram, dated shortly before WWI began, the Bavarian representative at the Vatican noted that the pope approved of Austria's[3] determination to take action against Serbia (Rasehorn 1988: 411). In an even more bizarre case, a court in Magdeburg found President Friedrich Ebert guilty of treason shortly before his death, because back in 1918 he had joined the leadership of a strike in order to help end it quickly (ibid.: 412). Rasehorn concludes that, for the judges, it was more important to be conservative and devoted to the fatherland (*vaterländische Gesinnung*) than to be loyal to the constitution. For this reason, a judge found a man innocent in 1930 for taking action that endangered the republic, because the revolution of 1918 had allegedly been an act of treason (ibid.: 417).

Brandt (1976: 93) notes that it was also difficult to punish civil servants who sabotaged policies, as the members of the disciplinary organs held conservative views as well. Peukert (1991: 50) adds that the opposition of many of the elites to the republic was an especially big problem among those "in the higher echelons of state…[whose] influence might be critical…" Schwabe (1988: 113) cites the attempt of a defense minister to ban Völkische *Beobachter*, the Munich national socialist newspaper after it had slandered some leaders. However, the commander of the seventh infantry division in Munich refused to carry out the order. When the minister demanded that the commander resign, the latter refused. Thus, the national government could not rely on Bavarian military units to carry out its orders.

Of course, during the Weimar Republic, the democratic regime was able to hire some democratically minded officials, but those with social democratic sympathies were still greatly underrepresented and Jews constituted only a very small percentage (Wunder 1986: 120ff.). As a result, social democrats complained constantly about the "reactionary" *Beamte* who opposed the republic (Grotkopp 1992: 31). Grotkopp (1992: 39–40) notes that, in 1920, the social democratic-led government passed a law authorizing the interior and finance ministers in exceptional cases to recruit people who did not meet the normal criteria to high positions. They could do so if the applicant had professional knowledge (professional training) and at least 3 years' experience in an administrative position. Even then, very few social democrats qualified. The Nazis were more successful in getting their sympathizers into the state bureaucracy: by 1930, 8.3 percent of Nazi party members were civil servants, as compared to 5.3 percent of the population. (p. 100). Mann (2004: 163) points to a survey of Nazi activists done in 1933 which showed that civil servants were four times as likely to become Nazis as Germans in general. Feuchtwanger (2001: 116) argues that bureaucrats were not only motivated by their conservative beliefs, as the Brünning government of 1930–1932 reduced the salaries of civil servants. In view of their dislike for Brünning's policies and manner,

> [t]he overwhelming majority of civil servants were … prepared to accept at face value the legality of the Nazi take-over in 1933, and to participate without reserve in the euphoria—the *Aufbruchsstimmung*—that took hold of much of German public opinion in the spring of 1933. Thus, the Nazi revolution was able to take advantage of continuity in the administrative sphere.…

Moreover, when the Nazis came to power, they quickly moved to purge those new employees who had liberal or social democratic leanings (as well as those of Jewish background) and to replace them with loyal cadres, who were often Party members (Brandt 1976). The legislation ensuring this, known officially as the "Law for the Restoration of the Professional Civic Service," was designed to purge the civil service of actual or alleged political appointees. It also included a clause requiring all Jews to retire unless they were veterans of the front or relatives of men fallen in the Great War (Burleigh 2000: 284). Furthermore, the law stated that civil servants must "unreservedly support the national state" (Grotkopp 1992: 112; law §4BBG from 1933). Those who had been social democrats were declared "enemies of the people" (p. 113) and forced to leave the civil service. A law in 1939 required *Beamte* to pledge loyalty to the Führer until death, and stated that anyone who did not support the national socialist state could be fired.

Nevertheless, not many employees had to leave the ministries in these purges, as most already had "national" values. Even when the previous republican authorities had created new ministries and thus had greater leeway in deciding whom to hire, most of the recruits to the new positions seem to have had very conservative values. Thus, Middendorf (2015) notes that, because the finance ministry was founded in 1919 by the new regime, the social democrats had an opportunity to fill its positions with their supporters. Still, not many had to leave the ministry when the Nazis came to power:

> When the Nazis came to power, [the ministry's] employees did not experience it as a rupture, but rather as a new start, especially as it became clear that their position as *Beamte* would not be in danger. As of March 1934, only about 3 percent had lost their job at the ministry. The new finance

minister, Lutz Graf Schwerin Von Krosigk, had worked at the ministry since 1920, and he had been leader of its budget department since 1929. (p. 152)

The biggest changes took place at the highest level of the bureaucracy, where Göring began replacing political appointees already in February 1933. This included state secretaries, presidents of the provincial governments (*Regierungspräsidenten*), district administrators (*Landräte*), the head of the provincial police and so on. Thus, for example, by September 1934, 31 of the 40 police presidents in Prussia were "old" Nazi members, who had joined the party before 1932 (Broszat 2007: 303). However, less than 10 percent of police functionaries at higher levels were old party members.

Even though the bureaucrats were generally conservative, antidemocratic and willing to support the Nazi regime,

> ...the real impetus for genocide...came from those Nazi organizations created to parallel and *subvert* existing state organs [emphasis in the original]. Preeminent among these were the SS-police complex and the economic administrative bodies created during preparation for war (particularly the labor offices and the office for the Four-Year Plan), and the various civil administrations appointed in occupied Eastern Europe. (Bloxham 2008: 210)

The people working for these organizations were thus even more loyal to the Nazis than the state bureaucrats were.

If the German bureaucracy was based on loyalty to an antidemocratic, conservative and nationalist state, then many of the actions of its members do make sense. It makes sense, for instance, that civil servants often obstructed policies during the Weimar Republic, because they did not consider it legitimate or deserving of their loyalty. If the German bureaucracy was based on conservative, antidemocratic values, then it also becomes more understandable why its members were so willing to cooperate with the new Nazi regime, which they regarded as more legitimate than the Weimar Republic. It also makes sense that at times they did not cooperate with the Nazi leadership, and in fact at times were even more radical than the political leadership. A famous example is when Eichmann and other Nazis in Budapest—in a very non-banal manner—refused to follow Himmler's order to call off the Holocaust. They probably saw this order as illegitimate and as a last-ditch effort on Himmler's part to save himself by selling out the Nazi cause to the West. When ordering the long march of Budapest's Jews against Himmler's wishes, Eichmann told his colleague Kastner:

> You forgot that Hungary is always under the Reich's shadow, and our arms are long enough to catch the Jews of Budapest....And now, listen: this new government obeys us. I am going to immediately establish contact with Minster [of Jewish Affairs] Kovarcz. The Jews of Budapest will be deported, this time on foot.... (Lozowick 2000: 265)

SUPPORT FOR THE NAZIS

Of course, it would not have been enough for the Nazis to gain the support of the bureaucracy if they were not able to get any support from the population. In this section, therefore, I examine the views of the population in general. Even though anti-Semitism was at the core of Nazi ideology, experts mostly agree that anti-Semitism was *not* of major importance for Nazi electoral advances in the early 1930s. Instead, economic factors account for the sudden rise in the Party's vote—from a little more than 2 percent in 1928 to 37.3 percent in 1932 (see, e.g., Childers 1983: 208). In fact, the Nazis downplayed their anti-Semitism in this period in order to gain electoral support (Childers ibid.; Levy 2016: 32). Brustein (1996: 58) adds that "[o]nly a few of the Nazi leaders came to the party because of anti-Semitism." Moreover, Hitler understood that his "rabid anti-Semitism lacked drawing power among the German masses." Thus, the party put the emphasis instead on the material needs of the population. Given the sorry state of the German economy with the onset of the Great Depression, changes in the economic situation seem to have been a more important factor for the Nazis' increased support than any sudden increase in anti-Semitism. Of course, there is an interaction between the two: the Weimar Republic already enjoyed little legitimacy, and far-right groups attacked it and argued for replacing it with a more authoritarian system—and in so doing they found it convenient to blame the Jews for the ills of the country. Studies of Nazi voters (see, e.g., Childers 1983) and Nazi members (see, e.g., Brustein 1996) show that support for the Nazis can best be explained by the material interests of voters. However, ideology does matter: there was never a perfect correlation between material interests and support for the Nazis. Those who found racism, anti-Semitism or authoritarianism abhorrent would not have voted for the Nazis regardless of their material interests.

As Weiss (1999: 260) notes,

Nazi voters, like Nazi campaigners, made no such separation [between anti-Semitism and material interests]; for them all issues were racial issues. Ignoring the racist mentality, most German historians have maintained, for example, that large numbers of voters supported Hitler because of his anti-communism. But they do not add that Hitler's voters believed communism was Jewish, nor do they point out that the Weimar Republic and all other parties were anticommunist as well. Neither Goldhagen nor his critics, therefore, see that the key to Nazi electoral power was neither simply universal "eliminationist anti-Semitism" nor other issues than racism. The Nazis gained millions of votes because they were able, as their campaign literature shows, to connect, of course falsely, old antisemitic myths to the practical dilemmas of millions already historically disposed to do so. Reformulating old stereotypes, the Nazis united constituencies otherwise divided by conflicting interests. Even so, a majority of Germans voted anti-Nazi, even when Hitler's vote reached 37 percent.

Browning (1992/2001: 202) also points out that, to the extent Nazi voters were anti-Semitic, they held various types of anti-Semitic beliefs, only some of which were eliminationist in character. He also notes that the main driving force for these voters was their rejection of certain aspects of the Weimar Republic, rather than pure anti-Semitism:

In my opinion, ordinary Germans in eastern Europe brought with them a set of attitudes that included not only the different strands of anti-Semitism found in German society and fanned by the regime since 1933, but much else as well. As the Treaty of Brest-Litovsk, the Freikorps campaigns, and the almost universal rejection of the Versailles Treaty demonstrate, refusal to accept the verdict of World War I, imperial aspirations in eastern Europe underpinned by notions of German racial superiority, and virulent anticommunism were broadly held sentiments in German society. I would argue that they provided more common ground for the bulk of the German population and the Nazis than did anti-Semitism.

Kershaw (2008: 156) also sees economic issues and the Weimar Republic's lack of legitimacy as the main driving force behind popular support for the Nazis:

[B]efore 1933...people "were drawn to anti-Semitism because they were drawn to Nazism, not the other way round." Anti-Semitism cannot, it seems, be allocated a significant role in bringing Hitler to power, though, given the widespread acceptability of the Jewish Question as a political issue—exploited not only by the Nazis—nor did it do anything to hinder his rapidly growing popularity. However, the relative indifference of most Germans towards the Jewish Question before 1933 meant that the Nazis did have a job on their hands after the "take-over of power" to persuade them of the need for active discrimination and persecution of the Jews.

Koonz (2003: 10) makes a similar argument:

> From 1928 to mid-1932, when electoral support for Nazi candidates leapt from 2.6 percent to 37.4 percent, antisemitism played little role in attracting voters to Nazism. Masses of Germans, disillusioned with a foundering democracy and terrified of communism in a time of economic catastrophe, were drawn to the Nazis' promise of a radically new order under Hitler's control. Archival research as well as memoirs and oral histories make it abundantly clear that Germans' attitudes toward "the Jewish question" began to depart from Western European and North American norms only after the Nazi takeover. Germans did not become Nazis because they were antisemites; they became antisemites because they were Nazis.

One should also keep in mind that, even when the Nazis came to power, they did not have an electoral majority. If the majority of the population had supported eliminationist anti-Semitism before the Nazis came to power, then the Nazis should have been able—as clearly the most anti-Semitic party—to win a majority of votes in the 1933 elections. As Gerlach (2016: 39) observes:

> In the general elections of March 5, 1933, the Nazis, despite their intimidation, did not win an absolute majority. In the months afterwards, however, they gained the often-enthusiastic sympathy of the vast majority of Germans who often flocked to Nazism of their own accord. This mass support was consolidated by an economic recovery stronger than in many other countries, a recovery that was built in no small degree on *dirigiste* measures—and especially on a massive rearmament effort—and accompanied by the rhetoric of class compromise that in reality gave entrepreneurs a free hand.

In other words, the Nazis did not originally enjoy the support of the majority, but they gained popular legitimacy because of the economic recovery. The population compared the economic recovery under Nazi rule with the depression under Weimar (both the hyperinflation of the early 1920s and then the Great Depression of the early 1930s). The population also remembered the helplessness they had felt during the period of forced disarmament under the Versailles Treaty to which the Weimar government had agreed. The Nazi rearmament gave them new pride. Germans in the 1930s associated the Nazi regime with order and the Weimar Republic with disorder. As a result, the Nazis enjoyed greater popular legitimacy than Weimar had done, regardless of the issue of anti-Semitism.

One should also keep in mind that, even though the Nazis increased their support upon coming to power, there were always people who were critical of them. However, given the regime's extreme repressiveness, it was able to destroy most of the opposition groups (for a discussion of this, see the articles in Nicosia and Stokes 1990/2015).

Even in the case of Nazi militants, anti-Semitism was usually not the main driving force for joining the party. In 1934, an American sociologist, Theodore Abel, got 581 Nazi militants to write essays on the topic: "Why I Became a Nazi." He recruited the militants by advertising in a Nazi journal. Mann (2004: 144) points out that 32 percent of the militants claimed they had joined because they supported the *Volksgemeinschaft* (folk community), "23 percent of the essays expressed 'super patriotism' (pride in Germany plus hatred of foreigners), 18 percent identified with Hitler as the embodiment of the *Volk*, 14 percent centered on anti-Semitism, 6 percent centered on 'blood-and-soil romanticism,' and 5 percent advocated military recovery of the lost territories—quite a narrow ideological range." Thus, only 14 percent gave anti-Semitism as their main reason for joining the Party.

In addition, Mann (ibid.) points out,

[t]hese militants were also very strong on "enemies." Marxists/communists/socialists were seen as the main enemy in 63 percent of the essays, Jews in only 18 percent, liberals/capitalists in 8 percent, and Catholics in 5 percent. A third of the essays showed no evidence of anti-Semitism, half revealed some, and 13 percent seemed obsessed by it. Some 22 percent showed hatred for foreigners abroad, 15 percent for "foreigners" in Germany, and 5 percent referred to a conspiracy between both. Almost all said they hated the Weimar Republic, 30 percent because it was run by Jews or other "un-Germans," 19 percent because it was a multiparty system, 9 percent because it was Marxist, 3 percent because it was liberal capitalist, 23 percent because it was "liberal or capitalist" *and* "Marxist," 6 percent because it was "black" *and* "red."

Levy (2016: 31) concedes that anti-Semitism was a major reason for recruits to join the Nazis in the early years, but among those who joined after 1930, only around 20 percent were "fanatical anti-Semites" or people who felt strongly that action had to be taken against the Jews. In conclusion, it seems that wanting to belong to the *Volksgemeinschaft* and feeling hatred for the Weimar Republic were much more important than anti-Semitism for recruiting militants to the Party.

This section proceeds with a look at which social groups supported the Nazis, followed by a more in-depth examination of the peasants. An important difference between Sweden and Germany was the fact that peasants were much better organized in Sweden, and they had their own party to represent their interests; whereas German peasants, being weaker and lacking their own party, were more likely to turn to totalitarian anti-system parties like the Nazis. Given that, in 1920, people involved in agriculture came to 43.7 percent of the workforce in Sweden and 30.7 percent in Germany (Luebbert 1991: 287), peasants accounted for a substantial portion of the electorate—one large enough to have a heavy influence on whether a democratically minded government or an authoritarian one came to power in either country.

Nazi Voters and Members

Studies of Nazi voters (see, e.g., Childers 1983) usually conclude that the main the main source of support came from peasants, civil servants and people from the lower middle-class (especially craftsmen and small businessmen). Artisans and owners of small family businesses were particularly hard-hit by the depression, and they had trouble competing with department stores and consumer cooperatives. Meanwhile, peasants suffered from a decrease in the price of agricultural products and a reduction in demand for their exports. The Nazis started to agitate among peasants and got many of their candidates elected to chambers of agriculture in Prussia (Childers 1983: 216). In 1931, a Nazi was even elected as one of the four presidents of the national farmers' association and succeeded in getting that organization to support Hitler in the presidential election of 1932. Thus, as Childers (pp. 222–3) shows, peasants and members of the "old middle class" (i.e., the petty bourgeoisie) were much more likely than others to vote for the National Socialists. As already discussed, moreover, civil servants tended to have conservative and antidemocratic values, and

Childers' study (p. 242) shows that they too were much more likely than the population as a whole to vote for the Nazis. When the working class is concerned, the situation was more ambiguous. On the one hand, the Nazis were right wing and anti-labor. On the other hand, they referred to themselves officially as a "workers' party" (their full name was the "National Socialist German Workers' Party"), and they claimed to support workers' interests in the creation of jobs and the fight against finance capital. According to Childers' investigation (pp. 254–5), the only workers who were likely to support the Nazis were those in the handicrafts, whose position was threatened by the large corporations.

While most studies have focused on voters, Brustein (1996) focuses on party membership. This gives an indication of who the most active supporters of the Nazis were. His data on party membership is more reliable than an analysis of voting can be, because he has concrete information on what kinds of people joined the party, whereas no survey data is available about which parties people voted for. Thus, analyses of voting can only look at the correlation between the percentage of a group in an area and how many votes different parties gained in that area. By contrast, Brustein had access to thousands of membership cards. His results, however, are basically the same as Childers'. For example, he notes that the old middle class was overrepresented in the party, accounting for 29 to 35 percent of those who joined from 1925 to 1932, although it only comprised 24 percent of the population as a whole (p. 104). He notes that the Nazis appealed to the middle class by opposing "unproductive" capital in speculation and lending while calling for support of small business. Thus they criticized big business, banks, the stock market, department stores and consumer cooperatives—all of which, they argued, hurt small business (p. 91).

Brustein (1996) also finds that some groups of workers were more likely to join the party than others. Even though the party was right wing, the party appealed to workers when the depression broke out by calling for large public-works programs to create jobs (p. 146). It especially appealed to skilled workers, because while the leftist parties emphasized equality, the Nazis appealed to the desire of such workers "to climb the social ladder" (p. 147). However, the Nazis' protectionist policies went against the interests of workers in the export sector. Consequently, those working in non-exporting sectors were more likely to join the party than those working in export-oriented sectors (p. 149). Altogether, around 40 percent of those who joined the party from 1925 to 1932 came from the working class.

Mann (2004: 27) maintains that fascist supporters in general (including Nazi supporters) came not so much from a particular class as from a certain section of the different classes. In his words:

> Fascists tended to come from sectors that were not in the front line of organized struggle between capital and labor. They were less likely to be workers in urban, manufacturing settings (though they were around Budapest and Bucharest because industry there was more part of the "statist" constituency). They were less likely to be small or large businessmen or their managers. Yet they were not "marginal" or "rootless." Their social location was (for the interwar period) relatively secure. But from their slightly removed vantage point they viewed class struggle with distaste, favoring a movement claiming to transcend class struggle.

In other words, anti-Semitism does not seem to have been a major reason for most people to support the Nazis; instead, material interests go a long way toward explaining their support. Given the weakness and minimal legitimacy of the newly created Weimar Republic, many citizens thought the Nazis might be able to create a powerful country with a strong functioning state. They thought the new Nazi regime could undo the humiliation of wartime defeat and of the subsequent Versailles Treaty. This is not to deny that many Nazi supporters were anti-Semites. At the very least, they probably would not have supported the Nazis if they had been strongly opposed to racism in general and anti-Semitism in particular. There was definitely a problem of anti-Semitism in the country, but most anti-Semites did not support an eliminationist form of that doctrine. Until the Nazis began their process of dehumanizing Jews, anti-Semitism was not a major factor in popular support for the regime; rather, the regime enjoyed support because much of the population regarded it as more legitimate than the failed Weimar Republic.

Peasants

As noted earlier, the Holy Roman Empire did not create a German country, and its rulers based their power on the support of local nobles—rather than on burghers as in France or on peasants as in Sweden. As a result, Germany remained divided into many principalities until the country was united in 1871. This path of development also meant that feudalism was much stronger in Germany than in the other three countries examined in this study and that German peasants were much weaker. Whereas serfdom was basically abolished in Sweden in the 1300s, the emancipation of peasants in Prussia did not begin until 1807–1808; and even as of 1860, many peasants still had not been released from their manorial duties (Jacob 1963: 20). Moore (1966: 435) links the early liberation of peasants from serfdom in England and France to the successful transition to democracy in those countries. However, at the same time that peasants were being liberated in England and France, serfdom was actually being strengthened in the German territories. For example, in northeastern Germany in the fifteenth and sixteenth centuries, the growth of grain exports prompted the Prussian nobility to force peasants more deeply into serfdom, so as to ensure themselves access to a suitably captive labor force.

Since peasants were much weaker in Germany than in Sweden, it was more difficult for them to organize politically. In Sweden, two peasant parties emerged right after democratization and then merged into a single highly influential party. In Germany, by contrast, peasants outside of Bavaria had no party that directly represented their interests.

Brustein (1996) explains the Nazis' ability to gain the peasant vote as follows. First, he notes that the other parties showed little interest in addressing the problems of German agriculture. Thus,

> the parties of the center and right retained their faith in the market; the left had little interest in defending private property. It is highly likely that in the eyes of many German farmers the Nazi Party's agrarian program offered fresh hopes for a better livelihood. (p. 72)

Then, when the agricultural crisis worsened in 1927, the Nazis took steps to mobilize farmers, shopkeepers and artisans. The party held local meetings for these groups and called for the creation of professional organizations to represent their interests. Moreover, "[t]he party's policies between 1928 and 1930 largely echoed the program of the emerging *Landvolk* [i.e., people from the countryside] movement. In particular, the NSDAP called for raising agricultural productivity through reductions in the cost of credit, production costs, trade margins, taxes, and land prices" (p. 92). From the standpoint of their material interests, then, peasants had good reason to support the Nazis. Indeed, Hildebrand (1973: 622) goes so far as to claim that Hitler had "developed a draft for an anti-modern agricultural utopia."

According to Moore (1966: 450), the Nazis also sought to appeal to peasants ideologically:

> The peasant became the key figure in the ideology of the radical right as elaborated by the Nazis. The Nazis were fond of stressing the point that, for the peasant, land is more than a means with which to earn a living; it has all the sentimental overtones of *Heimat*, to which the peasant feels himself far more closely connected than the white collar worker with his office or the industrial worker with his shop. Physiocratic and liberal notions found themselves jumbled together in these doctrines of the radical right. "A firm stock of small and middle peasants," said Hitler in *Mein Kampf*, "has still been at all times the best protection against social evils as we have them now."

Brustein (1996) claims that, although many peasants had ideological and material reasons for supporting the Nazis, the interests of peasants were not unitary: some groups among them had a stronger incentive to support the Nazis than others. He notes that self-employed farmers were overrepresented among Nazi party members, while agricultural workers were underrepresented (p. 100). His study of party members also shows that farmers involved in export had less incentive to join the party than other farmers, since the Nazis were against free trade (the reason being that farmers who exported their goods benefited more from free trade did than those who had to compete with imports) (p. 101). Interestingly, although the Nazis started out in Bavaria and first tried to come to power through a coup there, farmers in that state were less likely to vote for the Nazis, as they could vote for the Bavarian People's Party, which represented agricultural interests (p. 106). Thus, in contrast to the situation in Sweden, where a nationwide peasant party existed, the Nazis were able to benefit from the lack of such a party in Germany (outside of Bavaria). Thus, even though Bavaria was the birthplace of the national socialist movement, the Nazis had trouble getting peasant support there.

The difference between Sweden and Germany lay in more than just the fact that peasants in the former country had their own party and that the social democrats were able to coopt it; as Luebbert (1991: Chap. 8) shows, the existence of a peasant party also hinders social democratic parties from pursuing policies that put off peasants. In Sweden, for example, the social democrats never tried to gain the support of agricultural workers, even though they actually formed a larger proportion of society there than in Germany. The reason for this is that the peasants' organizations were so strong that the social democrats decided it was better to cooperate with them than to antagonize them by trying to organize agricultural workers. In Germany, by contrast, the social democrats actively recruited such workers, given the lack of a peasant party to deter them from doing so. Consequently, the German social democrats pursued policies aimed at helping agricultural workers at the expense of the small and mid-sized farms. This alienated the peasants and made it more difficult for the social democrats to coopt them. Thus, peasants in Germany tended to be left out of party-political negotiations, making them more likely to turn to an authoritarian antisystem party like the Nazis.

Thus, German peasants had a material incentive to support the Nazis, because no other political parties tried actively to represent their interests. The exception was in Bavaria, where a peasant party already existed. The historical background plays an important role here. The feudalist tradition of the Holy Roman Empire, based on cooperation between nobles and the rulers of the various small states, ensured that the aristocracy there would be stronger than its counterpart in Sweden or France. By contrast, the crown in Sweden based its power more on support from the peasants, and in France on support from the burghers. Feudalism, therefore, lasted much longer in the German territories than elsewhere, which helped make it more difficult to unite the various small states into a single country. Consequently, when Germany finally united (many centuries after Sweden and France did), the peasants were relatively weak and unorganized, which hindered the formation of a peasant party. German peasants were not alone in holding racist views—their Swedish counterparts did so too. However, the Swedish social democrats were able to coopt the Farmers' Party and to get it to share responsibility for building up the welfare state, thereby incorporating the peasants into the democratic system.

In conclusion, since the Nazis came to power legally, claimed to represent the German people and seemed to offer a functioning alternative to the weak Weimar state—an alternative that would wipe away the humiliation that Germans felt and make them proud again—millions of people were willing to follow them, regardless of how strong or eliminationist their anti-Semitism might be. The ability of the Nazis to create legitimacy for their rule then enabled them to institutionalize methods and structures aimed at gaining total control over how people thought and perceived the world.

ASSOCIATIONAL LIFE

In the previous chapter, I noted that some authors have claimed that associational life played an important role in the consolidation of Swedish democracy. I argued too that this connection is not so clear as some scholars have claimed—that the importance of associational life for the emergence of Swedish democracy has been exaggerated. Nevertheless, there is little doubt that civil society played a more positive role for the consolidation of democracy in Sweden than it did in Germany. This is not to say that civil society was stronger in Sweden than in Germany. On the contrary, one could argue that it was just as strong in Germany—perhaps even stronger. In Germany, however, many civil-society organizations played an active role in promoting a right-wing dictatorship; eventually, in fact, many of them helped the Nazis come to power.

Even though Germany had a very active civil society between the two world wars, it did not have the Swedish tradition of politically neutral "folk movements" and study circles that promoted democracy. In addition, in contrast to the situation in Sweden, where the social democrats were able to coopt the term *folk* on behalf of democracy, the welfare state and social solidarity, right-wing organizations in Germany colonized the term *Volk* and built up a racist, *völkisch* ideology around the term. This includes such organizations as the *Reichshammerbund, Dürerbund, Germanenorden, Thulegesellschaft, Uniclub, Herrenclub, Mittwochsgesellschaft, Nationaler Club von 1919*, the *Ring-Bewegung, Deutschvölkischen Schutz- und Trutz-Bundes* and the *deutschnational Handlungsgehilfenverband* (Mommsen 1999: 25). Moreover, the bourgeois reform movement that emphasized nature, sports, naturism (*Freikörperkultur*) and occultism tended to support ideas of racial hygiene and protest against the alleged dominance of Jewish capital (Mommsen 1999: 33).

Berman (1997: 420) notes that the Nazis were able to use civil-society organizations to recruit activists, who in turn helped them spread their message. Nazi party members also infiltrated already existing civil-society organizations. Their agricultural arm, for instance, worked actively to penetrate the national farmers' association (the *Reichslandsbund*). As mentioned above, in 1932 the Nazis succeeded in getting one of their members elected to that organization's four-member presidential council. Later that year, moreover, the *Reichslandsbund* endorsed the Nazis in the general elections. Consequently, one reason why many peasants supported the

Nazis was because the national socialists had been able to penetrate the main farmers' organization. Berman also argues that many people started turning to *völkisch* civil-society organizations because the party system was weak, and many farmers and members of the old middle class did not feel the established right-wing parties represented them. This induced them to become active in right-wing civil-society associations which eventually backed the Nazis.

Berman's (1997) main argument backs up this book's thesis about the role of state-building. As I have noted, in Sweden the state had existed for many centuries, so it was extremely stable and enjoyed great legitimacy. Germany, by contrast, was a newly created state with a regime that suffered from grave legitimacy problems. Berman (p. 427) concludes that if

> political institutions and structures are weak and/or the existing political regime is perceived to be ineffectual and illegitimate, then civil society activity may become an alternative to politics, increasingly absorbing citizens' energies and satisfying their basic needs. In such situations, associationism will probably undermine political stability, by deepening cleavages, furthering dissatisfaction, and providing rich soil for oppositional movements.

Weber (2015: 631) supports Berman, pointing out that "although Imperial Germany and the Weimar Republic witnessed a proliferation of voluntary associations, these intermediary organizations—because developed along the traditional ideological and religious fault lines of German society—weakened Germany's inter-war democracy and favored National Socialism's electoral successes." He notes that organizational life was "blossoming" already "no later than the beginning of the nineteenth century."

Reiter (2009: 23) mentions another important aspect of German state-building for explaining the antidemocratic influence of civil society. He emphasizes the "centrality of Prussian militarism" for the formation of both the German state and German society. This militarism encouraged the emergence of nationalist civic associations, "such as the *Thule Kampfbund*, the *Deutschvölkischer Schutz- und Trutsbund*, the *Reichshammerbund*, and the *Alldeutscher Verein*." He also points out that student fraternities, sports associations and occupational associations served as recruitment grounds for the Nazis (pp. 24–5).

In sum, the German state was weak, newly created, poorly institutionalized and lacking in legitimacy. This created a situation in which civil society undermined democracy rather than strengthening it. As Mann (2004: 171) puts it: "Germany was thus a very strong civil society, and Nazis were at its heart. Led by Nazis it became a strong but evil civil society." Whereas the social democrats in Sweden were able to coopt the term *folk* and use it to support the democratic state and to increase solidarity with weaker members of society, in Germany militaristic and nationalistic groups gained control over the term *Volk*. German civil-society organizations used *Volk* to support authoritarian racist alternatives to the democratic state. This helped the Nazis come to power.

THE DEVELOPMENT OF ANTI-SEMITISM

A common argument is that, before the industrial revolution, anti-Semitism was based on religion, so that Jews could avoid persecution if they converted to Christianity. Chap. 3, on Spain, shows that this is not true, as the view that Jews had different "blood" and constituted a different species was already widespread in medieval times, leading to the introduction of "pure-blood" laws.

Goldhagen (1996) takes the biological question one step further and claims that a special type of "eliminationist" anti-Semitism emerged in Germany that differed from that in other countries. Since this type of anti-Semitism based itself on the need to liquidate all people of Jewish ancestry regardless of their religion, the Nazis were able to gain the support of much of the German population for the Holocaust. Consequently, in contrast to the amoral banal murderers that Arendt saw, most of the perpetrators in Goldhagen's view believed in what they were doing. Part of his proof lies in the many examples of sadistic acts that he details, which show that the perpetrators did much more than would have been necessary to blindly follow orders.[4]

Goldhagen's thesis has been highly criticized, but at the very least it is important that he posed the question as to whether the perpetrators really believed in what they were doing. It had traditionally almost been assumed that they were not ideologically motivated and that they carried out their acts for such reasons as group pressure, obedience to orders and so on. Goldhagen makes a strong point that we should at least consider the possibility that they believed in what they were doing.

However, as this book will argue, even if the perpetrators believed in what they were doing, that does not necessarily mean that they did so because a unique eliminationist variant of anti-Semitism had developed in

Germany. In order to argue effectively for this thesis, at the very least one would need to conduct a comparative analysis of anti-Semitism among European countries. As Chap. 6 shows, Goldhagen would be correct if the comparison were limited to Sweden, as no eliminationist anti-Semitism developed in that country, even though anti-Semitism was so widespread there as almost to be taken for granted.

One obvious objection to concentrating on Germany is the fact that Hitler and many of those involved in the Holocaust—such as Eichmann—not Germans but Austrians (c.f. Mann 2005; Weiss 1996, 1999). In addition, two of the men who had great influence on Hitler's anti-Semitism—Houston S. Chamberlain and Henry Ford—were Anglo-Saxons (Chamberlain being British and Ford American).

Furthermore, even if Sweden did not harbor much eliminationist anti-Semitism, Germany's neighbor, France, *did*. Perhaps the most influential proponent of the notion of the superior Aryan race and the inferior Semitic one was the French author Joseph Gobineau, who in turn inspired such people as the French writer Maurice Barres and the German composer Richard Wagner (Derfler 2002: 19). As in Germany, "[a]nti-Semitism [in France] became a major weapon employed by opponents of liberalism and the republican state, and it consequently took on a political dimension." Moreover, "[t]he juncture of anti-Semitism and anti-Republicanism would resurface in twentieth century France, most notably in the Vichy government that collaborated with Germany during World War II and in the bitter campaigns waged against two Jewish prime ministers: Leon Blum in 1937 and 1938 and Pierre Mendes-France in 1954–1955)" (ibid.: 22).

Another important French proponent of anti-Semitism was Édouard Drumont, whose *La France juive* appeared in 1886. According to Derfler (2002: 24), this book sold better than any other political work in the century, going through two hundred printings; and when it was serialized in a popular newspaper, "it was even more widely read" (see also Brustein 2003: 118ff.). Furthermore, anti-Semitic literature increased in France during this period from an average of less than one publication per year from 1879 through 1885 to 20 such publications in 1889. Drumont founded the *Ligue nationale antisemitique* (National Anti-Semitic League) in 1889. Eight years later, Drumont's disciple, Jules Guérin, founded the *Ligue Antisémitique Française* (the French Anti-Semitic League) which had between 5000 and 10,000 members (Derfler 2002: 24–5). In contrast to anti-Semitical organizations in Germany, which the political Right dominated, the *Ligue* had a leftist and "socialist" orientation. Several more anti-Semitic groups emerged around this time, including the *Ligue des Patriotes* (League of Patriots) and the *Ligue de la Patrie Franqaise* (League of the French Fatherland). This last group was established by school teachers in 1899 and claimed to have 40,000 members. The *Action Française* was a breakaway from this group. The *Ligue de la Patrie Franqaise* developed into a fascist movement that cooperated with the Vichy regime in sending between 75,000 and 77,000 Jews to their deaths (p. 26). Not only did these groups see Jews as a biological race, some of them had clearly eliminationist views. For example, *L'Union nationale*, established in 1893, organized cells in 35 French *départements*. It demanded the removal of Jews from public life, and its members often shouted at meetings: "France for the French!" and "Death to the Jews!" (Brustein 2003: 121).

Brustein (2003: 122) gives many more examples of racial anti-Semitism in France. He notes that Jules Soury wrote about the upcoming racial and religious war between Semites and Aryans. Similarly, Vacher de Lapouge claimed Jews are an inferior race and a dangerous rival to Aryans. In his 1899 book, *L'Aryen, Son Rôle social*, De Lapouge argued that the inferior Jewish race represents a threat to the survival of the superior Aryan race. He predicted that, in the final battle between Jews and Aryans, the Jews would lose because they lacked spirituality and a political instinct, and were unable to fight. In 1928, the perfume magnate Francois Coty started an anti-Semitic newspaper, *L'Ami du Peuple*, whose circulation had reached one million by 1930 (ibid.: 125). Thus, Stern (1996: 129) points out, several scholars have claimed that anti-Semitism was stronger and more aggressive before WWI in France than in Germany, although the current in defense of Jews was also much stronger in France. Volkov (1985: 224) claims that, before the Nazis came to power, German anti-Semitism had been similar to the French version.

Even if there was a strong biological-racist anti-Semitic trend in France, political parties promoting such policies at least never came to power on their own. During the Nazi occupation, though, the German army installed the anti-Semitic Vichy government in the officially unoccupied part of the country. Yet, anti-Semitic governments *did* come to power in other European countries well before WWII and the Holocaust began. In July of 1938, delegates from 32 countries met in the French resort town of Evian-les-Bains to discuss ways to help Jewish refugees fleeing Germany. At this meeting, the Romanian, Hungarian and Polish representatives proposed that their countries also be relieved of their Jews (Brustein and King 2004: 35). To be sure, this does not mean they espoused an eliminationist anti-Semitism, but at the very least they wanted to eliminate Jews from their country. Moreover, in the Polish case, a sort of eliminationist anti-Semitism was considered: in the late 1930s, the Polish government negotiated with the French government over the possibility of transferring all Polish Jews to Madagascar, which was a French colony at the time (Evans 2005: 7; Midlarsky 2005: 129). Even if there was no talk of murdering the Jews, they could hardly be expected to survive alone on that isolated island. Furthermore, given the fact that Poland had several million Jewish citizens, the island would have been overcrowded and unable to provide enough food for the forced immigrants. Moreover, there were plans in Poland to pass legislation banning Jews from public life and depriving them of the means to live in the country, but the onset of WWII prevented this (Midlarsky, ibid.). Anti-Semitism was so widespread among the Polish political elite that even "the Prime Minister in exile, Władysław Sikorski, suggested the resettlement of 3.5 million Polish Jews to the British Foreign Minister, Anthony Eden, as late as in January 1942" (Gerlach 2016: 60).

One study of violent attacks against Jews between the two world wars shows that such attacks occurred less frequently per capita in Great Britain, France and Italy than in Germany; however, the number of anti-Semitic acts in Romania was three times higher than in Germany (Brustein and King 2004: 43). It is also well-known that the Nazis were able to find many helpers for their mass killings among Ukrainians and Lithuanians, who were more than willing to join the *Einsatzgruppen* in hunting down Jews when the German army had invaded the Soviet Union.

This is not to deny the existence of an eliminationist anti-Semitism in Germany, nor is it to deny its importance: if there were no anti-Semitism or if the anti-Semitism were much milder, then it would have been more difficult to find people willing to help carry out the Holocaust. Moreover, the lack of an eliminationist anti-Semitism in Sweden would have made it much more difficult for a genocidal, anti-Semitic totalitarian regime to come to power in that country. The point is that the sheer existence of such a strain of anti-Semitism is not enough to explain the Holocaust. If it were, then racist and totalitarian regimes could just as well have emerged in countries such as France, and perhaps Poland, Ukraine and other countries.

Another criticism is that the eliminationist approach cannot explain the changes in levels of support for anti-Semitism over time in Germany (e.g., Hilberg 1980; Levy 2016; Moses 1998; Rosenfeld 1999). Levy (2016: 21) reflects that studies of Jews living in Germany before WWI show that they did not feel threatened. Yet, most admitted that a "Jewish problem" existed in Germany. Rosenberg (1967) claims that the main reason why anti-Semitism increased in some periods and decreased in others was that leaders made Jews a scapegoat during economic crises. Rosenberg (p. 89) remarks that anti-Semitism was relatively weak in Germany from 1849 to 1873 when the economy was growing. When the economy slid into depression in 1873, on the other hand, anti-Semitism grew more intense and developed into racial anti-Semitism (p. 93; cf. Mommsen 1999: 30). However, anti-Semitism decreased in 1896–1914, when the economy picked up again (Rosenberg 1967: 95). Given this pattern, it is not surprising that the Nazis came to power during the Great Depression, when people's fears were existential. Midlarsky (2005: 153) mentions that "German anti-Semitic political parties had declined precipitously in their share of the Reichstag vote prior to World War I, achieving only 0.86 percent in 1912 compared with 3.70 percent in 1898." Thus, support for anti-Semitism was far from stable; rather, it varied over time.

In addition, when the Nazis came to power, they were able to use their propaganda to increase support for anti-Semitism. Anti-Semitism also increased as a result of German defeat in WWI, which the Nazis blamed on the Jews. Yet even then, as several authors have pointed out, the Nazis toned down their anti-Semitic rhetoric in order to increase their support: "In one of Hitler's key addresses in 1932, for example, he hardly alluded to Jews at all" (Stern 1996: 131; cf. Levy 2016: 32). Moreover, in the last free elections, about two-thirds of the electorate voted against the Nazi Party.

Furthermore, as Kershaw (2008: 156) emphasizes, the Nazis had trouble mobilizing society against Jews in the early years of their rule. Their boycott of Jewish shops on April 1, 1933, was not very successful,[5] so they never tried to institute a second boycott. Moreover, while legal measures such as the Nuremberg race laws (which deprived Jews of citizenship) did not elicit much opposition, open violence—such as the *Kristallnacht* attacks on Jews and Jewish property—met with widespread disgust (Kershaw, p. 180; Bajohr 2016: 47).

In Kershaw's (p. 180) words:

[O]bjections to the spoliation and plunder of "Crystal Night" were wholly compatible with unreserved approval of the draconian but "legal" form of "punishment" which the State itself decreed in the immediate aftermath of the pogrom. The response to the "legal" measures of 1938 was as positive and uncritical as it had been to the Nuremberg Laws of 1935. The Government President of Swabia reported, for example, that the decrees of the government, especially the imposition of the "expiation payment" and the measures to remove Jews from the economy were "generally appreciated and—especially the economic measures—approved in principle by ever more national comrades." In contrast to the pogrom itself, the "legal" measures against the Jews also found "fullest understanding" in Lower Bavaria and the Upper Palatinate. In Lower Franconia, where there was also general approval, it was said to be the "expiation fine" which was particularly welcomed. These generalizations of the Government Presidents find frequent confirmation in the reports of the lower authorities.

Other authors come to similar conclusions. Bajohr (2016: 45) asserts that the non-Jewish population did not support violent actions against Jews. One reason was material: boycotts of Jewish-owned stores hurt non-Jewish customers; attacks against Jewish businesses threatened the jobs of their non-Jewish employees; and so on. Secret reports from local security organizations also claimed that the majority of the population opposed violent attacks on Jews as a threat to public order (p. 46). On the other hand, "[a]ccording to the reports, the anti-Semitic Nuremberg Laws were viewed with 'substantial satisfaction' and enjoyed 'full recognition'" (p. 47). Repression carried out in a legal and orderly manner enjoyed much greater legitimacy and met with much less resistance among the population. Once the war started and the deportations began, security reports indicated that even "many of the older national comrades criticized" these steps (p. 52). "Particularly in the reports in 1943 and 1944, it became clear that many Germans were speaking about the treatment of the Jews in a kind of mélange of bad conscience, fears of future retribution, and projections of guilt" (p. 53). Gruner (2016: 72) adds that the eliminationist policies encountered some resistance. In February 1943, for example, approximately 4000 Jews working as forced laborers in factories in Berlin were able to go into hiding to avoid deportation. They could do so "after being warned by neighbors, company employees, even policemen."

In other words, even if there was widespread anti-Semitism, and even if those who opposed racism were afraid to protest against the regime, the majority of the population does not seem to have supported a brutal eliminationist anti-Semitism. Yet, the population did consider the regime to be legitimate and believed it had the legitimate right to pass discriminatory laws. Consequently, once repression passed certain limits, at least parts of the population started questioning the regime's anti-Semitic policies, and some people were willing to help Jews escape deportation.

Another common critique of Goldhagen is that he does not take the influence of Nazi propaganda into account. The regime's relentless propaganda was bound—especially when combined with measures to dehumanize Jews, such as forcing them into poverty and stripping them of their rights—to influence attitudes toward Jews and to contribute to increased anti-Semitic views. As Bajohr (2016: 50) notes, diplomats reporting on the situation in Germany observed that

> an anti-Jewish consensus...had crystallized after six years of National Socialist rule. This consensus meant that Jews were no longer viewed as Germans, and in keeping with this, no objections were raised to their expulsion.

Yet, this does not mean that the population at this point supported the mass murder of Jews. As noted above, the deportations actually did meet with disdain among groups of Germans. A dynamic process emerged: views changed over time, as Jews became more dehumanized, and anti-Semitic propaganda increased. Thus, Herzstein (2002: 92) writes, "Goldhagen, however, underestimates the extent to which Nazi propaganda radicalized and intensified the anti-Semitic strains in German society." He adds:

> In 1946 the U.S. Military Government in Germany discovered that only two percent of the Germans in the U.S. zone of occupation were free of anti-Jewish prejudices. In no way could anti-Semitism have been so pervasive in 1880 or 1928. Were the killers in 1943 really the products of a toxic culture dating back to Luther, or were they as much or more creatures forged by the National Socialist movement after the late 1920s? (p. 93)

Midlarsky (2005: 185) shows more nuanced results, reporting that

> [i]n October 1945, a survey of the German population in the American zone of occupation revealed that fully 20 percent of the respondents supported Hitler's treatment of the Jews, and another 19 percent "were generally in favor but felt that he had gone too far." As late as 1947, 55 percent of the population believed that "National Socialism was a good idea

badly carried out." And we know that these attitudes were not characteristic of Germans in 1933 at the start of the Nazi regime (e.g., the failed Nazi-sponsored April 1 boycott of Jewish businesses).

While I agree with Midlarsky that anti-Semitism among the German population was stronger in 1945 than in 1933, in my view Herzstein goes too far in his critique: the "toxic culture dating back to Luther" and the development of eliminationist anti-Semitism *do* matter. They provide a cultural backdrop in which certain views are widespread. Maybe not everyone holds these views and perhaps many of those who do hold them do not do so wholeheartedly. Yet, the mere existence of a strong eliminationist discourse made it much easier for the Nazis to go further in their propaganda than they could have in a country in which racism and anti-Semitism had previously been nonexistent.

My state-building approach allows for a much more dynamic model than Goldhagen's cultural argument. My starting point is that the state-building process made ethnicity a central question since the new rulers had to decide exactly who qualified as "German," and whether the German state was to be a state for ethnic Germans all over the world or a state for all people living within its borders. The unification project always had a strong ethno-nationalist element. After the Austro-Hungarian Empire collapsed at the end of WWI, the newly formed Austrian state faced similar existential issues: Was the new country simply a shrunken version of the old empire? Had a new Austrian people emerged? Or were Austrians a section of the German people that should be united with Germany?

From this perspective, it is not necessary to accept Goldhagen's hypothesis on the existence of an eliminationist brand of anti-Semitism that openly or latently was widespread over 100 years before the Nazis came to power. Instead, it is enough to argue that a large number of Germans and Austrians (and other groups of ethnic Germans living in other countries) basically accepted the legitimacy of Hitler's regime. Their main motive might not have been anti-Semitism, but rather a belief that Hitler could unite Germans and make them strong again after the humiliation of defeat and the resulting Versailles treaty, the suffering caused by hyperinflation and then the Great Depression and so on. Yet, given the fact that the Nazis blamed the Jews for these problems, some people may eventually have come to believe that the Jews actually did cause them and that they posed an existential threat. But a major reason why many Germans accepted these arguments was that they accepted the Nazis' legitimacy. They believed the Nazis came to power in a legitimate manner and they believed it was a legitimate task to replace the weak state of the Weimar era with a strong state that would unite Germans living in Germany, Austria and the Sudetenland. Then, once people accepted the regime's legitimacy, they became more susceptible to the Nazi arguments in other spheres, such as in connection with anti-Semitism. Of course, it helped that there was a relatively strong eliminationist discourse in the country. It would have been much more difficult for a government in Sweden to carry out anti-Semitic campaigns than in Germany because although anti-Semitism was widespread, an eliminationist element was lacking and even anti-Semitic groups opposed the Nazi policies, which seemed "barbaric" to them. Yet, this eliminationist element existed in other countries, but only a regime that enjoyed great legitimacy and which used this discourse as part of a state-building strategy to unite the state around the notion of promoting the "master race" could succeed in getting more than very marginal support for such policies.

Thus, a more dynamic approach would be to point out that a view had been widespread around Europe since medieval times that Jews are subhuman or even a different species. This led among other things to the purity-of-blood laws in Spain. With the advent of industrialism and the new faith in scientific explanations, the idea of social Darwinism and racial competition arose throughout the industrialized world. Moreover, since Germany was a new state which had to decide who belonged to it and who did not, there was a greater need in its case to decide what to base the state on. Even though the new state was to some extent based on language, ethnicity also became important as the rulers did not trust some ethnic groups (among them Jews) to be loyal to the new state. When economic crises occurred, as in the 1870s, anti-Semitism increased as people looked for a scapegoat. Of course, economic depressions took place in other countries as well. Moreover, as discussed earlier in this chapter, anti-Semitism was stronger until WWI in neighboring France than it was in Germany. However, since France had been a state for many centuries, it did not feel as threatened and anti-racist forces gained the upper hand.

It must be admitted that liberal intellectuals in Germany were also more afraid of Jews than were their counterparts in France. The national liberals worried that Jews would be an obstacle to unity in the new state unless they completely assimilated and gave up their Jewish traditions. Thus Heinrich von Treitschke, editor of the *Preussiche Jahrbücher*, wrote that Jewish citizens must become Germans and feel like Germans so that the emergence of a mixed culture could be avoided. He added that

[f]ierce struggles have unified our fatherland to a powerfully advancing Empire. Unity has been achieved because the feeling that necessity has welded us together carried the victory over the tribal and religious divisions that had fragmented our nation like no other. (Stoetzler 2008: 1)

Thus, Jews emerged as an outgroup that posed a threat to the unity necessary for building the new German state. In Sweden, by contrast, no serious intellectuals made similar claims about Jews being an obstacle to national unity, despite the existence of widespread anti-Jewish stereotypes and prejudices in the country. Incidentally, von Treitschke coined the phrase which the Nazis later used in their propaganda: "Jews are our misfortune" (Stoetzler 2008: 5). Nevertheless, it took the collapse of the imperial regime and the ensuing disastrous conditions in Germany after WWI for a strong anti-Semitic political movement to arise.

Finally, Brustein and King (2004: 47) point out that it is easier to mobilize people around anti-Semitism if Jews are linked to the political left. Many of the top leftist leaders and theorists in Germany were Jews. This made it easier for the Nazis to blame the destruction of the previous regime on some international Jewish plot tied with the Bolshevik movement. Consequently, the Nazis were also able to frame the war against the Soviet Union as not just a war against communism but a war against *Jewish*-controlled communism. As seen in the previous chapter, there was also some support in Sweden for the Nazi war against the Soviet Union, but as the Swedish left was not tied to Jews, the war against the Soviet Union did not lead to much increase in anti-Semitism in the country. The fact that people with Jewish backgrounds played a much greater role in the German than in the Swedish left is not central to my argument about state-building. Rather, it was simply a factor adding to the differences that already existed between Sweden and Germany, given their different paths of state-building.

GERMANY AND THE NON-BANALITY OF EVIL

An argument throughout this book is that people are more willing to carry out evil acts if the state is successful in presenting an outgroup as an existential threat. However, the regime has a much greater incentive to do so and a much greater chance of succeeding if it is creating a new state and is using this threat as part of its legitimizing strategy. Such a strategy involves either creating a political religion (as in the case of the

Nazis) or developing a politicized religion (as in Spain). Thus, while the Catholic monarchs in Spain decided to use Catholicism as a totalizing, homogenizing ideology to unite the newly created state, the Nazis decided to use the National Socialist nationalist ideology based on racial biology. Whereas the Spanish regime used the notion of "purity of blood" to purify the nation from the influence of "demonic" Jews and "inferior" Muslims, the Nazis further developed the purity-of-blood notion into the pseudo-scientific theory of racial biology. Thus, they used their racial-biological theory to create an outgroup that could be portrayed as an existential threat to the recently united country. Of course, Jews were not the only outgroup; this group also included communists and to some extent social democrats, Roma, mentally handicapped and so on. Yet, since Jews were portrayed as the biggest enemy (and the force behind both communism and liberal capitalism), they are the focus of this book.

In the case of Spain, the monarchs saw Jews as an existential threat because they could induce *conversos* to revert to Judaism. The *conversos* themselves posed an existential threat because some of them were marrying into noble families and thus threatening the legitimacy of the aristocracy, which had been based on its having "blood" superior to that of the peasants. Also, to the extent that some *conversos* might have been practicing Judaism secretly, they threatened Catholic hegemony in the country. Muslims who had converted to Catholicism also represented an existential threat, as they were a potential fifth column that might support an invasion by Berbers or the Ottoman Empire.

In the German case, the Weimar Republic lacked legitimacy among much of the population. The right blamed the Jews for the loss in WWI, for the Versailles Treaty and for the Great Depression. The Nazis built on this by making Jews the main outgroup that was presumably responsible for all of the country's ills. In Stern's (1996: 131) words:

> by 1917, when hope for total victory turned to apprehension of defeat, an enraged right wing fastened on violent, chauvinist, anti-semitic [sic] beliefs; but for many other Germans defeat was the result of internal enemies, the Weimar Republic was a Jewish excrescence in German politics, and both Marxism and Bolshevism were Jewish machinations.

In fact, as Mommsen (2009: 21) points out, the military leadership started already during the war to use anti-Semitism as a way to entice workers to distance themselves from the social democrats and to support the war effort more strongly.

Again, Goldhagen (1996) is correct in pointing out the existence of an eliminationist anti-Semitism, but such an ideology also existed in France and it is not at all clear that this ideology was stronger in Germany than in France. However, France was not creating a new state, so the regime did not have to find an outgroup against which to unify the country; nor was there any need to portray Jews as an existential threat, given the fact that France had won the war. Similarly, when Sweden lost Finland in its last war in 1809, the Swedish state had been long established, so it did not need to find an outgroup as part of a legitimizing strategy. Moreover, the only group it could have legitimately blamed for the loss would have been the Finns, on the ground that they had not fought against the Russians whole-heartedly enough. Yet, such a claim would have been in incompatible with any demands for reconquering Finland: why would Swedes want back the land of the people who had presumably betrayed them? Actually, the opposite happened: the Swedish elite continued to take a pro-Finnish view and many Swedes were willing to aid Finland during its "Winter War" with the Soviet Union in 1939.

Goldhagen is also correct in at least raising the issue as to whether the perpetrators believed in what they were doing. However, my argument is much more dynamic than Goldhagen's: yes, culture—as in the existence of an eliminationist type of anti-Semitic discourse—matters, but in itself, it is not enough. As Hinton (2005: 26) acknowledges, there is a "dialectic between instituted and mental models...." So, there is great variation. Not everyone was willing to carry out evil acts and even those who were willing to do so in the 1940s might not have been willing to do so in the 1920s.

My argument is not that Germans were necessarily more anti-Semitic culturally than other Europeans, but rather that, as long as they had some basic belief in the regime's legitimacy as the "true" representatives of Germans, then at least some of them were likely to believe that committing atrocities in the name of this regime was necessary and perhaps even legitimate. The regime's legitimacy was tied to a political religion that justified and encouraged taking part in evil acts of repression. And the leaders of this regime, in turn, had an incentive to present the Jewish outgroup as an existential threat, to mobilize support for their new regime. The existence of an eliminationist discourse upon which to build certainly helped, as it formed a core of the regime's political-religious ideology. Ehret (2007: 1245) sums it up as follows:

The Christian apocalypse, the prophecy of an *endzeit* struggle between the forces of light and dark before the chosen community can enter paradise, is projected onto Hitler's worldview of a fundamental struggle between the races, between 'Aryans' and Jews, that had to be won before the German people achieved the promised Reich. This National Socialist apocalypse is, according to Vondung "the only plausible explanation for the Holocaust."

The political religion could gain resonance among portions of the population in part because the two main variants of Christianity in Germany also had strong anti-Semitic traditions. Chapter 3 shows how Catholic Spain developed the ideology of blood. Weiss (1996: 85–6) notes that

> ...in 1876 the official Catholic journal *Germania* accused "Jewish" liberals in the Reichstag of seeking to rob the church of its legitimate rights because of their ancient battle against Christ. For the first time in a respectable periodical, a boycott of Jewish businesses was called for, and in the phrase the Nazis were to make infamous: "Do not buy from Jews." *Germania* also blamed Jews for the economic collapse of 1873, following the lead of Pope Pius IX, who declared them "The enemies of Jesus, they have no other God but their money." Some three hundred local Catholic newspapers in Germany were even more racist.

Lutheran traditions were no less anti-Semitic, Weiss (1996: 23–4) points out that

> Luther declared that a Jew could never be converted anymore than one could convert the devil they so early served. It was dangerous even to discuss religious matters with these satanic Jews, he insisted. It was enough to remind them of their historical fate since the destruction of the temple, for it proved well enough how the Lord hated their accursed race. Luther would not baptize a Jew even if asked, he wrote; instead he would drown him like a poisonous serpent....The princes of Germany should ban Judaism, destroy Jewish property, execute rabbis who continued to teach, burn their schools, synagogues, and houses, seize their wealth, destroy their prayer books and Talmudic writings, and either "drive them like mad dogs out of the land" or place them all "under one roof"—in short, a concentration camp. Following his advice, the princes of three Prussian provinces drove out the Jews.... Luther was a racist, pure and simple, bothered not at all that his hatred of the Jews denied the power of Christ to redeem all humanity. To him the Jew was simply not human. As the Protestant "German Christians" of the Nazi movement would later claim, the blood of a Jew was beyond redemption.

> For Luther, the devil walked on earth; he himself, he wrote, had seen Satan and often heard his vile voice.

Or as Maccoby (2006: 44) puts it: "Luther's proposals for the Jews fore-shadow in almost every particular the measures taken by the Nazis." Berger (1993: 601) adds that Luther denounced the Jews as Germany's special "plague," "pestilence" and "misfortune." Of course, not all Lutheran preachers in Germany continued Luther's anti-Semitic tradition, but Weiss (1996) and many other authors have argued that a large number of Lutheran preachers did openly support the Nazis and give anti-Semitic, pro-Nazi sermons (see, e.g., Burleigh 2000: 281).

Yet, despite the influence of Catholic and Lutheran traditions of anti-Semitism, a political religion with an eliminationist ideology was not able immediately to gain the full support of society for repressive acts, even if it had the support of some religious leaders and even if it based its political religion on Christian religious traditions. Germans did not give enthusiastic support to many of the regime's anti-Semitic actions, such as the boycott or the pogroms of Kristallnacht. But since the regime enjoyed great legitimacy, the population became open to its constant propaganda. A decade of anti-Semitic propaganda, along with many measures to dehumanize the Jews, made it easier to induce some people to engage in repressive acts against this outgroup.

It is also important to note that the Nazi regime did not want to eliminate just Jews. It was a genocidal regime in general. The first victims of mass murder were those whom the regime regarded as mentally insufficient. Lifton (1990: 33), writing about the doctors who participated in such mass killings, emphasizes the importance of "a genocidal ideology" that legitimizes such behavior. "In the Nazi case, that genocidal ideology included killing in the name of healing and a pseudo-biological or 'biomedical' worldview." As is well-known, the Nazis also massacred millions of Russians and Poles.

Thus, my more dynamic approach allows for great diversity and for changes in anti-Semitic views among people over time, in contrast to Goldhagen's model. An eliminationist discourse had existed in some European countries, but the combination of a political religion forming part of a state-building process with a decade of indoctrination and the progressive dehumanization of the outgroup in question made it easier for the regime to induce some people to engage in genocide. The Nazi regime was able to blame the destruction of the imperial German state on the

Jews and it similarly blamed the Jews for all of the ills of the Weimar Republic. This increased the tendency to see Jews as the outgroup, which represented an existential threat. Then, when the war with the Soviet Union began, the Nazis even linked this war to the race war, claiming that the Bolsheviks represented a "Jewish" regime that was their mortal enemy. The Nazis' political religion legitimized the mass murder of other groups than Jews; therefore, the Nazi genocide, while indeed being linked to ideology, cannot be explained merely by reference to an eliminationist anti-Semitism.

Even though authors such as Kershaw and Browning do not emphasize the role of legitimacy as much as I do, they still do agree to its importance. Thus, Kershaw (2008: 40) concludes:

> Building a "national community," preparing for the showdown with Bolshevism, purifying the Reich of its political and biological or racial enemies, and removing Jews from Germany, offered free license to initiatives which, unless inopportune or counter-productive, were more or less guaranteed sanction from above. The collapse in civilised standards which began in the spring of 1933, and the spiraling radicalisation of discrimination and persecution that followed, were not only unobstructed by but invariably found *legitimation in the highest authority in the land* [emphasis added]. Crucial to this "progress into barbarism" was the fact that in 1933 the barriers to state-sanctioned measures of gross inhumanity were removed almost overnight. What had previously been unthinkable suddenly became feasible. Opportunities rapidly presented themselves; and they were readily grasped.

Moreover,

> Where the Nazis were most successful was in the *depersonalization of the Jew* [emphasis added]. The more the Jew was forced out of social life, the more he seemed to fit the stereotypes of a propaganda which intensified, paradoxically, its campaign against 'Jewry' the fewer actual Jews there were in Germany itself. Depersonalization increased the already existent widespread indifference of German popular opinion and formed a vital stage between the archaic violence of the pogrom and the rationalized 'assembly-line' annihilation of the death-camps. (p. 184)

Browning (1992/2001: 202) did not emphasize legitimacy much in his original study of "ordinary men," but in revising the book and adding an afterword on Goldhagen, he now admits more clearly the importance of legitimacy. Thus, he describes how the mere act of being involved in a war that the regime defined as a race war also served to legitimize evil actions:

> And in eastern Europe ordinary Germans were transformed even more by the events and situation of 1939–41 than they had been by their experience of the domestic dictatorship of 1933–39. Germany was now at war; moreover, this was a "race war" of imperial conquest. These ordinary Germans were stationed in the territory where the native populations were proclaimed inferior and occupying Germans were constantly exhorted to behave as the master race. And the Jews encountered in these territories were the strange and alien Ostjuden, not assimilated, middle-class German Jews. In 1941 two more major factors, the ideological crusade against Bolshevism and "war of destruction," were added.

He adds (p. 203) that

> it is important to note that before the Final Solution was implemented (beginning on Soviet territory in the second half of 1941 and in Poland and the rest of Europe in the spring of 1942), the Nazi regime had already found willing executioners for 70,000 to 80,000 mentally and physically handicapped Germans, tens of thousands of Polish intelligentsia, tens of thousands of noncombatant victims of reprisal shootings, and more 2 million Russian POWs. Clearly, as of September 1939, the regime was increasingly capable of legitimizing and organizing murder on a staggering scale that did not depend on the anti-Semitic motivation of the perpetrators and the Jewish identities of the victims.

Finally, Browning concedes that he should have emphasized the role of legitimacy more in his original study (pp. 215–6):

> For the most part, they did not think what they were doing was wrong or immoral, because the killing was sanctioned by *legitimate* authority [emphasis added]. Indeed, for the most part they did not try to think, period. As one policeman stated: "Truthfully, I must say that at the time we didn't reflect about it at all. Only years later did any of us become truly conscious of what had happened then." Heavy drinking helped: "most of the other men drank so much solely because of the many shootings of Jews, for such a life was quite intolerable sober." …[In the original study] I noted the importance of conformity, peer pressure, and deference to authority, *and I should have emphasized more explicitly the legitimizing capacities of government* [emphasis added].

Herzstein (2002: 106) underlines that the perpetrators "did not need to suppress or 'double' [in the sense of living double lives] at all, for in killing Jews they were behaving in a legal and morally sanctioned manner."

As Berkowitz (1999: 248) shows, legitimacy also mattered in the case of Milgram's famous experiments, in which participants were supposed to give shocks to punish somebody when that person gave the wrong answer. In his original experiment, 65 percent of the participants were willing to give the maximum level of punishment when they were told the man leading the project was a scientist. However, in another experiment, when a "common man" gave the orders to the participants, only 20 percent were willing to administer the highest-level shocks. Thus, "[t]he majority of the ordinary people serving in the baseline study apparently believed they were so obligated to comply with the commands of a *legitimate* authority that they were even willing to hurt another person severely at the authority's behest" (emphasis added). Even in this case, though, as Berkowitz points out, those who were willing to give shocks were not comparable to the Nazi perpetrators, because they lacked the sadism that was common among the Nazis. That is, some participants were willing to give electric shocks to people because they thought the orders were legitimate coming from a scientist, but they were not filled with the enthusiasm and vigor of true believers following an ideology, and they did not perceive the victims in the experiment an existential threat or as members of an outgroup. For this reason, in contrast to those "ordinary people" who joined the police reserve battalion in Hamburg and carried out atrocities, many of the participants in Milgram's experiments suffered psychologically afterward, whereas none of the German police did. The latter did not have a guilty conscience since they believed in what they were doing (cf. Blass 1993; Fenigstein 1997).

Dehumanization always makes genocide easier: if the victims no longer look human, then killing them is likely to feel like killing a rat or an insect. As Herzstein (2002: 208) notes:

> Interestingly, the eloquent [Holocaust] survivor Primo Levi agreed at least in part with Franz Stangl, the notorious Treblinka commandant,…that the total debasement and humiliation of the victim facilitated the victim's dehumanization so essential to the actions of the perpetrator—"to condition those who actually had to carry out the policies. To make it possible for them to do what they did."

Emphasizing the need to dehumanize the outgroup, Berger (1993: 611) comments that

> the bureaucrats of the Third Reich constructed the "final solution" in an interpretive climate in which anti-Jewish policies were warranted in light of a commonly held collective representation that had dehumanized (and demonized) the Jews and a legal system that had juridically transformed them into "nonpersons." This made it possible for the bureaucrats to abandon any "residual sense of shared humanity" with their Jewish victims and view their actions as legitimate instances of solving a grave and pressing social problem.

Zukier (1994: 446) points out that the regime was not able to completely dehumanize the Jews right away; rather, it had to do so gradually over time. Changing the attitudes of the population is a process that cannot be done all at once:

> They became murderers not by leaps and bounds but by inches, insensibly, gradually, step by step. The spiral of murder is fueled, initially, by moral anxiety at one's prior actions. The Nazis did not kill the Jews in a battlefield frenzy nor out of depraved indifference but in the inner, moral frenzy that follows the silencing of the cannons.

Moreover,

> [t]he shaping of the murderous mentality follows a gradual, twisted psychological path. It involves an ineluctable progression from smaller initial offenses, seemingly devoid of larger significance, through moral conflict and psychological adjustment, to the ultimate atrocities. The string of small acts that leads to great crimes facilitates the incomprehension of the victims and of the perpetrators, who may fail to grasp their condition until it is too late. We tend to think of socialization into evil (and into heroism) as one continuous, smooth process. In fact, it consists of two contrary moments, animated by different motivations. The slide into evil is not self-starting, a simple slippery slope. But, at moment two, it is self-sustaining. The beginnings of the spiral, and the progression to new levels, require the pressure of a legitimate authority. (p. 447)

The dehumanization process even influenced the highest-level members of the system's elite. Burleigh (2000: 575) remarks that

[a]fter visiting the Łódź ghetto Goebbels wrote: "It is undesirable. These aren't human beings any more, these are animals. This is therefore not a humanitarian, but rather a surgical task. One must make cuts here, moreover really radical ones."

Hinton (2005: 29) calls this process of dehumanization "genocidal priming."

Finally, it is important to note that ethnic Germans were not the only ones who actively participated in the Holocaust. Even if the Nazis' rise to power and their drive to liquidate all Jews were what made the genocide possible, people in other countries actively participated. It is beyond the scope of this book to go into details about these cases, but it suffices to say that, if a special German eliminationist anti-Semitism were to blame, then we would not expect people in other countries to have assisted in the Holocaust. Even if the mass murder in other countries took place as part of the Nazi occupation rather than as part of a state-building strategy, my legitimacy argument goes far in explaining what happened. The occupation made it legitimate to kill Jews or to hand them in to Nazi authorities. The degree to which the local populations were willing to cooperate seems to have depended on the degree to which preoccupation regimes promoted anti-Semitism. For example, Dumitru and Johnson (2011) show that people were more willing to collaborate in killing Jews in Bessarabia than in Transnistria, because the former joined Romania after WWI, while the latter joined the Soviet Union. During the interwar period, the Romanian government carried out anti-Semitic policies, while the Soviet state officially disapproved of anti-Semitism. Consequently, those living in Soviet Transnistria had been taught that anti-Semitism is something bad, so they were less willing to cooperate in murdering Jews when Romania occupied their territory during the war. Those living in Bessarabia had been taught that anti-Semitism is something good, so they were much more willing to cooperate in persecuting Jews. These two areas make for a good comparison because they are neighbors and they were similar in the size of their Jewish populations, and both areas had belonged to the Russian empire before 1918.

Denmark and Poland are less comparable, but many scholars have pointed out that Denmark was probably the country where the population was the least willing to collaborate with the Nazis' anti-Jewish policies. When the Danish authorities found out that the occupying power was getting ready to deport the Jews, they helped most of the Jews escape to

Sweden. In Poland, by contrast, much of the local population was willing to cooperate with in catching and murdering Jews. As already noted, during the 1930s the Polish government had gone in an increasingly anti-Semitic direction. At the conference in 1938 on Jewish emigration, the Polish government was just as eager as the German one to find a way to deport all its Jews. So even though very few Poles thought the Nazi occupation was legitimate, it had already become legitimate to oppose Jews well before the Nazi occupation began. Studies have shown that the Nazis employed both positive and negative incentives for local populations to help them catch Jews in hiding. Positive incentives included rewards, such as getting bags of sugar for Jews whom they had brought in, as well as sometimes being able to take the clothes and other belongings of Jews who had been killed. Negative incentives included the fear that the village would be punished by the Nazis if Jews were found hiding there. Nevertheless, these incentives by themselves are not enough to explain the behavior of Poles who helped catch Jews. Statements they made in post-war trials, for example, indicate that much of the local population thought it was perfectly normal and legitimate to kill Jews. Sometimes even the Home Army, which was fighting against the Nazi occupation, killed Jews who volunteered to join them. This type of action cannot be explained by the rewards and incentives that the Nazis provided. However, since Jews were already being dehumanized and marginalized in society before the war began, and since the Polish government had already labeled Jews a threatening outgroup, it became legitimate to cooperate with the Nazis in supporting the Holocaust (see, e.g., Engelking 2012; Gross 2012; Grabowski 2013).

This section will exclude the Eichmann case since I discussed it in Chap. 3. It begins rather with a discussion of how the plans for committing genocide evolved, to show that far from being a totally top-down system in which bureaucrats followed orders, it was a system in which many bureaucrats—in addition to Eichmann—were instrumental in taking the initiative for plans to accomplish the Holocaust. In contrast to the people portrayed in Arendt's banality-of-evil thesis, these individuals were believers—or at least people who believed in the legitimacy of these policies—who did not act as they did merely because it was their duty. They committed atrocities because they believed that what they were doing was correct and legitimate. In contrast to Arendt's robots, they were both able to think and very flexible in figuring out what steps to take. Their thoughts were limited only by the constraints of the ruling ideology.

Finally, this section will analyze the "street-level bureaucrats"—that is, those who actually carried out mass murder. Since that topic might require a book in itself, this section is largely limited to discussing the allegedly "ordinary" men in Browning's famous study on the Reserve Police Battalion 101 from Hamburg (although it will also make reference to other groups of organized killers). The Reserve Police Battalion 101 is an important case because Browning (1992/2001) uses it to show that those who carried out the atrocities were not necessarily strong believers. Goldhagen (1996) agrees that these reservists were ordinary, but sees them as proof that ordinary Germans were adherents of eliminationist anti-Semitism. By contrast, I will argue that they were not so ordinary: that is, they were more inclined than the population, in general, to carry out atrocities, even if they may have been less inclined to do so than the more ideologically engaged soldiers of the SS. In other words, ideology matters: those who were stronger believers in the political religion—who were more indoctrinated in the political religion—were more willing to carry out atrocities.

The Development of the Holocaust

Since this book argues that the bureaucrats were not banal people who were merely doing their duty, but instead were often fanatical believers who took a lot of initiative, two questions naturally arise: First, how much initiative did they really take? Second, did their efforts to show initiative merely amount to finding creative ways of following orders? Among German historians, this has led to the great instrumentalism-versus-functionalism debate. Instrumentalists portray Hitler and the top elite as having had the critical impact, while functionalists see more influence from below, whereby bureaucrats created the Holocaust by competing with each other. The truth seems to be somewhere in-between: the leaders set the tone, but the bureaucrats took the initiative in figuring out how to do it in practice For example, Aly (2017: 40ff.) claims that the Holocaust was not originally planned[6]; rather, the Nazis were looking at first for a place to send Jews living in Poland (as well as Poles), so that they could resettle Germans in the parts of Poland that the regime incorporated into the *Reich*. So it was sort of a migration policy, which then logically developed into the Holocaust as Nazi bureaucrats struggled to find new solutions to the increasing number of Jews under their control. Originally, in September 1939, the destination was to be a

Jewish reservation on the new southeastern Polish border. Even though the bureaucrats did not talk about mass murder, all of the deportation plans would have led to the death of tens of thousands of Jews; later the numbers were in the hundreds of thousands. They would die through hunger, slave labor, police attacks and a lack of medicine. More would die in the winter transports when they had to walk long distances by foot or travel on trains in unheated freight cars. In December 1939, Eduard Könekamp at the German Foreign Institute wrote a report stating that the "destruction of these subhumans lies in the interests of the entire world" (p. 41).

The following year, Heydrich was still discussing Jewish policy as part of general resettlement policy. Thus, in connection with the development of the Madagascar plan in the summer of 1940, he saw the solution of Jewish policy in relation to general resettlement policy (Aly 2017: 100). It was not simply an issue of getting rid of Jews; it was also a question of finding living areas for ethnic Germans, who were to be resettled in the western part of Poland. Thus, goods confiscated from Jews and Poles would be used to help finance the resettlement of Germans (p. 119). After the conquest of Poland, there were 3.25 million Jews in the territories under German control, which was too many to make it possible to solve the Jewish "problem" through emigration (p. 121). In this situation, different organizations in the bureaucracy had different ideas, different interests and different bottlenecks to overcome. For example, one group wanted to solve the Jewish Question quickly, while another wanted to concentrate on improving conditions in the countryside in the poor regions of the Reich (p. 123). Thus, far from being passive bureaucrats, they were heavily engaged in developing policy proposals. In September 1941, Heydrich said that the Jews would be sent to camps in the arctic (that the Soviet Union had already built) as soon as the military situation allowed.

During the spring of 1941, various bureaucrats postponed the deportations because everyone assumed the Soviet Union would be defeated in the fall, and that all of the publicly and secretly formulated plans could be put into practices without any obstacles. The deportations would lead to the death of some; others would starve and freeze to death in the ghettos and camps; still, others would be worked to death. This program worked out in the spring of 1941, would have led to the destruction of European Jewry. It went much further than the Madagascar plan. However, it still did not provide for the mass murder in gas chambers that later took place

(Aly 2017: 234). On July 17, 1941, Heydrich reached an agreement with the *Wehrmacht* that active communists, members of the Soviet intelligentsia and all Jews should be taken from the prison camps and shot (p. 244). Thus, the bureaucrats were now openly advocating murder—but not yet total genocide.

That same month, Hans Frank (Governor-General of the occupied Polish territories) was discussing deporting Jews quickly toward the east rather than putting them to death in gas chambers (Aly 2017: 265). At around this time Rolf-Heinz Höppner, an SS officer, noted that it would not be possible to feed all the Jews during the winter. Therefore, it might be more humane to kill those who are not capable of working using something that would kill them quickly (p. 273). Still, he was not thinking at this point about killing all Jews, as those who could work would be concentrated in camps, while the others would be killed. In addition, he thought, all Jewesses should be sterilized, to prevent a new generation of Jews from emerging (p. 274). Thus, there were processes coming from below from people like Höppner, while at the top there were also discussions about how to solve the "Jewish question." Immediately after the Wannsee conference in January 1942, Heydrich brought up the arctic solution again, suggesting the Nazis should take over the Russian gulag camps (p. 231). This shows that it was not certain even then that the Jews would mostly be killed in death camps.

Where decisions from the top are concerned, for example, in January 1941 Himmler asked Philipp Bouhler from the Führer's chancellery to investigate whether it would be possible to sterilize all Jewish women using X-rays. This means that, by the early spring of 1941, Himmler and his associates were already thinking about the biological destruction of European Jews (Aly 2017: 275). Moreover, by the war against the Soviet Union began, they had already decided that prosecuting the "race war" required wiping out the entire "Jewish Bolshevik" enemy. Therefore, the commandos of the *Sicherheitspolizei* (security police) and the *Sicherheitsdienst*, with the support of the Wehrmacht, were to shoot all Jews who were capable of being soldiers. It had already been discussed in Wartheland that it would be good to find a quick way to get rid of those Jews who were not able to work in labor camps and therefore could not contribute to the economy. After Himmler visited the front in August 1941, the German occupation forces started "liquidating" Jews, Jewesses and their children (p. 277).

According to this evolutionary view, the inability to obtain a quick victory against the Soviet Union was a key factor impelling the Nazis to choose genocide, as they were no longer able to deport the Jews to Siberia. Consequently, they started thinking of new approaches, which led to the Holocaust. Thus, Aly (2017: 328) supports Mommsen's idea of "cumulative radicalization." In other words, the Final Solution was not one decision, but rather different decisions at different points in a process over time (pp. 323–4). Of course, it would not have been possible without approval from the top. Hitler had already warned in 1939 that all European Jews would face liquidation if they "started" another world war. But whether one supports those historians who put greater emphasis on decisions made at the top or those, like Aly and Mommsen, who stress local initiatives taken by problem-solving bureaucrats, it is clear that these bureaucrats were not banal desktop murderers who did not understand what they were doing. They were quite aware of the larger picture, and they took great initiative to come up with proposals for improving the process; indeed, they suggested the idea of committing mass murder to higher levels of authority. As Mann (2005: 278) remarks,

> the vast majority of those involved in actual killing knew what they were doing. Most thought there was good reason for it....Exterminist ideology emerged as a process and through institutions and subcultures. Radicalized Nazism was implemented through the careful selection of appropriate institutions and personnel that could employ hierarchy, comradeship, and career to accomplish genocide.

Kershaw (2008: 42) called this process "working towards the Führer." He notes that bureaucrats anticipated "Hitler's presumed wishes and intentions," seeing them as "guidelines for action" and knowing that their actions would be approved. He adds that "the tasks associated with 'working towards the Führer' offered endless scope for barbarous initiatives, and with them institutional expansion, power, prestige and enrichment." Gross (2012: 66) adds that the perpetrators were not merely following orders; rather, they were constantly improvising in an effort to work toward the Führer. In his words:

> [B]ureaucratic apparatuses and bureaucratic routines are devised with specific goals in mind. And to apply them to different tasks requires adaptation and initiative.

That idea accords with the argument in this book. Nazism was a political religion in which many of the perpetrators believed and which made it easier for them to work toward the Führer. But even those who did not believe in it (or did not do so completely) nonetheless believed in the legitimacy of the regime, and at the very least they knew that their actions would be seen as being legitimate. To some extent, moreover, "power, prestige and enrichment" served as carrots. No regime can ever succeed completely in its totalitarian indoctrination, and other motive will always matter somewhat depending on the person in question.

Gerlach (2016: Chaps. 4, 5, 9) agrees that the Holocaust was not planned from the beginning, but he places more emphasis than Aly on the critical issue of food. He basically argues that, from the Nazi viewpoint, food was in short supply, so it was hard to justify feeding Jews when the local populations did not have enough to eat. By killing Jews, they could increase food rations to people in the occupied territories, thereby decreasing the probability that the local population would rebel. In addition, the Nazis were afraid that Jews living in crowded ghettos would spread epidemics that would reach non-Jews outside the ghettos. Even though Gerlach agrees that the Holocaust was not originally planned and that it rather evolved, he ascribes much more responsibility for the decision to Hitler than functionalists do. He claims that Hitler gave the order to liquidate all of the Jews in German-held territory already in December 1941 (p. 80). So, even if the idea to murder all of the Jews was something that evolved, and even if lower-level bureaucrats played an important role in suggesting mass murder, Hitler made the final decision for genocide at a rather early stage of the war.

Ironically, just as the social sciences were abandoning the notion of "functionalism," some of the very historians who showed that the bureaucrats took great initiative in developing the Holocaust claimed to be providing a "functionalist" explanation. The concept of working toward the Führer implies a lot of room for individuals to take personal initiative, as does the idea of having bureaucracies compete with each other to come up with ideas for solving the "Jewish question." Despite this, one of the leading proponents of this approach, Mommsen (1983), claims that the notion of cumulative radicalization is functionalist and even goes so far as to support Arendt's claim that the evil of the bureaucrats was banal.[7] Yet, the evidence seems to show clearly that many of the bureaucrats were highly motivated ideologically and that even those who were not true believers showed great initiative, which does not make their behavior seem particularly "banal." They were aware of what they were doing, they saw the big picture and they knew that what they were advocating violated civilized norms, which is why they tried to hide the crimes that they were committing. Mommsen (1983: 383) rightly emphasizes the role that "duty," "loyalty," "honor" and "service to the nation" played within the German bureaucracy. This made it different than the Swedish bureaucracy, where loyalty and duty were not such an important component and bureaucrats had more freedom to follow their conscience. Nevertheless, this emphasis on duty and loyalty—which applied from the beginning as criteria for the recruitment of civil servants—meant that the bureaucrats saw the regime as legitimate and believed it was their duty to "work toward the Führer"; but it also means they believed that what they were doing was legitimate and honorable, so they took great initiative rather than merely passively following orders.

Rather than thinking in terms of individuals' being trapped in institutions that have certain functions—so that the individuals have no choices— a more dynamic approach would explain their behavior better. If we look at the question more in of dialectical terms, then we can say that those working within the different institutions basically believed in the ideology, or at least in the legitimacy of the regime. The rulers hinted at general policy directions and then various civil servants took upon themselves the task of working out competing proposals for how to turn these ideas into actual policies. The proposals and actions of the various bureaucrats, in turn, influenced the policy guidelines of the ruling elites. Thus, the bureaucrats were not passive cogs in a machine, but rather active participants in developing the regime's genocidal strategy. The forces of production highlighted by Marx are still important: for example, even if the ancient Greeks carried out genocides, they could not do so in the same industrial manner, as they did not have a series of modern means and methods at their disposal: mass transportation, factories, furnaces for burning bodies, gasses for killing thousands of people at a time and so on. The modern world has afforded other possibilities for committing genocide.

Meanwhile, even if the means and methods for implementing totalitarian rule and genocide necessarily differ at different stages in the development of the forces of production, institutional arrangements give varying incentives for how to solve the issues at hand. Sociological institutionalists have long pointed out that institutions create different norms for how to act, and that these norms combine with cultural values to create certain "logics of appropriateness."

In the Nazi system, there were various institutions with different and competing institutional interests. For example, the *Gauleiter* (party leader of a regional branch) had an interest in making his area *Judenfrei* (free of Jews) as quickly as possible, which meant deporting the Jews—usually to Poland. Meanwhile, those responsible for occupied Poland (the *Generalgouvernement*) had an interest in using the Jews as slave labor to keep up production levels; but they did not have an interest in taking in too many Jews, as doing so would lead to sanitary problems and make it difficult to feed everyone. At the same time, those in charge of Jewish issues within the *Sicherheitdienst* (security police) had an incentive to keep the "Jewish question" hot, so as to increase their own importance. Given these different institutional incentives, the different actors took different actions and made different suggestions; but within the institutional arrangements, they had substantial freedom to devise solutions in line with institutional norms, the logic of the ruling ideology and the rulers' general policy directions. In other words, there was continuous interaction between the different institutions, between individuals at the different institutions and between the institutions and the Nazi leadership. In contrast to the banal bureaucrats depicted by supporters of Arendt, these participants were able to think. They believed in the ideology (or at least accepted its legitimacy) and they took great initiative.

Several historians have shown that, during the Nazi era, the impetus for anti-Jewish measures often came from below. According to Gerlach (2016: 42),

> [t]he active role of city, county and town administrations demonstrates that the central German government, or Nazi leadership, did not prescribe everything in detail and that a considerable drive existed beyond the Nazi Party's organization. Local administrations took the initiative to exclude Jews from a growing number of aspects of public life. They dismissed local civil servants; it was they who erected the infamous signs declaring that Jews were not allowed to enter certain towns or localities. Such exclusions started in 1933, were extended in the mid 1930s to include public baths, sports grounds and park benches, and later extended to educational and recreational facilities like theatres, cinemas and libraries, as well as market stalls.

Similarly, Kulka (2009) documents how, long before the Holocaust started, the most important anti-Semitic measures were actually introduced after pressure from below. For example, the regime did not introduce the Nuremberg race laws until there had been a big increase in anti-Semitic attacks at the local level throughout the country. Noting that the number of internal reports of local anti-Semitic acts (such as demonstrations or local boycotts) had increased over six-fold from 1934 to 1935 (p. 89), Kulka observes:

> The mounting pressure from below as presented in the reports created a reality, in which the local and regional authorities acted on their own initiative by adopting quasi-legal measures, which actually preceded the anti-Jewish laws of Nuremberg on the Reich-level. The "Law for the Protection of German Blood and Honour" was preceded by the refusal of local registrars to perform marriages between "Aryans" and "Non-Aryans" and by the daily arrests of men and women who were accused of "race defilement." Also the "Reich Flag Law" forbidding Jews to fly the German state flag and the Swastika was preceded by local initiatives as well as by a Reich-wide directive of the Gestapo....All these kinds of radicalizing pressure from below, as presented in the reports, clearly influenced the political leadership of the Reich.

The fact that initiatives came from below does not mean, however, that they were necessarily popular. For example, according to a Gestapo report:

> The new laws announced in Nuremberg were not greeted by the population with unanimous approval. [...] The only aspect praised is that this legislation will prevent excesses in antisemitic propaganda and violence. (Kulka 2009: 92)[8]

In other words, many Germans opposed the repression which the laws involved, but they were even more opposed to outward violence—so they hoped that codifying some anti-Semitic measures would keep it under control. This indicates a society that was willing to accept anti-Semitic measures but still opposed to coarse violence and it indicates that radical anti-Semitic measures involving murder still lacked popular support. Just because local party activists took measures that inspired the leadership elite does not mean that the whole population shared this enthusiasm. Thus, from the very start, the Nazi totalitarian state was not simply a case of absolute top-down rule, in which local bureaucrats mindlessly followed orders. Instead, local-level activists took initiatives, which spread and influenced the top leadership.

The Holocaust was not predestined, even if Nazi ideology made it likely. The exact form it took was also far from predestined. It was not created by leaders who gave orders, which apolitical, neutral, banal bureaucrats merely accepted and implemented. Rather, the leaders set forth general ideas, which were then converted into practical plans by loyal and obedient civil servants who believed strongly in the legitimacy of the system and who often shared the radical anti-Semitic views of the leaders. The fact that different institutions had different interests, set off certain dynamics and caused certain problems, which required great initiative and ingenuity on the bureaucrats to solve. This evil was *not* banal—it required the active support of bureaucrats who understood that what they were doing was out of the ordinary, but who saw it as in line with the state ideology. These bureaucrats used code words like "special treatment" rather than murder, and they hid the killings at the camps and the like, precisely because they knew they were going beyond the bounds of what society considered to be acceptable. Himmler made it clear in his infamous speech to the SS at Posen in 1943 that they were doing a great thing for the good of the German race, but that their great deed had to be kept secret (e.g., Berkowitz 1999: 252; Browning 1992/2001: 74; Midlarsky 2005: 137, 170, 181–1). As Burleigh (2000: 316) concludes in his discussion of the bureaucrats at the Jewish division of the *Sicherheitsdienst*: "They were encouraged to show the maximum initiative in identifying and solving problems, an approach not easily reconciled with the idea of them robotically carrying out orders."

How Ordinary?

As Gerlach (2016: 15) points out, far from being desktop in nature, the killings all involved the active participation of many people. In fact, only about half of the Jews who were murdered were killed with gas. The other half died because soldiers and police shot them or because they starved to death or died of illness. Furthermore, many of the perpetrators who actually did the killing—for example, by shooting Jews or working at extermination camps—had built their careers in the Nazi era by accumulating experience in repression. Burleigh (2011: 401) notes that "2.9 million Jews were killed by men standing a few feet away from them, for there was nothing 'factory-like' or 'industrial' about how these people were killed." Mann (2005: 205) observes:

By the time they were asked to commit mass murder routinely, many had long experience of violence. Not all of them were real Nazis, but their work environments tended to produce bigoted, comradely, disciplined, and careerist killers. For these were Nazi and work careers in ascending violence.

Mann gives the concrete example of Höss, who became commander of the Auschwitz concentration camp. Höss

> began as a teenage volunteer soldier in World War I. After the war, at age 19, he joined a Freikorps, killing Latvians, Poles, and German Communists. His unit was dissolved after it killed one of its own members, a suspected traitor. The leading killer, Höss, was convicted of murder. Released in 1928, he went straight into the Artamen League, a Nazi agrarian organization; he was a full-time party militant until 1934, when he became one of the first concentration camp guards, at Dachau. He served in the camps until 1945. Höss may have been an efficient manager, but he certainly was a highly ideological Nazi, his adult life caged entirely within proto-Nazi and Nazi organizations, steeped in violence. It is difficult to picture him as an ordinary manager or as representing modernity. (p. 213)

In other words, the perpetrators were far from "ordinary" people.

Since Chap. 3 discusses the alleged "desktop" murders around Eichmann, this chapter will focus more on "street-level bureaucrats"—those, such as policemen, who did the actual killing. However, I want to point out that there is much evidence that even the desktop murderers, who were not part of Eichmann's group, were also far from being banal or ordinary. For example, Werner (2010) discusses the case of Alfred Meyer, who had been a manager at the ministry of the occupied eastern territories. He participated in the Wannsee conference as one of the many bureaucrats who took part there in planning the Holocaust. He had previously been a district party leader (*Gauleiter*). In promoting him to his position in the ministry, Alfred Rosenberg (head of ideology) wrote that "Dr. Meyer is an old national socialist fighter who sees the political problems clearly and from a national socialist viewpoint" (p. 61). Even though Meyer was a radical anti-Semite who supported the liquidation of the existential "enemy," he also pushed for a pragmatic policy toward certain groups of people living in the Soviet Union. He and his mentor, Rosenberg, were critical of the desire among Nazi leaders to oppress "non-Aryans" in the Soviet territories. Instead, he favored granting some degree of local autonomy (*Selbstverwaltung*) to the Baltic peoples, White Russians and

Ukrainians, so that they would cooperate more with the occupation authorities (p. 63). Such desktop murderers were fully aware of the situation, they understood that millions of people were being killed, they thought mass murder was acceptable to further their cause, and despite Arendt's claims they were clearly able to think—although they thought within the confines of their political religion.

Yet, the idea of perpetrators' being "ordinary" persists. Thus, although Goldhagen (1996) and Browning (1992/2001) have been very critical of each other, both accept the idea that the reserve police officers whom Browning studied were "ordinary" people from Hamburg without any special pro-Nazi or anti-Semitic traits. Despite their alleged ordinariness, however, they were able to carry out mass executions against helpless Jews in Poland. Goldhagen and Browning also both admit that none of these perpetrators were forced to participate in the killings and that those who refused were not punished (see also Dean 2000: 102). Goldhagen sees this as proof that even ordinary Germans shared an eliminationist anti-Semitic outlook, while Browning argues that group pressure combined with careerism accounted for their behavior. Those who refused to participate did not have to worry about their careers. In the 1960s, German courts began prosecuting many officers and police who had been involved in the mass killings. Browning (1992/2001: 57) points out that some of the officers who refused to participate in the killings explained that they had already had good civilian jobs, which they planned to go back to after the war, so they were not interested in a career in the police once the war ended. Those, who were younger and more interested in a career in the police had a stronger incentive to fully participate in all actions.

This is not to say that those who committed the atrocities were only motivated by careerism. When testifying at their trials, the former police officers did not show any regret. Yet, their testimony took place in a democratic country, where showing remorse would have mitigated their guilt and led to lower sentences. Instead, their testimony showed that their psychological problems did not arise from a bad conscience, but rather from the horror they felt from experiencing the events in question (e.g., Fenigstein 1997; Vetlesen 2005; Zukier 1994). In other words, they thought their actions were legitimate, so they did not have a guilty conscience, but that does not mean they all enjoyed doing the criminal acts.

However, it is questionable just how "ordinary" these policemen actually were. As is well-known, those who decide in all countries to become police tend to have more authoritarian personalities than the population in general. In addition, those who chose to join in the 1930s were well-aware they were joining a force that was under Himmler's control, so they would have expected this force to be more brutal and racist than a "normal" police force. Moreover, as police, they had to undergo indoctrination in Nazi race biology.

Breitman (2003: 23–5) underlines that Himmler started trying to train police in SS ideology even before the Nazis came to power—in 1929 when he became *Reichsführer* for the SS. At that time he established contacts with policemen throughout the country. Many police were dissatisfied with the Weimar Republic, making them open to Nazi doctrine. When Hitler became chancellor, Himmler began taking control over the national police step by step. He made sure the police schools used Nazi-SS propaganda. In 1936 he became head of the German Police at the Ministry of Interior, while Heydrich had responsibility for the security police that had been created by combining the gestapo (the secret police) with the kripo (criminal police). Kurt Daluege took over responsibility for the *Ordnungspolizei* (regular police). It was important to make sure policemen understood that their professional success depended on how much they had internalized the national socialist ideology. In April 1937 the SS founded the leadership school for the security police in Berlin-Charlottenburg. One had to attend its courses if one wanted a higher position within the security police, gestapo or kripo. Courses for criminal inspectors were shorter. In other words, even the regular police and reserves got indoctrinated in Nazi ideology more than the rest of society, and at that point society, in general, was also being subjected to anti-Semitic indoctrination. Breitman (2003: 38–9) adds that the bureau for the *Ordnungspolizei*, established in 1939, was responsible for teaching Nazi ideology to the police and indoctrinating them politically. Thus, even ordinary police officers had to go through extra ideological indoctrination in a totalitarian society that was already heavy on indoctrinating the population.

From the very beginning of Nazi rule, German police were encouraged—even if they were not members of the SS—to act much more violently than police normally would. Already in early 1933, Göring, as Reichskommissar for the Prussian interior ministry, wrote that the police must proceed severely against communists engaged in acts of terror. When necessary they should be "ruthless" (*rücksichtlos*) in using their guns. In dealing with mobs, they should always be ruthless (Rückert 2014: 34). Gruner (2016: 74) reflects that after 1933 the police had to enforce anti-Jewish restrictions in close contact with the Gestapo and in 1938 were specifically ordered to harass Jews in any way possible. The violent socialization of German policemen throughout the 1930s is a factor that is often overlooked, which may help to explain the ease with which many officers were able to participate in mass murder in the occupied east during the war.

Moreover, even Browning's own statistics indicate that the reserve police were not so ordinary. He admits that 22 of the 32 noncommissioned officers for which he has information were party members and seven were in the SS (1992/2001: 47). In addition, about one-fourth of rank-and-file policemen were party members—a substantially higher proportion than among the population at large. Welzer (2005: 83) argues that the SS carefully chose the members for the *Einsatzgruppe* to make sure they were politically reliable. He also gives the example that, in 1941, students from one class at the *Führer* School of the *Sicherheitspolizei* in Berlin-Charlottenburg were commanded to join an *Einsatzgruppe*. Thus, Burleigh (2011: 402) concludes,

> policemen in a police state were far from ordinary. They would already have accustomed themselves to blameless members of the public being cast outside the ambit of the law, while through ideological instruction and image the police had been gradually refashioned in the universally belligerent mould of the SS. Many of them belonged to the SS and wore its runes on their tunics and helmets.

Similarly, Langerbein (2004: 6) points out that, although most members of the Reserve Police Battalion 101 studied by Browning did not begin as fanatical Nazis, they nevertheless decided to work in the Police Reserve in the knowledge that the police "had come under increasing SS control after 1933," which meant they could be used by Himmler for his "nefarious purposes." In addition, Browning "does not sufficiently recognize the significance of pervasive anti-Semitism and the impact of Nazi propaganda, which had systematically denigrated the Jews and other groups of 'undesirables' to less-than-human status for many years preceding the events in Poland." Consequently, "even the battalion commander's simplistic and devised justifications before these large massacres—excuses such as, the Jews were being punished for starting the war or for the bombing of the policemen's hometown and other German cities—might have allowed these very ordinary men to validate their own behavior once they had been sent to occupied Poland" (Langerbein 2004: 6–7). Mann (2005: 214f.) argues in similar fashion. He points out that those working in the security police came into an organization that shared an institutional identity with Nazism. The escalating spiral of routine violence in which they engaged further socialized them into supporting radical Nazi policies, even if they were not party members. Discussing Browning's studies, Mann (p. 215) agrees that the perpetrators came from different backgrounds. However, he adds that this does not mean they were ordinary:

> But some variations were predictable. The higher the rank, the greater the Nazism; and there were more committed Nazis in core SS and party organizations than in auxiliary police forces. The higher *Einsatzgruppen* officers were ideological Nazis....Thus the higher ranks in core institutions were brimming with long-term Nazis.

Furthermore, high-ranking SS police officers usually had long experience of political violence. Klemp (2013: 8) gives the example of Erich Mehr, who was head of the first company of the police battalion 61, which was in charge of the Warsaw Ghetto. He prided himself on calling himself "The Number One Jew-Hater" (*Judenhasser Nr. 1*) or "The Number One Enemy of the Jews" (*Judenfeind Nr. 1*). The battalion liked to call itself "the Murder Battalion" (*Mord Bataillon*), while battalion 301 from Bochum was called the "Devil's Battalion." Klemp (2013: 12) adds that the police unit which Browning chose was not representative, pointing out that it was quite common for members of the battalions to be volunteers who joined for ideological reasons. Some were even psychopaths, although it is difficult to estimate how many suffered psychological pathologies. Nevertheless, Klemp gives examples throughout his book of how far from "normality" many of the perpetrators were who administered the Warsaw ghetto.

Concentration-camp commanders and those working on Eichmann's staff also tended to have had long careers within the Nazi movement. In a survey of SS members, Rohrkamp (2014: 49) concludes that over three-fourths of SS members in the 1930s had been members of another national socialist organization before joining the SS. This again shows that the perpetrators were often supporters of the ruling ideology. Even if some SS members were motivated more by careerism, it is highly unlikely that those who joined several national socialist organizations would do so unless they believed in the ideology (even if not necessarily strongly). Rohrkamp (p. 60) argues that, during the war, new recruits were even more supportive of Nazi ideology, as the younger generation had been thoroughly indoctrinated in the ideology at school.

Even at the local level on the ground, soldiers and police took great initiative because they had been trained to support the ideology of the regime, which they considered to be legitimate. Thus,

> [i]n some places, Wehrmacht soldiers killed Jews on their own and without an Einsatzkommando nearby. In Augustowo, Poland, an anonymous Wehrmacht unit shot one hundred Jews and Communists at the recommendation of the local Security Service commander, SS Capt. Wolfgang Ilges. In other cases, Wehrmacht soldiers and engineers helped to search the cities for hidden Jews and then prepared and closed the mass graves. Without specific orders, individual army soldiers from all ranks volunteered to participate in the massacres and contributed in other ways to the killing operations. Moreover, the army allowed the Einsatzgruppen to screen its POW camps for Jews, political commissaries, and other "undesirables". (Langerbein 2004: 32)

Mann (2005: 230) also argues that, even though Protestants in Germany had been more likely to vote for the Nazis than Catholics, Catholics (or "lapsed Catholics") were much more likely to become perpetrators once Austria had been incorporated in Germany. The reason for this is that, in Germany proper, Evangelical Lutherans supported the idea of a nationalist Protestant Germany based on Prussia, and they were wary of a Greater Germany that would include Catholic Austria. Thus, in Germany, Lutheran Nazi supporters tended to support a "small German" nationalism centered on Prussia. Their anti-Semitism was not as virulent as the one in Austria, and their goal was not as expansionist as the great German (*grossdeutsch*) nationalism stemming from Austria. In Catholic Austria, the pan-German movement developed a "distinctly Austrian anti-Semitism" (p. 232). In contrast to Goldhagen, who stresses the eliminationist anti-Semitism that emerged in Germany, Mann claims that anti-Semitism was more intense in Austria. According to Mann (ibid.), Austrian pan-Germanism

> retained the territorial ambition of the old Habsburg ideal of *grossdeutsch* nationalism (an eastward-tilting union of all Germans in a single Reich), while changing this from a cultural-political union to an ethnic-racial one.

These Nazis attacked Habsburg multiethnicity and Jewish cosmopolitanism....
.Nazi genocide resonated amid the more *grossdeutsch* eastern-tilting sentiments of former Catholics. Thus refugee ethnic Germans and those from
threatened border, Catholic, and Austro-Bavarian areas were all more likely
to become perpetrators because genocide flowed from their ethnic *grossdeutsch* imperialism. It was racist because it was eastern-oriented, anti-Slav,
and anti-Semitic. Jews and Slavs were murdered for reasons of imperial ethnic revisionism. They allegedly stood in the way of the unity and power of
the German nation. This explains the perpetrators' regional biases in terms
of the resonance in their regions of Nazi ideology as a whole, not merely of
its anti-Semitic component.

In other words, despite Arendt's (1963) claim that Nazi ideology and
anti-Semitism did not matter to the perpetrators, most perpetrators seem
to have been highly motivated ideologically. Because many believed in the
ideology and most affirmed the legitimacy of the regime, they eventually
accepted the Nazi claim that Jews were the major outgroup that posed an
existential threat to society. Consequently, the Nazis were even able to get
people to take the initiative to commit atrocities, rather than waiting passively for orders. People were willing to take the initiative because they
believed in the legitimacy of the regime and were susceptible to its indoctrination. Consequently, they were able to convince large portions of the
population step by step that Jews could not become part of the new state
and posed an existential threat to this new state. Those working in the
repressive units, such as the police—including the "ordinary men" of the
regular *Ordnungspolizei*—were more heavily indoctrinated in the Nazi's
racist, anti-Semitism ideology than truly "ordinary" people. In the words
of one perpetrator, who had shot to death around 200 Jews, "[m]an alive,
damn it, a generation has to go through this so that things will be better
for our children" (cited in Burleigh 2011: 405). Or as Welzer (2005: 69)
proclaims: "During the National Socialist period, Germans felt it was their
duty to follow a normative model which did not condemn the degradation
and persecution of other people, but rather supported it; and during the
last third of its rule, the Third Reich proclaimed it was both necessary and
good to kill people."

The case of Germany contrasts markedly with that of Sweden. The stable and long-established state had of the latter country had no need to
mobilize the population against any outgroup to gain legitimacy, for it was
already seen as legitimate. In addition, the Swedish bureaucracy was more
autonomous, less ideological and less based on loyalty to the regime. This

encouraged bureaucrats to do what they personally considered to be morally correct rather than supporting government policy.

CONCLUSION

Even though the two Germanic states of Sweden and Germany both had many inhabitants who believed in mythologies about superior Germanic peoples, and even though both countries had become centers for race biology, only Germany became totalitarian. In Germany, even liberals held racist views. In 1871, for example, Gustav Freytag wrote that the Germans were destined to be the pioneers and representatives of the fight for progress, through which culture would be passed on to civilization (Mommsen 1999: 48). This chapter shows that the main difference between the two countries is that Germany was a newly created state with legitimacy problems, while Sweden was a well-established state with great legitimacy. Another important factor was the difference in the way in which the state developed in the two cases. Perhaps the comparison should begin with the dynamics behind the losses suffered in war.

In 1809 Sweden lost a war against Russia, thereby losing its Finnish territories. In contrast to the German case after WWI, however, this did not lead to the collapse of the state's legitimacy, nor did it lead to a search for an ethnic group to use as a scapegoat. Instead, a military coup took place, the leaders of which found a king who they thought would be more competent than the previous one. Thus, the country did not change regimes and remained a kingdom. Then they started to carry out administrative reforms, believing that the country needed a more modern and merit-based bureaucracy if it was to survive and to be able to defend itself against its enemies. As a well-established country that had existed for many centuries, Sweden did not need to concern itself with the issue of who belonged to it and who did not, and in any case Jews were not yet emancipated in the country (so they could not influence politics or the military), and there were too few of them to have much influence on the economy. Meanwhile, the Sami in the north were too isolated from mainstream society in the south and center to be a major concern. Finally, Swedish leaders could hardly blame the Finns for the loss in the war, since they wanted to get Finland back and they could not argue for this if they claimed Finns were disloyal or inferior. In fact, Swedish nationalists generally had a pro-Finnish attitude. For example, when the Soviet Union invaded Finland, many Swedish nationalists wanted Sweden to fight openly on the Finnish side, under the banner: "Finland's cause is ours."

Some Swedish nationalists even volunteered to fight on the Finnish side—this despite the fact that race biologists such as Lundborg considered Finns to be members of a different and inferior race. Lacking ethnic groups to blame, therefore, Swedish leaders chose the more progressive and modernizing alternative of administrative reform. Swedish policymakers also developed a policy legacy of consensus and cooperation. Consequently, they were able to carry out a successful transition to democracy through compromises that were supported by all of the major political parties as well as by the king. This gave the conservative parties backward legitimacy. Then, since the democratic system enjoyed great legitimacy, it was difficult for authoritarian parties to get support. In contrast to the Weimar Republic in Germany, the democratic regime in Sweden enjoyed the support not only of all major political parties but of the bureaucracy as well. Thus, it was not subject to sabotage in the same way that the republic in Germany was.

In addition, the manner in which the state developed in the two cases mattered greatly. In Sweden, the peasants had always long wielded great influence, as the crown often relied on their support against the aristocracy. They were represented in the estates, and when the country democratized they were able quickly to build up a strong peasant party. This party, the Farmers' Party, shared the racist views found among many Swedish peasants, and it was the only party to have a racist clause in its party platform. However, the social democrats were able to persuade this party to join a worker-peasant coalition government that laid the foundations for the modern Swedish welfare state. This kept peasants within the democratic orbit, as they gained from the government's policies to support agricultural prices and so on.

This contrasts greatly with the situation in Germany, where the peasants had no mainstream party to which they could turn for a defense of their interests. This left the road open for the Nazis to start gaining peasant support. As for the situation in Sweden, the social democrats in that country made an important strategic choice in addition to their decision to form a coalition with the Farmers' Party—to start using the term *folk* (in an inclusive way), rather than leaving it to the right as did their counterparts in Germany (where nationalists used the term *Volk* in a racist manner). The existence of a stable state also facilitated the emergence in Sweden of an active civil society, which to some extent supported democracy—or at the very least did not actively oppose it, as in Germany.

Furthermore, in Germany, the newly founded state did not enjoy the same level of legitimacy as the long-established state in Sweden, because Germany was not united into one country until 1871. Moreover, even when it was united under one Kaiser, the country remained a collection of kingdoms and a collection of states and principalities, some of which had very strong regional identities. As a new state, furthermore, it had to try to gain the loyalty of bureaucrats. Therefore, it followed a policy of recruiting civil servants according to whether they were loyal to the Kaiser and had conservative, antidemocratic values. In addition, the state gave special privileges to these *Beamte*, such as high pensions and guaranteed life-long employment. These conservative bureaucrats generally opposed the Weimer Republic and made it difficult for the government to carry out its policies. It also showed its bias by punishing leftists much more severely than right-wing nationalists who carried out similar violent acts. Thus, when Hitler came to power, he inherited a bureaucracy that was basically willing to support him. For carrying out the harshest acts of repression, he relied on newly created organizations totally dominated by strongly committed believers (such as the SS and the *Sicherheitsdienst*). When a new state is created, the issue of who belongs to it becomes important. Questions arise as to what kind of state it should be and what should it be based on. Chancellor Bismarck and the conservative bureaucrats worried that Jews, French, Poles and other ethnic groups would not be loyal to the new state, especially in case of war. This concern led to an ethnic orientation in which Jews were seen as an outgroup that could never become fully German. Therefore, they were discriminated against in the public sector and found it difficult to get a job in the civil service, and they had great difficulty obtaining citizenship. In other words, the country's rulers defined Germanness to some extent in opposition to Jewishness.

Even if the imperial regime was starting to gain legitimacy, it collapsed with defeat in WWI. The democratic regime that replaced it lacked legitimacy in the eyes of much of the population, as aristocrats, conservatives and nationalists opposed it. Thus, the new regime lacked the backward legitimacy of the democratic regimes in Sweden, as many of the parties in parliament remained opposed to the Republic. Not only was the Republic founded by a revolution that nobody wanted—even the radical left opposed it, for not leading to socialism—its association with military defeat and with harsh war reparations made it unpopular. Nationalist groups found a scapegoat in the Jews, whom they blamed for the defeat, for the Versailles Treaty, for the instability of the democratic party system and ultimately for the Great Depression as well. Once the war against the Soviet Union began, moreover, Jews were also linked to Bolshevism—thus, the fight against the Soviet Union was also framed as a race war against "Jewish Bolshevism."

The fact that, in contrast to the new democratic system in Sweden, the recently founded Weimar Republic lacked backward legitimacy shows that it is not just important whether a state is old or new; the *manner* in which the state is formed also matters. In Sweden, where a consensual policy legacy had developed, the main political parties and the monarchy were able to agree on a compromise for the transition to democracy; as a result, all of the major political groups saw the democratic regime as legitimate. The conservative parties could also legitimize themselves backward, as they had supported democracy during the transition. In Germany, by contrast, conservative and nationalist groups continually questioned the legitimacy of the Weimar regime. As Berman (1997) argues, when the state is weak and unstable—as in Weimar Germany—then civil society tends to fill the political vacuum by offering antidemocratic alternatives to the poorly functioning democratic regime.

The manner in which the state was formed was also important in the sense that, before becoming one country, the German territories consisted of a variety of principalities and states. The Holy Roman emperors had based their power on support from the aristocracy (in contrast to the French kings, who had based their power on support from the burghers); this led to pronounced decentralization and made unification impossible for many centuries. In addition, this reliance on the aristocracy meant that the peasants were much weaker, and serfdom continued much longer than in France, Spain or Sweden. One long-term consequence of this was that peasants had difficulty organizing themselves so that in contrast to their Swedish counterparts they lacked their own political party (except in Bavaria). Many Swedish peasants held racist attitudes as well; the critical difference is that they had a party which represented their interests. German peasants did not. This encouraged them to turn to the Nazis, who took an interest in many of their problems.

In summary, the Nazis were able to create a totalitarian state by incorporating a political religion that could make sense of why the Weimar Republic failed. They could feed off the lack of legitimacy that the Weimar Republic entailed and gain legitimacy by promising to unite the country and make it strong again. Moreover, even rulers with totalitarian ambitions are bound to fail if they cannot get the bureaucracy to cooperate with them. If a totalitarian party had come to power in Sweden, it would have faced a hostile bureaucracy that was loyal to the democratic regime and which enjoyed great autonomy, which encouraged individual civil servants to make decisions they considered to be morally correct. The Nazis inherited a conservative and antidemocratic bureaucracy whose members had been indoctrinated to be loyal and faithful (i.e., to regimes which they regarded as legitimate). First, they were faithful to the Kaiser and then later to Hitler, both of whom they considered to be legitimate rulers; but they were not so faithful to the democratic Weimar Republic, which they saw as illegitimate.

However, even if the German bureaucracy was based more on loyalty and less on merit than the Swedish one, its members were still able to take a lot of initiative in developing policies that were in line with what the Nazi leadership demanded. In addition, the Nazis were able to create new organizations to carry out their most repressive policies, and these organizations were made up of loyalists who believed strongly in the political religion.

Next comes the question of evilness. According to the model in this book, a regime is more likely to become totalitarian and then to get inhabitants to carry out evil tasks if it is a newly founded state. A newly founded state needs to define itself and to decide who belongs to it and who does not, so it has an extra incentive to define an outgroup. Goldhagen is correct that an eliminationist anti-Semitism developed at the end of the nineteenth century against the Jewish outgroup, but other countries, such as neighboring France, also harbored eliminationist tendencies. A big difference is that France had already existed for centuries and the French state enjoyed much more legitimacy than its German counterpart, so large groups were willing to defend the state against anti-Semitic attacks as witnessed in the Dreyfus affair. Nevertheless, the existence of an eliminationist discourse in Germany made the Holocaust easier to carry out there than in Sweden, where the eliminationist discourse was very weak and where even some anti-Semitic groups were critical of the "barbarism" taking place under Nazi rule throughout Europe. If there is an outgroup, then during a crisis—such as that seen when the imperial German regime collapsed and then the Great Depression hit—leaders are likely to blame the outgroup for the country's problems. If they can convince the population that the outgroup presents an existential threat, they are more likely to succeed. In the case of Germany, the Weimar Republic lacked legitimacy and nationalist groups such as the Nazis blamed Jews for the loss in WWI, as well as for the Versailles Treaty, the unstable democratic party system and the Depression itself. In a stable system with a stable state, as seen in Sweden, the regime has much less reason to find an outgroup to blame and the population is less likely to feel threatened by outgroups.

Once in power, the Nazis were able, through their propaganda and the steps they progressively introduced to dehumanize Jews as a group, to gain more support for their policies. Many who supported the Nazis did not do so for their anti-Semitism. Economic factors seem to have been more important; however, the Nazis linked these economic factors to the "Jewish question." The regime also set up special groups to carry out repression, such as the *Sicherheitsdienst* and the SS, in which they could employ fanatical followers who were willing to commit mass murder to support the regime. Even "ordinary" men were willing to help to some extent. Yet, even if the reserve officers who carried out much of the killing were not chosen because they were fanatical Nazis, they still more likely to accept their murderous tasks than the average, truly "ordinary" person. First, those who volunteer for a police are more likely than the average person to have an authoritarian personality. Second, as police they were under Himmler's control, so they faced additional ideological indoctrination. Third, a large portion of their officers were, in fact, Nazi Party members. It should be noted, however, that around one-tenth of the police reservists still refused to take part in mass shootings, and they were not punished for their refusal. Therefore, it was not structurally determined that everyone would participate.

Even those who did not fully believe in the ideology could defend their actions on the grounds that they were following the orders of a legitimate state. No state can ever succeed in gaining complete totalitarian control over everyone. So not only did some refuse to carry out the orders, some of those who did carry out the orders were motivated to some extent by other factors than ideology, such as the desire to be promoted in police careers after the war. Similarly, as discussed in Chap. 2, many of the people who turned in their neighbors did so for personal reasons such as revenge or material gain rather than ideological commitment. Yet, even in these cases, political religion was important because the Nazi regime enjoyed a high level of legitimacy, and people could justify their actions—regardless of their real motivations—by claiming they were following the official state ideology.

Regardless of the motivations of the perpetrators, however, most of the killings and repressive acts were not banal: the perpetrators believed in what they were doing. They thought they were doing something good for the country (if they believed in the ideology), or they thought they were doing something good for themselves (if they were motivated more by greed and careerism). They were not simply following orders, and those who morally opposed actions did not need to participate in them. The desk murderers around Eichmann were mostly fanatical anti-Semites who took great initiative and went well beyond what was necessary to follow orders. Their great creativity and fanaticism they showed in taking the initiative to solve problems contradicts Arendt's thesis that banal evil-doers are unable to think and are void of ideology. Many of the actual murderers displayed a high degree of sadism that went well beyond what would have been necessary if they were merely unthinking robots doing their duty.

It would have been much more difficult for a totalitarian regime in Sweden to get the population to engage in genocide. First, anti-Semitism may have been widespread in Sweden, but not in its eliminationist variant. Second, the democratic regime enjoyed great legitimacy, so a totalitarian regime that overthrew it would have had much more difficulty establishing its legitimacy. Third, the Swedish bureaucracy enjoyed a relatively high level of autonomy and was based more on merit and less on ideology than the German one. Consequently, some Swedish civil servants took great initiative to save Jewish lives when they found out about the Holocaust. It is likely they would have done the same if the Holocaust had taken place in Sweden. One should keep in mind that in neighboring Denmark, which was similar to Sweden in not having much in the way of eliminationist anti-Semitism, civil servants helped most of the Jews escape to Sweden during the Nazi occupation.

This does *not* mean that nobody would have collaborated with the Nazis if the Germans had invaded Sweden. The Norwegian case shows that there are "Quislings" in every country who are willing to betray their country and to cooperate with occupying forces. But Quisling's party never got enough votes to gain seats in parliament before the Nazi occupation, which shows that the totalitarian rule was imposed from the outside rather than coming from the inside. In Sweden, there were small Nazi parties—although at least one changed into a fascist party in protest against the ruthlessness of the Nazis' anti-Semitic policies—and there were military officers and police who sympathized with Hitler. So, there would likely have been people who willing to collaborate with a Nazi occupation force. If a totalitarian regime occupies another country, it might succeed somewhat in installing totalitarian rule there, but the question asked in this book is under what conditions countries can become totalitarian on their own. The point is that a totalitarian regime probably could not have come to power in a country like Sweden. Moreover, even if a party with a totalitarian ideology had won a Swedish election, it is unlikely the bureaucracy would have supported the ensuing regime. In such a country, totalitarianism can only come from without—that is, when a totalitarian regime with a strong military occupies it.

NOTES

1. Büttner (2008: 36) claims that the independent socialists were also against a revolution originally. In addition, the democratic wing of the party was against establishing a socialist republic and instead wanted a parliamentary system, but it wanted stronger guarantees against a return to authoritarianism than did the social democrats.
2. Mann (2004: 198) similarly notes that, in the Weimar Republic,

   22 murders committed by leftists resulted in an average sentence of 15 years for 38 persons plus 10 death sentences; 354 murders committed by rightists resulted in average sentences of four months for 24 persons—and no death sentences. Though in 1927 the 22 rightist killers who were members of the "Black *Reichswehr*" conspiracy received six death sentences and six long prison sentences, the death sentences were commuted, and only two of the defendants were still in prison three years later. When the rightist paramilitary Stahlhelm marched, police protection was arranged; when leftists marched, the police harassed them.

   Grebing (1986: 152) gives slightly different statistics, but she reaches the same conclusions as the other authors cited here about the right-wing bias of the legal system.

3. Technically it was the Austro-Hungarian Empire and not Austria, but the text refers to Austria.
4. Other authors, who do not support Goldhagen's cultural argument, still agree with him about the sadism which many perpetrators displayed, which they see as evidence against the banality-of-evil thesis. See, for example, Burleigh (2011: 401ff.)
5. Many other scholars have also pointed out that the boycott was a failure; see, for example, Gerlach (2016: 47).

6. It is now generally accepted that the Holocaust was not originally planned. Even general books not written by historians share this view. For example, Weitz (2003: 104) writes: "No less than Lenin, Hitler had a clear ideological vision; he was never only concerned with power for its own sake, despite what many early observers thought. If class was the central element in the Bolsheviks' worldview, race constituted the essence of Nazism, and Jews the premier racial enemy. The specific policies, even genocide, were not preordained; they would emerge in the context of political and social developments—including, critically, total war—in the 1930s and 1940s."

7. Interestingly, although Mommsen's approach plays down the role of anti-Semitism among bureaucrats, Herzstein (2002: 117) notes that Mommsen has personal reasons for downplaying this aspect of Germany in the Nazi era:

> In 1935 Wilhelm Mommsen, father of Hans, published a book called *Political History from Bismarck to the Present*. In his foreword, Mommsen, according to Kautz, wrote about the younger, postwar generation as having grown up with a sense of "totally unbroken strength in the new Reich of Adolf Hitler, in whose rise it has to some extent already played a decisive role." Mommsen was speaking of his four sons, including Hans, the future historian. Mommsen senior, Kautz continues, also branded Karl Marx "a typical representative of Jewish intellectualism," and praised Richard Wagner for being "one of the first who saw the Jewish problem, not as a one of religion, but one with racial premises." No wonder, Kautz adds, that the younger Mommsen has preferred to dwell upon the history of bureaucratic institutions. Speaking of the trio Jaeckel-Wehler-Mommsen, Kautz even declared that "They seek to rid themselves of their past and thereby deny their origins."

8. Kershaw (cited above) and Gerlach (2016: 48) also point out that the Nuremberg racial laws did not elicit the same level of opposition as did the more violent boycott of Jewish stores.

References

Aly, G. (2017). *"Endlösung": Völkervershiebung un der Mord an den europäischen Juden* (Rev. ed.). Frankfurt am Main: Fischer.

Arendt, H. (1963/2005). *Eichmann and the Holocaust*. London: Penguin.

Bajohr, F. (2016). German Responses to the Persecution of the Jews as Reflected in Three Collections of Secret Reports. In S. Schrafstetter & A. E. Steinweis (Eds.), *The Germans and the Holocaust: Popular Responses to the Persecution and Murder of the Jews*. New York: Berghahn.

Berger, R. J. (1993). The 'Banality of Evil' Reframed: The Social Construction of the 'Final Solution' to the 'Jewish Problem'. *The Sociological Quarterly, 34*(4), 597–618.

Berkowitz, L. (1999). Evil Is More Than Banal: Situationism and the Concept of Evil. *Personality and Social Psychology Review, 3*(3), 246–253.

Berman, S. (1997). Civil Society and the Collapse of the Weimar Republic. *World Politics, 49*(3), 401–429.

Blass, T. (1993). Psychological Perspectives on the Perpetrators of the Holocaust: The Role of Situational Pressures, Personal Dispositions, and Their Interactions. *Holocaust and Genocide Studies, 7*(1), 30–50.

Bloxham, D. (2008). Organized Mass Murder: Structure, Participation, and Motivation in Comparative Perspective. *Holocaust and Genocide Studies, 22*(2), 203–245.

Bracher, K. D. (1957). *Die Auflösung der weimarer Republik: Eine Studie zym Problem des Machverfalls in der Demokratie.* Stuttgart: Ringverlag.

Brandt, E. (1976). *Die politische Treuepflicht.* Karlsruhe: C.F. Müller.

Breitman, R. (2003). 'Gegner Nummer eins': Antisemitische Indoktrination in Himmlers Welanschauung. In J. Matthäus, K. Kwiet, J. Förster, & R. Breitman (Eds.), *Ausbildungsziel Judenmord? 'Weltanschauliche Erziehung' von SS, Polizei und Waffen-SS im Rahmen der 'Endlösung'.* Frankfurt am Main: Fischer Taschenbuch.

Broszat, M. (2007). *Der Staat Hitlers: Grundlegung und Entwicklung seiner inneren Verfassung.* Munich: Marixverlag.

Browning, C. R. (1992/2001). *Ordinary Men.* New York: Harper Collins.

Brustein, W. (1996). *The Logic of Evil: The Social Origins of the Nazi Party, 1925–1933.* New Haven: Yale University Press.

Brustein, W. I. (2003). *Roots of Hate: Anti-semitism in Europe Before the Holocaust.* Cambridge: Cambridge University Press.

Brustein, W. I., & King, R. D. (2004). Anti-Semitism in Europe Before the Holocaust. *International Political Science Review, 25*(1), 35–53.

Burleigh, M. (2000). *The Third Reich: A New History.* London: Macmillan.

Burleigh, M. (2011). *Moral Combat: Good and Evil in World War II.* New York: HarperCollins.

Büttner, U. (2008). *Weimar: Die überforderte Republik 1918–1933.* Stuttgart: Klett-Cotta.

Childers, T. (1983). *The Nazi Voter. The Social Foundations of Fascism in Germany, 1919–1933.* Chapel Hill: University of North Carolina Press.

Confino, A. (1993). The Nation as a Local Metaphor: Heimat, National Memory and the German Empire, 1871–1918. *History and Memory, 5*(1), 42–86.

Dann, O. (1996). *Nation und Nationalismus in Deutschland 1770–1990* (3rd ed.). Munich: C.H. Beck.

Dean, M. (2000). *Collaboration in the Holocaust Crimes of the Local Police in Belorussia and Ukraine, 1941–44.* Basingstoke: Macmillan.

Derfler, L. (2002). *The Dreyfus Affair.* Westport, CT: Greenwood Press.

Dumitru, D., & Johnson, C. (2011). Constructing Interethnic Conflict and Cooperation: Why Some People Harmed Jews and Others Helped Them During the Holocaust in Romania. *World Politics, 63*(1), 1–42.

Ehret, U. (2007). Understanding the Popular Appeal of Fascism, National Socialism and Soviet Communism: The Revival of Totalitarianism Theory and Political Religion. *History Compass, 5*(4), 1236–1267.

Engelking, B. (2012). Murdering and Denouncing Jews in the Polish Countryside, 1942–1945. In J. T. Gross (Ed.), *The Holocaust in Occupied Poland: New Findings and New Interpretations*, Warsaw Studies in Jewish History and Memory Vol. 1 Hensel, J., & Kapralski, S. (Eds.). Frankfurt am Main: Peter Lang.

Esping-Andersen, G. (1990). *The Three Worlds of Welfare Capitalism*. Cambridge: Polity Press.

Evans, R. J. (2005). Zwei deutsche Diktaturen im 20. Jahrhundert? *Aus Politik und Zeitgeschichte, 1–2*(January 3), 3–9.

Fenigstein, A. (1997). Reconceptualizing the Psychology of the Perpetrators. In D. Shilling (Ed.), *Lessons and Legacies* (Vol. II). Evanston, IL: Northwestern University Press.

Feuchtwanger, E. (2001). The Transition from Weimar to the Third Reich: The Political Dimension. In P. Panayi (Ed.), *Weimar and Nazi Germany: Continuities and Discontinuities*. Harlow: Longman.

Gerlach, C. (2016). *The Extermination of the European Jews*. Cambridge: Cambridge University Press.

Gerwarth, R. (2008). Bismarck und die Weimarer Republik. *Aus Politik und Zeitgeschichte, 50–51*(December 8), 19–25.

Goldhagen, D. J. (1996). *Hitler's Willing Executioners*. London: Little Brown Group.

Grabowski, J. (2013). *Hunt for the Jews: Betrayal and Murder in German–Occupied Poland*. Bloomington: Indiana University Press.

Grebing, H. (1986). *Der "deutsche Sonderweg" in Europa 1806–1945: Eine Kritik, written with the cooperation of von der Breile-Lewien, D. and Franzen, H.J.* Stuttgart: Kohlhammer.

Green, A. (2001). *Fatherlands: State-Building and Nationhood in Nineteenth-Century Germany*. Cambridge: Cambridge University Press.

Gross, J. T. with Gross, I. G. (2012). *Golden Harvest: Events at the Periphery of the Holocaust*. Oxford: Oxford University Press.

Grotkopp, J. (1992). *Beamtentum und Staatsformwechsel: Die Auswirkungen der Staatsformwechsel von 1918, 1933 und 1945 auf das Beamtenrecht und die personelle Zusammensetzung der deutschen Beamtenschaft*. Frankfurt am Main: Peter Lang.

Gruner, W. (2016). Indifference? Participation and Protest as Individual Responses to the Persecution of the Jews as Revealed in Berlin Police Logs and Trial

Records, 1933–45. In S. Schrafstetter & A. E. Steinweis (Eds.), *The Germans and the Holocaust: Popular Responses to the Persecution and Murder of the Jews.* New York: Berghahn.

Hastings, A. (1997). *The Construction of Nationhood.* Cambridge: Cambridge University Press.

Herzstein, R. E. (2002). Daniel Jonah Goldhagen's "Ordinary Germans": A Heretic and His Critics. *The Journal of The Historical Society, 2*(1), 89–122.

Hilberg, R. (1980). The Significance of the Holocaust. In H. Friedlander & S. Milton (Eds.), *The Holocaust: Ideology, Bureaucracy, and Genocide-The San Jose Papers.* Millwood, NY: Kraus.

Hildebrand, K. (1973). Hitlers Ort in der Geschichte des presußisch-deutschen Nationalstaates. *Historische Zeitschrift, 217*(3), 584–632.

Hinton, A. L. (2005). *Why Did They Kill? Cambodia in the Shadow of Genocide.* Berkeley: University of California Press.

Hürten, H. (1988). Bürgerkriege in der Republik: Die Kämpfe um die innere Ordnung von Weimar: 1918–1920. In K. D. Bracher, M. Funke, & H. A. Jacobsen (Eds.), *Die Weimarer Republik 1918–1933* (2nd ed.). Bonn: Bundezentral für politische Bildung.

Jacob, H. (1963). *German Administration since Bismarck: Central Authority versus Local Autonomy.* New Haven: Yale University Press.

Jöhlinger, O. (1921). *Bismarck und die Juden.* Berlin: Dietrich Reimer.

Jones, N. (1987). *The Birth of the Nazis: How the Freikorps Blazed a Trail for Hitler.* London: Carroll & Graf.

Kershaw, I. (2008). *Hitler, The Germans and the Final Solution.* New Haven: Yale University Press.

Klemp, S. (2013). *Vrnichtung: Die deutsche Ordungspolizei und der Judenmord in Warschauer Ghetto 1940–43.* Münster: Prospero.

Koonz, C. (2003). *The Nazi Conscience.* Cambridge, MA: Harvard University Press.

Kühnl, R. (1996). *Deutschland seit der Französischen Revolutin: Untersuchungen zum deutschen Sonderweg.* Heilbronn: Distel.

Kulka, O. D. (2009). Popular Opinion in Nazi Germany as a Factor in the Policy of the 'Solution of the Jewish Question': The Nuremberg Laws and the Reichskristallnacht. In P. Corner (Ed.), *Popular Opinion in Totalitarian Regimes: Fascism, Nazism, Communism.* Oxford: Oxford University Press.

Langerbein, H. (2004). *Hitler's Death Squads: The Logic of Mass Murder.* College Station: Texas.

Langewiesche, D. (1995). Die Reichsgründung 1866/1871. In H. U. Wehler (Ed.), *Scheidewege der deutschen Geschichte: Von der Reformation bis zur Wende 1517–1989.* Munich: Beck.

Levy, R. S. (2016). Anti-Semitism in Germany, 1890–1933: How Popular Was It? In S. Schrafstetter & A. E. Steinweis (Eds.), *The Germans and the Holocaust: Popular Responses to the Persecution and Murder of the Jews.* New York: Berghahn.

Lifton, R. J. (1990). The Genocidal Mentality. *Tikkun, 31*(3), 32–33.

Lozowick, Y. (2000). *Hitler's Bureaucrats: The Nazi Security Police and The Banality of Evil* (H. Watzman, Trans.). London: Continuum.

Luebbert, G. M. (1991). *Liberalism, Fascism, or Social Democracy: Social Classes and the Political Origins of Regimes in Interwar Europe.* Oxford: Oxford University Press.

Maccoby, H. (2006). *Antisemitism and Modernity: Innovation and Continuity.* London: Routledge.

Mann, B. (1983). Zwischen Hegemonie und Partikularismus Bemerkungen zum Verhältnis von Regierung, Bürokratie und Parlament in Preußen 1867–1918. In G. A. Ritter (Ed.), *Regierung, Bürokratie und Parlament in Preußen und Deutschland von 1848 bis zur Gegenwart.* Düsseldorf: Droste.

Mann, M. (2004). *Fascists.* Cambridge: Cambridge University Press.

Mann, M. (2005). *The Dark Side of Democracy: Explaining Ethnic Cleansing.* Cambridge: Cambridge University Press.

Middendorf, S. (2015). Das Reichsministerium der Finanzen (1919–1945) in der Geschichte von Staatlichkeit im 20. Jahrhundert. *Geschichte und Gesellschaft, 41*, 140–168.

Midlarsky, M. I. (2005). *The Killing Trap Genocide in the Twentieth Century.* Cambridge: Cambridge University Press.

Mommsen, H. (1983). Die Realisierung des Utopischen: Die 'Endlösung der Judenfrage' im 'Dritten Reich'. *Geschichte und Gesellschaft, 9*(3), 381–420.

Mommsen, H. (1999). *Von Weimar nach Auschwitz: Zur Gesichte Deutschlands in der Weltkriegsepoche.* Stuttgart: Deutsche Verlags-Anstalt.

Mommsen, H. (2009). *Aufstieg und Untergang der Republik von Weimar 1918–1933* (3rd ed.). Berlin: Ullstein.

Moore, B. (1966). *Social Origins of Dictatorship and Democracy.* Boston: Beacon Press.

Moses, A. D. (1998). Structure and Agency in the Holocaust. *History and Theory, 37*(2), 194–219.

Nathans, E. (2004). *The Politics of Citizenship in Germany.* Oxford: Berg.

Nicosia, F. R., & Stokes, L. D. (1990/2015). *Germans against Nazism: Nonconformity, Opposition and Resistance in the Third Reich.* Oxford: Berghahn.

Panayi, P. (2001). Continuities and Discontinuities in German History, 1919–1945. In P. Panayi (Ed.), *Weimar and Nazi Germany: Continuities and Discontinuities.* Harlow: Longman.

Peukert, D. J. K. (1991). *The Weimar Republic: The Crisis of Classical Modernity* (R. Deveson, Trans.). New York: Allen Lane.

Ping, L. L. (2012). Gustav Freytag, the *Reichsgründung*, and the National Liberal Origins of the *Sonderweg. Central European History, 45*, 605–630.

Pollmann, K. E. (1983). Parlamentseinfluß während der Nationalstaatsbildung 1867–1871. In G. A. Ritter (Ed.), *Regierung, Bürokratie und Parlament in Preußen und Deutschland von 1848 bis zur Gegenwart.* Düsseldorf: Droste.

Rasehorn, T. (1988). Rechtspolitik und Rechtsprechung: Ein Beitrag zur Ideologie der 'Dritten Gewalt,'. In K. D. Bracher, M. Funke, & H. A. Jacobsen (Eds.), *Die Weimarer Republik 1918–1933* (2nd ed.). Bonn: Bundezentral für politische Bildung.

Reagin, N. R. (2004). Recent Work on German National Identity: Regional? Imperial? Gendered? Imaginary? *Central European History, 37*(2), 273–289.

Reiter, B. (2009). Civil Society and Democracy: Weimar Reconsidered. *Journal of Civil Society, 5*(1), 21–34.

Reuth, R. G. (2009). *Hitler's Judenhass: Klischee und Wirklichkeit.* Munich: Piper.

Rohrkamp, R. (2014). Die Reruitierungspraxis der Waffen-SS in Frieden und Krieg. In J. E. Schulte, P. Lieb, & B. Wegner (Eds.), *Die Waffen-SS: Neue Forschungen.* Paderborn: Verlag Ferdinand Schöningh.

Rosenberg, H. (1967). *Grosse Depression und Bismarckzeit.* Berlin: Walter de Gruyter.

Rosenfeld, G. D. (1999). The Controversy That Isn't: The Debate over Daniel J. Goldhagen's 'Hitler's Willing Executioners' in Comparative Perspective. *Contemporary European History, 8*(2), 249–273.

Rückert, J. (2014). Perversion der Verwaltung – Verwaltung der Perversion in der NS Zeit. *Juridica International, 21*, 29–45.

Schwabe, K. (1988). Der Weg der Republik vom Kapp-Putsch 1920 bis zum Scheitern des Kabinetts Müller 1930. In K. D. Bracher, M. Funke, & H. A. Jacobsen (Eds.), *Die Weimarer Republik 1918–1933* (2nd ed.). Bonn: Bundezentral für politische Bildung.

Sheehan, J. J. (1989). *German History 1770–1866.* Oxford: Clarendon Press.

Stern, F. (1996). The Goldhagen Controversy: One Nation, One People, One Theory? *Foreign Affairs, 75*(6), 128–138.

Stoetzler, M. (2008). *The State the Nation and the Jews: Liberalism and Antisemitism Dispute in Bismarck's Germany.* Lincoln: University of Nebraska.

Sturmer, M. (1981). Eine Skizze sozialer Krisenbedingungen und gesellschaftlicher Wirklichkeit. In O. B. Roegele, M. Stürmer, & H.-U. Thamer (Eds.), *Wie konnte es dazu kommen? Hintergründe der nationalsozialistischen Machtergreifung* (pp. 27–35). Munich: Bayerische Landeszentrale für politische Bildungsarbeit.

Vetlesen, A. J. (2005). *Evil and Human Agency.* Cambridge University Press.

Volkov, S. (1985). Kontinuität und Diskontinuität im deutschen Antisemitismus 1878–1945. *Vierteljahreshefte für Zeitgeschichte, 33*, 2221–2243.

Weber, P. C. (2015). The Paradoxical Modernity of Civil Society: The Weimar Republic, Democracy, and Social Homogeneity. *Voluntas: International Journal of Voluntary and Nonprofit Organizations, 26*(2), 629–648.

Wehler, H. U. (1970). Bismarck's Imperialism 1862–1890. *Past & Present, 48*(August), 119–155.

Wehler, H. U. (1985). *The German Empire 1871–1918* (K. Traynor, Trans.). Oxford: Berg.

Wehler, H. U. (1995). Der deutsche Nationalismus bis 1871. In H. U. Wehler (Ed.), *Scheidewege der deutschen Geschichte: Von der Reformation bis zur Wende 1517–1989.* Munich: Beck.

Weiss, J. (1996). *Ideology of Death: Why the Holocaust Happened in Germany.* Chicago: Ivan R. Dee.

Weiss, J. (1999). Daniel Jonah Goldhagen, *Hitler's Willing Executioners:* An Historian's View. *Journal of Genocide Research, 1*(2), 257–272.

Weitz, E. D. (2003). *A Century of Genocide: Utopias of Race and Nation.* Princeton: Princeton University Press.

Welzer, H. (2005). *Täter: Wie aus ganz normalen Menschen Massenmörder werden.* Hamburg: Fischer.

Werner, F. (2010). Der regionale Machthaber: Alfred Meyer. In F. Werner (Ed.), *Schaumburger Nationalsozialisten, Täter, Komplizen, Profiteure* (2nd ed.). Bielefeld: Verlag für Regionalgeschichte.

Wirsching, A. (2008). Die paradoxe Revolution 1918/19. *Aus Politik und Zeitgeschichte, 50–51*(December 8), 6–12.

Witt, P.-C. (1983). Kontinuität und Diskontinuität im politischen System der Weimarer Republik: Das Verhältnis von Regierung, Bürokratie und Reichstag. In G. A. Ritter (Ed.), *Regierung, Bürokratie und Parlament in Preußen und Deutschland von 1848 bis zur Gegenwart.* Düsseldorf: Droste.

Wunder, B. (1986). *Geschichte der Bürokratie in Deutschland.* Frankfurt am Main: Suhrkamp.

Ziblatt, D. (2006). *Structuring the State: The Formation of Italy and Germany and the Puzzle of Federalism.* Princeton: Princeton University Press.

Zukier, H. (1994). The Twisted Road to Genocide: On the Psychological Development of Evil During the Holocaust. *Social Research, 61*(2), 435.

CHAPTER 8

The End?

This book, which began many centuries ago at the start of the papal inquisition in medieval France, has sought to answer the question of whether or not totalitarianism is something modern. In contrast to such authors as Bauman (1991), Elias (1976), Giddens (1991), Heller (2010) and Horkheimer and Adorno (1944/1988), I argue that it is not necessary for a country to be modern for it to become totalitarian: even pre-modern states, such as Spain under the Inquisition, became totalitarian. I argue that Spain under the Spanish Inquisition became totalitarian but that France under its papal inquisition did not. Even if one disagrees with my explanation as to *why* Spain became totalitarian, the reader at least hopefully will be convinced by this book that pre-modern societies can, in fact, become totalitarian. If we dispense with the notion that totalitarianism is linked to modernity, we will be better able to understand the logic behind totalitarianism—a type of rule that can occur in both pre-modern and post-modern societies. Of course, the manner in which totalitarianism manifests itself will not be the same in different epochs. Just as the direct democracy of Athens differs from modern parliamentary democracy, pre-modern totalitarian regimes differ from modern ones; but that does not make them any less totalitarian, just as Greek democracy was no less democratic than modern representative democracy. When it comes to controlling people's thoughts and forcing them to prove beyond a doubt that they really believe in the "correct" ideology, it would be hard to find a more totalitarian society than Spain was under the Inquisition.

© The Author(s) 2019   287
S. Saxonberg, *Pre-Modernity, Totalitarianism and the Non-Banality of Evil*, https://Doi.org/10.1007/978-3-030-28195-3_8

Not only does this book argue against the widely held belief that totalitarianism is something modern, it also criticizes Arendt's (1963/2005) contention that evilness under totalitarianism was banal and that its perpetrators were motivated by a sense of duty rather than ideology. Those who committed evil acts usually believed in the ideology and thought they were doing something good. Moreover, even when they did not believe in the ideology, they at least believed that what they were doing was legitimate. Consequently, they often took great initiative. Far from matching Arendt's picture of banal bureaucrats unable to think, they were often extremely creative and capable of thought. However, they thought within the framework of the totalitarian ideology of the rulers.

It is relatively easy to argue against the widely held beliefs about the modernity of totalitarianism and the banality of evil. It is more difficult to explain when regimes become totalitarian and capable of inducing people to carry out evil acts. This book focuses on an aspect of this question which has been left out of the social-scientific discourse: the role of state-building. It argues that newly created states have a much greater incentive than well-established states do to follow totalitarian strategies and try to get the population to engage in evil acts. In addition, they are more likely to succeed in such endeavors than are old states, which tend to be relatively stable and to enjoy high levels of legitimacy.

A new state faces questions that old states do not face with the same degree of urgency. For example, on what criteria should the state be based? And who should belong? This tends to impel leaders of newly formed states to wonder whether any groups living within the new state lack loyalty to it and whether such groups ought, therefore, to be branded as outgroups. In choosing their scapegoat, the new rulers have an incentive to frame the group in question as an existential threat, thereby uniting members of the ingroup behind themselves in defense against the threat. By contrast, leaders of stable states with a high degree of legitimacy do not have the same need to find scapegoats or to try to enhance their support by uniting the majority against a minority group. In addition, even if they tried to do so, such leaders would discover that their depiction of the outgroup as an existential threat would be less believable and less likely to win adherents. Leaders of newly created states also have a greater incentive to try to create a political religion (or to politicize a religion) in order to enhance their legitimacy, thereby cementing the loyalty of the population to the new state. Old states do not have to worry about these issues, for they already enjoy high levels of legitimacy.

For example, while France was one of the most well-established countries during the era in which the Church introduced the inquisition there,
Spain had only just been united as a country. After defeating Granada, the
regime suddenly found itself with a large Muslim minority within its borders. It had reason to fear that these Muslims would support the Ottoman
Empire or the Berbers if they invaded—and that would still do so even
after having officially converted to Christianity.

Leaders of a newly created state also have a strong incentive to choose
civil servants based on their loyalty to the new state, rather than on their
merits. Germany and Sweden form an instructive contrast here. In
Germany, the imperial regime recruited conservatives who held antidemocratic beliefs. This made it harder for the subsequent democratic
regime to carry out its policies—and easier for the Nazis to carry out
theirs since they inherited a bureaucracy that sympathized with them.
Thus, German civil servants were more willing to help the regime carry
out evil acts of repression and genocide. In Sweden, by contrast, the
state had enjoyed a high level of legitimacy for many centuries; so, when
the country carried out administrative reforms in the nineteenth century,
merit became more important than political loyalty for getting a job in
the civil service.

Neither is the issue of whether the state is old or new the only important one; the manner in which it develops also matters. In France, the
crown supported the burghers over the aristocrats in order to centralize
the system. In Sweden, the kings often turned to the peasants for support
against the nobles, enabling the former group to acquire considerable
influence. The peasantry grew so strong, in fact, that it comprised one of
the parliamentary estates. Then, when the country democratized, farmers
were well-organized, and they quickly created their own party to represent
their interests. Like their counterparts in Germany, peasants in Sweden
often held racist views; and the Farmers' Party had race hygiene in its program. Yet, the social democrats were able to coopt this party and to gain
its support for the democratic regime. Indeed, the Farmers' Party ended
up helping the social democrats build up the Swedish welfare state. Thus,
Swedish peasants gave firm support to the democratic system. In Germany,
by contrast, the Holy Roman Emperors relied on support from local aristocrats, leading to a decentralized system with many small states and principalities. When the country was finally able to unite in 1871, regional
identities were still very strong, making it difficult for the new state to gain
legitimacy. Moreover, since the peasants were very weak, and since the

various territories (except Bavaria) remained somewhat feudal even well into the nineteenth century, peasant parties did not emerge in the united country. This lack of a peasant party made it easier for the Nazis to gain support in the countryside.

Similarly, France and Spain form a contrast. French rulers did not feel they faced existential threats in the way that their Spanish counterparts did. French Jews, for example, posed no threat to the regime during the period of the inquisition, as very few had converted. Furthermore, even if converted Jews had married into the aristocracy, that would not have presented a problem, for the French aristocracy was not based on "blood" in the same way as its Spanish counterpart. In France, it was quite common, for example, for burghers to be ennobled. The main group targeted by the inquisition were the Cathars, who had the same "blood" as other French, and who therefore were not seen as a threat by virtue of their ancestry or ethnicity. Thus, it was more difficult to frame them as an evil "other." In Spain, by contrast, the aristocracy based itself much more on blood; and hundreds of thousands of Jews had converted. Some of the more successful *conversos* had married into aristocratic families, which started to threaten the legitimacy of the aristocracy because it could no longer so easily defend its right to rule on grounds of "superior blood." In addition, as already noted, having conquering an area where the vast majority of the population was Muslim, Spain's rulers now feared that this group represented a potential fifth column that would support an invasion of the country by Islamic powers.

The manner in which democratization occurs is also important. The Weimar Republic came into being through a revolution, while the democratic regime in Sweden emerged through a negotiated transformation. The new Swedish regime enjoyed backward legitimacy, as even the conservative parties and the king had supported the democratic reforms. The democratic regime, therefore, met with wide acceptance, granting it great legitimacy and making it difficult for antidemocratic movements to challenge it. This smooth transformation was helped by the consensual policy legacy long established within the country, in which the various groups would try to reach a consensus on important reforms. In Germany, by contrast, the democratic regime came into being through a revolution which none of the major parties wanted. Radical leftist groups did not support it, as they had hoped for a socialist revolution; while the social democratic, liberal and Catholic parties had wanted gradual change and a constitutional monarchy. Conservative groups, meanwhile, rejected democracy altogether. Thus, lacking the backing of any major group, the new regime had little legitimacy.

According to the model developed in this book, a totalitarian state is able to induce people to commit acts of evil if it chooses an outgroup and portrays it as an existential threat in a period of crisis. It must also succeed in dehumanizing that group. By the time Aragon and Castile united to become Spain, the dehumanization of Jews had already begun. Throughout Europe during that period, there was a trend to see Jews as members of a subhuman species allied with the Devil. They had inferior "blood," which threatened to dilute the superior blood of the aristocracy. Furthermore, since even Jews who had converted allegedly maintained their old religious practices in secret, their improper thoughts—or "thought crimes" in Orwell's terminology—threatened the homogeneity upon which the Catholic state was built. Similarly, the rulers portrayed Muslims as a threat to the country's existence, as they might ally themselves with Muslim invaders from the Ottoman Empire or the Berber areas of northern Africa.

In the German case, the process of state formation gave rulers and civil servants reason to believe that certain groups—such as French and Poles— would not be loyal to the new state. Due to the prejudices, they harbored, furthermore, they believed Jews would not be loyal either. As an eliminationist anti-Semitism developed in the area, some conservative groups embraced this way of thinking. When the Kaiser lost and abdicated, conservative groups rejected the democratic Weimar Republic as illegitimate. The Nazis portrayed Jews as an existential threat—as having been behind the country's defeat in the war, the founding of the "illegitimate" Weimar Republic, and even the unpopular Versailles Treaty and its demands for heavy reparations.

Many—perhaps most—of those who voted for the Nazis did not necessarily do so for anti-Semitic reasons. Instead, they saw Hitler's regime as a legitimate replacement for the illegitimate Weimar Republic, and as a way to restore order in the country. In the Nazi political religion, this was all connected to defeating the Jewish enemy—the existential threat. Even if many Nazi voters did not necessarily share the Party's deep-seated anti-Semitism, they were at least willing to accept it; after all, if fighting anti-Semitism had been a key issue for them, they would have voted for other parties. At first, the Nazis had trouble gaining support for their anti-Semitic activities, such as their boycott of Jewish stores. However, they were able to change the general attitude toward Jews over time, by enacting measures that dehumanized them more and more. Meanwhile, the

population was influenced by the constant onslaught of anti-Semitic propaganda. Finally, when WWII expanded to include the Soviet Union, the
Nazis portrayed it as a "race war" against "Jewish Bolshevism," thereby
tying anticommunism into anti-Semitism. By contrast, in a firmly established country such as Sweden, fears of disloyalty were largely absent, even
if it was commonly believed that Jews were racially different and so could
never become "true" Swedes.

In emphasizing the state-building process, this book might seem overly
deterministic. I should, therefore, point out that, while structural developments yield incentives for certain types of behavior, they do not necessitate
them. For example, the Nazis' assumption of power was not an inescap-
able fate; it was not certain that a racist and totalitarian party would come
to power. There were many factors involved here. Before the Great
Depression, after all, the Nazis were a very minor party, never getting
more than a few percent of the vote. Furthermore, even once the
Depression had begun, a Nazi takeover could still arguably have been prevented—if, for example, the *Zentrum* chancellor Brünning had tried less
orthodox economic policies and, rather than introducing austerity measures, had instead tried stimulating the economy as the social democrats
did in Sweden. And even after Brünning's government failed, moreover,
the next chancellor (von Papen) could have pursued different policies.
Hindenburg, in turn, could have refused to appoint Hitler chancellor. My
point, however, is that it was much easier for a totalitarian movement to
come to power in a country such as Germany—given its recent founding
and the manner in which it had developed—than in a country such as
Sweden, where the regime enjoyed much greater legitimacy and institutions were far older and much more stable. The incentive to choose an
outgroup to serve as a scapegoat was also much greater in Germany than
in Sweden.

Moreover, once having come to power, a totalitarian movement will
likely find it much easier to carry out its policies in a newly formed state
than in a long-established one. Thus, in Germany, the Nazis could count
on assistance from a well-disposed bureaucracy; in Sweden, by contrast,
civil servants enjoyed much more independence than in Germany, which
encouraged them to take greater moral responsibility. Many German
bureaucrats held antidemocratic views and saw the Weimar Republic as
illegitimate and the Nazi regime as legitimate. Many of them, finally,
believed in the political religion to some extent and were therefore willing

to take great initiative in planning and carrying out evil deeds such as genocide.

Similarly, even though the idea of an inquisition is very totalitarian, the inquisition faced much greater resistance in France than in Spain, making it much more difficult for the rulers of the former country to use it to create a totalitarian regime. In the French case, the inquisition did not form part of a state-building strategy, as the state already existed (although it was not a "modern" state, and its territory was still growing). Neither did the crown use its inquisition to unite the country; on the contrary, that institution actually had the opposite effect in France—of *dividing* it. Furthermore, the inquisition in France was not directed at an ethnic "out-group" perceived as an existential threat to the country. Ethnically and in terms of "blood," the Cathars and "heretics" were the same people as the other French. Moreover, since many denizens of the southern areas saw the Church as an exploitative landowner, even those who did not join the Cathars still tended to sympathize with them. Even local aristocrats who did not share the religious views of the Cathars wanted to protect them against encroachment from Rome. In view of these various factors, it took many decades to subdue the Cathars. Thus, the inquisition in France was not part of a politicized religion which the rulers used to unite the country behind a totalitarian regime. In fact, the inquisition in France was officially "papal" and Vatican-run (even though in reality it was dependent on support from the French monarchy to be able to carry out its tasks).

As rulers of a new state, the Spanish monarchs did not face the same opposition to their inquisition as did their French counterparts. Instead, the Spanish Inquisition became to a large extent a popular event, uniting much of the population behind the crown and its politicized religion. Yet, just because totalitarianism was much easier to instigate in Spain than in France (and in Germany than in Sweden), this does not mean that Spain and Germany *had* to become totalitarian. Theoretically, Isabella and Ferdinand could have chosen a different path of development. The "Catholic monarchs" could have decided that the *conversos* did *not* represent a real threat, and they could have decided not to instigate an inquisition. They could even have decided that, since there were such large Jewish and Muslim populations within the country, it would be economically and culturally beneficial to continue the centuries-long policy of relative tolerance and to leave those groups in peace. It is not predetermined, then, that rulers at a "critical juncture" will choose a certain path and a certain ideology. However, certain structural and cultural factors encourage some choices more than others. Moreover, once rulers make these choices and the country goes down a particular path, it becomes more difficult to change direction.

The example of the United States may be instructive here. Even if a totalitarian movement came to power in that country, it would find it very difficult to carry out its policies and to make the country totalitarian, because the American republic is relatively old and well-established, and it enjoys a high level of legitimacy. We can see this in the election of Donald Trump to the presidency. Trump is not totalitarian, but he definitely has authoritarian tendencies, and he has little respect for the law or for institutions. Yet, he has faced numerous barriers to the enactment of his policies, as when the courts twice found his travel ban on Muslims to be unconstitutional, forcing him to revise his law proposal for a third time. His power has been further checked by the outcome of the mid-term elections, in which his party lost control of the House of Representatives. Moreover, despite his open contempt for the mass media, he has not been able to take any measures to curb its freedoms. When he wanted to ban a news reporter from CNN from press conferences at the White House, the courts ruled that the reporter had to be reinstated. Finally, despite his disdain for the Mueller investigation into his possible collusion with Russia (which he calls a "witch hunt"), he was unable to shut it down.

This book has taken up just four cases: medieval France as compared to medieval Spain and Nazi Germany as compared to democratic Sweden. Further studies may be able to ascertain how general this model is. For example, there has been a tradition within research on political religions to claim that only modern societies can become totalitarian; and furthermore, that totalitarian regimes cannot be based on a religion, because they furnish a secular substitute for religion. Yet, the Spanish case in this book shows that a politicized religion can also form the basis for a totalitarian regime. Actually, given the rise of radical political Islam, my claim that a totalitarian regime can be based on a politicized religion should not be very controversial. Yet, few studies have so far been undertaken of how such totalitarian Islamic regimes function.

For example, it is clear that the Islamic State (ISIS) is based on totalitarian principles, and it seems too that they rule in a totalitarian manner. How well does this fit into the scheme proposed in this book? At the very least, it seems clear that ISIS tried to create a new state on territory it had taken from several existing states, and from which of course it hoped to expand. This could make for an interesting comparison with Iran, which was the first country in which a fundamentalist Islamic regime came to power. To be sure, Iran is dominated by Shia Muslims, while ISIS adheres to the Sunni interpretation of Islam. Nevertheless, they share the idea that an authoritarian theocracy should rule society. Yet, even though Iran is undeniably an authoritarian country, it does not class as totalitarian. For example, it holds elections with multiple candidates. The religious authorities do ban many candidates if they consider them too "liberal," but they still usually allow some minimal degree of choice. Sometimes "moderate" candidates win over the more orthodox ones that obviously enjoy the support of the mullahs. Perhaps, then, an important reason why the Islamic regime in Iran did not become totalitarian is that the revolutionaries took over a well-established state in that case; whereas ISIS is less constrained, as it is trying to build a completely new state.

REFERENCES

Arendt, H. (1963/2005). *Eichmann and the Holocaust*. London: Penguin.
Bauman, Z. (1991). *Modernity and the Holocaust*. Oxford: John Wiley & Sons.
Elias, N. (1976). *Über den Prozess der Zivilisation. Soziogenetische und psychogenetische Untersuchungen*. Frankfurt: Suhrkamp Verlag.
Giddens, A. (1991). *The Consequences of Modernity*. Stanford: Stanford University Press.
Heller, A. (2010). Radical Evil in Modernity: On Genocide, Totalitarian Terror and the Holocaust. *Thesis Eleven, 101*(May), 106–117.
Horkheimer, M., & Adorno, T. (1944/1988). *Dialektik der Aufklärung*. Frankfurt am Main: Fischer.

Index[1]

A

Adrian VI, Pope, 130
Age of Liberty, 158
Albigensian Crusades, 11, 97
Anti-Semitism
  biological, 147
  eliminationist, 25, 71–74, 155,
    189–191, 208, 224, 225, 232,
    235, 236, 238, 241, 242, 246,
    249, 253, 255, 265, 269, 275,
    277, 291
  racial, 56, 70, 71, 73, 122–129,
    237, 239
  religious, 73
  role in support for the Nazis,
    71
Arendt, Hannah, 6, 8, 13, 16, 51–65,
  70, 176, 235, 254, 259, 261,
  265, 270, 277, 288
Associational life, 166, 233–235
Atlantica, 180

B

Bagge, Gösta, 169
Banality of evil, 6, 8, 17, 24,
  51–53, 60, 62, 176, 207, 254,
  288
Barres, Maurice, 236
Bavaria, 17, 22, 154, 169, 196,
  210–212, 230–232, 240, 274,
  290
Beamten, 21
Begin, Menachem, 3
Benns, Gottfried, 216
Bibliskt Månadshäfte, 190
Bismarck, Otto von, 20, 21, 28, 153,
  154, 179, 205, 208, 211–214,
  217–219, 273, 279n7
Björk, CG, 169
Bondeförbund, 169
Boniface, Pope, 89
Branting, Hjalmar, 163, 181, 188
Brask, Bishop Hans, 157

---

[1] Note: Page numbers followed by 'n' refer to notes.

© The Author(s) 2019   297
S. Saxonberg, *Pre-Modernity, Totalitarianism and the Non-Banality
of Evil*, https://doi.org/10.1007/978-3-030-28195-3